THEY HAD
FACES THEN

THEY HAD

FACES THEN

STARS AND STARLETS OF THE 1930's

by JOHN SPRINGER
and
Jack Hamilton

CITADEL PRESS   *Secaucus, New Jersey*

First edition

Copyright © 1974 by JOHN SPRINGER and JACK HAMILTON
All rights reserved

Published by CITADEL PRESS
A division of LYLE STUART, INC.
120 Enterprise Ave., Secaucus, N.J. 07094

In Canada: George J. McLeod Limited
73 Bathurst St., Toronto, Ontario

Manufactured in the United States of America by
Halliday Lithograph Corp., West Hanover, Mass.

Designed by A. Christopher Simon

Library of Congress catalog card number: 73-90954

ISBN 0-8065-0300-9

To our beloved Beulah Bondi

ACKNOWLEDGMENTS

To the Springer/Bettmann Film Archives for all pictorial material used . . .

And to the Publicity Departments and Still Departments of Columbia Pictures, M-G-M, Paramount, RKO Radio, Republic, Twentieth Century-Fox, United Artists, Universal, Warner Brothers-First National.

CONTENTS

THEY HAD FACES THEN

INTRODUCTION

The film flickers in the private screening room—a long, loving closeup of a misty-eyed girl. A woman watches—a woman with the same face as that she sees on screen, but eroded, lined, cruelly ravaged. Yet she gazes avidly at the girl she was.

"We had faces then," cries Norma Desmond. Her words may have come from the pens of *Sunset Boulevard* screenwriters Charles Brackett, Billy Wilder and D. M. Marshman, Jr., but the sentiment was Swanson's. And ours.

Faces they were—strong, stunning, individual. Where is the countenance of a star, whose career was generated in the sixties or seventies, that can compare with any one of a couple of dozen of the thirties? Jane Fonda perhaps. Julie Christie, Glenda Jackson, or Vanessa Redgrave. Who else?

You might not have known the names of all the people you saw in the movies of that bygone era but there wasn't a bit player not instantly recognizable. (The occasional exception quickly passed out of the screen world.) How many of today's film and television small-part players would be familiar on second or third sight?

They had faces then—and, by the thirties, they had voices, too.

There they were so many times larger than life but so much more than shadows.

Has one of us not been influenced, somehow, sometime, by at least one of these goddesses? (Even Einstein, they tell us, was a Garbo devotee—and Hitler had an unrequited passion for the cool, silvery image of Marlene Dietrich.)

For many of us they were the first "crush"—after Mommy but before the real thing came along.

They set styles in fashions, manners, morals. There were the Unattainables—and the Too-Attainables. But always they were there on the screen or in the columns or headlines, not really in "real life" at all.

And that's how we treat them here. No attempt at learned analysis of their "art"—simply notes about them as they appeared to all of us up there on the screen where they lived.

This book must be a very personal report. Forgive us if we can't quite summon up the enthusiasm that may be yours about Gloria Glamour. Pardon our "overboard" attachment to Mimi Moviestar. They're our thoughts, our feelings, and yours may not agree at all.

But they all belong—these darlings—to you and to me and to all of us—the ladies in all our lives.

JOHN SPRINGER

Note: Since there must be some limits, this volume deals only with those actresses who spoke on the screen—and in English—from those first halting stutters in 1928 and 1929 through the great days of the thirties. All pictures mentioned in any detail have been seen by the author, most of them recently. Jack Hamilton's biographical notes and occasional opinions follow the Springer comments, set off in another type face.

SPRINGER LIST OF FAVORITE PERFORMANCES

The emphasis is on two words—"personal" and "favorite." There are performances and actresses embraced by the critics, but you won't find them here—just because of those two words.

There must be some limitations, the editors insist, so the list is arbitrarily limited to twelve, with one picture per player, no matter how many "best" performances any one personality may have given.

Is the list capricious? Probably. Who, for instance, is Nova Pilbeam? Only someone who gave the most poignant child performance in memory. Why Nancy Carroll? Throw in those words "personal favorite" again—an underrated performance by an underrated actress.

But the pangs of elimination become sharper. How can Jean Arthur not be there? Simply because her best thirties work was as leading lady, not star. Will Joan Crawford forgive? Despite her great star image in this era, her more demanding roles came in later days.

What about Dietrich? Hers were frequently performances as well as glamour—but the latter quality predominated.

And there can be no argument with someone who would make a case for the inclusion of an Irene Dunne, a Barbara Stanwyck, a Claudette Colbert, a Marie Dressler, a Janet Gaynor, a Helen Hayes, a Miriam Hopkins, a Mary Pickford, or even a Jean Harlow or Mae West. How can the joys given to us by Rosalind Russell, Ginger Rogers, Claire Trevor, Olivia de Havilland or Madeleine Carroll (if only for that face), be overlooked? What about the character actresses, ranging from Fay Bainter and Aline MacMahon to Flora Robson and Dame May Whitty, not to forget Ouspenskaya and Edna May Oliver? Ingrid Bergman's glowing debut, Ann Harding's earlier pre-"noble lady" work, Joan Blondell's breeziness, the remarkable acting of Bonita Granville and Marcia Mae Jones in *These Three*, the freshness of the young Judy Garland, and some extraordinary work by actresses like Betty Field, Marsha Hunt, Geraldine Fitzgerald, Jane Bryan, Wynne Gibson—how wrenching to eliminate them and so many more. And why wouldn't the editors allow a list of fifty? But would even that number be adequate to list all the really notable performances? However, their tributes come in the individual sections about them—all those unforgettable moments from all those unforgettable ladies.

So a dozen it remains and, after much soul-searching and memory-jogging, here is the list—the twelve top feminine screen performances of the thirties:

Beulah Bondi in *Make Way For Tomorrow*
Nancy Carroll in *The Shopworn Angel*
Bette Davis in *Dark Victory*
Greta Garbo in *Camille*
Katharine Hepburn in *Alice Adams*
Wendy Hiller in *Pygmalion*
Vivien Leigh in *Gone With the Wind*
Carole Lombard in *Nothing Sacred*
Myrna Loy in *The Thin Man*
Nova Pilbeam in *Little Friend*
Sylvia Sidney in *You Only Live Once*
Margaret Sullavan in *The Shop Around the Corner*

BETTE DAVIS lies down to await death in *Dark Victory*

BEULAH BONDI in the unforgettable telephone scene from *Make Way for Tomorrow*

NANCY CARROLL had both sweetness and toughness in *The Shopworn Angel*

GARBO's incomparable Camille (with Robert Taylor)

4

KATHARINE HEPBURN was heartbreaking in her gaiety in *Alice Adams* (here with Grady Sutton)

WENDY HILLER, the "draggle-tailed guttersnipe" of Shaw's *Pygmalion*

VIVIEN LEIGH as Scarlett O'Hara in *Gone With the Wind*

CAROLE LOMBARD was brilliantly comic in *Nothing Sacred*

Cool and lovely, MYRNA LOY escaped forever from stereotyped vamps as Nora opposite William Powell's Nick Charles in *The Thin Man*

NOVA PILBEAM in one of the most poignant child performances on record in *Little Friend* (with Jimmy Hanley)

SYLVIA SIDNEY in a stunning dramatic characterization opposite Henry Fonda in *You Only Live Once*

MARGARET SULLAVAN, tender and delightful, with James Stewart in *The Shop Around the Corner*

7

THEY HAD

FACES THEN

KATHARINE ALEXANDER in *The Great Man Votes* with Peter Holden, John Barrymore, Virginia Weidler

KATHERINE ALEXANDER

Always a competent character actress, never an exciting one, Katherine Alexander played dignified women, wronged wives and society snobs. She moved elegantly from the royal court and the social whirl in pictures like *Should Ladies Behave?*, *After Office Hours*, and *Cardinal Richelieu*, to the more earthy atmospheres of *Sutter's Gold*, in which she played the neglected wife of Sutter (Edward Arnold), and *The Great Man Votes*, with John Barrymore.

ELIZABETH ALLAN

Every inch the modern maiden was Elizabeth Allan as she appeared opposite Leslie Howard in *Reserved for Ladies*, a 1932 British comedy. Imported to the states, she seemed rather wan and went through a great deal, whether as the browbeaten mother of *David Copperfield* or the nurse, expiring sadly after a fling with Dr. Clark Gable in *Men in White*. These were her American film high spots. She also played some leads in *Tale of Two Cities*, *The Soldier and the Lady*, *Camille*, *Slave Ship*, *A Woman Rebels*, and *Mark of the Vampire*. But she was much more lively in such enjoyable melodramas as *Mystery of Mr. X* and *Solitaire Man*.

GRACIE ALLEN

You can have your Judiths and Elizabeths—our Allen is Gracie. Was there ever a more enchanting scatterbrain? We had heard her on the radio, burbling and babbling to an exasperated George Burns. How wonderful that on the screen she looked exactly the way we expected Gracie Allen to look, in her frilly dresses and pawky hats, and behaved with even more disarming *joie de vivre*. The most satisfying Burns and Allen picture was *Damsel in Distress*, which costarred Fred Astaire. Their others had them performing little more than a collection of skits, but with Gracie and George, they were all merry. And Gracie was Gracie in them all—*International House*, *College Humor*, *Six of a Kind*, *We're Not Dressing*, *Many Happy Returns*, *Love in Bloom*, *Here Comes Cookie*, *Big Broadcast of 1936*, and *of 1937*, *College Holiday*, *College Swing*, *Honolulu*, and *The Gracie Allen Murder Case*.

JUDITH ALLEN

Judith Allen should have had it made. She began her screen career in 1933 with publicity drums beating, as Cecil DeMille's personal discovery for *This Day and Age* and then went right on, playing opposite Bing Crosby in *Too Much Harmony*. But the DeMille movie was a hysterical youth-age hodgepodge which did nothing for anyone. And most of Bing's leading ladies in the thirties were just there while he sang. She went through the decade in undemanding leads in pictures like *Hell and High Water*, *Thundering Herd*, *The Witching Hour*, *The Old Fashioned Way*, and *Bright Eyes*. Finally, her jobs became parts in quickies and cowboy flicks for Republic and Monogram. All in all, her marital adventures provided more copy than her acting.

ASTRID ALLWYN

Scratch a chilly "other woman" and if she were not Helen Vinson, she usually turned out to be Claire Dodd. Or Astrid Allwyn. Allwyn had a seductive, dishonest smile, crimped blonde hair, and bedecked herself in silver fox furs.

Astrid was the girl with whom Herbert Marshall and Fred MacMurray briefly dallied before they returned to the warmer attractions of Sylvia Sidney and Carole Lombard in *Accent on Youth* and *Hands Across the Table*. She created comparable turmoil in the lives of leading ladies in pictures like *Follow the Fleet*, *Servant's Entrance*, *The White Parade*, *Love Affair* and *Mr. Smith Goes to Washington*. But she was unexpectedly touching as a Depression victim living in Central Park in *One More Spring*.

ADRIENNE AMES

Brunette Adrienne Ames was primarily decorative, but how she dressed up a scene! When she played a

ELIZABETH ALLEN, the mother of David Copperfield (Freddie Bartholomew)

JUDITH ALLEN

GRACIE ALLEN with, of course, George Burns

ASTRID ALLWYN in *Accent on Youth* with Herbert Marshall and Sylvia Sidney

ADRIENNE AMES opposite
W. C. Fields in *You're Telling Me*

11

society girl in Paramount's *24 Hours* in 1931, the publicists insisted that she was a real socialite. And she played the part—all satin hauteur. Girls like Carole Lombard and Helen Twelvetrees had some bad moments when their true loves strayed Ames-ward in pictures like *Sinners in the Sun* and *Disgraced*.

She sometimes made it as a leading lady herself—usually scared (*Guilty as Hell, The Death Kiss*). But you could never believe that anything could really frighten Adrienne Ames.

Once, though, she enjoyed herself in the movies—and so did her audiences—when she was the royal lady involved with W. C. Fields in *You're Telling Me*. In this, she was charming and humorous—which, incidentally, was the way she was known off-screen. On screen, however, it was usually just the sleek chignon, the ice-blue eyes in a fashionably impassive face, with its mouth carefully painted into a semi-sneer—and with yards and yards of silks and furs and dangling earrings.

LONA ANDRE

One of those "Film Fun" cuties—a sort of minor-league brunette Toby Wing—Lona Andre made more publicity stills than movies. She came to Hollywood through the "Panther Woman" contest, which was won by Kathleen Burke. But Lona was put under contract by Paramount, where she posed for lots of fan magazine leg art and played a bit here and there. By 1935, she was working for a quickie company, Liberty, in *School for Girls*, and later frolicked with Iris Adrian in Laurel and Hardy's *Our Relations*.

HEATHER ANGEL

Heather Angel. That name (her real one, incidentally) still evokes the delicate, wistful loveliness of her performance as the girl Leslie Howard loved when he went backward in time to Georgian England in *Berkeley Square* (1933). It should have made her a star, somewhere on the Janet Gaynor level, but nothing much really happened in her career thereafter. She played a lot of lead roles but mostly in unimportant pictures. There were a couple of other parts that stood out: as a prim murderess in *Springtime for Henry*, and as the sorrowing sister of the victim in *The Informer*. There were a few more of some note—*The Mystery of Edwin Drood, The Last of the Mohicans, The Three Musketeers, Daniel Boone*, but the roles were ordinary leading lady parts. By the end of the 1930s, she was the girl in the *Bulldog Drummond* series made by Paramount for the lower half of double bills.

ANNABELLA

Although Annabella had two classic French films, Rene Clair's *Le Million* and *Quatorze Juillet*, it was a British movie, *Wings of the Morning*, which made her

12

ADRIENNE AMES with sometime leading man and real-life husband, Bruce Cabot

ROSEMARY AMES in *I Believed in You* with John Boles

ANNABELLA starred opposite Tyrone Power in *Suez* and married him in real life

a star. Made in 1936, it was England's first Technicolor film and the leading man was the upcoming new American, Henry Fonda. Annabella played a dual role —a girl who raises horses and, in flashback, the girl's grandmother, a gypsy princess. In the modern-day sequences, she spent most of the movie disguised as a boy, and managed it very convincingly indeed—quite the most engaing "boy" of that era in which such ladies as Katharine Hepburn and Miriam Hopkins were also doing such impersonations.

Her other British pictures—*Dinner at the Ritz* and *Under the Red Robe*—gave her much more conventional roles, and so did her subsequent American movie, *The Baroness and the Butler*, with William Powell, a sorry attempt at sophisticated comedy. She was a gamine again in *Suez*—one of the few bearable things about that ponderous epic, although this time she overworked the cuteness a bit. Tyrone Power was the star of *Suez*, and Annabella became his off-screen wife—probably her most famous American role—in a March 1939 wedding.

EVE ARDEN

There had never been anybody quite like Eve Arden until Eve Arden. Nobody was so deadly accurate with verbal barbs which slid lazily from an artistically-created mouth. She was too languid to play romantic leads, even though she was a handsome, long-limbed, green-eyed blonde.

Under her real name of Eunice Quedens, she made

an appearance in *Song of Love* with Belle Baker, in 1929. It wasn't until she had a success on the Broadway stage that she started her real movie career, in 1937, playing a gun moll in *Oh, Doctor*, with Edward Everett Horton. Her first hit was as an unemployed showgirl in a theatrical boarding house in *Stage Door*, the same year. Here, with a cat named Henry draped around her neck, she lounged about, being quite delightfully bitchy about everybody. Other Arden films of the decade were *Having Wonderful Time* and *Letter of Introduction.*

JEAN ARTHUR

Jean Arthur was a perfectly awful ingenue. That was in the early talkie days when Paramount tried to make her look and act like Mary Brian, the perennial sweetheart. But Jean succeeded only in looking like somebody who knew just who she was and where she was going; not at all like the clinging vine who was the normal leading lady of the time. She had to do the usual leg art—they hadn't started calling it "cheesecake" then—and posed for the usual silly publicity shots. But her heart (and intelligence) wasn't in it.

Occasionally she had screen dates with such all-American boys as Buddy Rogers, Richard Arlen, and Jack Oakie. There were some rather effective oddball roles—Clara Bow's nasty sister in *The Saturday Night Kid*, a deceptively sweet young thing who tries to kill off her entire family in S. S. Van Dine's *The Greene Murder Case*.

But, eventually, there were no pictures at all for Jean Arthur. So off she went to Broadway, and there wasn't much dancing in the streets about that either. Even then, though, such critical pundits as Brooks Atkinson saw something special in her performances. In spite of the scant success of the three plays she appeared in, Miss Arthur said later, "Those two and a half years on Broadway were the happiest years of my life. I loved the stage."

And then she was back and suddenly bewitching. There was that cracked, child-woman voice—how could they have once considered it a liability because it was "different"? She was blonde now—fresh and trim and just tough enough to hold her own in the big city world in which she moved, but warm and tender, too. She was a knowing vis-à-vis to *Mr. Deeds* (Gary Cooper), and *Mr. Smith* (James Stewart) . . . an amusing, if improbable, Calamity Jane, in Cecil De-Mille's *The Plainsman* (who would not have been Calamity if she looked like Jean) . . . a moderately normal member of the madcap menage of *You Can't Take It With You* . . . an innocent stenographer engulfed in comic scandals in *Easy Living* . . . a flippant showgirl-drifter in *Only Angels Have Wings* with Cary Grant . . . and assorted, unconventional leading ladies for men like Edward G. Robinson, William Powell, and Charles Boyer.

13

EVE ARDEN

JEAN ARTHUR with James Stewart in *Mr. Smith Goes to Washington*

It would not be until the 1940s that Jean Arthur would really come into her full powers as a star in her own right, but the Jean of the late 1930s made us all very happy indeed.

MARY ASTOR

The 1930s were an interim period for the adaptable Mary Astor. No longer the obedient silent-screen ingenue whose principal function was to be clutched to the manly breasts of Douglas Fairbanks and John Barrymore, and not yet the fascinating villainess she would become in the 1940s, she rode through the 30s in a variety of pictures. There were the worthy parts and performances—like Paul Muni's neurotic wife in *The World Changes,* and the good-time girl of *Convention City* . . . the selfish sister of Ann Harding in

Holiday, and the cheating wife with a yen for Gable in *Red Dust* . . . mistress of the villain caught up in the intrigue of *The Prisoner of Zenda* . . . and, best of all, the drifting, lonely widow who brings affection and understanding to Walter Huston in *Dodsworth.*

But there were many other Mary Astor pictures, too, with leading roles in lesser pictures, and lesser roles in bigger ones. As she has said in her autobiography, *My Story* (1959), her career has always been filled with erratic ups-and-downs.

But to all of her roles, she brought calm dark beauty and poise. She had a kind of sensual side to her, tinged with wickedness that suggested a sub-layer of violent passions. This would be tapped in the forties. Probably though, the Mary Astor of the thirties was known best, not for any picture, but as the central figure in a long real-life courtroom drama.

14

JEAN ARTHUR

JEAN ARTHUR, as Calamity Jane, with Gary Cooper in *The Plainsman*

JEAN ARTHUR in starlet era pin-up pose

16

MARY ASTOR with Walter Huston in *Dodsworth*

MARY ASTOR opposite Paul Muni
in *The World Changes*

17

MARY ASTOR

STELLA ADLER renamed Ardler

RENEE ADOREE with John Gilbert in *Redemption*

ADRIANNE ALLEN (center) with Lila Lee, Clive Brook in *The Night of June 13*

NOTES ON OTHER "A" LADIES

Stella Adler, of the foremost Yiddish Theatre acting family, allowed Hollywood to bill her as *Stella Ardler* in the nonsensical *Love on Toast*. Her many drama students in the following decades do not hold that early mistake against her . . . *Renee Adoree*, the peasant girl of *The Big Parade*, made only three all-talkies, none in lead roles, before her lingering illness of tuberculosis and "burn-the-candle" life had begun to show their marks . . .

The days of the reign of *Iris Adrian* as brassiest babe of them all did not arrive until the 1940s. But you got some indication in a few thirties films—all played at high decibels with her bray-like voice . . . *Adrianne Allen*, of London West End plays, scored in American movies chiefly as a psychotic housewife-suicide in *The Night of June 13* and was a major reason for the small success of this interesting minor film . . . *Rosemary Ames* was to be Fox's hot new star, according to hopeful advance publicity on *I Believed in You*, but the picture was a bomb and Fox believed no more in Rosemary . . .

When "the man of one face," George Arliss, needed a cosy, comfortable wife in films, who better than his own cosy, comfortable wife? *Florence Arliss* played with her husband on stage and in several films . . .

No hot tamale Velez was *Armida*, flashing and tragic by turns as the gypsy bride of Barrymore in *General Crack*. Sadly no roles of consequence followed —only below-border senoritas . . .

IRIS ADRIAN

JUDITH ANDERSON in *Blood Money* with George Bancroft, Chick Chandler

GWILI ANDRE

LONA ANDRE

FLORENCE ARLISS with her distinguished husband

Gwili Andre was like a walking page out of *Harper's Bazaar*—all cheekbones, fake eyelashes and glistening lips. And her screen animation was scarcely more pronounced than that of a photo in the magazine . . .

In passing, some others—*Mary Alden, Agnes Ayres* and *Gertrude Astor,* who once had had more prominence . . . *Sara Allgood,* notable in Hitchcock's early *Blackmail* and *Juno and the Paycock,* as well as in *Storm in a Teacup,* all almost unseen in this country, but with *How Green Was My Valley* still to come . . . *Judith Anderson,* rather a grotesque leading lady for George Bancroft in *Blood Money*—but with *Rebecca* waiting in the forties . . . *Kathryn Adams, Agnes Anderson, Mary Anderson,* nothing special, although the latter would attain more importance than her *Gone with the Wind* bit . . . *Katharine Aldridge* more familiar on magazine covers . . . *Dorothy Adams,* who would be a regularly working character actress in the

PEGGY ASHCROFT and Walter Huston in *Rhodes, the Empire Builder*

ARMIDA opposite John Barrymore in *General Crack*

forties . . . *Anna Appel*, a Jewish mother, most notably in *Symphony of Six Million* . . . *Muriel Angelus*, a leading lady in British pictures unseen in this country but with only one unimpressive lead in an American movie of this period (*The Light That Failed*) . . . *Maria Alba, Dorothy Appleby, Dorothy Arnold*, each with a forgettable lead or two . . . *Bobbe Arnst, Ann Andrews, Jean Adair* and *Edith Atwater*, stage, but not movie, names . . . and *Cupid Ainsworth*, whose wonderful name turned up at the bottom of some cast lists even though the face that went with it has faded from memory. And a nod to *Fern Andra, Alice Adair, Alice Ardell, Pearl Argyle, Betty Amann, Lissi Arna*, the latter in one inconsequential loanout from German films where she was a star.

And there was a brilliant vignette by an actress, unknown to us at the time. The picture was Hitchcock's *39 Steps*—the actress, *Peggy Ashcroft*.

21

OLGA BACLANOVA with Harry Earles in *Freaks*

B

OLGA BACLANOVA

The hard-breathing, teeth-baring type of acting projected by Olga Baclanova (sometimes billed as just Baclanova) seemed outdated for talkies. But she did make a few of them—*A Dangerous Woman*, *The Wolf of Wall Street*, *The Man I Love*, *Cheer Up and Smile*. There was also Tod Browning's famous *Freaks*. She played the sadistic circus queen who marries a midget for his money, and betrays him with the strong man. The horrifying moment when the freaks of the circus take their revenge—silently slithering through the night storm in their hideous pursuit of Baclanova—has given nightmares to a whole generation.

FAY BAINTER

Fay Bainter was our favorite aunt, or the nicest neighbor on the block. Everybody has had a Fay Bainter in his life.

She may have received an Academy Award nomination for it, but we didn't really believe that our smart, viola-voiced Miss Bainter could ever be the clod of a Mary Worth housekeeper that she played in *White Banners*.

But as the most charming of modern mothers, she was always so right. That was the role she played in her first movie in 1934 (although on the stage from childhood, she didn't make a movie until she was 41)— with Lionel Barrymore in *This Side of Heaven*. She was to play such roles again many times, most notably in Leo McCarey's *Make Way for Tomorrow*, as the daughter-in-law who gives bridge lessons to supplement the family income, and whose clash with her husband's mother is made more painful because Fay is not an unfeeling woman, but a most sympathetic one.

She had similar roles in *Yes, My Darling Daughter*, and *Daughters Courageous*, and others. She won an Academy Award in 1938 as best supporting actress as Aunt Belle, who must constantly reprimand Bette Davis for her naughty ways in *Jezebel*.

A many-sided and most sophisticated actress, she alternated such roles with other characterizations—a stabbing vignette as Michael Strogoff's tortured mother in *The Soldier and the Lady*, the fluttery old-maid sister of fluttery old-maid Katharine Hepburn in *Quality Street* and a dowager standing up against terrorism in *The Lady and the Mob*.

There would be many more Bainter performances of distinction in the decades to come (her last was in *The Children's Hour* in 1962) but her individuality contributed importantly to the films of the thirties.

LUCILLE BALL

She was that tall blonde in the background of Rogers and Astaire musicals (*Roberta*, *Follow the Fleet*) and some lesser efforts.

Later we learned that Lucille Ball was red-headed, but that was about the time she was playing second and third bananas to the likes of Ginger, Katharine Hepburn and Irene Dunne. Even then she had a way with a droll line or a slapstick situation, and those eyebrows were already astonished.

She was a chum to the heroines in *Stage Door*, *Having Wonderful Time* and *Joy of Living*. And she was off on her own in some little program pictures. The best of these were two about a rattlebrained movie star, *Affairs of Annabel* and *Annabel Takes a Tour*.

She may have been flattened by the frantic steamroller of the Marx Brothers in *Room Service* but she had some moments all her own as a good natured trollop in *Five Came Back*. All of these films were made for RKO, the studio she later owned, which first paid her $50 a week.

In the 1930s, Lucille Ball was already fun to have around—but she was a long way yet from becoming a national institution.

TALLULAH BANKHEAD

In 1931, Paramount Pictures proclaimed, in advertising for *Tarnished Lady*:

FAY BAINTER, Eddie Nugent, Mae Clarke in *This Side of Heaven*

FAY BAINTER, with Claude Rains, Bonita Granville, in *White Banners*

LUCILLE BALL with Harpo, Chico and Groucho in *Room Service*

COMING! COMING!
TALLULAH, THE GLAMOROUS
TALLULAH, THE MYSTERIOUS
TALLULAH, THE WOMAN
WE GAVE YOU MARLENE DIETRICH—
NOW WE GIVE YOU TALLULAH BANKHEAD!

So why in the world did they tone down the high-powered personality of Tallulah Bankhead when they brought her to the movies? She was given roles completely removed from those that had made her an

LUCILLE BALL in starlet publicity pose

international celebrity. She was the most flamboyant and vibrant of sophisticates—so they made her one of those more sinned against than sinning heroines in heavy melodramas like *My Sin* and *Tarnished Lady* and, loaned to MGM, *Faithless*. Nor were the phony "Garbo" roles she had in *The Cheat* and *Thunder Below* much improvement. She was rather well turned-out as an adulterous wife in *The Devil and the Deep*—she was married to Charles Laughton, and had both Gary Cooper and Cary Grant waiting on the sidelines. But not until a couple of films of the forties did movies let her flip out the acerbic retort in that wonderfully masculine bellow. In the thirties, there was never a chance to camp it up . . . never a chance to be Tallulah.

VILMA BANKY

Blonde and ethereal—promoted as "The Hungarian Rhapsody"—was Vilma Banky, contrasting so well with the swarthy Ronald Colman and Rudolph Valentino. But along came talkies and Vilma spoke—in accents guttural. They tried to tailor her roles—an immigrant girl in *This Is Heaven* . . . a made-for-Banky version of *They Knew What They Wanted*. It didn't work. Banky didn't pound on the doors and quit while she was still ahead, for domesticity, real estate investments and golf.

LYNN BARI

As Claire Trevor moved on to better things, her position as Queen of the B's at 20th Century-Fox was taken over by Lynn Bari, a lush, no-nonsense brunette. Miss Bari was apple-cheeked and had a gleaming sense of humor. You could imagine her doing well in Rosalind Russell-type roles.

What Fox did give her were adventures with Mr. Moto, Charlie Chan, and the Cisco Kid, as well as such programmers as *Battle of Broadway, Speed to Burn, News Is Made at Night,* and *Pack Up Your Troubles*. She also showed up in minor roles in pictures of somewhat more ambition but no more achievement—*Always Goodbye, The Baroness and the Butler,* and Elsa Maxwell's *Hotel For Women*. Better roles in better pictures—there were a few—were not to come until the 1940s.

BINNIE BARNES

One of the four (others being Merle Oberon, Wendy Barrie, Elsa Lanchester) who started their successful careers as the consorts of Charles Laughton in *The Private Life of Henry VIII*, was Binnie Barnes, who played Katherine Howard. She arrived on our shores in 1934 as one of those long-suffering mistresses in *There's Always Tomorrow*. She was sprightly as Lillian Russell in *Diamond Jim*, and in *The Lady is Willing* and *Rendezvous*. But her true forte was rather tart,

24

TALLULAH BANKHEAD and Gary Cooper in *The Devil and the Deep*

TALLULAH goes maternal with Baby Rosemary McHugh in *Tarnished Lady*

TALLULAH BANKHEAD in *The Cheat*

VILMA BANKY

LYNN BARI

enameled comedy and she brought a great deal of bite to a series of secondary roles—the blondined, gold-digging man hunter of *Three Smart Girls* being a well-remembered example. Other such Binnie Barnes roles would include the remake of *Holiday*, *Always Good-bye*, *Wife, Husband and Friend*, *Three Blind Mice*, and as the notorious Milady de Winter (who hid state-secrets papers in her ample bosom) in the Ritz Brothers' version of *The Three Musketeers*.

WENDY BARRIE

Wendy Barrie played the sluttish Jane Seymour, the fat king's second wife, in *The Private Life of Henry VIII* in 1933, and, along with his other "wives"— Merle Oberon, Binnie Barnes, Elsa Lanchester—she moved on to Hollywood. The vivacious Wendy fared only moderately well in her Hollywood career. For instance, she was teamed with Spencer Tracy in her first American movie, 1935, *It's a Small World*, but that meant not a thing—it was one of the few Tracy movies that was never heard of again. She appeared in some twenty-five movies during the 1930s—they ranged from *College Scandal* and *Big Broadcast of 1936* to *Hound of the Baskervilles* and *Five Came Back*—but only three of them gave her a chance to stand out. She was a breezy heroine in *Wings Over Honolulu*, with Kent Taylor and Ray Milland; was the kept girl in *Dead End* who fought back her love for slum-born Joel

McCrea; and played, quite against her usual type, the underworld honey with whom Edward G. Robinson got involved in *I Am the Law*.

ETHEL BARRYMORE

One of the few real superstars of the Theatre con-descended only once in the thirties to set foot on a Hollywood sound stage. Ethel Barrymore joined her brothers in *Rasputin and the Empress* and the experi-ence must have unnerved her. She would not return to the screen until the mid-forties, when she won an Academy Award as Cary Grant's cockney mother in *None But the Lonely Heart*. Actually Lionel Barry-more dominated *Rasputin and the Empress* as the mad monk, and there may not be a hammier performance on record. John was dashing as his assassin. That left little for Ethel except to stand about imperially as the doomed Czarina. Occasionally there were glimpses of the Great Lady—a roll of those magnificent eyes, a few words in that magnificent voice. But it was really an inauspicious talking picture debut for Ethel Barry-more and it would be a dozen years before she tried again.

LOUISE BEAVERS

Back in those days, the few possible roles for a black actress would be a hallelujah-singing Mammy or a domestic, ranging from low comedy to warm-hearted. Specialist in the latter field was Louise Beavers. Where Hattie McDaniel could be gruff and bossy, and Butterfly McQueen squeakily idiotic, the Beavers image was all big protective bosoms and benevolent smiles. Some of her more memorable maids served Mae West in *She Done Him Wrong*, Jean Harlow in *Bombshell*, Constance Bennett in *What Price Hollywood?* Fay Bainter in *Make Way for Tomorrow* and Carole Lombard in *Made for Each Other*.

But certainly the best-remembered Beavers role is Aunt Jemima, who parlayed her pancakes into big business with the help of Claudette Colbert in *Imitation of Life*. A pretty soggy sentimental drama, it had the then fairly unusual theme of the broken-hearted mother of a black girl (Fredi Washington) who has left home to pass as white. That Miss Beavers had to play a role saddled with every Negro cliché did not take away from the gentle impact of her personality or the honest strength of her performance.

JANET BEECHER

Janet Beecher was a forthright actress who generally was cast in what you might call "midway roles"— women not quite as fluttery as Spring Byington, not quite as hard as Jean Dixon, not quite as affecting as Fay Bainter. Alert-eyed and square-jawed, she played stalwart wives, staunch mothers, and sympathetic friends in *Gallant Lady*, *The President Vanishes*, *The Mighty Barnum*, *So Red the Rose*, *Good Old Soak*, and many more. She was the dependable kind of actress who never particularly stood out, but whose presence in a movie was always welcome.

MADGE BELLAMY

Madge Bellamy, a brunette with big brown eyes, was popular in the silents but made only a few talkie appearances. Her last talkie of note was her first—a part-dialogue film, *Mother Knows Best*, in which she was a stage personality, supposedly possessed of more talent than she was able to display. After that, she was the screeching heroine in a horrible horror film, *White Zombie*, with Bela Lugosi, and appeared in a Universal serial, *Gordon of Ghost City*, with Buck Jones. Later her name moved toward the bottom of the cast lists of *Charlie Chan in London*, *The Daring Young Man* and *The Great Hotel Murder*.

CONSTANCE BENNETT

Constance Bennett was model-slender, had round china-blue eyes, a marcelled blonde bob—and style. My, what style! Sometimes she uttered wisecracks in the husky voice that was a trademark. But then there would come a time when she suffered and suffered— men and babies taking advantage of her. But she somehow managed to be refined, even when she was being

LOUISE BEAVERS and Claudette Colbert in *Imitation of Life*

BINNIE BARNES with Don Ameche in *The Three Musketeers*

WENDY BARRIE with Charles Laughton in *The Private Life of Henry VIII*

ETHEL BARRYMORE with her brothers, John and Lionel, and Tad Alexander in *Rasputin and the Empress*

JANET BEECHER in *So Red the Rose* with Margaret Sullavan, Randolph Scott

MADGE BELLAMY in *Mother Knows Best* with Barry Norton and Louise Dresser

CONSTANCE BENNETT and Lowell Sherman in *What Price Hollywood*

a wide-eyed maid seduced by the son of her wealthy employer. This was in *Common Clay*, and it was typical of the way Connie took it on the chin from men in those days. There was more of the same—*The Easiest Way* and *Bought*, *Rockabye* and *Bed of Roses* among them.

Bennett also went the Glamour route—the Glamour spies of *Three Faces East* and *After Midnight*, the Glamour performer in *Moulin Rouge*, the Glamour model in *Ladies in Love*. And since she had created quite an off-screen reputation as a New York and Paris society swinger, she played lots of society girls, from a very upper-class member of the drawing room set in Maugham's *Our Betters*, to that wild Iris March, of *The Green Hat* notoriety, in a remake, called *Outcast Lady*.

One of her best performances, and her own favorite, was as the Brown Derby waitress who becomes a Hollywood star in *What Price Hollywood?*. She was also a very modern Renaissance duchess in *The Affairs of Cellini*.

CONSTANCE BENNETT

CONSTANCE BENNETT with her father, Richard Bennett, (right) and Ben Lyon in *Bought*

CONSTANCE BENNETT and Clark Gable in *After Office Hours*

JOAN BENNETT in *Private Worlds*

JOAN BENNETT and Fredric March in *Trade Winds*

There was a while there, back in the early 1930s, when she was the highest paid star on the screen—her $150,000 net for four and a half weeks' work on *Two Against the World* for Warners in 1932 was the highest salary paid any film player up to that time. When she moved from one studio (Warners) to another (RKO), it was in the manner of a queen trading in a small kingdom for a much more opulent one.

But then there came the period when her pictures became almost as much of a drag at the box office as they were with the critics. She lost her RKO studio contract, flitted around, took much less important roles as a freelance. She finally even had to make a movie (*Everything Is Thunder*) in England, at that time the haven of has-been American movie stars.

When she did return to Hollywood, it was to a picture for Hal Roach, and everybody knew he only made slapstick shorts. But this time he made *Topper*, and Constance Bennett positively scintillated as the most blithe and saucy lady ghost to turn up in movies. She was quite delightful, too, as the dizzy post-debutante in another of those comedies of the *My Man Godfrey* school—but a good one—*Merrily We Live*.

But then her career dipped again, and she rounded out the last two years of the decade with three misfires. The Bennett career was never to regain its full lustre, except for an occasional moment, in the decades to follow. But she certainly made her mark on the thirties.

JOAN BENNETT

Much less showy than her sisters, Constance and Barbara, was Richard Bennett's youngest daughter. Joan Bennett started out in 1929, her soft blondness (but never soft personality) making her right for the dark good looks of a Ronald Colman in *Bulldog Drummond*, or a Robert Montgomery in *Three Live Ghosts*. She embellished the scene with all manner of men—from John Barrymore to Bing Crosby. Every so often, she had a chance to do something a little more than just be a passive leading lady. She was a pert Amy in *Little Women*, and she was really quite moving as the wife of a psychiatrist who teeters on the brink of insanity herself in *Private Worlds*. She went the route from Cary Grant to Jack Benny. Mostly, her parts were bland, and even when she had the chance to play one of those stylish ladies-with-a-past in *I Met My Love Again* (Henry Fonda was the "I"), the picture was so novelettish that it wasn't much of an improvement. Unexpectedly though, she suddenly came along looking quite unlike the usual poker-faced demure Joan Bennett—actually she was a near-ringer for Hedy Lamarr—in a jazzy comedy-melodrama called *Trade Winds*, with Fredric March, in 1939. Not only had her appearance changed, but so had her personality

—to brunette and sultry. Then she went back to the routine roles. But there would be more of the gutsy ones in the forties.

INGRID BERGMAN and Gosta Ekman in the Swedish *Intermezzo*

LEILA BENNETT and Janet Gaynor in *The First Year*

LEILA BENNETT

Leila Bennett turned up in small roles and bits in a number of pictures of the thirties—a vivid closeup of a lynch-excited onlooker in *Fury* was one example. Her best remembered role was as one of those slovenly Negro maids in *The First Year*. Since she was not a Negro and played it in blackface, it added insult to the injury of a stereotype. But, of course, they didn't think of it as insult in those thankfully past days.

INGRID BERGMAN

Ingrid Bergman flashed into international screen prominence at the very end of the 1930s. One of the most radiant of all actresses, she had been brought to America by David Selznick to repeat a role she had played in 1936 on the Swedish screen, in *Intermezzo*. It was a terribly old-hat triangle story—the great musician (Leslie Howard), his considerate wife (Edna Best), and the romantic girl who falls madly in love with him. But since Bergman was so young and eloquent, the picture achieved a high mark it shouldn't have rated, and it began one of the most fabulous careers in Hollywood.

INGRID BERGMAN and Leslie Howard in the American remake of *Intermezzo*

31

ELISABETH BERGNER in *Escape Me Never*

EDNA BEST and Leslie Howard in *Intermezzo*

ELISABETH BERGNER

Viennese Elisabeth Bergner was all darting eyes, breathless little gasps and giggles, and other affectations that some found cloying, others artistic. In Central Europe, she was considered a major actress in Shakespeare, Ibsen and Shaw. She made her English-speaking debut on the London stage as the gamine Gemma Jone in *Escape Me Never*, and her Broadway debut in the same play in 1935. She won ecstatic notices in the theatre and, to be fair, in films. But to us, she was almost entirely too much for movies.

All of her British-made films had distribution in the States. She repeated *Escape Me Never* for the screen in 1935, and, as Rosalind in *As You Like It*, her German accent made mincemeat of Shakespeare's poetry.

Probably her most satisfactory screen job was in the title role of *Catherine the Great*, her first English-language movie, in which her excesses were overshadowed by the wild overacting of Douglas Fairbanks, Jr., as her mad consort. Others included *Dreaming Lips* and *Stolen Life*, in which she played twins.

EDNA BEST

That excellent English actress Edna Best appeared in British pictures like *The Calendar* and *Michael and Mary* which got very limited distribution in this country, and in Hitchcock's *The Man Who Knew Too Much*, *South Riding* and *Prison Without Bars*, which were shown only slightly more extensively. She made one American movie in 1934—*The Key*, opposite William Powell—but it was one of his weakest. So she was relatively unknown to American moviegoers until 1939, when she finally played in an American film in which she was impressive, *Intermezzo*. Even so, as the wife deserted by Leslie Howard, she had to take a back seat to a breathtaking new Swedish girl, named Ingrid Bergman.

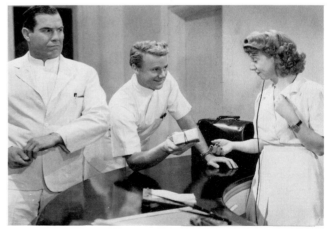

MARIE BLAKE as Dr. Kildare's receptionist (with Nat Pendleton and Van Johnson)

MARIE BLAKE

Marie Blake played small roles, and her name isn't one to stay with any but the most fervent buff. But look at a picture of her and recognition should be immediate. Of course! She's the telephone operator at

32

Blair General Hospital, for Drs. Kildare and Gillespie. She did other pictures, but it is as the doctors' side-kick that she survives in memory.

SALLY BLANE with Lee Tracy in *Advice to the Lovelorn*

CLARA BLANDICK in *The Show Off* with Henry Wadsworth, Spencer Tracy, and Madge Evans

CLARA BLANDICK

On April 15, 1962, an old lady had her hair done, got dressed in her best, spread out pictures and mementos of a long career that had made her face—if not her name, which was Clara Blandick—known to millions of movie fans, took a mammoth dose of sleeping pills, and lay down to die. She could no longer face the failing of her eyesight and growing arthritic agony.

In the 1930s, Clara Blandick played character roles in dozens of pictures. She would be the crabby woman down the road, then she would turn up as an apple-pie mom. She showed up well in pictures like *As the Earth Turns, A Star Is Born, Drums Along the Mohawk, Swanee River* and a number of others. And she was everybody's aunt—fussy, kindly—among others, Aunt Polly in Jackie Coogan's *Tom Sawyer* and *Huckleberry Finn*, and in the later non-Coogan *Tom Sawyer, Detective*. She was Judy's Auntie Em in *The Wizard of Oz*, and everyone in that was touched with immortality.

SALLY BLANE

After Loretta Young was established, her comely sisters made their move. Polly Ann Young, the eldest, didn't stick it out long, and Georgianna, the youngest, merely joined the others as Loretta's screen siblings in *The Story of Alexander Graham Bell*. But Sally Blane had a modest career. She was Rudy Vallee's girl in *The Vagabond Lover*, in the days when Rudy was America's idol, and Kate Smith's sister in *Hello Everybody*, at the period when Kate was something of a sweetheart too. After a couple of minor leads with Lee Tracy and Edmund Lowe, Sally—she briefly spelled it "Sallie"—was relegated to B-pictures and Westerns.

JOAN BLONDELL

Joan Blondell had the face of a corrupt Kewpie doll and the personality of a hip Orphan Annie.

Only once or twice did she play a dumb blonde and, because Joan Blondell was always one of our brightest actresses, she even made you believe that she could be one. But usually she played wise, warm and honest girls who know the score.

She was discovered for the screen in a sleazy little play, *Penny Arcade*, on Broadway in 1930, and both she and James Cagney were imported to Hollywood by Warners to make the screen version, renamed *Sinners' Holiday*. Blondell and Cagney formed a happy, well-matched team in *Public Enemy, Blonde Crazy, The Crowd Roars, Footlight Parade, He Was Her Man*. But then it seemed as if Joan were in every other picture put out by Warners in the 1930s.

She was frequently a Broadway gold-digger—all shades from the dumb-bunny of *The Greeks Had a Word for Them* to the calculating biddy of *Stage Struck*. You'd also find her teaming up with Glenda Farrell—they were a sort of higher-class Thelma Todd and Patsy Kelly.

Joan was good in her Blondell way in just about everything she did, but her best roles—and therefore her best performances—cast her opposite Leslie Howard in *Stand In*, as a sharp-witted studio girl pitted against a naive babe in the Holly-woods . . . opposite Fernand Gravet as the second half of the title, *The King and the Chorus Girl*, and in two trivial but quite pleasing comedies, *There's Always a Woman* and *Good Girls Go to Paris*.

Our own favorite Blondell moment was her song, as the torchy streetwalker, in *Gold Diggers of 1933*, in which she begged us all to "Remember My Forgotten Man" (the World War I veterans who were

33

JOAN BLONDELL with frequent co-star and once-husband, Dick Powell

BLONDELL and Cagney made many films together—*He Was Her Man* being one of them

now in the Army of the Unemployed). Don't tell us that Miss B. was not well aware that the number was sheer camp—away back before camp was invented.

ELEANOR BOARDMAN

Eleanor Boardman had reached the apex of her career in King Vidor's *The Crowd*, in which her well-bred manner made her seem wrong casting. But she overcame it to give a performance of some depth.

She made only a few talking pictures—Henry King's *She Goes to War*, *Mamba*, *Redemption*, *The Flood*, *The Great Meadow*, *Women Love Once* and a re-make of *The Squaw Man*. While none was any great shakes, they were not bad enough to send her to quickies. But after 1931, she dropped out. Then surprisingly, two years later, her name turned up at the bottom of the cast following those of people like John Darrow, Merna Kennedy, Natalie Moorhead, Matthew Betz and Mickey Rooney in something called *Big Chance*, a film thoroughly poverty-row in all other respects.

MARY BOLAND

Madcap mothers were a staple of the 1930s and, by some stroke of film chance, they were invariably played by actresses whose names began with "B"—Brady, Byington, occasionally Bainter, and always dear Billie Burke.

One of the earliest—and maddest—was the befuddled Mrs. Rimplegar of *Three-Cornered Moon*, as brought to life by the bountiful Mary Boland. It was Mrs. Rimplegar who gave away the family fortune to a swindler because he had struck her as being "such a nice young man."

More often she was the chattering, henpecking wife of Charlie Ruggles in a series of domestic farces with titles like *Mama Loves Papa*, *People Will Talk*, *Early to Bed*, and *Wives Never Know*. Since the Boland roles were almost all the same, the success of her performances depended on the pictures. When *they* were good, *she* was wonderful.

Among other roles away from the Ruggles slapstick series, although Ruggles was still present, she was the social climber in *Ruggles of Red Gap*, who brings back from Europe to her Western tank town an impeccable butler, played by Charles Laughton. And she was the Revolutionary War mama of Joan Bennett in *Pursuit of Happiness*.

Once in the 1930s, Paramount, for whom she made most of her pictures, let her play a serious role—she had occasionally appeared that way during a long stage career. But the movie, *A Son Comes Home*, was a particularly maudlin mother-love drama, and no movie audience would accept a suffering Mary Boland.

So it was back to the dingalings with a special one to see out the thirties—the ribald Countess in her un-

JOAN BLONDELL and Jimmy Cagney were discovered for the screen in the play *Penny Arcade*

JOAN BLONDELL

ELEANOR BOARDMAN gave her most noted performance in the silent, *The Crowd* with James Murray

MARY BOLAND and her frequent team-mate, Charlie Ruggles

ceasing alcoholic quest for "l'amour" in *The Women*. Throughout all the occasional vulgarity of her roles, she managed to maintain a quality that reminded you that she had once been one of the great beauties of the American theater.

LILIAN BOND

A dark, curvacious girl, Lilian Bond usually played roles that called for her to lure the hero away from the leading lady for a moment or two—with such stars as Nancy Carroll, Sylvia Sidney, Loretta Young, Ann Harding, and Joan Blondell among the temporary victims. There was a period (1932-1933), in which she had some fifteen such roles. She even worked her wiles on Joe E. Brown in *Fireman, Save My Child* and was also one of the visitors to the scary *Old Dark House*, with Charles Laughton and Boris Karloff.

BEULAH BONDI

When you are speaking of the most moving movie scenes of all times, certainly you're going to choose several from Leo McCarey's *Make Way for Tomorrow*. There's the heartbreaking final moment when the old man is going away and the old lady is at the train station to see him off. He doesn't know—but she does, and you do—that they will never see each other again. There's their warm, wonderful second honeymoon when they go for a ride in a car that's being hopefully demonstrated—but they think the salesman is just a friendly, obliging man. There is the tentative attempt at a little waltz—but the music turns to swing. There is the absolutely devastating scene when the old lady gets a telephone call from her husband so many miles away—and pours out her love and loneliness to him, oblivious of the annoyed, then ashamed, then strangely touched guests at a card party in the room where she is on the phone. Try to see that without choking up.

I yielded to no one in admiration for Victor Moore, but the person who tore you apart at all of those moments was the beloved Beulah Bondi, surely the most versatile character actress on all levels the movies have known. She wasn't one of those darling lavender-and-old-lace ladies. Her Lucy Cooper in *Make Way for Tomorrow* could be a cranky, cantankerous old girl. But she was so real, she was frightening. Academy Oscars ceased to have their full value the year she did not get a nomination for *Make Way for Tomorrow*.

She had been nominated in 1936 for her Rachel Jackson, the pitiful, pipe-smoking wife of President Andy in *The Gorgeous Hussy*, a Joan Crawford-Lionel Barrymore film that had little else to recommend it. And she was perfection in so many other roles—as Mrs. Jones, the archetype of all tenement slatterns in *Street Scene*, her film debut in 1931 (she had created the role on the stage) . . . Melissa Tolliver, gentle

MARY BOLAND as Mrs. Rimplegar in *Three Cornered Moon* with Tom Brown, William Bakewell, Wallace Ford

LILIAN BOND and Charles Laughton in *The Old Dark House*

BEULAH BONDI and Victor Moore in *Make Way for To-morrow*

BEULAH BONDI in *Street Scene*

BEULAH BONDI as Rachel Jackson and Lionel Barrymore as President Andy in *The Gorgeous Hussy*

mountain mother, crying out against the blood lust of her clan in *The Trail of the Lonesome Pine* . . . as the half-crazed crone trying to regain her youth in *Maid of Salem* . . . the sacrificing wife of stern preacher Walter Huston, and mother of thoughtless soldier James Stewart in the Civil War drama *Of Human Hearts* . . . and in so many other roles of infinite variety that continued through the 1940s, the 1950s, and into the 1960s. In the twenties, she had created roles in the theatre. In the 1940s, and 1950s she would be sweet again, and evil again, and elegant or drab. But, in the 1930s, she was all of those women—the loving mothers, the harridans, the aristocrats, the frontier women, the religious psalm singers. And she was the pince-nezed, righteous wife of Rev. Davidson in *Rain* . . . the greed-driven Mrs. Haggerty in *The Late Christopher Bean* . . . the prototype of the mother to come home to at Christmas in *Remember the Night* . . . the beautiful old lady who goes so willingly with Death in *On Bor-*

rowed Time and the once-inhibited, once-repressed wife of a college dean in *Vivacious Lady*. But, above all, she was Lucy Cooper of *Make Way for Tomorrow*. That alone—if she had done none of her others—would make her a screen immortal.

OLIVE BORDEN (center) with Jack Oakie, Mary Brian in *A Social Lion*

OLIVE BORDEN

Olive Borden—whippet-slim, dark-eyed, dressed to kill—the very picture of the wilful flapper—had had a short silent-screen career as a star (*Fig Leaves, Joy Girl, Pajamas*, etc.) but she made only a few talkies. She was the other girl in Jack Oakie's *Social Lion*, but the rest were principally quickies. Among these were *Half Marriage, Dance Hall, Wedding Rings* and *Hotel Variety*.

VEDA ANN BORG

There's a smarty-pants set which considers the height of something to be reference to the movies of Veda Ann Borg. Actually, outside of her name, which may now have a "Film Fun" ring, Miss Borg was not unattractive—tawny and tall. She may have been in forgettable pictures (mostly at Warners: *The Singing Marine, San Quentin, Alcatraz Island, She Loved a Fireman, Over the Wall* were some in the thirties), but the name and visage of Veda Ann Borg lingers on to the true movie connoisseur.

THE BOSWELL SISTERS

So you thought it was Elvis and his contemporaries who first sang "Rock and Roll" in movies. Wrong. A song of that name was highlighted in the 1934 Nancy Carroll-Jack Benny movie, *Transatlantic Merry Go Round*, and it was put across by three ladies named Connie, Martha and Vet, the Boswell Sisters. They had a few years singing on radio, on records and in short movies as well as features like *The Big Broadcast*. Then Martha and Vet took off and Connie—who made herself "Connee" for the occasion—continued to sing all by herself. Tuneful recollection—Connee's velvety "Whispers in the Dark" from *Artists and Models*.

CLARA BOW

By the beginning of the 1930s, the "Brooklyn Bonfire" had just about burned out. Clara Bow was still curvy and red-headed but the old "It" just wasn't there any more.

She had had her share of scandals, but they didn't hurt her nearly as much as did pictures like *True to the Navy* and *No Limit*. We still went to see her for a while because after all, she was Clara Bow, and just a couple of years back she had been the jazz baby who typified the age.

And when she wasn't cutting it as a jazz baby any more, Paramount half-heartedly tried to change her image by giving her the role of the faithful wife of an ex-convict who helps him to reform in *Kick In*. It didn't work. She herself bowed out of *City Streets* and *Secret Call*, thereby giving opportunities to a couple of striking new faces—Sylvia Sidney and Peggy Shannon—who replaced her.

There were a couple of last gasps when Fox attempted to revive her career in roles similar to those she had played in her heyday. But both *Call Her Savage*, based on Tiffany Thayer's novel about a part-Indian girl, and *Hoopla*, in which she played a carnival dancer, were, to put it as kindly as possible, terrible. And that was the movie end of one of Hollywood's really legendary stars.

VEDA ANN BORG

CLARA BOW and Fredric March in *True to the Navy*

CLARA BOW

DORRIS BOWDEN

Dorris Bowdon, described as "a blonde, hazel-eyed little lady from Tennessee, with the cool oval face of one of those pretty 19th century German madonnas and the figure of a Balinese dancing girl" (Michael Mok, *New York Post*), played minor roles in *Young Mr. Lincoln* and *Drums Along the Mohawk*, both with Henry Fonda. But she got most attention in those last months of the 1930s with the announcement that she would be the Rose of Sharon of the film version of John Steinbeck's classic *The Grapes of Wrath*.

GRACE BRADLEY

Redheaded Grace Bradley began as a contract player at Paramount in 1933, as one of the girls in *Too Much Harmony*, with Bing Crosby. Her roles were unimportant—she was a minor-league sex-pot who showed up better in publicity stills than on the screen. After she was finished at Paramount, Grace occasionally did make it as a leading lady but at small-time studios.

OLYMPE BRADNA

Olympe Bradna was a brunette French actress, not too notable as a leading lady at Paramount. She probably was better-known for the publicity campaign on how to pronounce her name—"Say O-Lamp!"—than for any of her performances. Still she played conventional leads in such conventional movies as *Stolen Heaven, Say It in French* and *Night of Nights*.

ALICE BRADY

Alice Brady was an emotional actress on the stage, but in films she was much more likely to be a giddy one. From 1933, she giggled and simpered through a spate of films like *Should Ladies Behave, When Ladies Meet, The Gay Divorcee, Three Smart Girls*, and most notably as the moronic mother of a zany millionaire family in *My Man Godfrey*.

GRACE BRADLEY (right) with Una Merkel and Harold Lloyd in *The Cat's Paw*

OLYMPE BRADNA and Gene Raymond in *Stolen Heaven*

But unlike other such sisters of the cinema as Mary Boland and Billie Burke, Miss Brady was accepted on screen by audiences in more serious roles. She was a grasping, pushing *Stage Mother* to Maureen O'Sullivan. She played spunky country women—one who helped a distraught movie queen find her kidnapped baby is *Miss Fane's Baby Is Stolen*, and another whose family gets involved in a murder case defended in court by *Young Mr. Lincoln*, her final film. She was the shanty Irish Mrs. O'Leary, whose cow started the big fire in *In Old Chicago*, and she won an Academy Award for that one.

But we recall most vividly her vaudeville soubrette, Lulu Hackett, in one of those youth-to-old-age cavalcades, *Broadway to Hollywood*. It had a scene which should have been awful: the old vaudeville couple, Alice Brady and Frank Morgan, go to watch their grandson, who has become a big-time movie director, as he films a scene. And during the scene, the old man dies as his wife watches, not crying out for fear of ruining the take. On second thought, the scene *was* awful. But the stricken eyes of Alice Brady keep it alive in the memory.

EVELYN BRENT

Evelyn Brent was a smouldering-eyed brunette whose look was supposed to be sultry but could just as well have been described as sullen. Through the 1920s she played women of dubious reputation—particularly gun molls (e.g. "Feathers" McCoy in Josef von Sternberg's *Underworld*)—in the silent era.

She moved easily enough into talkies as the blackmailer in Paramount's first all-talking picture, *Interference*, and went into other such roles—from the vengeful Pearl in *Broadway*, to vamping Jack Oakie in *Fast Company*. Her contract with Paramount ended in 1930 with *Slightly Scarlet*. Suddenly it seemed, her name moved further and further down in the cast lists, or turned up in pictures best described as "cheapies." But she did return to Paramount briefly in 1937 in bits in *Night Club Scandal* and *Daughter of Shanghai*.

MARY BRIAN

Mary Brian was such a nice girl. Open-faced, with nice blue eyes and a nice white smile. She was nice as Buddy Rogers' leading lady and she was nice as Richard Arlen's. Or Gary Cooper's. Or Lee Tracy's. The only trouble was that she was exactly the same nice girl in everything. Wendy grown up. But just a little. For instance as the eldest daughter and "guardian" of the children of divorce in *Marriage Playground*.

She finally did try hard to change the image—how else to explain the inappropriate *Hard to Handle* part with James Cagney. And blonde! Not our Mary. Better Alice White had done it.

40

ALICE BRADY in *Lady Tubbs*

ALICE BRADY as Mrs. O'Leary in *In Old Chicago*

EVELYN BRENT in *Why Bring That Up?*

MARY BRIAN and Buddy Rogers in *River of Romance*

MARY BRIAN and Douglas Fairbanks, Jr. in *It's Tough To Be Famous*

But mostly she was Mary, sweet as any girl could be —not exactly electric, but such a nice girl.

FANNY BRICE

Fanny Brice could do no wrong on Broadway or in countless radio shows. But movies almost never used her properly.

She was one of the earlier stars to make the trek from Broadway when talking pictures put such names in demand. But both of her starring pictures—*My Man* and *Be Yourself*—were wretched affairs, enlivened only fitfully by a couple of her specialty numbers.

She did come back as Funny Fanny herself, discovered by William Powell as *The Great Ziegfeld*, and her scene was a high spot in the film of high spots. But she had barely started to sing her incomparable "My Man" before Ziegfeld-Powell shut the door to his office and shut Fanny and "My Man" out of the rest of the picture. It was a big let-down.

There was one more film in the thirties, *Everybody Sing*, with Judy Garland, which gave Fanny a chance to make a few faces and reprise her impersonation of Baby Snooks. But it was to take decades before the movies—through a girl named Barbra Streisand—really did right by our Fanny.

FANNY BRICE and Guinn Williams in *My Man*

FANNY BRICE as Baby Snooks, with Judy Garland in *Everybody Sing*

42

HELEN BRODERICK

Helen Broderick, of the big bug eyes and acid tongue, did a lot for Broadway revues (*The Band Wagon, As Thousands Cheer*) with her dry, economical way with a putdown. Salute her in movies of the 1930s for the same reasons, although generally she had fairly unrewarding roles as the duenna-friend of the stars.

These included Fred Astaire and Ginger Rogers in *Top Hat* and *Swing Time*. She did other musicals in similar roles but these were nothing to remember, and and Miss Broderick's presence was among their few assets.

Her employer, RKO, seemed to want to turn her into an Edna May Oliver replacement. She had Miss Oliver's role in a remake of *Ladies of the Jury*, now called *We're on the Jury*, and in *Murder on the Bridle Path* in which she played Hildegarde Withers, the school marm detective originated by Oliver in *Penguin Pool Murder*. But whereas Edna May was the very personification of a persnickety old maid, Broderick was much more "with it."

She did a number of pictures with Victor Moore—she had been with him on Broadway—but these were third-rate; they never scored nearly as well as a team as did a Mary Boland and Charlie Ruggles, or Aline MacMahon and Guy Kibbee.

SHEILA BROMLEY

There was a girl with blue eyes and light brown hair—Sheila Mannors (sometimes spelled Manners) was her name—who played in movies, mostly Westerns, with obscure titles.

In 1937 a new name began to turn up on cast lists, Sheila Bromley. It would be nice to say the change of name gave Sheila Mannors-Bromley a change of luck in her movie roles but, though she's listed in some sixteen or more over the next three years, most produced by Warners, they were all bottom-of-the-barrel.

Anybody remember Sheila Bromley in *West of Shanghai*? In *King of the Newsboys* or *Making the Headlines*? Or in *Rebellious Daughters*, or *Torture Ship*? Those were typical Sheila Bromley pictures, which may explain why few remember seeing her in anything.

BETTY BRONSON

In silents, Betty Bronson was an elfin Peter Pan and the Cinderella of *A Kiss for Cinderella*. But although she remained quite as winsome, her talkie career didn't measure up. She appeared with Al Jolson in *The Singing Fool* and without him in *Sonny Boy*. And there were *The Medicine Man* with Jack Benny, *The Locked Door* with Barbara Stanwyck and *The Bellamy Trial*. Then she disappeared, returning in 1937 in a Gene Autry Western, *The Yodelin' Kid from Pine Ridge*.

HELEN BRODERICK and her son, Broderick Crawford

HELEN BRODERICK and Danielle Darrieux in *The Rage of Paris*

SHEILA BROMLEY

BETTY BRONSON

LOUISE BROOKS in *Beggars of Life*

LOUISE BROOKS

Nobody ever would have predicted that Louise Brooks would one day become the subject of a worshipping cult. Certainly, producers who wrote her off as "washed up" after talkies came in showed no appreciation of her worth.

She had been one of the singular screen beauties in the silent era, with her straight black eyes, her carved features, her famous patent leather bob, her frank, direct look. But she was treated like a second-class cinema citizen. Clara Bow, Colleen Moore and others of the flapper age got the big pictures, and Louise Brooks took what was left over—which wasn't much.

She also admits that she was irresponsible, and somewhat of a playgirl then. Because she was having a ball on someone's yacht in Europe in 1929, she refused to go back to Hollywood to dub *The Canary Murder Case*, which she had already made as a silent. Paramount was furious and she had had it in the movies. (Margaret Livingston spoke the lines, although it was still Brooks who appeared physically as "The Canary.")

Thereafter she did secondary roles—with Frank Fay in *God's Gift to Women* and *It Pays to Advertise*—and she was occasionally announced for a comeback. But all that remained were a Buck Jones picture, *Empty Saddles*, in 1936, and a 1939 *Overland Stage Raiders*, with John Wayne (in the era when Wayne was making Republic Western quickies). Years later, depressed and forgotten, she would find that rediscovery of her stunning performances in Pabst's *Pandora's Box* and *Diary of a Lost Girl*—largely unseen at release because they were silent in a talking era—had made her an idol among film historians and critics.

PHYLLIS BROOKS

Phyllis Brooks had the kind of petulant blonde good-looks that you expected to see in the magazine illustration of 1930s illustrators like McClelland Barclay and Bradshaw Crandall. She was their model until she was brought to the screen by Universal in 1934, to play opposite Chester Morris in *I've Been Around*.

There's not much to say about her movie roles, except that she was an adequate actress when called upon to act, which was not often (*City Girl* and *Walking Down Broadway* almost alone stick in mind.) But she was decorative in pictures with Shirley Temple, the Ritz Brothers, and Charlie Chan.

IRENE BROWNE

One of those very capable English actresses, Irene Browne came over with the whole British contingent who appeared in the screen version of Noël Coward's *Cavalcade*, and stayed around for similar stints in *Berkeley Square*, *Peg o' My Heart*, *My Lips Betray* and *Christopher Strong*. Then it was back to Blighty, where she was something rather more important in the theatre than just a small-part character actress.

LOUISE BROOKS in *The Canary Murder Case*

PHYLLIS BROOKS

LOUISE BROOKS

IRENE BROWNE (left), with Diana Wynyard, Frank Lawton, Clive Brook, in *Cavalcade*

45

VIRGINIA BRUCE and her husband, John Gilbert, at a Hollywood costume ball

VIRGINIA BRUCE

Virginia Bruce was that fairest of Goldwyn Girls—you know, the one who looked like Vilma Banky—and she was a lady-in-waiting to Jeanette MacDonald in *The Love Parade*. Paramount used her opposite stars like Richard Arlen and Buddy Rogers, but she was far down in the leading lady line.

So Virginia left Paramount and her roles began to get better—nothing special, but better. She was Jimmy Cagney's girl in *Winner Take All* and John Gilbert's in *Downstairs*—offscreen she was briefly married to Gilbert. She even was *Jane Eyre* in an atrocity from Poverty Row. And she was Jenny Lind to Wallace Beery's *Mighty Barnum*.

But most of the thirties she spent at MGM, and here she was used for everything—as the lead in lots of their program pictures (take *Times Square Lady*, *Stronger Than Desire* and *Between Two Women*, as examples) and as a lesser player in bigger budget pictures, like *Yellow Jack*, where she was a rather superfluous leading lady . . . *The Great Ziegfeld*, in which she was a showgirl with designs on the great man . . . and *Born to Dance*, in which she introduced a song that still remains a standard—Cole Porter's "I've Got You Under My Skin."

Away from MGM, she showed up well in pictures like *Wife, Doctor and Nurse*, *There Goes My Heart* and a nice little romance called *When Love Is Young*. She never became a star of rank and never gave a performance of much note, but she was always agreeable to see.

JANE BRYAN

When we were in school, the very ideal of the ideal girl would have to be somebody like Jane Bryan. She was so pretty—nothing so obvious as beautiful, mind you, but clear-eyed, slim, with a sprinkling of freckles—just about the most clean-cut American girl you've ever seen. Jaded characters like Bette Davis in three of her pictures (*Marked Woman, Kid Galahad*, and *The Old Maid*), and Kay Francis in *Confession*, went to desperate lengths to protect Jane's innocence; but Jane, though fresh and vulnerable, seemed much too clever to really get in trouble. She was the most likable of *These Glamour Girls*, the girl who had the surprise baby in *Brother Rat*, and the good girl in the life of convict James Cagney in *Each Dawn I Die*.

After serving so attractively, she was handed a very unexpected role—a refugee, stranded German dancer, who is aided by Dr. Paul Muni in *We Are Not Alone*, and who, with him, becomes the victim of malicious slander and false accusations that lead to their death. With no attempt to glamorize the role, Jane Bryan gave a stunning emotional performance.

DOROTHY BURGESS

In Old Arizona, 1929, was the first oudoor talking picture, and Warner Baxter got an Oscar for his performance as The Cisco Kid. Not so fortunate was Dorothy Burgess, who played his faithless Tonia. She continued getting parts, but the leads were mostly in pictures made for studios, like Mayfair, Allied, Equitable, and Tower. In major studio product, she sneered and seethed darkly in second leads or less in movies like *Hold Your Man, I Love That Man, Fashions of 1943* and *Hat, Coat and Glove*.

BILLIE BURKE

Who ever twittered quite so delightfully as Billie Burke? Spring Byington perhaps, but we knew that was a put-on—we had already seen her as all those sensible mothers.

Billie Burke had a serious dramatic role to start off her talking-picture career—she was the distraught woman who has terminated her marriage to a mental patient and is about to be married again when he reappears. This was in *A Bill of Divorcement* in 1932, and her quiet performance was rather overshadowed by the pyrotechnics of John Barrymore, in one of his best roles, and the spectacular debut of a young actress playing their daughter, Katharine Hepburn. She was with Hepburn again in *Christopher Strong* and also had a role in *Only Yesterday*, which introduced another young actress, Margaret Sullavan.

But then came *Dinner at Eight*, and as Lionel Barrymore's society wife, distracted over problems of a dinner party while everyone around her is wrestling with life-and-death problems, Billie Burke carried away

VIRGINIA BRUCE, Warren William and Melvyn Douglas in *Arsene Lupin Returns*

Paul Muni and JANE BRYAN in *We Are Not Alone*

VIRGINIA BRUCE in an early pin-up

JANE BRYAN

47

DOROTHY BURGESS, Warner Baxter, and Edmund Lowe in *In Old Arizona*

a good share of the laurels from an all-star cast. There were other frivolous matrons for her to play, and it was only a short step to the flibbertigibbets—all fluff and flutter—which became her stock-in-trade. She was so pretty, with a swirl of red hair, blue eyes that she could bat so blankly, and that little bird voice.

She was the wife who drove Will Rogers up the wall with her aspirations to little-theatre acting in *Doubting Thomas*, movie version of George Kelly's *The Torch Bearers* . . . the exasperating, scolding mate of *Topper* . . . and similar empty-heads. And best of all, she was the bemused vis-à-vis to Roland Young in that deft and witty comedy-drama, *The Young in Heart*. And, away from her usual vague burbling, she was a rebuffed neighbor to Rosalind Russell's *Craig's Wife*, and Glinda, the Good Witch, helping Judy Garland and her companions through their trip to see *The Wizard of Oz*.

BILLIE BURKE and Louise Closser Hale in *Dinner at 8*

BILLIE BURKE

KATHLEEN BURKE, Richard Arlen and "animal men" in *Island of Lost Souls*

KATHLEEN BURKE

In one of its periodic attempts to hypo sagging business during the Depression, Paramount ran a "Panther Woman" contest for its *Island of Lost Souls*, in 1933. They say that 60,000 girls entered the contest. The winner, Kathleen Burke, seemed to be satisfactorily pantherish.

But Paramount didn't give her much more work except for minor roles in pictures like *Murder in the Zoo, Torch Singer,* and *Good Dame,* and occasional Westerns with Randolph Scott and Buster Crabbe. Kathleen did have one of the few non-action moments in *Lives of a Bengal Lancer*—that was a bit, too, but she was the only woman in the cast and looked exotic enough to provide a pleasant break in the general wild activity for Gary Cooper and Franchot Tone. Her last job was a small role in *Rascals* in 1938, with Jane Withers at 20th Century-Fox.

MAE BUSCH

Mae Busch was a von Stroheim star and played with people like Lon Chaney. But that was in the silents. By talkie time, she was used strictly for walk-ons and bits—even these declining sharply after the early thirties. (Her greatest fame came probably as the result of a running gag on the Jackie Gleason television shows of the fifties. Naming the "casts" of old pictures, he always wound up with "and the ever-popular Mae Busch.")

SPRING BYINGTON

Spring Byington wasn't in every other picture made during the mid- and late thirties—she just seemed to be. Her top role, of course, was as Penny Sycamore, the fledgling "authoress" who used her cat as a paper weight, and was writing a novel because somebody had

SPRING BYINGTON (right) in *The Jones Family* series with Helen Ericson, Kenneth Howell, and Jed Prouty

MAE BUSCH

MARION "PEANUTS" BYRON

left a typewriter at the house by mistake in *You Can't Take It With You*, and she was every bit as happily addled as were such similar ladies of the period as Billie Burke, Alice Brady and Mary Boland.

But she wasn't always one of the "screwball set." Her first movie, *Little Women*, in 1933, had her playing an unsugary Marmee and she was quite lovely as the worried mother in Eugene O'Neill's *Ah, Wilderness*. She was a gossiping trouble-maker in *Way Down East* and again in *Theodora Goes Wild*, and a homey neighbor in *Dodsworth*.

She did some other mothers, in a couple of "Penrod" pictures, for instance, and in the first of what turned out to be the "Andy Hardy" movies—this one being *A Family Affair*.

She was already trapped —and "trapped" is the best possible word—in a family series of her own. This was the insufferable group known as "The Jones Family." Let us quickly add that Miss Byington remained as believable as possible. It seemed that every time you hit a movie house, there would be a second feature with another "adventure" of "The Jones Family." Spring Byington alone survived them.

MARION BYRON

At Warners, she was sometimes billed as Marion "Peanuts" Byron, because of her petite height (five feet). She played chorines and collegiennes in pictures like *Broadway Daddies* and *Forward Pass* and was also in the early Warners musicals *Song of the West* and *Golden Dawn*, both with Vivienne Segal. But after these early talkies, she was seen only occasionally in small soubrette roles.

SPRING BYINGTON in *Ah, Wilderness* with Eric Linden and Lionel Barrymore

BELLE BENNETT

MONA BARRIE in *Mystery Blonde*
with John Halliday

IRENE BORDONI in *Paris* with Louise
Closser Hale and Jack Buchanan

NOTES ON OTHER "B" LADIES

Beginning with a brace of Belles, who could hardly
give thanks for talkies, we had *Belle Baker*, running
right back to two-a-day after a deadly talkie debut in
Song of Love . . . *Belle Bennett* had been the silent
Stella Dallas and *Mother Machree* but there were only
a few dismal attempts (like *Courage, Recaptured
Love*) in audible films . . . Other Bennetts—*Barbara
Bennett*, the second of Richard Bennett's three daughters and the only brunette, unlike sisters Constance
and Joan, had only a brief, unimpressive screen career
. . . *Enid Bennett*, no relation, had been leading lady
to Douglas Fairbanks in *Robin Hood* and to Milton
Sills in *The Sea Hawk* in silents but, in talkies,
was known primarily as Jackie Cooper's mother in
Skippy. . . .

Irene Bordoni, like Belle Baker, was a theatre name
to reckon with but, although she did her typical oo-la-
la in *Paris* and *Show of Shows*, it wasn't enough to
turn her into a screen star. . . .

Silent character actress *Gladys Brockwell* was confined to two or three primitive early talkies . . . And
The Queen of Sheba of the silents, *Betty Blythe*,
found only her name—not her roles—registering as a
reminder of past glories as it moved far down in cast
lists of talkies . . .

Florence Britton, a spruce brunette, looked good
enough in small roles in pictures like *A Devil to Pay*
and *Confessions of a Co-Ed* to make you wish they
had been big roles . . . *Phyllis Barry* got her first attention as Ronald Colman's melancholy shopgirl love in
Cynara but then moved from Colman to Keaton,

HELEN BURGESS

51

NANA BRYANT

GLORIA BLONDELL

EDWINA BOOTH and Duncan Renaldo in *Trader Horn*

TALA BIRELL, Cesar Romero, and Walter Pidgeon in *She's Dangerous*

Durante, Wheeler and Woolsey romances . . . *Mona Barrie*, a poor man's Kay Francis, played clothes-horse second woman and a couple of artificial leads in B's. . . . *Edwina Booth* was the ill-fated "White Goddess" of *Trader Horn*. . . .

Whitney Bourne started well—in *Crime Without Passion*—but her parts quickly became low-grade leads and less . . . *Nana Bryant* usually played roles that were interchangeable with those played by such actresses as Marjorie Gateson and Nella Walker—most often as haughty matrons . . . Youngest and most excited of the girls going to *Winter Carnival* was *Joan Brodel*, who, within a year, would turn up as a leading lady named Joan Leslie . . .

May Boley was a burlesque comic in *Dance of Life* and the bawdy house proprietress in *The Informer* and had other, if less colorful, bits . . . The movie high for *Gloria Blondell* was as Ronald Reagan's leading lady in a programmer, *Accidents Will Happen*—otherwise she just had some minor roles at Warners, the studio at which her sister, Joan, was a star . . . *Tala Birell* never became the Garbo they hoped for but you saw her occasionally in lesser roles in pictures like *Bringing Up Baby* and *Crime and Punishment* . . . *Lina Basquette* got some notice when she played for DeMille in *The Godless Girl* at the end of the silents—but the notice was more from the movie magazines and even that stopped by the talkie period when her roles were in Poverty Row quickies . . . *Eugenie Besserer* has a place in history as the one to whom Jolson sang his first *Jazz Singer* song—her other talkie roles, though, were inconsequential . . . *Marjorie Beebe* had a part or two

FLORENCE BRITTON

in features but was better known to the short comedy afficionados . . .

Helen Burgess, not quite 21 when she died of pneumonia, made four Paramount pictures, with the De-Mille/Gary Cooper *The Plainsman* the only one of note . . . *Betty Burgess* danced opposite Johnny Downs in *Coronado* . . . *Gladys Blake* was one of those slangy Iris Adrian carbons who played waitresses and such . . .

Bessie Barriscale, Sylvia Breamer, Miriam Battista, Fritzi Brunette, Lucy Beaumont, Barbara Bedford all dated back to silents—most of them had scarcely more than a look-in or two in talkies . . . *Baby Sandy* was a fetching miss (as babies go), particularly opposite Bing Crosby in *East Side of Heaven* . . . *Baby Rose Marie,* the moppet vaudevilian, had a number in *International House*—she's a well-known TV comic in her post-Baby years . . . *Ferike Boros* went by in a number of pictures (like *Bachelor Mother, Make Way for Tomorrow*) as a number of cheerful Jewish ladies . . .

And a quick nod to some others—*Jane Baxter, Monica Bannister, Margaret Bannerman, Virginia Brissac, Joan Barclay, Barbara Barondess, June Brewster, May Beatty, Irene Bentley, Mozelle Britton, Lucile Brown, Mona Bruns, Faith Bacon, Marion Ballou, Judith Barrett, Olive Brasno, Judith Barrie, Jean Bary, Elaine Barrie* (she was John Barrymore's "Ariel"), *Phyllis Barrington, Finis Barton, Lauri Beatty, Sylvia Beecher* (played opposite Chevalier in his first, *Innocents of Paris,* but, while he went on, she dropped out), *Carol Ann Beery* (with a bit in her father's *China Seas*), *Daisy Belmore, Bertha Belmore, Edna Bennett, Irene Biller, Carmen Barnes, Joan Blair, Beatrice Blinn, Virginia True Boardman, Betty Boyd, Margaret Breen, Joan Breslau, Ann Brody, Helen Brown, the Brox Sisters, Veda Buckland, Michelette Burani, Marion Burns, Jessie Busley, Rosita Butler, Carol Borland, Loie Bridge, Esther Brodelet, Lora Baxter, Mildred Boyd, Constance Berger, Betty Balfour, Jerry Bergh.*

Peter Lorre, Marion Marsh, MRS. PAT CAMPBELL in *Crime and Punishment*

MRS. PATRICK CAMPBELL

"Oh, yes," oozed Mrs. Patrick Campbell, when asked about a queenly movie actress she had met, "she has such pretty little eyes—and they're so close together."

Shaw's original Liza of *Pygmalion* was much more famous in Hollywood for such quips than for any screen role she ever played. By the time she hit the movies, her glory was long past. So there were only a few minor character roles for her to play—acidulous dowagers in *Riptide*, *One More River* and *Outcast Lady*, and the evil, spiderlike pawnbroker of *Crime and Punishment*.

KITTY CARLISLE

It was Kitty Carlisle to whom Bing sang "Love in Bloom" and "June in January" . . . to whom Allan Jones sang "Alone" . . . to whom Carl Brisson sang "Cocktails for Two." The songs were more memorable than the roles, yet Kitty was pretty—with a singing voice to match—in *She Loves Me Not*, *Here Is My Heart*, *Murder at the Vanities* and *A Night at the Opera*. The trouble is that when you talk about those pictures, you think of Bing and Groucho and his brothers, not of Kitty Carlisle. So Kitty went back to

KITTY CARLISLE, Carl Brisson in *Murder at the Vanities*

Broadway, and later to TV, where she was a star in her own right.

MARY CARLISLE

Most of Bing Crosby's leading ladies of the 1930s were virtually interchangeable. They would be Leila Hyams, Ida Lupino, Frances Farmer, or Joan Bennett. The only stipulation seemed to be that they be blonde and pose adoringly while Bing crooned his love songs.

Mary Carlisle, with shimmering blonde hair catching the light, fitted the bill so well with Bing in *College Humor*, 1933, that she repeated her job in *Double or Nothing* and *Doctor Rhythm*. She was just as pictorial in other movies, often as a co-ed: *Sweetheart of Sigma Chi*, *Saturday's Millions*, *Hold 'Em Navy* and *Touchdown Army*. Too, there was *Palooka*, in which she could have stepped right out of the comic strip as Anne Howe.

SUE CAROL

Sue Carol had been a brunette flapper in the last days of silents and she was carried over into the early talkie days in pictures like *Dancing Sweeties* and *Check and Double Check*, with Amos 'n' Andy. She also introduced the dance "The Breakaway," with David Rollins, in one of those "all star" studio musical revues, *Fox Movietone Follies*.

She wasn't much of a singer, but you wouldn't have guessed it from sheet music covers. Her face appeared on some of the most popular of these—songs like "Kiss Waltz" and "Three Little Words," from movies in which she appeared, as well as on "Sweet Sue," which she supposedly "inspired." And, oddly, her acting career died with the first demise of the movie musical.

MADELEINE CARROLL

The definitive Madeleine Carroll role just has to be the Princess Flavia of *Prisoner of Zenda*. Not because it is the most demanding role she has played, not because she gave a particularly remarkable performance —just because only the role of a princess could do justice to her beauty.

There was something regal about Madeleine Carroll —something that made it hard for you to accept her as a drifter, no better than she should be, and involved in shady activities with shadier characters in *The General Died at Dawn*. Actually it may have been her best movie performance because she had warmth and spirit in that one. That wasn't usually the case—most movies concentrated on her face but the characters were rather chilly and, yes, regal.

But just looking at Madeleine Carroll was one of the great treats of going to movies in the thirties.

She did some British pictures which seldom were

MARY CARLISLE

SUE CAROL

MADELEINE CARROLL and Tyrone Power in *Lloyds of London*

MADELEINE CARROLL and Ronald Colman in *The Prisoner of Zenda*

seen in this country until one of them—*I Was a Spy*—was picked up for American release by Fox. Miss Carroll received excellent critical notices and Fox, impressed, brought her over. But her initial American film, *The World Moves On*, despite direction by John Ford, was wearisome enough to send her scuttling back across the sea.

All to the good. Because back in England, Alfred Hitchcock had a couple of films that called for beauteous blonde leading ladies. So Miss Carroll played damsels in distress in *39 Steps* and *Secret Agent*, becoming the model for blondes Hitchcock would use many times again as played by Grace Kelly, Kim Novak, Janet Leigh, Joan Fontaine, Vera Miles, Eva Marie Saint and Tippi Hedren.

The international success of *39 Steps* was enough to cause new interest among the American filmmakers. So back she came to team with Gary Cooper in *The General Died at Dawn*; Ronald Colman in *Prisoner of Zenda*; Tyrone Power in *Lloyds of London*; Henry Fonda in *Blockade*; Francis Lederer in *It's All Yours*; Fred MacMurray in *Cafe Society* and *Honeymoon in Bali*. She showed a lively sense of humor in a diverting Irving Berlin musical, *On the Avenue*, but most of her films called for little more from her than to look the way she looked. It was quite enough.

The off-screen Madeleine Carroll was casual about that fabulous face. And she could joke about herself as a sex symbol. When a contingent of collegians selected her as "The Girl with Whom We'd Most Like to Be Marooned on a Desert Island," her response was that it would be fine with her, as long as a good obstetrician was also cast away.

NANCY CARROLL

If Madeleine Carroll was, to many, the most beautiful star of the thirties, Nancy Carroll was certainly the prettiest. Consider those eyes—big Irish orbs of a color supposedly requested of her decorator by Ethel Barrymore ("I want drapes of a special shade of blue—the blue of Nancy Carroll's eyes"). Think of the flame of hair . . . a child's pert nose . . . The face of Nancy Carroll was something all her own—completely individual and a joy.

With a face like that, and a dancer's legs and trim body, you wouldn't expect any dividends. The fact was that Nancy Carroll was also an actress—a sparkling comedienne and highly proficient in emotional drama.

She was the first star made by talkies—others in the early days of the new medium had made their reputations in the silents or came to films from the theatre. But, after only a couple of non-talkies, Nancy Carroll was singing, dancing and making conversation right from the beginning. Although at her peak (1930-31) she was the most popular girl in pictures, that period was surprisingly brief. A combination of poor movies and some private problems (a temper that made im-

MADELEINE CARROLL and Gary Cooper in *The General Died at Dawn*

NANCY CARROLL

NANCY CARROLL (with Morgan Farley) in *The Devil's Holiday*

NANCY CARROLL and Stanley Smith in *Sweetie*

portant enemies; a young daughter whose existence she refused to hide in the days when movie sweeties were not supposed to be off-screen mothers) killed off her career in the mid-thirties. There were two comeback attempts in 1938—small, unworthy roles in *There Goes My Heart* and *That Certain Age*—and that was the movie end of Nancy Carroll.

So she is barely known to the current generation of moviegoers. Most of her films have been unavailable to television or revival theatres. Still, many of her films are being screened by film societies, and shops specializing in old pictures cannot keep her stills in stock.

The first Nancy Carroll to beguile us was that delectable doll of all those youthful comedies. She romanced with Buddy Rogers or similar types, danced a bit, and sang now and then in a funny, cooing, but wholly irresistible little voice. The pictures ranged from *Abie's Irish Rose*, which was quite controversial in its day, to fluffs like *Sweetie, Honey, Follow Through* and *Close Harmony*.

Then there was Nancy the actress, in a succession of quite extraordinary characterizations—her uncompromising portraits of a hard-as-nails show girl finding tenderness in a romance with an idealistic young soldier (*Shopworn Angel*) . . . the loyal burlesque dancer in *The Dance of Life* . . . a greedy, avaricious manicurist, reformed by love—and Carroll won an Academy nomination for her performance in *The Devil's Holiday* . . . the society wife in the brilliant *Laughter* . . . the pathetic streetwalker having a last fling at happiness in *Stolen Heaven* . . . the taxi dancer of *Child of Manhattan*.

There were other notable Carroll performances—as an accidental murderess in *Woman Accused* and a blithe adulteress in *Springtime for Henry*; in unusual roles, as a Budapest beauty in *The Kiss Before the Mirror* and as a Fräulein in Lubitsch's *The Man I Killed*.

But there was also *Night Angel*, in which she was incredibly miscast as a gamin of Prague. It was a notoriously bad picture and did her career irreparable damage, which only an outstanding follow-up picture could have overcome. And trivialities like *Hot Saturday* and *Personal Maid*, to mention only two of the better ones, couldn't do it.

By the time her Paramount contract was finished, that once-so-hot film career well-nigh burned out. And she never got a strong enough film to revive it.

HELEN CHANDLER

"I'll take vanilla," chirped Helen Chandler in *The Last Flight*, as Nikki, the determinedly wacky waif who joined a band of Hemingwayesque ex-airmen in their carousing through Europe. That was her best movie role.

She had another as one of the would-be young suicides in *Outward Bound*, but was overshadowed by Leslie Howard and Beryl Mercer. In *Dracula* she was

57

wispy enough to look anemic even before she became a victim of the bloodthirsty Count. *Mother's Cry, A House Divided* and *Long Lost Father* were among her other films.

Thereafter, she commuted between stage and screen, and had better luck on Broadway in *Springtime for Henry*, the title role in *Lady Precious Stream* and repeating her film role in *Outward Bound*, this time with Laurette Taylor.

ILKA CHASE

Ilka Chase was certainly a celebrity of the 1930s— but not for any of her occasional movie appearances. She was frequently on radio, appeared on Broadway, wrote with panache, and was widely quoted for her café society bon mots.

On screen, her roles were minor (she even played a servant in Lenore Ulric's *South Sea Rose*) and there were only rare opportunities for her caustic personality to register. It did—but only momentarily—in *Rich People, The Animal Kingdom, Soak the Rich* and *The Lady Consents*.

RUTH CHATTERTON

Brittle—that was the Ruth Chatterton character. Brittle, tense, overwrought. She might have been sorely tried by some domestic situation—indeed she usually was—but she invariably reacted with a kind of strained nervousness . . . a quick, mirthless, mechanical smile . . . a staccato outpouring of clipped words . . . perpetually on the edge of the jitters.

She was in her element when she moved in high circles—the world of *The Rich Are Always With Us* and *Charming Sinners*. But in spite of giving a performance that is technically one of her best, she seemed out of place in *Dodsworth*. A silly Midwest matron, gullibly playing into the hands of international parasites—not our Miss Chatterton. You might have admired her performance but you just knew she was smarter than any of them.

There were actually two types of Chatterton characters. The more standard was the lady who made small talk and committed polite adulteries in the drawing rooms of Lonsdale and Barry.

But then there was the Chatterton who suffered a lot—our old friend *Madame X*, the mothers of *The Right to Love, Sarah and Son* and *Frisco Jenny*. She could play floozies (e.g. *Anybody's Woman* and *Lilly Turner*), and she even gave us an early dose of women's lib as the automotive tycoon who ran her company along Catherine-the-Great lines in *Female*.

Our own particular favorites—the socialite with the uncontrollable giggle in *The Laughing Lady*; the neglected wife in Philip Barry's *Tomorrow and Tomorrow* and of course, miscast or not, the restless, demanding Fran, so fearful of the onrush of age in *Dodsworth*, the last picture of her Hollywood career.

ANCY CARROLL in *Child of Manhattan*

HELEN CHANDLER

ILKA CHASE (right), and Miriam Hopkins in *Fast and Loose*

RUTH CHATTERTON and Fuller Mellish, Jr., in *Sarah and Son*

RUTH CHATTERTON and David Manners in *The Right to Love*

MADY CHRISTIANS (center) with Jean Parker and Betty Furness in *A Wicked Woman*

MADY CHRISTIANS

We know Mady Christians was an actress of distinction. But there is small proof of that in her films.

Miss Christians made her American screen debut in *A Wicked Woman*, 1934, a tacky study of a downtrodden wife who murders her drunken lout of a husband, and must bring up her three children under the shadow of this misdeed. She did as much as she could with the role but it was a disaster. And she couldn't recover with poor roles in her pictures that followed—*Escapade, Come and Get It, The Woman I Love, Seventh Heaven,* and *Heidi.*

MARGUERITE CHURCHILL

A dark and intelligent girl, Marguerite Churchill played in enough movies to have made her mark. But most of her pictures were second-rate, or worse, and her roles were not much better.

She started in 1929 as Paul Muni's sister in *The Valiant.* She played the heroine in *The Big Trail*, with John Wayne, a tedious Western with epic pretensions; and opposite her future husband, George O'Brien, in *Riders of the Purple Sage.*

Twice she was with Will Rogers, once as his daughter in *They Had to See Paris,* and as the Queen of the mythical kingdom of Sylvania in *Ambassador Bill.* She also appeared in such chillers as *The Walking Dead,* with Boris Karloff, and *Dracula's Daughter,* without Bela Lugosi.

BERNICE CLAIRE

If the moment had been right, brunette Bernice Claire might have preceded Jeanette MacDonald as the queen of movie operettas. In one year, 1930, she sang her way through such very early examples of the genre as *Song of the Flame, Spring Is Here* and *No, No, Nanette,* all with Alexander Gray, and Victor Herbert's *Mlle. Modiste,* later retitled after its best-known song, *Kiss Me Again,* with Walter Pidgeon.

VIRGINIA CHERRILL with Charles Chaplin in *City Lights*

VIRGINIA CHERRILL

With the decided exception of Paulette Goddard, the leading ladies of Charles Chaplin never got very far in films after their moment with the Little Tramp. Virginia Cherrill, the fairest of them all, had only a few other roles—in things like *The Brat* and *Girls Demand Excitement.* The latter was opposite a young actor who had also starred in a big picture (*The Big Trail*) but dropped quickly to minor movies. John Wayne came back, though. Virginia Cherrill did not.

Even so, as the blind flower girl of *City Lights,* her place in the sun is assured. She shared one of the unforgettable scenes of cinema history when the girl, her sight restored, suddenly realizes that the comical little character at whom she is laughing is the man she had adored in her blindness.

Even here though, it was Chaplin's scene—it was his face, registering the varying emotions of still another rejection in life, that haunts the memory.

MARGUERITE CHURCHILL with Paul Muni in
The Valiant

INA CLAIRE, Joan Blondell, and Madge Evans in *The Greeks
Had a Word For It*

BERNICE CLAIRE and Alexander Gray in *No, No, Nanette*

But these singing pictures were bland and static, and
came at a time when movie musicals had become a
drug on the market and the advertisements were promising "*This* is *not* a musical!"

INA CLAIRE

Ina Claire, was the star of a few early silents, done
in New York between 1915 and 1920, but did not
make any more pictures until talking films in 1929,
when she was thirty-seven. Although Miss Claire displayed a light soap-bubble comedy style, her *Awful
Truth* and *Rebound* were over-talky versions of drawing room comedy dramas. (Leo McCarey's direction
was to turn the remake of *The Awful Truth* into one
of the best comedies of the late 1930s, but Irene
Dunne inherited the Claire role.)

INA CLAIRE and Robert Ames in *Rebound*

Then, there was *The Greeks Had a Word for
Them*. Miss Claire was fetching, but whatever fun
had been in the play was pretty thoroughly squeezed
out by the moviemakers.

That left *The Royal Family of Broadway*, 1931, and
eight years later *Ninotchka*. The first of these was
pretty stagey, too, but it remained effective in its satire
of the Barrymores. Miss Claire had the Ethel role, but
Fredric March's slick take-off on John attracted most
of the kudos. And in *Ninotchka*, she was a gay Duch-

ess in contrast to Garbo, the glum peasant Russian girl. But who ever really noticed anyone else but Garbo in a Garbo film? What a loss that Hollywood didn't use Miss Claire's frolicsome talents more boldly.

MAE CLARKE

Because of a cruel movie moment (which has become a classic movie still), poor Mae Clarke is always thought of with a grapefruit in her face. Her role in *The Public Enemy* was really rather short—just a dame for James Cagney on his way to gangland eminence. But it cinched Mae Clarke's claim to fame.

Mae Clarke did have more rewarding roles, and she played them, well. She was the unhappy hooker of the first *Waterloo Bridge*. Vivien Leigh made it her own when she played the same role nine years later, but Miss Clarke was as notable in her day. And she was a pathetic Molly Malloy in *The Front Page*.

She also did things like *Impatient Maiden*, *Frankenstein* and *Night World* then, when Miss Clarke was a frizzy blonde. Later she became a sleek, boyish-bobbed brunette to play opposite a rapidly fading John Gilbert in *Fast Workers*, or a Lee Tracy on the downgrade in *Turn Back the Clock*.

And then she had a series of second-rate parts, and third-rate movies. By 1938, there were no more movies for Mae Clarke, until she would begin to turn up in unbilled bits and extra parts.

JUNE CLYDE

The thirties had more than their share of amiable blondes who had a few years of steady work. June Clyde was such a starlet.

She played in RKO's first musical, *Tanned Legs*, in *Hit the Deck* and with Wheeler & Woolsey in *The Cuckoos*, but she spent more time doing fan magazine photos than actual film appearances. The latter ranged from bits in such "big" pictures as *Back Street* and *Only Yesterday* to leads in program features.

CLAUDETTE COLBERT

Nobody was ever quite as totally feminine as Claudette Colbert. Her fussy little gestures . . . the way she had of cocking her head . . . her flair and chic . . . it was all very French (although she seldom played Frenchwomen), all very girlish (although her roles were almost always womanly), and very individually her own.

DeMille saw her as an alluring siren, but although you might enjoy watching her soaking in her milk bath or tantalizing Caesar and Antony, glamorous evil was hardly her bag. Naughty perhaps, as in *Midnight*. But she had too much humor and too much—yes, femininity—to be the femme-fatale.

Actually she wasn't all that chic—nor even all that pretty—when she first came to the screen. Having made one silent film, *For the Love of Mike*, to which the public responded negatively, she had gone back to the theatre, where she was doing fine.

But with the talkie advent she succumbed and, while she didn't immediately race to Hollywood, she did a few pictures at Paramount's East Coast Astoria studios. The first of these—*The Hole in the Wall*, 1929—had no more merit than had her one silent film. But things got better with *The Lady Lies* in which she played opposite Walter Huston as one of those maligned mistresses who later became such a staple of 1930s movies.

Even then she had those great dark eyes. But her face was wide—at some angles, heavy—and she hadn't yet discovered either her trademark bangs or the photogenic "Colbert good side." Nor was she dressed with any particular care. So, for a while you were seeing her as a rather matronly leading lady for Maurice Chevalier, George M. Cohan, Fredric March and Gary Cooper.

Then came DeMille with *The Sign of the Cross* and Colbert as Poppaea. She may have been less than convincingly depraved, but at least you looked at her in a new way. Matronly no more. And the Poppaea bangs, with variations, remained as an integral part of the Colbert look.

She had a couple of moderate successes—in *Three Cornered Moon*, for instance, although that was really Mary Boland's movie—but nothing to make her big enough to be able to protest at being loaned to Columbia, a Poverty Row studio, for a "madcap heiress" role already turned down by better-established actresses. She was teamed with another reluctant loan-out, Clark Gable, who also didn't have enough box-office strength to refuse.

And so Claudette Colbert and Clark Gable did *It Happened One Night*. And the rest, as they say, is history. The producers didn't low-rate Claudette again —or not for a long, long time.

There followed *Imitation of Life*, one of the most unabashedly tear-drenched and most successful of all women's pictures; *Cleopatra*, under DeMille again; *Private Worlds*, a forceful drama of the intertwined lives of doctors and patients in a mental hospital; and *The Gilded Lily*, an amusing comedy. She made many more of the latter, best of which were *I Met Him in Paris*, *Bluebeard's Eighth Wife* and *Midnight*.

She did stumble a bit as the can-can dancer *Zaza*, but nobody could have done much with that tired old war-horse. Mixed in with the comedies came other roles—as Cigarette in *Under Two Flags* and as the Puritan lass accused of witchcraft in *Maid of Salem*. She was beautifully right as the White Russian princess, now a lady's maid, in *Tovarich*, and the pioneer wife of *Drums Along the Mohawk*. All in all, in this decade, she made thirty-five films, most of them for Paramount.

MAE CLARKE and George C. Stone in *The Front Page*

JUNE CLYDE

MAE CLARKE and Douglass Montgomery in *Waterloo Bridge*

CLAUDETTE COLBERT as Poppaea in the milk bath in *Sign of the Cross*

CLAUDETTE COLBERT

Having entered the thirties as a competent, rather plain and unexciting leading lady, she finished out the decade as one of the screen's most shining stars.

CONSTANCE COLLIER

With the theatre behind her, Constance Collier, the marvelously stately British actress, moved to Hollywood in 1929 and found a place for herself as a drama and voice coach for film players in the days of the early talkies. In her later years, among her pupils were Mae West, Katharine Hepburn, Shelley Winters, Marilyn Monroe.

But Miss Collier also made her presence felt on the screen, and at one time she was under a seven-year contract to 20th Century-Fox. Because she was an imposing figure and an actress in the grand manner, she showed up as a grande dame in such films as *Professional Soldier*, *Wee Willie Winkie*, *Damsel in Distress*, and *Zaza* . . . as a martinet school mistress in *Girls' Dormitory* and, quite enjoyably, as a formidable dowager turned amateur detective in *Shadow of Doubt*.

But she will be best remembered as the drama coach, elegant if a bit seedy, of *Stage Door*, who gave Katharine Hepburn the same kind of a "Go-on-that-stage" pep talk that was usually given to Ruby Keeler by Warner Baxter or James Cagney. Her screen roles continued until 1950.

CORA SUE COLLINS

A ubiquitous face of the 1930s was that of child actress Cora Sue Collins. She might be the daughter of such mirthless mothers as Wynne Gibson in *The Strange Case of Clara Dean*, Claudette Colbert in *Torch Singer* or Sylvia Sidney in *Jennie Gerhardt*, or she might be the young Merle Oberon in *The Dark Angel*.

She was in any number of pictures, generally far down in the cast list and no threat at all to Shirley Temple. By the close of the thirties, she had reached adolescence and was still appearing in movies like *Adventures of Tom Sawyer*, and *Stop, Look and Love* —but ever so briefly.

JUNE COLLYER

The epitome of lady-like loveliness was June Collyer. She didn't exactly make it big as an actress, although it was always gratifying to watch her opposite Gary Cooper in *The Man from Wyoming*, Richard Dix in *The Love Doctor*, Jack Oakie in *Dude Ranch*, and Buddy Rogers in *River of Romance* and *Illusion*.

But with June Collyer, it wasn't the roles. It was her face—one of the most luminous, with the most dazzling dimples ever.

CLAUDETTE COLBERT in *Private Worlds*

CLAUDETTE COLBERT as Cleopatra

65

CONSTANCE COLLIER (center) in *Stage Door* with Eve Arden, Katharine Hepburn, Jane Rhodes and Lucille Ball

CORA SUE COLLINS in *Jennie Gerhardt* with Sylvia Sidney

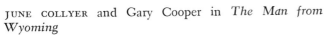

JUNE COLLYER and Gary Cooper in *The Man from Wyoming*

BETTY COMPSON and Richard Barthelmess in *Weary River*

BETTY COMPSON

Betty Compson was one of the few silent screen names who received a new lease on life with the coming of talkies. Over a couple of years she played in at least twenty talking pictures, among her roles the carnival-girl friend of Milton Sills in *The Barker*, the cabaret-girl friend of Richard Barthelmess in *Weary River*, and the temperamental star in *On With the Show*. She also sang and played the violin in *Street Girl*, competed with a dummy for the affections of ventriloquist Erich von Stroheim in *The Great Gabbo*, did her best to pass as a Russian peasant girl in *The Case of Sergeant Grischa*, and was the saloon belle Cherry Malotte in *The Spoilers* with Gary Cooper.

But this flurry in talkie leads was short-lived, and although the Compson name showed up in many cast lists throughout the 1930s, it was mostly in pictures from lesser studios, or in a tiny bit in a major studio film, like *A Slight Case of Murder*.

JOYCE COMPTON

It seems now that Joyce Compton was in just about every other movie shot in the 1930s.

Joyce always played approximately the same role—the archetypal belle with a sugary drawl, who might be a waitress or a chorine, a night club chantoosie or just one of those babes on the fringe of things. At this distance, she lives in memory, but all the parts she played run together, making it hard to remember just what she did in what.

The possible exception would be as a night club blonde, named Dixie Belle Lee—Toots for short—with whom Cary Grant became hilariously involved in *The Awful Truth*, to get back at his ex-wife, Irene Dunne. To Grant's embarrassment, Miss Dunne witnesses Miss Compton's performance singing a song called "Gone with the Wind," clad in a dress that blows up over her head at every chorus.

PEGGY CONKLIN

For someone of such accomplishment in the Broadway theatre—she had the original leads in plays like *The Pursuit of Happiness*, and *The Petrified Forest*, with Leslie Howard and Humphrey Bogart—Peggy Conklin had a particularly unsatisfying screen career.

She made almost no impact at all in such pretty good movies as *The President Vanishes* and *The Devil Is a Sissy*, although she had better screen presence in a lesser picture, *One Way Ticket*. Unfortunately *Ticket* sold few tickets.

Her screen career finally wound up with her as one of the vacationing girls in *Having Wonderful Time*, but here she was just around, while more aggressive types, Ginger Rogers, Lucille Ball and Eve Arden, took the limelight. Miss Conklin returned to the stage, where things were always better for her.

JOYCE COMPTON (left) with Dorothy Wilson and Loretta Young in *The White Parade*

PEGGY CONKLIN with Mickey Rooney, Freddie Bartholomew and Jackie Cooper in *The Devil Is a Sissy*

DOLORES COSTELLO

INEZ COURTNEY and Jean Harlow in *Suzy*

DOLORES COSTELLO

Dolores Costello, who had started on the screen as John Barrymore's leading lady—later his wife—became one of the first of the Warner Bros. stars to be used in talkies. And she was used—and used—in a series of dismal melodramas (*Tenderloin*, *Madonna of Avenue A*, *The Glad Rag Doll* and worse).

One of her pictures, *Glorious Betsy*, in which she played Baltimore's Elizabeth Patterson in love with Napoleon's brother, Jerome, had a certain period charm. Miss Costello looked every bit the Baltimore belle, but audiences hooted at the ripe dialogue.

She disappeared from the screen until the mid-1930s when she returned as Dolores Costello Barrymore. Of her later films (*Yours for the Asking*, *The Beloved Brat*, *King of the Turf and* a dreadful thing with Bobby Breen called *Breaking the Ice*), the only role of any value was as the placid mother, Dearest, in David Selznick's *Little Lord Fauntleroy*.

There would be one more important Costello role —as Isabel Amberson in Orson Welles' *The Magnificent Ambersons*—but not in this decade.

HELENE COSTELLO

Helene Costello was the sister of one star (Dolores) and daughter of another (Maurice). Her only other movie distinction—a historical, but hardly histrionic, one—was that she was leading lady in the first all-talking picture, *The Lights of New York*, in 1928. That may have been enough to guarantee her name in the record books; it did nothing to assist her career as an actress.

INEZ COURTNEY

As a Broadway musical soubrette, Inez Courtney came to the screen in the early days of movie musicals for substantially the same kind of roles (in *Spring Is Here*, *Song of the Flame*, *Sunny*, etc.). When this musical cycle nosedived, Miss Courtney moved into straight roles as one of those sharp-tongued girl friends who hovered peripherally around the plot lines (Nancy Carroll's friend in *Jealousy*, Jean Harlow's in *Suzy*, Ginger Rogers' in *Having Wonderful Time*, etc.). And she showed up in dozens of similar roles into the 1940s—never a name but always a face to appreciate.

JOAN CRAWFORD

If you pick one personality to typify the words "Movie Star," it has to be Joan Crawford. Not that she was the best actress—although she was considerably more accomplished than many of her critics would admit. Not that she was the most beautiful— but she made capital of what might have been called her defects, emphasizing them for a look that was her own, not just a copy of a prevailing type. If her mouth

JOAN CRAWFORD in *Our Dancing Daughters* (with Dorothy Sebastian and Anita Page)

JOAN CRAWFORD and Polly Moran in *Paid*

JOAN CRAWFORD and Clark Gable in *Love on the Run*

was generous, she would exaggerate it. When pretty little eyes, topped by penciled lines, were the mode, Crawford would intensify her already-outsized orbs and bring back real eyebrows. Her shoulders were square so, abetted by Adrian, she dressed in clothes that made them even wider.

She painstakingly cultivated an off-screen image that complemented the roles she played. Just as she was so often the shopgirl who rose to great lady, she never let it be forgotten that the Star who was Crawford had started as a dancer of no social pretension. Her rise to her position as one of the most influential and authoritative of all screen personalities was the result of her own ambition, her own unrelenting work, her own immense drive. Never did Joan Crawford suggest the girl next door. She was, and is, a movie star—The Movie Star—every moment, in even her most unimportant public appearances. But Joan Crawford never makes unimportant public appearances—a trip to the supermarket for her would be An Event.

Having started out in the silent era as a straight leading lady, she quickly established the Crawford personality. If flappers were in vogue, for instance, Crawford would be the super-flapper—the very model of all of *Our Dancing Daughters*, both on and off the screen.

She was still jazzy in her first couple of talkies but, even before that era had waned, the Crawford style had changed. Now she would be the slum girl fighting her way up to luxury and the Adrian originals in which fans expected Joan Crawford to be dressed. She was a garish but less than successful Sadie Thompson, because who could ever believe that Joan, if not Sadie, would let such an impressive stumbling block as the Reverend Davidson not only stand in her way, but actually destroy her.

But when she was wreaking revenge on the man who had sent her to jail by marrying his son in *Paid* (the film version of the hardy old *Within the Law*) . . . when she was rising from poverty to penthouse as the paramour of a politician who was Clark Gable (*Possessed*) . . . when she was tripping from burlesque to Broadway stardom in *Dancing Lady* . . . or in such various other up-the-ladder experiences as in *Sadie McKee, Chained, Mannequin* and more—this was the Crawford we knew and understood.

Sometimes she was at the top of the social heap right from the beginning—as in *Letty Lynton* or *Forsaking All Others*—but it was a sure thing that she would encounter a good many obstacles, mostly emotional, before the inevitable happy ending.

She had her misfortunes—contrived and hokey things like *The Bride Wore Red* and *Love on the Run* . . . *The Gorgeous Hussy*, in which inappropriate casting saw her standing by, the typical Joan Crawford in everything but costuming, while a group of capable actors fit more realistically into the period . . . *Ice Follies of 1939*, which was just ridiculous.

JOAN CRAWFORD as Sadie Thompson in *Rain*

But there were the Crawford triumphs, too—Flaemm-chen of *Grand Hotel*, still effective today, although the extravagant performances of most of the other stars have dated . . . *The Shining Hour*, in which she held her own against the competition of Margaret Sullavan and Fay Bainter . . . *The Women*, her first unsympathetic role, as the conniving wench who gave such a hard time to Norma Shearer.

By this time an exhibitor had labeled her "box-office poison" and, while the old Joan would probably have settled for nothing less than Norma's leading lady part, this time she seized on the opportunity of a bitchy character role into which she could sink her teeth.

And by the forties, she would be back with a whole new career—the kind that wins awards.

JOAN CRAWFORD and Spencer Tracy in *Mannequin*

72

LAURA HOPE CREWS

The most monstrous mama of them all—the proto-type of Philip Wylie's *Generation of Vipers* Mom—was the clucking, fussing Laura Hope Crews in *The Silver Cord*.

Miss Crews knew how to suggest pure poison hidden beneath honeyed endearments and the picture explored her machinations to keep her sons bound to her and out of the clutches of Irene Dunne and Frances Dee. At the end of the thirties came the other famous Crews role—as that silly old Aunt Pittypat, in *Gone With the Wind*.

In between were assorted eccentrics in films like *Behold My Wife*, *Idiot's Delight*, *Camille* and *Her Master's Voice*, in which she had appeared on the stage but which lost whatever merriment it may have had in transit to films.

HENRIETTA CROSMAN

Another onetime theater luminary who extended her career into her old age by a series of screen character roles was Henrietta Crosman. She was incisive as the Dowager Queen of *The Royal Family of Broadway*, and did a complete reverse as an embittered gold Star mother in John Ford's *Pilgrimage*. The latter might have been mawkish, but Miss Crosman's characterization avoided all those dangers.

She was the stiff-necked Southern lady, fallen upon hard times, in the film version of *The House of Connelly*, renamed *Carolina* as a Janet Gaynor vehicle. She had other good roles as well—an aged actress in her last days in *The Curtain Falls* . . . a wise mother in the film version of Maugham's *The Secret Flame*, retitled *The Right to Live* for the screen . . . the amused grandmother of a tempestuous movie star (Margaret Sullavan) in *The Moon's Our Home*. She left films after appearing with Jean Harlow in *Personal Property*, and returned to the stage until 1939.

CONSTANCE CUMMINGS

Of course, Constance Cummings was a much better actress than the usual leading lady, so it is too bad that most of her film roles were not much more than usual leading-lady parts. Chic and charming even as a starlet, she won considerable note when she left films for Broadway's *Accent on Youth* in 1934. One would have thought that this would inspire the movie moguls to find better things for her to do in films, but at her return, she was given the same kind of roles.

Not that all her parts were bad, nor were most of her pictures. Her early ones—like *American Madness* and *Washington Merry-Go-Round*—were timely and entertaining, and she was more than up to her undemanding roles. In *Movie Crazy*, she actually achieved the feat of standing out in a Harold Lloyd picture—one of his best, by the way. Lloyd's leading ladies had usually no more to do than be pretty and passive.

Again—even with the competition of Wynne Gibson, Alison Skipworth, and Mae West—she was particularly effectual in *Night After Night*, as the girl who frequents George Raft's speakeasy because her family used to live in the mansion that houses it. One might mention a few departures from her norm: a man-chasing menace to Irene Dunne's marriage in *This Man Is Mine* . . . an erring wife in a bore called *Glamour* . . . one of the group who discover that a murder has happened during an alcoholic binge in *Remember Last Night* . . . and conventional, but crisp, leading ladies in two minor British melodramas, *Channel Crossing* and *Seven Sinners*.

CECIL CUNNINGHAM

Cecil Cunningham, with her rasp of a voice and horsey face, usually just played bits but enough of them so that she was never a stranger. She showed up, briefly but recognizably, in such pictures as *Susan Lenox: Her Fall and Rise*, *We Live Again*, *Come and Get It*, *Swing High, Swing Low*, and a good many others. She scored most attention as the lively aunt of Irene Dunne in *The Awful Truth*—but everyone scored in that, didn't they?

CONSTANCE CUMMINGS and Frank Albertson in *Billion Dollar Scandal*

CONSTANCE CUMMINGS and Harold Lloyd in *Movie Crazy*

HENRIETTA CROSMAN in *Pilgrimage*

CECIL CUNNINGHAM and Irene Dunne in *The Awful Truth*

LAURA HOPE CREWS and Greta Garbo in *Camille*

LOUISE CAMPBELL, John Howard and John Barrymore in *Bulldog Drummond's Peril*

LOUISE CARTER with Sylvia Sidney in *Jennie Gerhardt*

DOROTHY COONAN (top) with Ann Hovey and Frankie Darro in *Wild Boys of the Road*

JULIETTE COMPTON

NOTES ON OTHER "C" LADIES

There are some familiar names from other eras among the other "C" ladies—*Georgia Caine* and *Mary Carr*, *Ethel Clayton* and *Ruth Clifford*, rotund *Mathilde Comonte* and spare *Theresa Maxwell Conover*, *Virginia Lee Corbin*, *Grace Cunard*, *Mrs. Leslie Carter*, *Helene Chadwick*, *Naomi Childers*, *June Clayworth*—but their thirties opportunities are skimpy. A bit part in a quickie here, a tiny character role there. No *Over the Hill* for Mary Carr. No *Quicksands* for Helene Chadwick. Nothing, alas, but a Western (*Rocky Mountain Mystery*) for Mrs. Leslie Carter, far from her days with Belasco.

Wyn Cahoon is a pretty ingenue in a very few movies you never heard of and *Margaret Callahan* has a few, too, including yet another version of *Seven Keys to Baldpate*—this one aimed at the bottom of dualers. *Kathryn Crawford*, a blue-eyed brunette among all the blondes in *Safety in Numbers*, wins Buddy Rogers but doesn't do as well with her career which contains only a few more secondary roles before it ends. Of course, you know *Anita Colby*—"The Face," they called her with good reason—but you know her from the newspapers and magazines, not for any major movie role.

Louise Campbell was one of those able actresses who come and go, creating no great stir, but playing opposite stars like Bing Crosby and Fred MacMurray, as well as playing the girl in three of the *Bulldog Drummond* series . . . *Judy Canova*, movie leads still to come, was a guest entertainer in celluloid variety

MOVITA CASTENADA and Franchot Tone in *Mutiny on the Bounty*

HELENE COSTELLO and chorines in *Lights of New York*

GLADYS COOPER and George Arliss in *The Iron Duke*

KATHRYN CRAWFORD (left), Carole Lombard, Virginia Bruce, Josephine Dunn, Geneva Mitchell surround Buddy Rogers—in *Safety in Numbers*

shows like *Artists and Models* . . . Louise Carter seemed a particularly inarticulate and inexpressive character actress in a stream of doleful bits, best of which was the bereaved German mother in Lubitsch's *The Man I Killed* . . . Lynne Carver was busier with movie magazine publicity stills than movie acting but she had some starlet roles in MGM films . . . *Juliette Compton* was one of those brunettes who generally played socialites—and almost always unpleasant ones . . .

You can remember some of the others for a role of the period—*Jean Cadell*, bright-eyed in the background

75

as Mrs. Micawber, while W. C. Fields took all the attention in *David Copperfield* . . . *Mamo Clark* and *Movita Castenada*, known by just their first names as the dusky lovelies with whom Gable and Tone shared tropic bliss in *Mutiny on the Bounty* . . . *Dorothy Coonan,* a pretty feminine member of the *Wild Boys of the Road* . . . *Mabel Colcord*, the faithful old family servant of the *Little Women* of Hepburn and her group . . . *Jean Colin,* who was Yum Yum in *The Mikado* . . . *Marjorie Cooley,* of *The Great Commandment* . . . *Mady Correll,* who had the official lead in a low-grade sobber called *Midnight Madonna*, which also introduced *Kitty Clancy*. And they hoped Kitty would be the next Shirley Temple but there wasn't a "next" one. A more promising youngster was *Fay Chaldecott,* who played Little Emily in *David Copperfield* and the child, Lucie, in *A Tale of Two Cities* but soon disappeared from the film scene. And there was *June Carlson,* who grew through adolescence in that ghastly *Jones Family* series.

There are some character actresses you'd recognize —by sight if not by name. You'd see *Nora Cecil* occasionally, but briefly, as a stern-visaged crone. *Irene Cattell* repeated her stage role in *Another Language* but the movie part was reduced to little more than a walk-on. *Dorothy Christy* was a statuesque foil for Buster Keaton in *Parlor, Bedroom and Bath*, for Laurel and Hardy in *Sons of the Desert*, and for various other comics, including many in shorts.

And more "C" ladies—*Helen Cohan,* better known as the daughter of George M. than for any movie roles . . . *Betty Ross Clarke,* the Aunt Milly of a couple of Hardy Family movies . . . *Nell Craig,* a nurse in Dr. Kildare's hospital . . . *Gladys Cooper,* with only a minor role in Arliss' *Iron Duke*, in this decade . . . *Cicely Courtneidge, Lenora Corbett, Mary Clare*—names in England but hardly to American audiences . . .

And a nod to still others, whose names may evoke a fleeting memory—*Iphigenie Castiglioni, Aileen Carlyle, Ruth Channing, Lita Chevret, Ann Christy, Joyce Coad, Rose Coghlan, Claudia Coleman, Marcelle Corday, Cecilia Callejo, Dolores Casey, Janet Chapman, Jean Chatburn, Jean Carmen, Shirley Chambers, Phyllis Crane, Nina Campagna, Ann Codee, Ruth Coleman, Jane Clayton, Janet Chandler, Diana Churchill, Antoinette Cellier, Joan Carol.*

MADY CORRELL and child, KITTY CLANCY, with Warren William in *Midnight Madonna*

ESTHER DALE and Claudette Colbert in *Private Worlds*

D

ESTHER DALE

Esther Dale had no heart of gold beneath that gruff exterior. Unpleasant to the end—that was Esther.

In her parade of domineering servants, brutal prison matrons and gossiping drabs (she had a couple of dozen of such roles in the thirties), there were two standouts. She was the old-line head nurse who fought the advanced thinking of psychiatrists Claudette Colbert and Charles Boyer in *Private Worlds*. And she was formidable as Ralph Bellamy's dragon mother in *The Awful Truth*.

LILI DAMITA

Lili Damita started off promisingly enough in the last days of the silent era as a leading lady to Ronald Colman and as the fiery dancer of *The Bridge of San Luis Rey*. But then talkies came, and although Lili had a good role or two, she was to make much more news offscreen as the first and most flamboyant of the wives of Errol Flynn.

"Flamboyant" may have also been the word for her in *The Cockeyed World*, the most successful Mc-Laglen-Lowe follow-up to *What Price Glory?* And there were a few other flashes of that piquant per-

sonality as a girl going West with Gary Cooper in *Fighting Caravans* . . . a typical French-farce blonde in *This Is the Night* (Cary Grant was introduced in that one, but Roland Young stole it) . . . and a lady being torn among the affections of an unlikely three-some—Adolphe Menjou, Erich von Stroheim and Laurence Olivier—in an old-fashioned melodrama, *Friends and Lovers*.

BEBE DANIELS

Something went out of Bebe Daniels when she started to talk. In silents, she was an athletic, knock-about girl in things like *She's a Sheik* and *Senorita*. But she seemed to lose all her dash with the advent of the microphone.

Actually she got her first audible attention for her singing, which may not have been startling, but was worthy of note in those days when silent screen stars were considered to have made it if they could speak a dozen consecutive words in anything approaching a dulcet tone. Miss Daniels sang quite well in the title role of *Rio Rita*, but outside of proving she could, the picture did very little for her.

Even so, you would have thought they could have found something better for her to follow than three extremely thin program pictures (*Love Comes Along, Alias French Gertie, Lawful Larceny*). Apparently *Dixiana*, an "original movie musical," was their idea—but this, though lavish for its day, was even more foolish in plot than *Rio Rita* and without the *Rita* value of popular songs.

Whether that finished Bebe Daniels with Radio Pictures or vice versa, one could hardly blame her for severing studio ties. She played opposite Douglas Fairbanks, Sr., in *Reaching for the Moon* but any leading lady to Fairbanks (except for Miss Pickford) was just there to be there—and Daniels was no different.

There came a spell at Warners in things called *My Past* and *Honor of the Family*, as well as the lead in the first movie version of *The Maltese Falcon*. It was not in a class with the Bogart version and Miss Daniels' performance didn't come close to doing for her what the remake did for Mary Astor. Rounding out her American movie career—except for one or two quickies, best left unmentioned—were the roles of the second wife in *Silver Dollar* and the secretary in *Counsellor at Law*. Miss Daniels was competent in both roles but the pictures belonged to their male stars, respectively Edward G. Robinson and John Barrymore.

But there is the Daniels characterization that has become practically pop art—the temperamental musical comedy star who breaks a leg just before the big show to give Ruby Keeler her chance to tap-tap to stardom. That was in *42nd Street* of course; and this role, an old star giving way to a new, is the only one that survives for the present generation.

BEBE DANIELS had wild silent screen experiences, such as her mustached male impersonation in *Senorita* with William Powell

LILI DAMITA and Edmund Lowe in *The Cockeyed World*

JANE DARWELL as Ma Joad, with Henry Fonda as Tom, in *Grapes of Wrath*

BEBE DANIELS (with Ruby Keeler and George Brent) in *42nd Street*

MARION DAVIES in *Peg o' my Heart*

MARION DAVIES in *Page Miss Glory*

BEBE DANIELS, with John Boles and George Renevant in *Rio Rita*

DANIELLE DARRIEUX and Charles Boyer in *Mayerling*

LINDA DARNELL as "Daytime Wife" to Tyrone Power

MARION DAVIES in *Polly of the Circus*

With her husband, Ben Lyon, she moved to London, where loyalties are less fleeting, and became a well-loved personality all over again—this time via the radio airwaves.

LINDA DARNELL

Only the gossip columns gave away that Linda Darnell was surprisingly young when she came to the screen in 1939. Her personality may have been juvenile but her dark-eyed beauty was already quite mature. Her first picture, *Hotel For Women*, had her play a small-town girl, protégée of a gabby Elsa Maxwell, who presented her to New York as something pretty exciting. "Exciting" wasn't quite the word—nor was "believable"—for her next movie, *Daytime Wife*. Here she was Tyrone Power's wife, competing for him with his secretary, Wendy Barrie. But she certainly adorned a movie.

DANIELLE DARRIEUX

While it is true that this book concerns only performances in the English language, it would be unfair to Danielle Darrieux to limit discussion of her thirties film career to her one American picture. Actually *The Rage of Paris* was not bad at all—ordinary farce but gaily played, with Miss Darrieux, eyes wide and guileless as Hollywood's version of a Ma'mselle.

But if you had seen her in French—say in *Club de Femmes*—you would have found her much more spicy. And of course, the role that gave her instant world-wide recognition and brought her over here in the first place was that of the young Baroness of *Mayerling* in which, in spite of that astonishing beauty, she was truly tragic. It's tougher for ladies who look like that to break your heart.

JANE DARWELL

The role that would make Jane Darwell more than just a nice, stout character lady—Ma Joad in *The Grapes of Wrath*—didn't come along until 1940.

She was all over the screen in the thirties—mother to everyone from Nancy Carroll and Betty Grable to Jesse and Frank James . . . confidante to Shirley Temple, Will Rogers and the Dionne Quintuplets . . . able to stand up to the demanding *Craig's Wife* of Rosalind Russell . . . settling fates of student nurses like Loretta Young in *The White Parade* . . . running the small-scale Darwell gamut from housekeeper to landlady, nurse to prison matron.

But, there was Ma Joad to come.

MARION DAVIES

Marion Davies was hardly the enormous star that the Hearst papers insisted she was. But she wasn't nearly as hopeless as her detractors—fortified by Orson Welles' portrait of Susan Alexander in *Citizen Kane*—would have you believe.

In the silent era, her clowning and irreverent mimicry of Hollywood hot shots made her one of the screen's real comediennes. But then came the talkies.

They say she had an off-screen stammer. It never obviously interfered with her screen speech but perhaps it inhibited her. The fact remains that most of her dialogue performances were curiously flat. There was nothing in such comedies as *Bachelor Father*, *It's a Wise Child*, or even as Dulcy, in *Not So Dumb*, to compare with the delights she had dispensed just a couple of years before in pictures that didn't talk, like *The Patsy* and *Show People*. There was some mirth in *The Florodora Girl*, *Operator 13*, *Going Hollywood* and *Marianne*, but memory indicates that this too was basically pantomime.

For the rest of it, she went for all the tried-and-true things—playing quaint and cute in *Peg o' My Heart* . . . misunderstood in *Polly of the Circus* . . . pretending to be homely and bespectacled (*Ever Since Eve*) . . . or trotting out her impersonations, which didn't work as well when you had to listen to them, too. She seldom tried drama but, when she did (*Five and Ten*, *Blondie of the Follies*, *Hearts Divided*), the results were lamentable.

Her own company, Cosmopolitan, wound up its long stay at MGM in 1934 and it looked like well-deserved retirement for Miss Davies—going out without much glory but in no particular disgrace.

A year and some odd months later, she returned. This time, Hearst's Cosmopolitan set up shop at Warner Bros. and proceeded to spare no expense to bring back Marion Davies. They brought her the most-in-demand leading men (Clark Gable, Robert Montgomery, Dick Powell), filled her supporting casts with top comics and character actors, gave her expensive productions.

While Louella Parsons faithfully trumpeted "Marion never looked lovelier," the star moved through the uncomplicated plots like a walking doll. All personality gone now, she resembled a Nell Brinkley drawing of the Marion Davies who was—profusions of white-blonde, marcelled hair framing a face artfully painted on a blank.

There were four of these pictures (*Page Miss Glory*, *Hearts Divided*, *Cain and Mabel*, *Ever Since Eve*) before Hearst threw in the sponge. His star had obviously given up a long time earlier.

She finished her post-star days as Hollywood's most fabled and popular hostess.

BETTE DAVIS

And here is The Big One!

The Movie Queen of the era? It had to be Bette Davis.

BETTE DAVIS

JESSICA'S GIRL

BETTE DAVIS and Humphrey Bogart in *Dark Victory*

Crawford, Loy, Lombard, Hepburn, Colbert had their glories. Garbo and Dietrich, of course. Sylvia Sidney, Margaret Sullavan, Nancy Carroll, Jean Arthur —dear to our own dreams.

But *the* star of the thirties—and into the forties, too —Davis; it was. Not that she always had the best pictures. For every *Jezebel*, there must have been three like *That Certain Woman*. But even with *Parachute Jumper* and *Bureau of Missing Persons*, you had to know that this was somebody who went beyond the bland, blonde roles she was playing.

It would be nice to be able to say that the Bette Davis who would be, was immediately apparent. But the skinny little wren who started on the screen as the good sister in *Bad Sister* and followed in *Seed, Waterloo Bridge, The Menace, Way Back Home* and *Hell's House* was just about as nondescript as the roles she played.

Blonder and better made up, she did begin to make an impression in *The Man Who Played God, So Big, The Dark Horse* and especially *The Rich Are Always With Us*. Now an unusually vigorous ingenue, the first real hints of the Bette to come could be seen in an otherwise fairly dreary Richard Barthelmess picture,

Cabin in the Cotton. What fun she was, coquettishly tantalizing, outrageously flirting ("I'd like to kiss you but I just washed my hair"), with that magnolia drawl that would eventually serve her so well in *Jezebel*.

There were other roles in pictures like *Three on a Match* . . . in 20,000 *Years in Sing Sing*, as Spencer Tracy's faithful sweetheart . . . in George Arliss' *Working Man* as a spoiled brat . . . in her own starring programmer, *Ex Lady*, as a "liberated" modern girl. There was *Fog Over Frisco*, just a B melodrama, but one in which she had a chance to go into one of those frenzies—eyes spitting fire, voice crackling—which would do credit to the Bette of her palmiest days.

Then came a loanout to RKO to play Mildred, the Cockney waitress, in *Of Human Bondage*. This was a Leslie Howard vehicle and he was intense in the best Maugham manner—but it was Bette Davis who grabbed all the laurels. In a performance that compromised not at all with the prevailing ideas of screen glamour, she underscored all the commonness and vulgarity, bringing the character to a dazzling display of near-madness.

81

BETTE DAVIS as "The Old Maid" with Miriam Hopkins

BETTE DAVIS in *Bordertown*

BETTE DAVIS as Mildred in *Of Human Bondage*

There was another flashy role as the psychopathic, murdering wife in a Paul Muni movie, *Bordertown*. But then it was back to the nondescript. Eventually, though, somebody at Warners must have realized that she should be treated as more than a leading woman for Pat O'Brien and George Brent. She had been up for an Academy Award for *Of Human Bondage* and there were press and public rumblings about her not having won it. So at last, Warners decided to treat her like an Academy Award-style star. They gave her her own vehicle, *Dangerous*, and this time, helped by the backlash from *Of Human Bondage*, she won the Award (which she claims she named "Oscar.")

Actually *Dangerous* was a pretty bad picture—a plot straight out of the women's magazines about a fading actress destroying herself and the men in her life. But give Bette Davis such a role and you'll get a performance with fireworks exploding.

In *The Petrified Forest*, she offered a subdued but sensitive characterization as Gaby, the desert girl, learning about the life that exists beyond the roadside diner from a poetic wanderer. *The Petrified Forest* is best known now as the picture that brought Bogart so dynamically to the screen; then, it was for Leslie Howard's repeating his stage characterization. But Bette Davis' performance should not be overlooked.

By this time, she had her Oscar and her reputation, but to Warners she was still just a contract player. So we had her in *Golden Arrow*, and in one of the worst movies ever made, a mishmash called *Satan Met a Lady*, libelously "based" on Dashiell Hammett's *Maltese Falcon*.

There was *Marked Woman*, a good, gutsy melodrama in which the "café hostesses" (read "prostitutes") turned against their underworld bosses in a story more than vaguely suggested by Thomas Dewey's investigation of the Luciano empire. As usual, Miss Davis made the most of every opportunity.

She was involved with the underworld again via the prizefight racket as a night club singer in *Kid Galahad* and as a once-moll trying to live down her past in *That Certain Woman*, a shameless soap opera.

But then came one of her few comedies—*It's Love I'm After*—and, she gave what could be considered a preview of her characterization of an even more uninhibited stage lady—the Margo Channing of *All About Eve*, which wouldn't come along for another dozen years.

And there was *Jezebel*—the headstrong belle who could give Scarlett O'Hara a lesson or two in sheer witchery. Many of your most vivid Bette Davis memories must be of her Julie—scandalizing the countryside with her perversities . . . defiantly decked out in her scarlet gown at a white dress ball . . . taunting a fiercely rigid Henry Fonda . . . slyly fomenting a duel to the death. And there was the other Julie—humbling herself before the lover she had lost, begging for the chance to atone for her sins. It was a Bette Davis field day and she played it to the hilt.

But there was even more variety in her Judith Traherne of *Dark Victory*. Here again she was an arrogant society girl but this time she learns she is dying of a brain tumor. Did she take it gracefully? Not our Bette—not very likely. Shots of Bette on the town, living it up, drinking too much, moving from man to man. But then there was true love and courage to face the death that was to come. Sounds mawkish, and it very easily could have been. But *Dark Victory* skirted all the pitfalls. Everything worked. And over it all, the unforgettable performance of Bette Davis.

She was moving in *The Sisters*, harassed as she was by everything from a ne'er do well Errol Flynn to the the San Francisco earthquake. Her Carlotta in *Juarez* was little more than a cameo—Muni and Brian Aherne had most of the footage—but the Davis mad scene was one for the books.

There was *The Old Maid*, a sentimental, old-fashioned but very affecting movie with one of her most underrated performances.

To wind up the Davis films of the thirties, we had *The Private Lives of Elizabeth and Essex*. This was the first of several times as the Good Queen for Miss Davis and, as if to compensate for the fact that she was less than immediately physically recognizable, the Davis mannerisms were out in full. She stamped and shouted but the picture, with its court intrigue, seemed still bound by a proscenium. With all its flaws, *Elizabeth* was still another major portrait in the Davis gallery.

And so ended the thirties for Bette Davis—with so much still to come.

JOAN DAVIS

The comedy of Joan Davis was an acquired taste. If you could get your guffaws out of a gangling, raucous woman with a habit of punching herself in the jaw, Joan Davis was for you.

Truth be told, she seemed to have been for a lot of people. If Alice Faye or Sonja Henie—or even Shirley Temple or Jane Withers—needed a sidekick, there would be Joan. *Wake Up and Live*, *Thin Ice*, *Life Begins in College*, *My Lucky Star*, were some of the titles of movies in which she had a spot. But there were many more.

LARAINE DAY

Laraine Day was the name picked for her when she played in Wallace Beery's *Sergeant Madden*. Before that, she had been Laraine Johnson in George O'Brien Westerns.

Came a bit in a Tarzan movie, and then the role of Molly Lamont, the nurse every patient would like to see when he comes out of anaesthetic—the sweetheart of Dr. Kildare. There were two in 1939—*Calling Dr.*

Kildare and *Secret of Dr. Kildare*—but there would be many more. And there would be lots of Laraine Day leads all through the forties.

FRANCES DEE

Frances Dee was sweet, refined and very beautiful indeed. Most of her roles called for little more than that. But every so often, when the role gave her a chance, she revealed unsuspected capabilities. She had such a chance, for instance, in *The Gay Deception*, really a very minor little comedy but quite a charming one. And one of its principal charms was the entrancing presence of Frances Dee. She got well away from the standard ingenue also in *The Silver Cord*, as the girl who strikes out against the silken menace of her fiancé's mother.

Her placid loveliness was in welcome relief to the skittishness of Miriam Hopkins in *Becky Sharp*. In fact, she was frequently used as contrast to more volatile stars. She was the haven to whom Leslie Howard gratefully escaped after his bout with Bette in *Of Human Bondage*, and served similarly as distraction for Phillips Holmes from the entreaties of Sylvia Sidney in *An American Tragedy*. (Von Sternberg used her mostly as a symbol, never gave her the full-fledged characterization that was Elizabeth Taylor's under George Stevens' direction in the *Place in the Sun* remake.) And she was a quiet Meg to Katharine Hepburn's tomboy Jo in *Little Women*.

She played opposite her real-life husband, Joel Mc-Crea, in *Wells Fargo*, but their youth-to-old-age romance was dwarfed by the events of the bringing of the railroads to the West. She was a beauteous medieval princess for Ronald Colman in *If I Were King*.

In all ways, she was everything a movie leading lady should be—whether the man in her life was Chevalier or Gary Cooper, Douglas Fairbanks, Jr., or Jack Oakie. And when her pictures were bad—as they sometimes were (*Finishing School*, for example)—there was always the compensation of just looking at her.

LARAINE DAY and Alan Curtis in *Sgt. Madden*

FRANCES DEE and Francis Lederer in *The Gay Deception*

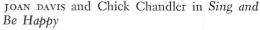

JOAN DAVIS and Chick Chandler in *Sing and Be Happy*

FRANCES DEE and Joel McCrea

OLIVIA DE HAVILLAND and Errol Flynn in *The Adventures of Robin Hood*

OLIVIA DE HAVILLAND as Melanie in *Gone With the Wind* with Hattie McDaniel and Vivien Leigh

OLIVIA DE HAVILLAND

Before Olivia de Havilland began to be taken seriously as an actress, she was a leading lady. James Cagney, George Brent, Dick Powell, Brian Aherne, and even Joe E. Brown were some of the actors opposite whom she played—but mostly Errol Flynn had the pleasure. He swashed and buckled through such adventure pieces as *Captain Blood, Charge of the Light Brigade* and *Adventures of Robin Hood*, while Olivia, with her brown, melting eyes and Mona Lisa smile, provided inspiration for his heroics. Roles in such "big" pictures as *A Midsummer Night's Dream*, in which she played Hermia, and *Anthony Adverse*, as Anthony's lost love, were not much more taxing. But, as usual, she served them well.

She did have two opportunities to score on her own in the 1930s and she pounced on them: as the lovelorn daughter of Ian Hunter and Frieda Inescort in *Call It a Day*, and as the dizzy debutante in *It's Love I'm After*. The latter called on her seldom-exploited gift for comedy as a girl with a stage-door crush on a famous actor, Leslie Howard. Typical of the fun was a sequence in which Howard, determined to turn her against him, locks her in a bedroom and advances. "What are you going to do?" asks Olivia, wide-eyed. "Some," he leers, "call it the fate worse than death!" Livvy, ecstatic: "Oh, goody!"

To round off the decade, came *Gone With the Wind*. Olivia was Melanie, such a milky figure in contrast to the full-bodied Scarlett. But one thinks of others who might have played it and is grateful for the gentleness and graciousness Olivia de Havilland brought to the role. And her success was enough to guarantee that there would be no more young things panting after Dick Powell and Joe E. Brown in her future.

CLAUDIA DELL

Claudia Dell's movie debut in *Sweet Kitty Bellairs* promised all sorts of things. She looked like a Valentine in those Regency costumes. But the movie was boring—operetta without song.

After that it was even worse. She played opposite Al Jolson in *Big Boy* but Jolson never gave anybody else much chance and this was one of his poorest pictures. Then she was a straight-woman for people like Winnie Lightner, Joe E. Brown and Olsen and Johnson in *Sit Tight* and *Fifty Million Frenchmen* . . . played very subordinate roles in major studio minor pictures (*Bachelor Apartment, Confessions of a Co-Ed*) and was already on Poverty Row not much longer than a year after her movie career had started.

There were a couple of returns to the screen but her roles in the Colbert *Cleopatra* and in Boyer's *Algiers* were not much more than glimpses.

OLIVIA DE HAVILLAND and Leslie Howard in *It's Love I'm After*

DOROTHY DELL

Dorothy Dell had the potential to become a star—maybe a Paramount Alice Faye, maybe better. She had the blonde good looks and a combination of wise-gal tongue and soft-gal heart. She used both, dealing respectively with Adolphe Menjou and Shirley Temple in *Little Miss Marker*.

She also was the only asset of a bad picture, *Wharf Angel*. In a better one, *Shoot the Works*, she sang the haunting "With My Eyes Wide Open, I'm Dreaming." And there was no more.

Dorothy Dell was killed in an automobile accident just as she was beginning to make it.

DOLORES DEL RIO

You automatically accept the fact that Dolores Del Rio was (and is) one of the great beauties of the century. Ebony eyes, raven hair, flawless features—but why proceed with the inventory? The face of Dolores Del Rio was sufficient to carry her through an acting life that hasn't stopped yet.

Certainly her first talkies should have been enough to nip any other career in the bud, and most of those which followed through the thirties were not much better. She had been Charmaine and Ramona and the downtrodden Katusha Maslova in the silent era. But her first talkie, *The Bad One*, was something that might have been thrown together.

There wasn't another Del Rio movie for almost two years but it was hardly worth the wait—a tired remake of the creaky old melodrama *The Dove*, here called *Girl of the Rio*. Another chestnut, *Bird of Paradise*, followed, but at least this one gave her a chance to get away from below-the-border dance hall girls and into some becoming Polynesian skirts.

Flying Down to Rio was a happy musical but people came away talking about the dancing of Fred Astaire and Ginger Rogers—not the thin romance involving Del Rio and Gene Raymond. She danced again in *Wonder Bar* but in a subordinate role. Other musicals, *In Caliente* and *I Live For Love*, could not have been more trivial. There was *Madame Du Barry* but again the rewards were purely visual.

To finish off the thirties, she had two entertaining potboilers, *Lancer Spy* and *International Settlement*. Not a very notable batch for an entire decade. So. Del Rio returned to Mexico, where she remains a major star, to return to Hollywood only occasionally thereafter.

KATHERINE DeMILLE

Sloe-eyed, full-lipped Katherine DeMille never seemed to have much fun. Katherine was always jealous, always sullen, always angry. But that was her part and she played it all the way in pictures like

CLAUDIA DELL in *Sweet Kitty Bellairs*

DOROTHY DELL, Preston Foster in *Wharf Angel*

DOLORES DEL RIO in *Madame Du-Barry*

DOLORES DEL RIO and Joel McCrea in *Bird of Paradise*

KATHARINE DE MILLE, Henry Wilcoxon and Loretta Young in *The Crusades*

GLORIA DICKSON

MARLENE DIETRICH and Cary Grant in *Blonde Venus*

MARLENE DIETRICH and Charles Boyer in *Garden of Allah*

Viva Villa, Belle of the Nineties, The Crusades and *Ramona.*

GLORIA DICKSON

Gloria Dickson had a strong role for her first film—as the wife of the innocent victim in the lynch law drama *They Won't Forget.* But although Warners kept her under contract for several years, they gave her absolutely nothing of any worth. So she played secondary blondes in things like *Gold Diggers in Paris* and *On Your Toes* and leads opposite actors like Dick Foran and Dennis Morgan in programmers.

MARLENE DIETRICH

When she first appeared on the screen, the magazines heralded Marlene Dietrich as "another Garbo." That was absolutely ridiculous of course, because there never was "another Garbo." And Marlene Dietrich was the least likely candidate to be "another anybody."

Very much her own person, Marlene, and there hasn't been another like her. But there came a time when Josef von Sternberg and other directors would use her like a piece of expensive scenery, allowing her almost no flicker of animation.

That came later. The first Marlene we saw was the blowsy, heartless strumpet of *The Blue Angel.* And just a casual glance at this Fräulein was not enough to indicate what was in store.

In the off-stage scenes, she was heavy, Teutonic, even dowdy.

But when she stepped to the apron of the sleazy cabaret stage, she was Lola-Lola—and Lola-Lola was something else. You could see how an Emil Jannings could sink to "cock-a-doodle-do" degradation over infatuation for such a woman.

There were the legs—double wonders of the world. And the voice—not yet the cross between purr and growl that it would become—but unique.

Then came Hollywood and a more—but expertly—glamorized Dietrich. The hair became a golden halo. The cheekbones—those matchless works of art—appeared. The eyebrows flew up like arrows over insinuatingly staring eyes—then later would curve into pencilled arcs.

And always there was the sublime unconcern, the unblinking acceptance of men, of sex, of life. No emotional turbulence for Marlene.

Even then, as now, they asked about her age. The answer—then as now—was the same. Marlene was ageless. Always the woman of the world—she who had been through everything. Nothing could upset that vast Dietrich composure.

She was the mysterious one, out of nobody's experience but out of everybody's imagination—as feathered Amy Jolly in *Morocco* and as a veiled Shanghai Lily in *Shanghai Express.*

MARLENE DIETRICH in *The Devil Is a Woman*

MARLENE DIETRICH

Then the pictures started to go wrong and there was only Marlene to admire—certainly not those hoary plots. There was a spy thing called *Dishonored*, a mother-love soap opera, *Blonde Venus*, and another, *The Song of Songs*, that produced only ennui. And, finally, just a series of breathtaking pictures of Marlene—posed against sables and gargoyles (*The Scarlet Empress*), shot through Spanish fans and mantillas (*The Devil Is a Woman*, which happens to be her own favorite picture). Seen today, it is erotic and intriguing, if slow. But then only the slowness came through and, if the Dietrich glamour was startling, the Dietrich performance was less so.

Ernst Lubitsch brought out sparkle—and even a pinch of warmth—in her performance in a smooth comedy, *Desire*, nominally directed by Frank Borzage and only produced by Lubitsch but with such an identifiable "Lubitsch touch" that almost nobody gave poor Borzage any credit at all.

But after *Desire* it was back to the mannequin roles in *Garden of Allah* and *Knight Without Armour*. And even a Lubitsch repeat, *Angel*, was in the same mold. Eventually an unchivalrous exhibitor was taking a trade ad, labeling her (as well as Crawford, Hepburn, Astaire, others) "box office poison."

Wait: That's not the end of Marlene Dietrich in the thirties.

Because there was *Destry Rides Again* and, who would believe it, Marlene bawdy, boisterous and battling—scratching, tearing, gouging and kicking those shapely limbs. She was a Western wildcat—never less than alluring of course, but with a new zing she hadn't shown before.

As the thirties began with a languorous Lola-Lola, they ended with a razzle-dazzle *Destry* Frenchie—both of them Dietrich at her peak.

JEAN DIXON

Jean Dixon had an astringent quality and a dry way with a wisecrack. Too bad the screen never gave her a role nearly as rewarding as some of her plays—*Once in a Lifetime* being a notable example.

On screen, it was just one best friend after another —always welcome appearances but of a regrettable sameness. Some of the better ones—the cynical maid, the only sane member of the household, in *My Man Godfrey*, the distraught sister of Sylvia Sidney in *You Only Live Once*, the witty, unpretentious Susan Potter of *Holiday* and various pals of ladies like Myrna Loy, Joan Crawford, Nancy Carroll, Claudette Colbert and Carole Lombard.

CLAIRE DODD

Claire Dodd was a slender blonde with a delicately dimpled face and an air that practically guaranteed she would play characters no lower than high society

girls. But what society girls! Let Dodd come into a scene, ever so briefly, and it was rocky times ahead for Stanwyck or Blondell or Dvorak or whoever the lady of lowlier station might be.

For Miss Dodd's presence was undeniably a threat. Of course, the star usually wound up with her man in the end—after he finally found out how two-timing was Miss Dodd.

In the approximately forty films she made during the thirties, she went from bits to leads (she was Della Street in a couple of Perry Mason mysteries), but primarily she was the enticing other woman. A few of those films—*Babbitt*, *Roberta*, *Footlight Parade*, *The Glass Key*, *Gambling Lady* and many, many more.

RUTH DONNELLY

Ruth Donnelly had such a salty way with a sharp comment that her screen career was almost entirely spent in playing secretaries, shrewish wives and others whose dialogue would be composed largely of repartee.

She was one of the Warners stock company, which meant that she would generally turn up as wife to Guy Kibbee or second banana to someone like Glenda Farrell. So her roles were predictable but she made them entertaining. Among her movies are *Convention City*, *Footlight Parade*, *Havana Widows* and about three dozen others. Her best-remembered role—by us anyway—was the dreadful mother out to see that her daughter lands a rich man in Jimmy Cagney's *Hard to Handle*.

MARY DORAN

Mary Doran was the rival to Bessie Love in the famous *Broadway Melody*. For the rest of her roles—there were a couple of dozen—she was a name far down in the cast list. Even when she had a lead, in *Remote Control*, it was opposite William Haines at his most obnoxiously smart-alecky—and there was no fate quite so bad for a leading lady.

FIFI D'ORSAY

Fifi D'Orsay, with her varnished black bob, her spitcurl, her rolling eyes and her "oui, oui, m'sieu" was just the girl to make Paris Paree for Will Rogers and Victor McLaglen. She did that in her first two pictures—*They Had to See Paris* and *Hot for Paris* respectively.

Then there were some others in which she wasn't nearly as kicky—*Mr. Lemon of Orange* with El Brendel, and such. And by the time she got back to Will Rogers again (*Young as You Feel*), the Fifi vogue was pretty well past.

She came back—but this time in unsuitable heavy roles in *The Life of Jimmy Dolan*, with Douglas Fairbanks, Jr., and *Going Hollywood*, in which Bing Crosby sang "Temptation" to her through a cham-

JEAN DIXON, Katharine Hepburn, Lew Ayres and Edward Everette Horton in *Holiday*

RUTH DONNELLY in *Blessed Event* with Lee Tracy, Mary Brian

FIFI DORSAY and Victor McLaglen in *Women of All Nations*

CLAIRE DODD

MARY DORAN, Anita Page, Bessie Love and Charles King in *Broadway Melody*

pagne haze. And, except for a few, widely-spaced roles, that was the end of the screen career of Fifi D'Orsay.

But in 1971, Hal Prince gave her a Broadway rebirth in the hit *Follies*, with a number recalling the Fifi of old.

CATHARINE DOUCET

If only for her performance as the destructive Lily Mortar of *These Three*—the stock actress who sponges on her niece and thoughtlessly disrupts several lives—Catharine Doucet should rank with the most important character actresses of the thirties. But there were other good roles, too—as a romantically befuddled American abroad in *As Husbands Go*, the loose-moraled mother of the title character in *Little Man, What Now?* and of course, the disdainful adversary for W. C. Fields in *Poppy*.

91

BILLIE DOVE

CATHERINE DOUCET

FRANCES DRAKE, with Edward Everett Horton and Cary Grant in *Ladies Should Listen*

LOUISE DRESSER and Will Rogers in *Dr. Bull*

BILLIE DOVE

Let's first admit that the face of Billie Dove was almost reason enough to see any picture she made. Almost, but not quite.

Even the pleasure of looking at Miss Dove couldn't compensate for sitting through any of the miserable little melodramas she made in her first year as a talkie star. Consider the list—*Careers*, *The Man and the Moment*, *A Notorious Affair*, *Sweethearts and Wives*, *One Night at Susie's* and *The Lady Who Dared*.

Howard Hughes, said to be smitten, tried to save the day by tailoring two films for her. But they were too little and too late—*The Age for Love*, a yawn-inducing domestic drama, and *Cock of the Air*, a laughless farce. There was one more, a second lead to Marion Davies in *Blondie of the Follies*.

Then Miss Dove had the very good sense to retire for marriage—before she, like so many of her contemporaries, became the victim of bit parts and quickies.

FRANCES DRAKE

Frances Drake had big, big eyes—the better to widen in horror, which is what she had to do in many of her movies. Being menaced by Peter Lorre in *Mad Love* was tough enough but Frances had to put up with both Karloff and Lugosi in *The Invisible Ray*. And there were other gaspers for her in murder movies like *The Preview Murder Mystery*, *The Lone Wolf in Paris*, *There's Always a Woman* and more.

Less harried roles had her losing Robert Montgomery to Joan Crawford in *Forsaking All Others* and giving up George Raft to Carole Lombard in *Bolero*. (But George was all hers in *The Trumpet Blows*—no great win, we'd say.)

LOUISE DRESSER

The most unsentimental of all actresses who played mother roles was Louise Dresser. She had none of the jolly heartiness of a Jane Darwell nor the old lady shticks of—well, you name them. Nor was there a hint of old lace.

Instead, she was brusque, stern—and, although occasionally capable of generous impulses, completely without sugar.

After a long period in the theatre and in silent films, she entered talkies with one of her best roles—the title character in *Mother Knows Best*. Here she was a stage mother of the most domineering stripe.

For the rest of her talking picture career, the Dresser characterizations that come most readily to mind include five with Will Rogers (*Lightnin'*, *Doctor Bull*, *David Harum*, *The County Chairman* and most nota-

MARIE DRESSLER as Carlotta Vance in *Dinner at 8*

MARIE DRESSLER

bly as Melissa Frake, the farm woman of *State Fair*). Others would be her roles as the Empress Elizabeth in *The Scarlet Empress*, the Mother Superior in *Cradle Song* and a woman caught up in the witchcraft hunts in *Maid of Salem*.

MARIE DRESSLER

As much a phenomenon in the early thirties as was Shirley Temple in the later part of the decade was Marie Dressler. There were other elderly comediennes (May Robson, Alison Skipworth, etc.) who would play leads but none of them ever had such an uncommon career in their twilight days.

Actually Marie Dressler had once been a star of the theatre; but by the time she hit the silent screen, those days were long past. She played supporting roles in silents and moved easily into talkies in the same kind of lowdown, rowdy performances. Dressler frequently made bad pictures bearable. But it wasn't until *Anna Christie* that there was a preview of what would come.

Anna Christie, of course, was Garbo's first talking picture and all the news centered around that. The Dressler role was small—as Marthy, the barfly, whose saloon encounter with the disillusioned Anna set the stage. It was a characterization, rather than the roughhouse comedy in which she had specialized, often in company with Polly Moran.

She continued with Polly in a series of increasingly popular topical comedies—*Caught Short*, *Reducing*, *Politics*, *Prosperity*. But in the meantime, she was mining a much richer vein of character acting.

Min and Bill, for instance, was a surprisingly sordid film for Miss Dressler. She still had her slambang, roughhouse sessions with Wallace Beery, but her role was more serious, ultimately tragic, and she was sincerely poignant in her final scenes.

There were touching moments for her too, in *Emma*, *Tugboat Annie* and *Christopher Bean*, although all of them had their obligatory Dressler slapstick sequence. In *Dinner at Eight*, she was laughprovoking in a more worldly way.

There were those who felt that Marie Dressler exaggerated her performances and overdid everything. Certainly "subtlety" was not a word that could be applied to her—and "mugging" sometimes was. But she was an audience pleaser and, in her own special way, she was frequently hilarious, occasionally very moving, and always impressive.

ELLEN DREW

Terry Ray celebrated her promotion from bit parts to leads by changing her name. And it is as Ellen Drew that she became known. Just getting going in the thirties, she appeared as Fred MacMurray's girl in an entertaining Bing Crosby film, *Sing You Sinners*

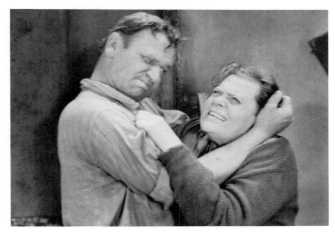

MARIE DRESSLER and Wallace Beery in *Min and Bill*

ELLEN DREW

MARGARET DUMONT, with Groucho, Chico and Harpo in *A Night at the Opera*

. . . as George Raft's lady love in a not-so-entertaining *Lady's From Kentucky* . . . as the yearning Huguette who loses Ronald Colman in *If I Were King* . . . and as a suspect in *The Gracie Allen Murder Case*.

MARGARET DUMONT

Margaret Dumont was a wondrous lady. She was statuesque and imposing, and only Groucho could attack her dignity. (Groucho may have seemed strange to her on occasion but she was much too well bred to appear to notice.)

Groucho, of course, was always after her because she was very rich. Perhaps that's why her last performance—a comeback in *What a Way to Go*—was so disappointing. Who could believe her as poor?

She was Mrs. Rittenhouse and Mrs. Upjohn, Mrs. Claypool and Mrs. Dukesbury—all ladies of serene and unflappable aplomb—and we'll probably never see their like again.

STEFFI DUNA

Remember Steffi Duna, the vindictive border belle of *La Cucaracha*, derisively singing the title song to the lover who had cast her off and spitting out every syllable? That first Technicolor musical short was the highlight of Miss Duna's American career.

She did a similar role in *Dancing Pirate*, but, although this was also in the new Technicolor, it was a pallid thing. She was an inarticulate Eskimo in *Man of Two Worlds*, an abused German girl in an exploitation quickie, *Hitler, Beast of Berlin*, and Neleta, the dancer, in *Anthony Adverse*. The latter had been reasonably important in the marathon book, but the picture cut down the character to a few shots of Miss Duna sulking. For the rest, she wound up playing minor stooges to the likes of Jane Withers, Joe E. Brown and worse.

Bobby Breen *was* worse, wasn't he?

DIXIE DUNBAR

She had roles in which she spoke lines and everything, but nobody is going to remember Dixie Dunbar for them. What they will remember is a tiny, dark-eyed Dixie, dancing energetically through some of those enjoyable thirties Fox musicals—pictures like *Sing, Baby, Sing, Pigskin Parade, King of Burlesque* and *Alexander's Ragtime Band*.

MARY DUNCAN

In spite of her homey-sounding name, Mary Duncan is chiefly recalled as a rather slinky temptress of silent films, carrying on into talkies, where she continued to play such roles in pictures like *Thru Different Eyes*, *Kismet* and *Boudoir Diplomat*.

She had one final role of some importance, the temperamental actress in *Morning Glory*. But of course, that was Katharine Hepburn's first Academy Award winner and nobody else got much attention.

Miss Duncan didn't need it. She retired from the screen to become Mrs. Laddie Sanford, one of the leading ladies of another world—international society.

THE DUNCAN SISTERS

The Duncan Sisters were darlings of vaudeville and Broadway but that was never insurance for movie success. Back in the silent days, they transferred their biggest hit, *Topsy and Eva* (which they had been playing since 1924), to celluloid without much luck (except that Vivian briefly married the leading man, Nils Asther).

They tried again as "the Hogan sisters, Casey and Babe," in a backstage talkie, *It's a Great Life*, but it was just one of the numerous examples of the genre that were crowding the screens in that year.

Vivian was the pretty one, Rosetta the one who made you laugh—at least that was how they established themselves on stage. But, in this movie, Rosetta hardly produced a titter and Vivian owed no gratitude to her cameraman.

JOSEPHINE DUNN

Josephine Dunn was a narrow-eyed blonde who played a few early talkie meanies after having done the same in late silents. Most of her talking picture work was in minor supporting roles—she had given Al Jolson a hard time in *The Singing Fool* and her career never seemed to recover from it. (She played the same kind of wife for Eddie Leonard in *Melody Lane*—and *his* movie career never recovered either.)

Miss Dunn may be one of the more forgettable Hollywood blondes—but anybody who was mean to both Jolson *and* Sonny Boy couldn't have been all bad.

IRENE DUNNE

Irene Dunne is a lady—right to the tip of her patrician nose. Maybe that's why we always liked her when she was pretending to be unladylike—as a repressed Theodora going wild . . . a lively divorcee impersonating a dese-dem-and-dose chorine in *The Awful Truth* . . . a worldly-wise girl in *Love Affair*.

But it was all pretense. In *Love Affair*, she had a line that referred to all the best things in life as being either "immoral, illegal or fattening." You couldn't imagine Irene Dunne being involved in any of those eventualities.

Forgetting her debut in a dim item called *Leathernecking*—and we hope she has—Irene Dunne got her real start in a strong and moving characterization of Sabra Cravat, a well-born Southern girl who becomes

STEFFI DUNA

JOSEPHINE DUNN in *The Singing Fool*

IRENE DUNNE and Cary Grant in *Penny Serenade*

DIXIE DUNBAR

IRENE DUNNE, Charles Boyer and player in *Love Affair*

MARY DUNCAN and Otis Skinner in *Kismet*

THE DUNCAN SISTERS, Vivian and Rosetta

an Oklahoma pioneer woman in Edna Ferber's *Cimarron*. It was one of those films in which the principal characters go from youth to old age, and Miss Dunne was completely believable all along the way.

Even with such an auspicious launching, the Dunne career faltered. Actually she was never less than lovely but it was well toward the end of the thirties before her flair for comedy was discovered and that was when she hit her high. Up to that time, she had to move through a series of films that alternated between domestic dramas—*Consolation Marriage, No Other Woman, If I Were Free,* by and large dismal—and women's sob stories like *Back Street, Ann Vickers* and *The Magnificent Obsession.*

Among the films in this period were a few of value —*The Age of Innocence* and, particularly, *The Silver Cord,* in which she took on her powerhouse mother-in-law, Laura Hope Crews. And certainly both *Back Street,* in which she was the noble mistress of a married man, and *The Magnificent Obsession,* in which

95

she was a blinded widow who regenerates a playboy, were extremely popular. Miss Dunne's cool authority gave even the worst of them some measure of distinction.

Before movies, she had been a musical comedy star and had a trained soprano voice just right for the songs of Jerome Kern. Most of her musicals had his tunes. *Sweet Adeline*, for instance, partially compensated for its tiresome story line with songs like "Don't Ever Leave Me" and "Why Was I Born?" Astaire and Rogers garnered most of the kudos for *Roberta* but it was Miss Dunne who got to sing "Smoke Gets in Your Eyes," "Lovely to Look At," "Yesterdays" and "The Touch of Your Hand." Then her *High, Wide and Handsome* was a musical drama of some sweep with a good original Kern score. *Joy of Living* had Kern songs, too, but they were little better than the picture, a moronic comedy.

But there was also *Show Boat*, the "great American musical" up to that point. Miss Dunne was the ideal Magnolia, and the picture was the best of three versions that have been made.

One thing that had been notably absent from the Dunne repertoire was comedy but, with what was called "the screwball cycle" in full swing and all kinds of unlikely people taking part, she was plunged into it in *Theodora Goes Wild*. This was a pleasant outing about a proper small-town girl who casts off her inhibitions when she admits to being the writer of a scandalous best-seller.

The Dunne comedy technique was refined by director Leo McCarey, who cast her with Cary Grant in *The Awful Truth*. She was absolutely delightful—and so was the picture. The magic worked again for McCarey and Dunne in the sophisticated, but tender, *Love Affair*.

Her final pictures of the 1930s were *Invitation to Happiness*, a comedy-drama, rather good of its kind, about a society girl and her boxer-husband (Fred MacMurray), and *When Tomorrow Comes*, an attempt to repeat the success of *Love Affair* with Dunne and Boyer again teamed. But this was machine-made and didn't work at all. One such mistake didn't change the general picture at the end of the decade, with Irene Dunne sitting securely on top of the movie world.

IRENE DUNNE and William Bakewell in *Back Street*

IRENE DUNNE in *High, Wide and Handsome*

MINNIE DUPREE

It's really unfair to Minnie Dupree that her performance in *The Young in Heart* is haunted by the ghosts of what might have been. She was certainly winsome as an old lady who reforms a reprobate family.

But before Miss Dupree was cast and to the accompaniment of maximum publicity, Selznick first announced that Laurette Taylor was to play the role, then that it would be Maude Adams. Stories vary about why neither of them wound up in the film but the fact remained that, while watching the much more obscure, though satisfactory, Miss Dupree, you could not help wondering how it would have been with one of those legendary ladies giving one of her legendary performances.

MINNIE DUPREE and Janet Gaynor in *The Young in Heart*

DEANNA DURBIN

Personalities as unlikely and varied as Mae West, Shirley Temple and King Kong are credited with "saving" studios in the dark days of the thirties. It seems that Deanna Durbin did just that for Universal, which had been in pretty bad financial shape. But the Durbin pictures caught on and the studio flourished again.

Deanna was a reject from MGM (she and Judy Garland had done a short, *Every Sunday*, for that studio—and MGM kept Judy) who was brought to ailing Universal to play a sunny Miss Fixit in a program picture, *Three Smart Girls*.

It was the first of the entertaining adolescent comedies to star the teen-age Deanna. She was a thoroughly winning youngster who grew up in those last years of the thirties to become a personable young lady. (Her last movie of the decade, *First Love*, saw her receiving her "first kiss," a widely publicized event.)

There was joy in her bubbling personality, infectiousness in her smile. Her singing voice was very much an asset, too, and she handled light concert and opera pieces with the same ease as songs written for her, like "I Love to Whistle" and "Serenade to the Stars."

Each of her thirties movies was tailor-made for her —a simple plot line in which she got into some kind of innocent trouble and then happily extracted herself. In *Three Smart Girls*, she set out to save her father from the wiles of fortune-hunting Binnie Barnes. *One Hundred Men and a Girl* saw her braving the forbidding Stokowski to help some unemployed musicians headed by her father (Adolphe Menjou). *Mad About Music* (our favorite) cast her as the hidden-away daughter of a Hollywood star (Gail Patrick) who invents a "father" and then sees him turn up in the person of Herbert Marshall.

In *That Certain Age*, she developed puppy-love for Melvin Douglas but recovered in time for a finale with Jackie Cooper. Having managed her father's love life

DEANNA DURBIN and Jackie Moran in *Mad About Music*

DEANNA DURBIN, Adolph Menjou, Leopold Stokowski and Mischa Auer in *100 Men and a Girl*

DEANNA DURBIN (center), Nan Grey, Barbara Read and Alice Brady in *Three Smart Girls*

in *Three Smart Girls*, she took over to help her sisters with theirs in *Three Smart Girls Grow Up*. And in *First Love*, she finally had the real thing with Robert Stack—first kiss and all.

There would be unsuitable Durbin roles in the next decade and some unfortunate pictures after she grew up and before she retired. But during the thirties, she was pure delight.

ANN DVORAK

Ann Dvorak was an actress of intensity only occasionally properly utilized by the moviemakers. You might not have noticed her in movie chorus lines but, when she broke out of them, she had an immediate impact.

She gave a compelling performance as Paul Muni's sister in *Scarface* and was efficient even in such tawdry melodramas as *Three on a Match* and *The Strange Love of Molly Louvain*.

Lithe and leggy, with a gift of humor, she was extremely likable in such comedies and musicals as *Sweet Music*, *Bright Lights* and *Thanks a Million*. To her list of thirties performances, add good ones with Paul Muni in *Dr. Socrates*, James Cagney in *G-Men* and Chester Morris in *Blind Alley*. But that left a couple of dozen other pictures which used her poorly, or hardly at all.

ANNE DVORAK and Paul Muni in *Scarface*

ANN DVORAK

98

LIL DAGOVER and Walter Huston in *The Woman From Monte Carlo*

PRISCILLA DEAN had her heyday in silent thrillers (menacer unknown)

FRANCES DADE with Phillips Holmes and Cyril Maude, in *Grumpy*

NOTES ON OTHER "D" LADIES

In a roundup of other "D" ladies, you'll come across some familiar names—but they are familiar from other eras, not for any of the bit parts or Z pictures they did in the thirties. The few pictures credited to *Priscilla Dean*, for instance, would not have been shown in a first-run theatre anywhere, and being a leading lady for Douglas Fairbanks was far in the past for *Marguerite de la Motte* in this last gasp of her career.

The pretty *Day* sisters, *Alice* and *Marceline*, did their little sister song-and-dance in *The Show of Shows* and Alice had an undemanding lead in Richard Barthelmess' *Drag*. But their other films were just program quickies. *Frances Dade* was pretty, too, in some 1930 and '31 pictures (*Raffles*, *Grumpy*, etc.) but is best remembered, if at all, as an early victim of *Dracula*.

Lil Dagover may have been a name with which to reckon in German films but her one American movie, *The Woman From Monte Carlo*, was a full-fledged calamity on every count. *Nancy Drexel*, one of Murnau's *Four Devils*, had only one or two lesser roles in pictures that talked. *Florence Desmond*, very much a star of the London music halls, just had a couple of her impersonations in a Will Rogers picture, *Mister Skitch*.

Now the *Dionne Quintuplets* were certainly "stars" —can you imagine any other reason for seeing *The Country Doctor*, *Reunion* and *Five of a Kind?*—but would you list them with the movie stars? And *June*

JUNE DUPREZ and John Justin in *Thief of Bagdad*

99

IRENE DELROY

YOLA D'AVRIL and Lew Ayres in *All Quiet on the Western Front*

VIOLA DANA and her sister, Shirley Mason

FLORENCE DESMOND

Duprez in *Four Feathers* only hinted that you'd pay her more heed in the forties. *Ann Doran* started her career of low-billed roles, which still continues, in the thirties.

Emma Dunn, never less than competent, was cliché casting for the mother of Lew Ayres in the Dr. Kildare series and dozens of other movie mothers—all exactly the same . . .

Jan Duggan would seem to have been the ideal W. C. Fields lady stooge in *The Old Fashioned Way* but her other roles were minimal. *Doris Dudley,* better known on the stage and eventually as the real-life mother of Butch Jenkins, had a role in the worst Katharine Hepburn picture, *A Woman Rebels. Ray Dooley* repeated her Broadway role in Eddie Dowling's *Honeymoon Lane,* which did nothing for her or for Dowling. *Irene Delroy,* also from the stage, didn't

make it in *Life of the Party* or *Divorce Among Friends.*

Yola d'Avril turned up as all the French girls not already preempted by Fifi D'Orsay but Yola's were usually only bits. *Adrienne d'Ambricourt, Anna Demetrio* and *Rose Dione* were also around when Latin or Gallic types were needed. *Geraldine Dvorak* got some publicity as a Garbo look-alike. *Luli Deste* had leads in *She Married an Artist* and *Thunder in the City* but caused no thunder herself. *Evelyn Daw* was James Cagney's least memorable leading lady in his least memorable movie, *Something to Shout About.*

Others who may stir a dim recollection—*Irene Dare,* a half-pint Sonja Henie . . . *Jean Darling,* once an "Our Gang" darling, later a secondary ingenue . . . *Adrienne Dore, Dorothy Dare* and *Maxine Doyle,* pretty but unimportant . . . *Jeanne Dante,* fresh from a stage triumph but unable to make even a one-day wonder in her one film, *Four Days' Wonder* . . . *Shirley Deane* of the Jones Family series . . .

And a nod to the rest—*Tamara Desni, Milla Davenport, Shannon Day, Jill Dennett, Dorothy Dix* (not the lovelorn adviser), *Doris Day* (not "Our Doris"), *Claire DuBrey, Arletta Duncan, Shirley Dunstead, Grace Durkin, Donna Damerel* (of "Myrt and Marge"), *Margaret Dale, Doris Dawson, Virginia Dale, Norma Drury, Live de Maigret, Adalyn Doyle, Elspeth Dudgeon, Florence Dudley, Marga Ann Daighton, Amanda Duff, Mary Doyle, Sheila Darcy, Nancy Dover, Vondell Darr,* and *Patricia Deering.*

JEANNE EAGLES shoots Herbert Marshall in *The Letter*

E

JEANNE EAGELS

Broadway's tempestuous Jeanne Eagels died too soon to establish herself on the screen. There were only two talking films for her, and one of these was poor—a talkative, melodramatic version of the French play *Jealousy*, with the star giving a frantic performance as a frantic wife.

The other, *The Letter*, was more like it, with Miss Eagels rising to dramatic heights in the final, emotion-charged sequences. With all due respect to the considerable reputation of Miss Eagels, can one suggest that Bette Davis was even more imperative in the remake—consistently suggesting the nuances and perversities beneath a well-bred exterior? Miss Eagels was not nearly as telling in these earlier sequences, apparently saving herself for the big scene at the end. Still, it was enough to show that she could have brought to the screen the same kind of flair that had made her a stage notable.

She was to have next been seen in *The Devil's Holiday*, as a character slightly related to her Sadie Thompson—a manicurist who gets paid for "parties" on the side and who is reformed by true love. At Miss Eagels' untimely death, a song-and-dance girl, Nancy Carroll, got the dramatic role and—but that's a story already told in these pages.

MAUDE EBURNE

If they needed a feisty old lady in movies of the 1930s, chances were they'd cast Maude Eburne. She was the roostery old hen in leather skirts who helped the perfect butler (Charles Laughton) become a rootin' tootin' Westerner in *Ruggles of Red Gap*, and she sniffed her way—how she overworked that sniff—through assorted "ma" and housekeeper parts in pictures that ranged from *The First Year*, to *Valiant is the Word for Carrie*, to *Meet Dr. Christian*. She was an Amazon in *The Warrior's Husband* and a reformatory matron in *Ladies They Talk About*. Whatever her role, she was always exactly the same.

HELEN JEROME EDDY

Helen Jerome Eddy had had bigger roles in the silents, and she played mournful women—unfulfilled spinsters, tenement mothers, widows, servants—all through the 1930s. From this distance, it is difficult to remember Helen Jerome Eddy roles—but you remember *her* . . . she was Sooky's mom in *Skippy*, the wife of the railroaded anarchist in *Winterset*, and she had parts in a couple of dozen other films. The roles may not have etched themselves into your memory, but once seen, you can't forget the sad, sweet face of Helen Jerome Eddy.

SALLY EILERS

When Mack Sennett put Sally Eilers into his first romantic feature, *The Goodbye Kiss*, he called her "the most beautiful girl in movies." That may have been stretching it a bit but Sally *was* something to see—with wistful eyes and a flashing smile in a heart-shaped face.

The Goodbye Kiss was a silent picture, but Sally continued on into talkies, playing small roles and lesser leads. She might have been forever the girl in the background if it had not been for Frank Borzage and *Bad Girl*.

Bad Girl had been a best-selling novel and, as a play, it first had drawn attention to the young Sylvia Sidney. Fox bought it, reportedly, as a vehicle for its young-love team of Janet Gaynor and Charles Farrell. It is Borzage who is credited with the offbeat casting. For the boy, he brought in a blithe youth from the stage, James Dunn. And the girl was that veteran of Hoot Gibson and Buster Keaton pictures, Sally Eilers.

They were very real as New York kids in a bitter-sweet romance and marriage that more than most of the many movies before and since—notable exception being King Vidor's *The Crowd*—dealt believably with young people in conflict with the big city.

You would have thought Sally Eilers had it made. You would have thought wrong. She and Dunn continued as a team for a while and she did many films

JEANNE EAGELS and Fredric March in *Jealousy*

MAUDE EBURNE, Rochelle Hudson in *Poppy*

HELEN JEROME EDDY with Arthur Hoyt and Stuart Erwin, in *Make Me a Star*

SALLY EILERS and James Dunn in *Bad Girl*

SALLY EILERS, Tom Brown and Richard Barthelmess in *Central Airport*

on her own. But none were good enough to make her the star she had shown every indication of becoming.

On her own, she played the carnival girl in *State Fair*, which suited her even though it was basically a subordinate role.

She went on through the thirties, doing her best in unrewarding roles—leads in programmers, leading lady to actors like Robert Montgomery, Richard Barthelmess and even Eddie Cantor in their least likely films.

She might have been just a pretty girl you liked in a lot of nondescript movies of the period. Because of *Bad Girl*, she ranks much higher in the parade of actresses of the thirties.

FLORENCE ELDRIDGE

Florence Eldridge is one of our more distinguished actresses, but you'd never know it from most of what she was given to play in the 1930s. She was austere and spiteful as Queen Elizabeth, adversary to Katharine Hepburn's Mary of Scotland, and pitiable as Fantine in *Les Miserables*—but both of these were small roles. And she had a scene or so as the slatternly Ruby Lemar, in *Story of Temple Drake*, but everything about that picture, based on William Faulkner's *Sanctuary*, was too bad for comment. That left colorless, secondary roles in colorless, secondary pictures like *The Great Jasper* and *A Modern Hero* and some ladies involved with murder, in *The Studio Murder Mystery*, *Thirteen Women* and *The Greene Murder Case*, in which she had a fight for life with Jean Arthur on a roof overlooking the turbulent Hudson River. She won, too.

MARY ELLIS

In the wake of Grace Moore came other divas to the screen. None of them even approached the same success. But certainly Mary Ellis—whose stage career ranged from Metropolitan Opera to the original *Rose Marie* to Shakespeare and Eugene O'Neill—was one prima donna who seemed a sure bet for the screen. Alas, her *All the King's Horses* and *Paris in Spring* were flimsy things, and *Fatal Lady* an outright horror. And they were at the end of that particular musical movie cycle. So Miss Ellis went back to the London theatre, having made scarcely a ripple in films.

PATRICIA ELLIS

From 1932 through 1937, Patricia Ellis seemed to be in just about every other Warner Bros. picture made, and she even had time for loan-outs. That was all to the good. For while her roles were ordinary youthful leads and gave her little chance to contribute anything but decoration, that seemed quite enough.

She appeared opposite actors who ran the gamut from James Cagney to Joe E. Brown, and she played the daughters of gentlemen of all types—George Arliss, Adolphe Menjou, Guy Kibbee. Among her films were *Elmer the Great*, *Picture Snatcher*, *The Circus Clown*, *Easy to Love*, *Sing Me a Love Song*, and more, many more.

Eventually she wound up in London, where she starred in *The Gaiety Girls* with Jack Hulbert, in a role that really gave her a chance to sing, dance and play with vivacity. But her days as an in-demand leading lady were just about over, and although there were a few other minor movies (*Blockheads* with Laurel and Hardy, *Back Door to Heaven*, and *Fugitive at Large*), her next stop was Broadway, where she sang and danced in *Louisiana Purchase*.

MADGE EVANS

There was very little required of Madge Evans in the 1930s movies except to be lovingly there when the star needed her. She did that so well that she turned up—always agreeably—in pictures all through the decade.

Did Robert Montgomery need a special kind of dream girl in pictures like *Lovers Courageous* and *Fugitive Lovers*? There was Madge Evans. And she was as lovely opposite Montgomery in *Made on Broadway*, *Hell Below* and *Piccadilly Jim*; opposite Ramon Novarro (*Huddle*, *Song of India*); an early Clark Gable (*Sporting Blood*). She played with Lee Tracy in *The Nuisance*, James Cagney in *The Mayor of Hell* and Spencer Tracy in *The Show Off*. And she yearned at songs of Al Jolson in *Hallelujah, I'm a Bum* and Bing Crosby in *Pennies from Heaven*.

She was a virtuous Agnes Wickfield, who would be waiting there when David Copperfield's Dora died. She was Lionel Barrymore's rebellious daughter, infatuated with the matinee idol of John Barrymore in *Dinner at Eight*. Even in the rare role of "the other woman" in *What Every Woman Knows*, she was far too nice to give any real worry to the star, Helen Hayes.

It was the common denominator of all of her roles. Madge Evans was *nice*—but she was nice to have around too.

MARY ELLIS in *Paris in Spring*

MADGE EVANS

FLORENCE ELDRIDGE and Katharine Hepburn in *Mary of Scotland*

MADGE EVANS and Robert Montgomery in *Hell Below*

PATRICIA ELLIS

JILL ESMOND and Ricardo Cortez in *Is My Face Red?*

MARY EATON

PEG ENTWHISTLE

NOTES ON OTHER "E" LADIES

Jill Esmond, a British player, came to this country with her husband, Laurence Olivier. She played secondary socialites (in *State Attorney*, *Is My Face Red?* *Thirteen Women*) and he fared little better so they went home. He would return. *Wera Engels*, another import, had one unimportant lead (opposite Richard Dix in *The Great Jasper*) and roles in quickies.

Alice Eden won a radio contest which gave her a screen name and one movie role (in *Career*). *Peg Entwhistle* had only one film role, too (in *Thirteen Women*), but made headlines when she jumped from a letter in a Hollywood sign . . . *Ruth Etting*, one of the song stylists of the time, had merely a few tunes—none for The Hit Parade—to croon in *Roman Scandals*, *Hips, Hips Hooray* and *Gift of Gab* . . .

Mary Eaton was special on Broadway but her first talkie, *Glorifying the American Girl*, did nothing to glorify anyone involved. She was also in *The Cocoanuts* but what is more superfluous than a girl in a Marx Brothers movie unless she is being chased by Harpo or stalked by Groucho? . . . As in vaudeville, *Vilma Ebsen* partnered her dancing brother, Buddy, in *Broadway Melody of 1936*. *Daisy Earles* was the midget sweetheart in *Freaks*. *Bess Ehrhardt* did her skating in *Ice Follies of 1939*.

Three familiar faces, although they seldom played more than bits, belonged to *Sarah Edwards, Fern Emmett* and *Effie Ellsler*—respectively the priggish spinster, the rural wife and the landlady types. Others with occasional credits include *Muriel Evans, Margaret Early, Edith Elliott, Lillian Elliott, Helen Ericson, Helena Phillips Evans, Ann Evers, Helyn Eby-Rock, Marcelle Edwards.*

RUTH ETTING and Bing Crosby

FRANCES FARMER

F

FRANCES FARMER

Frances Farmer, a clean-cut leading lady for Bing Crosby (in *Rhythm on the Range*) and in other program pictures, so beautified the screen that only a stickler would care whether or not she could act.

But, surprise, she could. The thanks for guessing it must be given to producer Samuel Goldwyn and/or to either or both of the co-directors, William Wyler and Howard Hawks. One or all of them cast her in *Come and Get It* and, in a dual role, she gave highly impressive performances. She was a tawdry North Woods saloon singer and, eventually, the well-brought-up daughter of the original character. Her beautifully controlled acting avoided all the pitfalls inherent in both characterizations.

She wasn't as happily cast as Josie Mansfield in *Toast of New York*, and her home studio, Paramount, could find nothing better for her than routine roles in *Ebb Tide*, *Exclusive* and *Ride a Crooked Mile*. So Miss Farmer took off for New York where she was to prove her talent all over again as the original leading lady of Clifford Odets' *Golden Boy*, in 1937.

GLENDA FARRELL

Glenda Farrell was one of those gangland blondes in pictures like *Little Caesar* and *I Am a Fugitive*. Fortunately somebody noticed her way of dropping a caustic quip from a curled lip. And her slightly acerbic comedy manner complemented those of such other Warners wisecrackers as Joan Blondell. So Glenda stopped being unsavory and went in for brash comedy.

The trouble is that Warners, having discovered this, kept using it. They put Glenda in everything—good picture or bad, mostly the latter. A girl can be sharp and funny just so often and, when she had the role and the lines, Glenda was up to it. But for every *Lady For a Day* or *Hi, Nellie*, there were a lot of things like *Girl Missing* and *Heat Lightning* in which her gifts were thrown away.

The first few of her teamings with Joan Blondell were rewarding but the studio used them too often. And her Torchy Blane series quickly fell into the rut.

Even so, when you think of all those hot-shot news-hens and all those wiseguy gold-diggers, you have to think of Glenda Farrell. When her role gave her half a chance, she was one of the best of the bunch.

ALICE FAYE

Alice Faye started out as an imitation Jean Harlow. And a cheap copy she was—with platinum, frizzed hair, beaded lashes, crayoned eyebrows, pouty lips smeared with goo. Years later, she would caricature her early screen self as the Barbary Coast belle in *Alexander's Ragtime Band*.

But like the sweetheart of Alexander, Miss Faye quickly learned the virtues of the natural approach. The honey-blonde Alice was much more appealing and her roles reflected the new look. One still wouldn't cast her as a Park Avenue deb, but she wasn't limited to burlesque queens either.

She shared closeups with Tyrone Power or Don Ameche—and, if it were a particularly big picture, she'd have them both. There were *In Old Chicago*, all about the big fire, and *Alexander's Ragtime Band*, all about the American dance-band world before and after the first World War—with appropriate Irving Berlin music. There was also *Rose of Washington Square*, in which Alice didn't attempt to be Fanny Brice although the scenarist owed the plot to Fanny's life. She echoed everyone from Mabel Normand to Constance Bennett in *Hollywood Cavalcade*.

Actually, the happiest Faye pictures were the light topical comedies—*Sing, Baby, Sing*, *Wake Up and Live*, *On the Avenue* and *You Can't Have Everything* being examples. The titles recall the title tunes, and there were many more—"This Year's Kisses," "I'm Shooting High," "You Turned the Tables on Me," "I Feel a Song Coming On," "Goodnight, My Love," "There's a Lull in My Life," "Afraid to Dream," "Now It Can Be Told"—all sung in the smoky, hit-making voice which was probably Alice Faye's number one attribute.

LOUISE FAZENDA

There was a time when Louise Fazenda was always around. She was the "comedy relief" in the first mystery talker (*The Terror*), the first movie operetta (*The Desert Song*), the first color backstage musical (*On With the Show*) and she performed similar functions in several dozen films all through the thirties. Miss Fazenda was inclined to make a lot of faces. But, actually, most of the pictures and most of her roles were so bad that even a Beatrice Lillie couldn't have helped.

She could be amusing when the role gave her half a chance, for instance as the brawny blacksmith in *Swing Your Lady*; the Louella-type in *Once in a Lifetime*; the woman's club representative in *First Lady*; the newly-rich mother of a child movie star in *Forbidden Adventure*.

EDITH FELLOWS

Edith Fellows proved—as had Bonita Granville and Jane Withers—that brats have more fun. And they're easier to take among movie children. Edith, a competent child actress—finally had her chance to shine in *She Married Her Boss*. Therein, Claudette Colbert found that her troubles were just beginning after her marriage. Principal trouble was the boss' daughter, a holy terror. Edith Fellows played her so realistically that there was applause when she finally got her comeuppance.

Young Edith was obstreperous too, in *Pennies From Heaven* with Bing Crosby—although that plot eventually skirted bathos. But then she was a crippled girl in a sob story, *City Streets*, and finally was playing "Little Mother" in that abysmal movie series *Five Little Peppers*.

BETTY FIELD

At the end of the thirties came the first two screen performances of Betty Field. Already a character actress, she demonstrated her versatility in the two widely varying roles. In *What a Life*, she repeated her stage role—as well brushed and squeaky-clean a high school heroine as any teenager could ask.

Then, in a completely different—and striking— performance, she was Curley's wife in Lewis Milestone's screen version of John Steinbeck's *Of Mice and Men*. Sluttish and provocative, yet strangely vulnerable, she made her few moments count as strongly as anything in that film.

VIRGINIA FIELD

Virginia Field, a British blonde, was frisky enough as a barmaid in *Lloyds of London* in 1936 to justify

FRANCES FARMER, Joel McCrea, Edward Arnold in *Come and Get It*

GLENDA FARRELL, Ross Alexander in *Here Comes Carter*

GLENDA FARRELL, as Torchy Blane, with Barton McLane

ALICE FAYE, Tyrone Power, Don Ameche in *Alexander's Ragtime Band*

ALICE FAYE

ALICE FAYE with Tony Martin in *Sally, Irene and Mary*

LOUISE FAZENDA, W. C. Fields in *Tillie's Punctured Romance*

BETTY FIELD, Jackie Cooper in *What a Life*

EDITH FELLOWS, with Mary Astor, Jackie Moran, Melvyn Douglas in *And So They Were Married*

BETTY FIELD, Bob Steele in *Of Mice and Men*

107

VIRGINIA FIELD, Tyrone Power in *Lloyds of London*

GERALDINE FITZGERALD

GRACIE FIELDS

your thinking that her studio (20th Century-Fox) would give her better roles. They didn't though. She continued to play secondary parts and less, her only nominal leads being in pictures featuring Charlie Chan, Mr. Moto and Jeeves. And of course, anybody except those title characters had to be an "also-ran."

GRACIE FIELDS

Oh, how they loved Gracie Fields in jolly old England! Hearty and robust she was, but, like many national idols, she wasn't quite so gladsomely received outside her own country. In the forties, she would come over to the States to make three films. But during the late thirties, we saw only a few of her British-made pictures, and only a very few of us saw them. The Lancashire Lass may have been hot stuff in Piccadilly, but Times Square and Main Street couldn't have cared less.

GERALDINE FITZGERALD

At the end of the decade came two films that still rank among the best, *Wuthering Heights* and *Dark Victory*. In them, a young Irish actress made her bow to American audiences, making much of roles that could have become merely cardboard figures.

Geraldine Fitzgerald never found the great screen roles to match her talents and beauty. But she was superb in these lesser ones. As poor, foolish Isabella, maddened by her infatuation for Heathcliff and eventually a beaten drab, old while still in her youth, she was never overshadowed by the more theatrical characterizations of the lovers. And as the best friend of Bette Davis, she was gracious and unsentimental in a role that she never allowed to become sloppy.

SUSAN FLEMING

Susan Fleming was named Angela in *Million Dollar Legs*. The picture was laid in Klopstokia and all Klopstokian girls are named Angela—except, of course, for Mata Machree (Lyda Roberti), the international spy. Miss Fleming was the prettiest Angela of them all.

She never had another movie chance except for an occasional bit or two. But anyone who played in *Million Dollar Legs* deserves our compliments. (Miss Fleming must have had quite as zany a time off-screen. She became the real-life wife of Harpo Marx.)

JOAN FONTAINE

We weren't going to know until the forties that Joan Fontaine was any more than the sister of Olivia de Havilland—something less, say, than a Sally Blane to Olivia's Loretta Young. She was the leading lady in pictures like *Gunga Din* and *The Duke of West Point* —but they were the kind of movies which really could

GERALDINE FITZGERALD, Laurence Olivier in *Wuthering Heights*

SUSAN FLEMING

JOAN FONTAINE, Douglas Fairbanks, Jr. in *Gunga Din*

JOAN FONTAINE, (right) with Rosalind Russell, Phyllis Povah in *The Women*

have dispensed with leading ladies. As the youngest of the about-to-be-divorcees in *The Women*, she was in the shadow of her more vicious associates. And she joined Fred Astaire in *A Damsel in Distress*, but she didn't have a chance to do the Ginger kind of things.

So there was nothing that would lead you to suspect Hitchcock, *Rebecca* and an Oscar in her future. But they'd be along very soon, right after the beginning of the next decade.

LYNN FONTANNE

Only once did Lynn Fontanne and Alfred Lunt face the terrors of the talking picture camera in star roles. Then, victorious, they returned to their own world of the theatre resisting every further Hollywood overture (up to and including that of Ross Hunter to cast them in support of Doris Day).

But in *The Guardsman*, they—it is almost impossible to separate them as actors—gave the brilliant, witty, incandescent performances that had raised them several notches above anybody else playing in the theatre. Fontanne, most adroit of comediennes, played an actress, "deceived" by the masquerade of her own husband. The Molnar dialogue was enhanced by the melodious laughter of her voice . . . the lightly mocking manner of her playing belied her seeming acceptance of her husband's disguise. Did she really know? Of course she did. Lynn Fontanne knew everything— even to the right moment to leave the screen forever.

SIDNEY FOX

Sidney Fox was very petite, very dark, and, very briefly, she got a star buildup. She had the title role in *Bad Sister*, for instance—with another newcomer, Bette Davis, relegated to the role of the ugly duckling "good sister." She was also given "cute" roles in pictures like *Strictly Dishonorable* and *Once in a Lifetime*. "Cute" she was—almost insufferably so—but the comedy talents needed to make those parts work just weren't part of her equipment. So, instead of establishing her, these good roles doomed her to routine ingenues. And then oblivion—except that you remember that there once was an actress who had a man's name.

KAY FRANCIS

They picked on poor Kay Francis—ridiculed the way she talked, substituting "w's" for "r's" and generally treated her efforts as an emotional actress fairly cruelly. Still she was a stunner—tall and so brunette, so sleek and with such chic. She was always called a "best dressed woman" and somehow she managed to live up to the title. There were those fans who went to a Kay Francis movie simply to see what the lady was wearing, and never mind the movie. That was good advice for many of the movies.

109

LYNN FONTANNE, Alfred Lunt in *The Guardsman*

SIDNEY FOX, Paul Lukas in *Strictly Dishonorable*

KAY FRANCIS, Ian Hunter in *The White Angel*

KAY FRANCIS, Miriam Hopkins in *Trouble in Paradise*

She started out very early in talkies, playing adventuresses opposite everyone from Walter Huston to Harpo Marx and Jack Oakie. Gradually she began to move to the right, softening her mannish hairdo and becoming a leading lady for the likes of William Powell and Ronald Colman.

She might have gone on that way, handsome and competent if not inspired, if Warners hadn't taken her on as their "women's pictures" star. Then it was soap opera time, with one sudsy plot after another while Miss Francis endured all the agonies of unfaithful husbands, villainous lovers and ungrateful children. The nadir was probably reached with *My Bill*, in which she was a struggling widow, turned against by kith and kin except for the faithful small boy of the title. But this was just one among a number of such roles, all played with scarcely a flicker of expression by Miss F.

There were a few pictures among these dozens in which her performances were almost as impressive as her glamour. George Cukor and Ernst Lubitsch

brought out an unexpected talent for comedy in *Girls About Town* and *Trouble in Paradise* respectively. *One Way Passage* was one of the all-time best tearjerkers and Miss Francis couldn't have been more lovely as the dying heiress on a last romantic ocean voyage. And she was sincere as Florence Nightingale in the ponderous biographical film, *The White Angel*.

But then there were all those others—*Mary Stevens, M.D., Comet Over Broadway, Secrets of an Actress, Another Dawn* and many more. All tiresome problem dramas notable chiefly for the perennial Francis fashion parade.

NOEL FRANCIS

Noel Francis played underworld blondes, seeming smarter—or, at least, more cunning—than the usual movie lady of the species. Although she was normally relegated to the lower depths as someone encountered along the way, she was apt to be in the best bad company for as long as she lasted. So we saw her with such gents as Jimmy Cagney in *Blonde Crazy*, with Cagney and Edward G. Robinson in *Smart Money*, with Spencer Tracy and Humphrey Bogart in *Up the River*, with George Raft in *Under Cover Man*, with Paul Muni in *I Am a Fugitive*.

PAULINE FREDERICK

Pauline Frederick was a heavy emotional actress of the stage and silent screen. After a few early talkies (*On Trial, The Sacred Flame, Evidence*) she was down to domineering mother roles. And how she chewed the scenery as she poured her vitriol on hapless daughters-in-law like Nancy Carroll and Claire Trevor!

FRANCES FULLER

Frances Fuller had the sharpest widow's peak on the screen. She also had a nice, unpretentious manner just right for the nice, unpretentious wives she played in film versions of two plays, *One Sunday Afternoon* and *To the Ladies*. The latter—it starred Helen Hayes on stage—was strangely turned into a vehicle for George Bancroft and retitled *Elmer and Elsie*. Elsie was played down on screen and Miss Fuller returned to the theatre, where she was used to meatier roles.

BETTY FURNESS

Betty Furness was always much too brisk and efficient for the innocuous roles she played (leads in things like *Midshipman Jack*, smaller parts in bigger pictures like *The Magnificent Obsession*). She was much too sharp to waste her time in such unrewarding work, but who could have prophesied that she'd "make her name" opening refrigerator doors on TV? ("You can be *sure* if it's Westinghouse.") And eventually, becoming known in federal and New York City administrations.

KAY FRANCIS, William Powell in *Behind the Makeup*

NOEL FRANCIS, James Cagney in *Blonde Crazy*

FRANCES FULLER, George Bancroft in *Elmer and Elsie*

PAULINE FREDERICK, Nancy Carroll in *Wayward*

BETTY FURNESS

TRIXIE FRIGANZA, (right) with Anita Page, Robert Montgomery in *Free and Easy*

JANE FROMAN (right), Jean Muir, James Melton in *Stars Over Broadway*

PEGGY FEARS

NOTES ON OTHER "F" LADIES

There are some "names" among the other "F" ladies—but they're not necessarily movie names. *Kirsten Flagstad*, for example, boomed a Wagnerian aria in *The Big Broadcast of 1938* and *Frances Faye* shouted scat in *Double or Nothing*—but that was the extent of their screen activity. *Sylvia Froos* sang in *Stand Up and Cheer* and *Vivien Fay* whirled through a ballet in *A Day at the Races*. And the velvet voice of *Jane Froman* was featured in *Stars Over Broadway* and *Radio City Revels*. *Irene Franklin*, of vaudeville, had a number of bits and *Trixie Friganza* had some, too. *Peggy Fears*, who wowed them in the Follies and in Manhattan café society, even played a secondary lead in a less than secondary picture (*Lottery Lover*). And a beauty of the theatre and the silent screen, *Elsie Ferguson*, had only one unfortunate film, *Scarlet Pages*, to show for her talking picture career. Names they might have been—but movie names they certainly were not.

Nor were *Jinx Falkenberg*, making her debut in a Tex Ritter Western, or *Nanette Fabares*—she didn't become "Fabray" until the forties—as a pretty lady-in-waiting to Queen Bette Davis in *The Private Lives of Elizabeth and Essex*. Later maybe—but not in this era. *Phoebe Foster*, who played leads on Broadway, was reduced to supporting roles in thirties films. *Mary Field* would be more familiar in films of the succeeding years but she was beginning to be recognized in thirties bits.

JULIA FAYE

MARY FORBES in *Sadie McKee* with Franchot Tone, Joan Crawford

HELEN FLINT, with Humphrey Bogart, in *The Black Legion*

EMILY FITZROY (head of table) in *The Man From Blankley's* with Loretta Young, John Barrymore, others

Susanna Foster trilled in *The Great Victor Herbert* and everybody thought she might become a star. (She didn't, of course—after Deanna, the rest were really minor leaguers, weren't they!)

Phyllis Fraser would become known as Mrs. Bennett Cerf but her film roles were minor. So were those of *Brenda Forbes* although her brother, Ralph, was a well-know leading man and their mother, *Mary Forbes*, had her innings as various stately dowagers. The vinegar-visaged *Blanche Frederici* turned up in—it seemed like dozens of movies—but never for long. Her sister in style—*Emily Fitzroy*—had much bigger roles in the silent days but, by talkies, she was practically finished. *Dot Farley* had few roles in talkie features but she did keep busy in shorts—usually as the personification of all mother-in-law jokes. Others whose silent celebrity didn't carry over into their few talkies appearances included *Betty Francisco, Elinor Fair, Virginia Browne Faire, Dale Fuller, Mabel Forrest, Flora Finch, Cissy Fitzgerald, Audrey Ferris, Maude Fulton* and *Julia Faye*, a DeMille silent player who continued getting billed in all of his pictures—though usually in bits without dialogue.

And, for the record, some other "F" names—*Bess Flowers* (just a bit player but eventually to become the most recognized extra, with a cult of her own, in the forties and fifties), *Helen Flint*, who had minor roles, two of which (the whores in *Ah Wilderness, The Black Legion*) rate special mention, *June Filmer*,

NANETTE FABARES (later Fabray) and Olivia de Havilland (lute) in *The Private Lives of Elizabeth and Essex*

Helen Freeman, Helen Foster, Gloria Foy, Mary Foy, Patricia Farr, Patricia Farley, Wilma Francis, Gloria Franklin, Barbara Fritchie, Hazel Forbes, Jean Fenwick, Florence Fair, Betty Farrington, Brenda Fowler, Margaret Fielding, Almeda Fowler. Just names now—most forgotten—but once they all, at least, got those names into movie cast lists.

FRANCISKA GAAL, Fredric March in *The Buccaneer*

G

FRANCISKA GAAL

Franciska Gaal, heralded as Hungary's gift to the American cinema, turned out to be distressingly coy in her Hollywood movies. Of course, each of them presented her in one of those roles that seems especially designed for European starlets with accents. Miss Gaal was well reported in her Magyar movies, but here she was a taste that was never acquired. For the record, her three American movies—there never was a fourth—cast her opposite Fredric March in *The Buccaneer*, Bing Crosby in *Paris Honeymoon* and Franchot Tone in *The Girl Downstairs*.

KETTI GALLIAN

Another in the big parade of Continental leading ladies who made the trek to Hollywood with visions of Garboesque eminence was Ketti Gallian. Mlle. Gallian was a blonde with a face made up á la Dietrich although, in personalty, she was closer to a Gallic Alice Faye.

She landed with a thud in her first picture—a melodramatic mishmash entitled *Marie Galante*—and *Under the Pampas Moon* wasn't the picture to pull her up. A couple of years later, she showed up in support-

ing parts in *Espionage* and *Shall We Dance?* and then was seen no more.

GRETA GARBO

How do you write about Greta Garbo?

What can possibly be said that hasn't been written over and over again—but so seldom with any emerging true picture of Garbo, the artist and woman? For Garbo is sublime.

Not that all of her pictures lived up to the glory that is Garbo. *Camille, Ninotchka, Queen Christina, Anna Karenina, Anna Christie*—then what?

Garbo took her time about talkies. Except for Chaney and Chaplin, she was the last of the silent stars to move over to the new medium.

When it happened, it was in a particularly well-chosen role—a complete switch from the sabled, silken sirens of her silent days.

The billboards shouted "Garbo Talks!" But it was more than just a talking Garbo—it was a new Garbo, light years removed from the creature who nuzzled John Gilbert on bearskin rugs. Here we met an unutterably weary Anna Christie, opening the door to that waterfront saloon. The first words in that startling baritone—"Give me a whisky."

Garbo's Anna Christie was a remarkably timeless characterization which still looks contemporary some forty-odd years later, even though the Eugene O'Neill play dates badly and now seems naive.

Even then, some of her other films—if not her performances—looked old hat, out of her silent past. There was *Romance*, with its creaky tale of the love of a passionate diva and a righteous cleric. And *Inspiration* had Garbo seeming more bored than ever before as one of those standard courtesans seducing a callow Robert Montgomery.

And there were the lending library romantics of *Susan Lenox, Her Fall and Rise*, in which even the addition of Gable failed to generate much steam . . . *As You Desire Me* with its muddled mysticism and with Garbo unbecomingly gowned and coiffed (in a white fright wig) . . . *Mata Hari*, passé even then in its tale of the international spy going to her death for love . . . *The Painted Veil*, a triangle drama out of the lowest shelf of the works of Somerset Maugham. These were all bad pictures and that they were worth seeing is a tribute to the Garbo who was always arresting. No better for Garbo was *Conquest*, although it was a rich production with an impressive characterization of Napoleon by Charles Boyer. But her role of Walewska was passive.

That still left a half-dozen (including *Anna Christie*) in which the pictures themselves were worthy vehicles for the portrayals of their star. All of them presented variations of the most immediately recognizable Garbo characterization—the cynical, disillusioned woman of experience falling heedlessly, giddily, recklessly into a young girl's love. Garbo was unexcelled when it came to portraying such all-consuming rapture. Picture her Christina, memorizing every detail of the room in which she has found such bliss . . . her Grusinskaya, well-nigh swooning in ecstasy . . . her Camille, defenses down and vulnerable . . . even her Ninotchka—"GARBO LAUGHS!"

Camille may be the best of all possible Garbos—the role that carried her extraordinary combination of enigmatic worldliness and radiant girlishness, that entrancing joy, inevitable doom, to its nth degree. And *Ninotchka* presented the same combination in rare comic terms, one of the most devastating displays of comedy technique ever exhibited.

And there were the others—the *Grand Hotel* ballerina . . . the masquerading *Queen Christina* . . . the doomed *Anna Karenina*.

Garbo needed only that face to become the most magical of all screen stars. Wasn't it an incredible bonus that she was one of the greatest actresses who ever lived, as well?

JUDY GARLAND

There was always something happening in those big MGM *Broadway Melody* movies—and when, in *Broadway Melody of 1938*, a girl went up to her room, picked up a picture and began to moon over it, you were prepared for an unusual stage wait.

What you got, of course, was Judy Garland, and it was a sequence to cherish—the first of so many to come. If the idea of a teenager singing her heart out in an adolescent crush on a movie star strikes you as silly and slightly sticky, you just don't know Our Judy. And you can't possibly remember "Dear Mr. Gable."

Judy had been noticeable before—in an innocuous short subject (*Every Sunday*) in which she appeared with another girl, named Deanna Durbin. And there was *Pigskin Parade*, in which you could not help noticing the little girl with the big voice even though all kinds of crazy people were doing all kinds of crazy things in the foreground. Judy was somewhat in the background in *Broadway Melody* too, but she came forth long enough for her session with Gable's photograph. That moment was all she needed.

Judy—a happy, wholesome, chunky youngster. Enormous eyes, a button nose, the most infectious laughter in the world. And that voice—full throated, with an irresistible quaver. There were pictures that are less than milestones—*Thoroughbreds Don't Cry, Everybody Sing, Listen, Darling*. But you couldn't ignore Judy for a second even then.

There was *Love Finds Andy Hardy*, most disarmingly pleasurable of the series with calf-love finding Judy—not a child anymore but not a grown-up either. Or as she sang it—"In Between."

KETTI GALLIAN, Warner Baxter in *Under the Pampas Moon*

GRETA GARBO, Ramon Novarro in *Mata Hari*

GRETA GARBO in *Queen Christina*

115

GRETA GARBO
in *Queen Christina*

GRETA GARBO, George Marion, Charles Bickford in *Anna Christie*

JUDY GARLAND, Mickey Rooney in *Love Finds Andy Hardy*

JUDY GARLAND, Buddy Ebsen in *Broadway Melody of 1938*

JUDY GARLAND in *The Wizard of Oz*

Judy and Mickey Rooney, bursting with youth and loaded with talents, singing and dancing, impersonating and just having fun in *Babes in Arms*.

And *The Wizard of Oz*—Judy, the pigtailed Dorothy with her Toto, meeting all the most engaging companions a little girl ever had. All of them skipping down a Yellow Brick Road to a fabulous Emerald City. And scarcely a reason to wonder about the treasure that lay "Over the Rainbow."

Because everything was so joyous for Judy on this side—now and all the time. Or so it seemed. Or so it seemed. . . .

117

GREER GARSON, Robert Donat in *Goodbye Mr. Chips*

MARJORIE GATESON, Patricia Ellis, George Arliss in *The King's Vacation*

JANET GAYNOR

GREER GARSON

Certainly one of the most fortunate things about Mr. Chips, that paragon of British public school masters, was Mrs. Chips. As played by a new actress, Greer Garson, Mrs. Chips was the very ideal of a warm and sympathetic wife. Indeed one was so taken by her that it is tempting to overlook Miss Garson's only other picture of the thirties—*Remember!*—and chalk up her affected performance to the fact that it was such a comedown from *Goodbye, Mr. Chips* to this trifle.

There would be enough good Garson in the era to come to help you forget *Remember!*

MARJORIE GATESON

It is odd that a most persistent memory of Marjorie Gateson is of her demonstrating some fancy footwork as she learns boxing from Harold Lloyd in *The Milky Way*. Particularly odd, in that Miss Gateson was one of our most stately and sophisticated matrons. But of course, that was what made the scene comic. And memorable.

It's easy to remember Miss Gateson. She had a distinctiveness which set her apart from the Nella Walkers and Nana Bryants and others who played similar roles. It isn't so easy to remember most of the roles. Miss Gateson did so many pictures—almost always in a lesser, if welcome, part—that her appearances tend to run together. But picking a few representative roles, she was George Arliss' one-time love in *The King's Vacation*, now interested in advancing herself socially . . . a social registerite who tries to give Mae West her come-uppance—to her regret, naturally—in *Goin' to Town* . . . a Washington hostess in *First Lady* . . . and various other upper-crusters in films like *Street of Women, Melody Cruise, Chained.*

JANET GAYNOR

For a star who continues to be one of the most cherished of her time, Janet Gaynor had remarkably few talking pictures that could be called good and only a handful that were better. *Adorable* and *Delicious* are titles of two, and they suited her. But they also gave a clue to what was wrong with her movies. They sound like sugary little comedy romances, and that's exactly what they were. That's exactly what most of Janet Gaynor's pictures were—excepting those which were creaky, sentimental adaptations of musty plays and novels.

Yet, in spite of most of her roles, Janet Gaynor was so endearing with her dainty, dimpled face . . . her luminous eyes . . . her whispery, small girl voice. "Sweet" may have been the word for her—but not "saccharine." She had too much humor for that, and you even felt that there might be a little steel in that fragility.

Her silent pictures—particularly *Seventh Heaven,*
Sunrise, Street Angel—had established her as a wistful,
sensitive actress who was a combination of child and
woman. But talkies, perhaps because of the child-like
voice, practically eliminated the woman. There were
some musicals—*Sunny Side Up, High Society Blues,*
and the aforementioned *Delicious* and *Adorable.* Miss
Gaynor was no Jeanette MacDonald in the vocal department—but she sang chirpily and at least two of the
pictures—Gershwin's *Delicious,* with its title song and
"Somebody From Somewhere," and DeSylva, Brown
and Henderson's *Sunny Side Up,* with four hit songs—
contributed to the movie musical treasury. But the
books of all four were banal or worse.

The others? There was *The Man Who Came Back,*
which presented Miss Gaynor as a drug addict with
makeup under the eyes to point up her degenerated
state. Her constant co-star, Charles Farrell, one of the
most unexciting of all actors, was incredibly inept as
an alcoholic, but Miss Gaynor, who usually won out
over bad material, was swamped too.

Realizing their mistake at casting their prize in such
a role, Fox then gave Miss Gaynor a series of pictures
unmatched by any since Mary Pickford was a teenager.
Any one of them—*Daddy Long Legs, Merely Mary*
Ann, The First Year, Tess of the Storm Country,
Paddy the Next Best Thing—was harmless enough on
its own. But all together, one following on another,
they were too much for even the strongest stomachs.
In a sense, the fine *State Fair* was more of the same
with Miss Gaynor as the country girl meeting a city
slicker.

Finally, Janet Gaynor was growing up, but her pictures lagged behind. There would be something rather
nice, like the fantasy of *One More Spring.* But then you
would have a trite and contrived thing like *Servant's*
Entrance or *Change of Heart.* *The Farmer Takes a*
Wife had its points, although perhaps Janet Gaynor
was a bit too gentle to be the required firebrand contrast to bashful farmer Fonda. *Small Town Girl* and
Ladies in Love were enjoyable too, in their small way,
and Miss Gaynor gave her routine roles better than
they deserved.

But then came *A Star Is Born.* All the things everyone had loved about Janet Gaynor were intact but
there was a new depth, a new maturity in her performance in the most adult drama of Hollywood presented on the screen up to that time. The cliché for
Janet Gaynor was "A Star Is Reborn"—and everybody
used it.

Riding high, she did two more pictures. Neither was
anywhere close to *Star* for her, but they were still
among her better ones. *Three Loves Has Nancy* was
diverting, if slight, while *The Young in Heart* was one
of the most sparkling comedy-dramas of its day. And
on this high note, she didn't take any chances. She
left the screen, still very much the star.

JANET GAYNOR, Charles Farrell in
Lucky Star

JANET GAYNOR, Fredric March in
A Star is Born

JANET GAYNOR, Charles Farrell in *The Man Who Came*
Back

GLADYS GEORGE

Leave it to Hollywood! Gladys George became the
talk of Broadway for her vulgar, sexy comedy in *Per-*
sonal Appearance. So, they brought her to the movies.
And what did they give her? *Madame X!* She was into
melodramatics in *They Gave Him a Gun* and her
biggest picture, *Valiant Is the Word For Carrie,* wound
up as something like a woman's radio serial.

Even so, *Carrie* did give you a chance to see the
real George in excellent action as the slangy "shady
lady" (Hollywood didn't recognize whores in those
days) who takes in a couple of stray kids who think
she's some kind of angel. It was only after Carrie ran
away with the kids to start a new life and bring them
up that the plot began to get sudsy. It still was worthy
for Miss George.

When they finally gave her the comedy that had
been her meat, they had her playing straight for Bob
Burns and Mickey Rooney. But at the end of the thirties, she got the role on which most of her subsequent
ones would be modelled. Texas Guinan was the obvious
inspiration for the night club queen she played in *The*
Roaring Twenties and she was brassy, boisterous and
warm-hearted.

GLADYS GEORGE, Spencer Tracy in *They Gave Him a Gun*

WYNNE GIBSON, George Bancroft in *Lady and Gent*

LILLIAN GISH, Roland Young in *His Double Life*

MARY GORDON, Pat O'Brien, James Cagney in *The Irish in Us*

WYNNE GIBSON, Sylvia Sidney in *Ladies of the Big House*

WYNNE GIBSON, Richard Bennett in *If I Had a Million*

MINNA GOMBELL, William Powell in *The Thin Man*

BETTY GRABLE

120

PAULETTE GODDARD, Charles Chaplin in *Modern Times*

PAULETTE GODDARD as a Goldwyn Girl

BETTY GRABLE, Jack Whiting, Bob Hope in *Give Me a Sai*

WYNNE GIBSON

When this book was announced, a former actress called—not about herself (although she's in it, too) but to remind us of a friend. "She was such a fine actress—I'd hate for you to forget her."

Forget Wynne Gibson? We'd as quickly forget Garbo. Some of our most indelible memories of thirties movies are of Wynne Gibson, mouth tight, green eyes blazing. (They had to be green eyes—nobody else ever so completely personified rampant jealousy.) Then there was Wynne Gibson, curiously touching.

If I Had a Million presented her as one of the beneficiaries of an eccentric millionaire—a weary street-walker, who rents a hotel suite with palatial bed and prepares to use it, all by herself, remembering to remove her stockings just before she goes to sleep. (You're lucky if you saw that sequence—censors cut it out of most prints.)

And she was stinging in *Lady and Gent*, as the tough night club hostess who turns to the country life and motherhood—but with minimum of sloppy sentimentality. The same could hardly be said of her other mother love pictures—*The Strange Case of Clara Deane* and *I Give My Love*—in both of which she had to go to jail for crimes she didn't commit, to be released finally, aged and hanging around in the background of the lives of her offspring, who didn't know she was their mother. Shades of Madelon Claudet and Madame X! Miss Gibson, being as capable as she was, played those roles well enough but they were pretty exhausted old girls by the time she got to them.

She was much more in her element as all those venomous tramps who gave everybody such a hard time—in *City Streets, Man of the World, Ladies of the Big House, Night After Night*, and a couple in which she was as hard-boiled as ever but just a softie way down deep—*Aggie Appleby, Maker of Men* and *Her Bodyguard*.

Forget Wynne Gibson? It can't be done.

LILLIAN GISH

Lillian Gish, one of the most important stars of the silent screen, didn't wait for the talkie fate that overtook most of her contemporaries. She didn't give it a chance. Before her first talking picture was released, she was already winning new respect as a star of the theatre. Except for one New York-made film, she did not return to the screen until the forties, when she could come back as an occasional, and exceptional, character actress.

On the evidence of that first talking picture, *One Romantic Night*, it would appear that her decision was wise. In this hackneyed version of Molnar's *The Swan*, she was serene and regal but the film was pale and Marie Dressler was allowed to ham so outrageously that Miss Gish was left rather in the shade. (Most of the other actors just walked through without even seeming to try.)

Her New York-made film, *His Double Life*, a screen version of Arnold Bennett's *Buried Alive*, was much more worthy, although it was such a quiet little comedy that it attracted scant attention. (Gracie Fields and Monty Woolley would play the same roles much more successfully—if with considerably less subtlety—in *Holy Matrimony*, in the forties.)

It really didn't matter to Lillian Gish. No silent screen has-been she, but a distinguished lady of the theatre.

PAULETTE GODDARD

Although the date was some eight years after talkies came in, Paulette Goddard had her first movie role in a silent picture. That is if you discount the walk-ons, such as her Goldwyn Girl spot in *The Kid From Spain*.

But Paulette, as a leading lady, started in *Modern Times* and, since Mr. Chaplin's little tramp had not yet decided to talk, Goddard was silent too. It was another two and a half years before her talking picture debut, which wasn't unusual. Most of Chaplin's leading ladies have found themselves in no special demand after their appearances with the Great Man.

It was different with Goddard. She had secondary roles in *The Young in Heart* and *Dramatic School* but they were enough to let you realize that she had a glittering, very up-to-date quality. And she proved it as one of the vixens of *The Women*, even surrounded, as she was, by Roz Russell, Joan Crawford and the other shrews.

She finally had her own leading role at the end of the thirties. *The Cat and the Canary* was a Bob Hope picture and Hope's leading ladies generally are merely that. But Miss Goddard kept pace with Hope every step of the way. There was no question after that that she would be very much with us all through the forties.

MINNA GOMBELL

Minna Gombell was always one of our favorite people—at least in the few pictures of the many she made which gave her more to do than react snappishly in the background. Miss Gombell, with her pursed mouth and tight dimples, was one of our best snappers.

She could also be a fast friend to Sally Eilers in *Bad Girl* . . . an uninhibited ex-burlesque queen in *Stepping Sisters* . . . a critical houseguest in *The First Year* . . . a nagging wife of the type who could drive a husband to murder in *Babbitt* . . . a callous mother in *The Thin Man* and a callous daughter in *Make Way For Tomorrow* . . . in other words, she could play a variety of roles and play them well.

BONITA GRANVILLE, Joel
McCrea in *These Three*

MARGOT GRAHAM, Victor
McLaglen in *The Informer*

BONITA GRANVILLE (center)
with Peter Willes, Olivia de
Havilland in *Call It a Day*

MITZI GREEN

MITZI GREEN, Jackie Coogan
in *Tom Sawyer*

CHARLOTTE GREENWOOD, Bert Lahr in *Flying High*

MARY GORDON

Since brogues and burrs were interchangeable in the Hollywood of the thirties, you were apt to see Mary Gordon turning up whenever there was a call for Scottish or Irish or even English characters. Generally she had parts, frequently unbilled, that were too minor for Beryl Mercer, the favorite old lady of those locales.

But in the Jimmy Cagney-Pat O'Brien comedy, *The Irish in Us*, their darlin' old Mom was very important in the family. That was Mary Gordon—and darlin' she was.

BETTY GRABLE

In the thirties, who would have thought that Betty Grable would be the Musical Comedy Queen and the Pin Up Girl of World War II. It might as well have been Toby Wing or Mary Carlisle—Toby was as perky and blonde, and Mary had bigger parts.

But all through the thirties—and Betty went most of the way through them—she was around, with all the equipment that would eventually be the reason for her pin-up pictures. Sometimes she had a lead—but then there would be no role at all, just singing in the back line while Ginger Rogers took center stage in *Follow the Fleet*. Mostly Betty was a co-ed tapping and shagging through *Collegiate*, *College Swing*, *Campus Confessions*, *Student Tour* and *Pigskin Parade*.

MARGOT GRAHAME

You remember Margot Grahame as Katie, the bedraggled Dublin streetwalker for whom Gypo betrays his best friend, in *The Informer*. Sadly, it may be the only thirties role for which you remember her, although she was seen in a dozen or so.

She was the wicked Milady de Winter in *The Three Musketeers*, but it was in the pedestrian version that cast Walter Abel as D'Artagnan. And she played opposite Fredric March in *The Buccaneer*, but most of the scant feminine footage went to Franciska Gaal.

For the rest of it, Miss Grahame had to do her best in things like *The Arizonian*, *Counterfeit*, *Night Waitress* and *Criminal Lawyer*. She finally gave it up and went back to London, where it can't be said that she did very much better than she had been doing in Hollywood.

Even so, she did have *The Informer*—and that counted for plenty.

BONITA GRANVILLE

You might have noticed Bonita Granville as the blonde tot who skipped through pictures like *Cavalcade*, *The Life of Virgie Winters* and *Westward Passage*.

But there was nothing to prepare you for the amazing performance she gave as the dark, baleful Mary

Tilford of *These Three*, the intelligent screen version of Lillian Hellman's *The Children's Hour*. The lesbian undertones of the play may have been too much for a motion picture of 1936 to handle, but they were eliminated without disaster in a film adaptation by the playwright herself.

The portrait of a malevolent child remained, without any attempt to soften the impact. Young Miss Granville played it with honeyed evil. She followed it with another vicious youngster—the hysterical "witch" accuser in *Maid of Salem*.

There was still another notable Granville performance—as the moonstruck adolescent in that underrated domestic comedy *Call It a Day*.

Most of her other naughty girls of the thirties—in *Merrily We Live*, *It's Love I'm After* and the rest—were given more to mischief than malice. And she ended the decade taking part in several adventures of that favorite heroine of very small girls, "Nancy Drew."

MITZI GREEN

"I got a secret!" chortled Mitzi Green in *Honey*, as a demonic youngster, forever snooping and selling. Young Miss Green—or Little Mitzi, as she was originally billed—was a Dutch-bobbed dumpling with a brattish manner. She was also adept at imitations—George Arliss, Maurice Chevalier and Helen Kane being among the staples of her repertoire.

She romped through pictures like *Forbidden Adventure* and *Finn and Hattie*, playing to the hilt her role of enfant terrible. She was more conventionally cast in *Skippy* and *Sooky* and as Becky Thatcher in *Tom Sawyer* and *Huckleberry Finn*, but she helped things along there, too. She was also *Little Orphan Annie*—the picture was even worse than the comic strip, but Mitzi played it with as much glee as possible.

Then she began to grow up and, except for her impersonations in *Transatlantic Merry-Go-Round* (her scenes were cut before general release), she was finished on the screen. But before the thirties were over, she came back strong as the former kid movie star in Broadway's *Babes in Arms*. Too bad she didn't have a chance to repeat in the movie version.

CHARLOTTE GREENWOOD

Charlotte Greenwood preceded Joan Davis in a brand of comedy playing chiefly distinguished by raucous outcries and a high-kicking of limber legs. If that appealed to you, you could get your fill for about a year and a half. During that time, she made her talkie debut in a screen version of one of her more popular Broadway shows, *So Long, Letty*, and followed up with similar roles opposite Buster Keaton, Eddie Cantor and Bert Lahr in, respectively, *Parlor, Bedroom and Bath*, *Palmy Days* and *Flying High*, among others.

By the time Miss Greenwood returned to movies in the forties, it would be as a character actress, at least partially subdued.

NAN GREY

Nan Grey was the blonde third of *Three Smart Girls* and *Three Smart Girls Grow Up*. That's about as much as can be said—Deanna really took them over. But Miss Grey was very pretty, both as a "smart girl" and as the others she played in films like *Crash Donovan*, *The Man in Blue*, *Ex-Champ* and *Tower of London*.

VIRGINIA GREY

They put Virginia Grey in many pictures and that was thoughtful of them. She never had very much to do but she was one of the most lissome of movie blondes.

Once upon a time, in the silent days, she had been Little Eva in *Uncle Tom's Cabin*. But when she returned to us in the late thirties, she was all grown up and gorgeous. So you would see her as one of Gable's "Blondes" in *Idiot's Delight*, in Beery's *Thunder Afloat*, in which she had a lead if not much of one, and in fleeting appearances in pictures like *The Women*, *Broadway Serenade*, *Test Pilot* and *Another Thin Man*.

CORINNE GRIFFITH

Corinne Griffith pointed up the plight of actresses who might have been considered silent screen stars but who were quickly washed up in talkies. Miss Griffith's last two silents were a spectacular and expensive drama about Lady Hamilton and Lord Nelson, *The Divine Lady*, and a screen version of Maxwell Anderson's Broadway hit, *Saturday's Children*.

Yet, in talkies she had only *Lilies of the Field* and *Back Pay*. Her voice was acceptable, so that wasn't it. The pictures were tiresome, but actresses have survived worse. But Miss Griffith, as was the case with some other silent stars of her stature, never had a chance to recover.

A few years later, she attempted a comeback in a British drama, *Lily Christine*, but that didn't make it for her either. So she faded away.

SIGRID GURIE

Sigrid Gurie—from Norway, they said in the publicity, but there were whispers that it was really Brooklyn—was another of Samuel Goldwyn's exotic imports. She was one of the Oriental treasures found by Gary Cooper in his *Adventures of Marco Polo*, but the picture made much more of such other discoveries as gunpowder and spaghetti, so she was just another ornament in the court of Kublai Khan.

Miss Gurie, given the Anna Sten heave-ho by Goldwyn, showed up later as the vengeful half-caste in *Algiers,* replacing Sylvia Sidney, who had decided this would be just another tenement girl in bangles. Sidney was right—Hedy Lamarr got the attention.

Miss Gurie finally looked like herself in *Rio,* and you could see why there had been interest in the first place. If only *Rio* had been a passable picture. . . .

CORINNE GRIFFITH, Colin Clive in *Lilly Christine*

NAN GREY, John Sutton in *Tower of London*

VIRGINIA GREY

SIGRID GURIE, Gary Cooper in *Adventures of Marco Polo*

ANN GILLIS in *The Adventures of Tom Sawyer*

ETHEL GRIFFIES

PEGGY ANN GARNER, with Carole Lombard, Cary Grant, in *In Name Only*

NOTES ON OTHER "G" LADIES

There are some well-known names among the other "G" ladies. You think of *Gilda Gray*, *Margalo Gillmore* and *Tamara Geva*, *Jetta Goudal*, and *Peggy Ann Garner*, *Pauline Garon*, *Carmelita Geraghty*, *Helen Gibson*, *Luella Gear*, *Betty Garde*, *Virginia Gilmore*, *Maria Gambarelli*. Each of them appeared in at least one film of the period—but it was not their finest hour.

Miss Gilmore peeped into *Winter Carnival*, for instance, but her leads would come in the following decade. Peggy Ann Garner's scenes in *In Name Only* gave no hint of the exceptional adolescent actress who would prove herself later. The Misses Gray and Gambarelli were in just for their regular specialty numbers (Miss Gray to teach the hootchie-kootchie to Jeanette MacDonald in *Rose Marie* and Gambarelli for ballet in *Here's to Romance* and *Hooray For Love*). It's doubtful if Misses Gillmore and Geva would list their roles in *Wayward* and *The Girl Habit* in any recapitulation of their career highlights, nor would Miss Garde, also for *The Girl Habit*, and Miss Gear, for *Carefree*. Jetta Goudal was reduced to playing a foil for Will Rogers in one of his least-remembered movies (*Business and Pleasure*) and such other silent luminaries as Miss Gibson and the pretty Misses Garon and Geraghty were down to bits and quickies by talkie time.

Then there was *Texas Guinan*, the "Give the little girl a big hand" urger, who played herself in *Queen of the Night Clubs* and *Broadway Through a Keyhole*, and *Alice Gentle*, of opera, who was in *Golden Dawn*

HELEN GAHAGAN in *She*

125

TEXAS GUINAN (standing) with Hugh O'Connell, Blossom Seeley, Paul Kelly in *Broadway Through a Keyhole*

CARMELITA GERAGHTY

JETTA GOUDAL, with Will Rogers, Dorothy Peterson in *Business and Pleasure*

PAULINE GARON

and *Song of the Flame*, in which she sang the title song.

Otherwise, there were some who had a little more to offer the movies. *Ann Gillis* was not only a pretty Becky Thatcher but an excellent actress in *Adventures of Tom Sawyer*. . . . *Lucille Webster Gleason*, of the popular family, played gruff characters in films like *The Shannons of Broadway*, *Klondike Annie* and *Rhythm on the Range* . . . *Ethel Griffies*, a busy British actress who played everything from nobility to charwomen, mostly in bits . . . *Shirley Grey* showed up as a secondary blonde (in films like *Back Street*, *Transatlantic Merry-Go-Round*, *From Hell to Heaven*) . . . *Helen Gahagan*, better known as a political figure, but an impressive *She* in her only movie . . . *Dorothy Gulliver*, who segued from the silent short series *The Collegians* into a talkie feature, *College Love*, based on that series . . . *Eleanor Griffith*, wan leading lady to Chester Morris in *Alibi*. . . .

Other "G" girls would include *Florence George*, who played in *College Swing* . . . *Gwen Gaze*, opposite John Wayne, but in a picture, *I Cover the War*,

too unimportant to be remembered, even probably by Mr. Wayne . . . *Helen Gilbert*, briefly the object of the affections of Andy Hardy (*Gets Spring Fever*) and one of the patients of Dr. Kildare (*Secret of—*) . . . *Nora Gregor*, imported after Continental success but with only one American role in a lesser Robert Montgomery movie, *But the Flesh Is Weak* . . . some character actresses like dour *Julia Swayne Gordon*, dowager *Maude Turner Gordon*, sour *Eula Guy*, buxom *Jody Gilbert* and *Vera Gordon*, who had better Yiddish momma roles in the silents . . . *Dorothy Granger*, who played bits in features and leads in shorts . . . *Leatrice Joy Gilbert*, daughter of two famous silent stars but barely on screen herself . . . *Everly Gregg*, who didn't find the fame that came to the other wives of *Henry VIII* . . . *Greta Grandstedt*, who played very minor roles but quite a few of them . . .

And a nod to still others, whose names, if not their roles, may stir a twinge or two. They would include *Linda Gray*, *Lorna Gray*, *Sally Gray* and *Dorothy Gray*, *June Gale*, *Joan Gale* and *Roberta Gale*, *Anne Grey* and *Gloria Grey*, *Miriam Goldina*, *Rosina Galli*, *Ruth Gillette*, *Anita Garvin*, *Ara Gerald*, *Kay Griffith*, *Diana Gibson*, *Grace Goodall*, *Helena Grant*, *Greta Gynt*, *Renee Gadd*, *Gwenllian Gill*, *June Gittleson*, *Mildred Gover*, *Betty Jane Graham*, *Charlotte Granville*, *Frances Grant*, *Mona Goya*, *Kathryn Givney*. And of "G" girls, let's not forget *The Sisters G*, who were present for a minute or two in *The King of Jazz*.

LOUISE CLOSSER HALE

H

LOUISE CLOSSER HALE

Louise Closser Hale was that smothering mother in *Another Language*—the one who always had a convenient heart seizure to end any family crisis, usually caused by her in the first place. In a time when terrible movie moms abounded, Mrs. Hale's was one of the most realistic in one of the best character performances of the time. But she died before the picture was released.

She had had a number of other such parts, usually as a crotchety old woman—a passenger on the *Shanghai Express*, a companion for Joan Crawford's *Letty Lynton*, an American abroad in *Paris*, the poor relation of the hostess of *Dinner at Eight*, and a dowager, inadvertently mixed up with Harold Lloyd's clowning in the hilarious "magician's outfit" sequence of *Movie Crazy*.

MARGARET HAMILTON

Margaret Hamilton—the Wicked Witch of the West! Her face turned into a green hatchet for the occasion, her voice became a cackling shriek, her garb the traditional black gown and conical hat. She traveled through the air on her broom, terrifying Judy and her companions and giving delicious nightmares to all

the lucky children who were able to see her. And, thanks to the perennial TV return of *The Wizard of Oz*, they still can.

That the Witch is the first—and frequently the only—role that comes to mind when you mention Miss Hamilton is an injustice to her. She played several dozen movie roles—gossips, maids, landladies and harridans—and she made her presence felt, even if it was only in a one- or two-line part like those she had as the suspicious Yankees in *Nothing Sacred* or *You Only Live Once*.

She made her movie debut in 1933 as the only likable in-law of Helen Hayes in *Another Language*, a role she had created on stage. And audiences applauded when she finally gave Bonita Granville that deserved whack in *These Three*.

Most of her roles were small. You don't necessarily remember them. But you don't forget Margaret Hamilton.

ANN HARDING

Fairly early in her film career, Ann Harding played the title role in a picture called *Gallant Lady*. Never was a title more apt. That was Miss Harding—gallant lady, understanding and misunderstood wife, self-sacrificing mistress. Such nobility had to grow wearing, and there came a time when any self-respecting cynic would run a mile to avoid an Ann Harding film.

But before she became carried away by her own sanctity (supposedly she had contractual approval of the roles she would play), she contributed more than her share of luminous and graceful moments to the screen. She had a pale and patrician beauty quite unlike that of anyone else in films. And when somebody like Philip Barry gave her tart and amusing dialogue, she had the wit to make the most of it.

She was the ideal Barry heroine and her very best roles—Linda in *Holiday*, the wife in *Paris Bound*, Daisy in *The Animal Kingdom*, and the other wife in *When Ladies Meet* (certainly a Barry role, even if written by Rachel Crothers)—had that characteristic brave masquerade when the lady quips to hide the sorrow beneath the surface.

But controlled and well-bred martyrdom was the name of the game for Ann Harding and, as one picture after another piled it on, she grew ever more taut and overwrought. Eventually even the most simple utterance from that melodious, throbbing voice was charged with emotion.

And the radiant Ann Harding grew more and more tiresome through *The Life of Virgie Winters*, *The Right to Romance*, *The Fountain*, *Enchanted April* and others. We would except *Peter Ibbetson*, in which the Harding personality was attuned to the dream-like love story.

It was a throwback to the Ann Harding we had loved—the Ann Harding we want to remember.

MARGARET HAMILTON, Spring Byington in *Way Down East*

ANN HARDING

ANN HARDING, Leslie Howard, Myrna Loy in *The Animal Kingdom*

ANN HARDING, Gary Cooper in *Peter Ibbetson*

JEAN HARLOW

Jean Harlow was one of the best rowdy comediennes in the business. She was also one of the worst dramatic actresses. She proved the latter every so often but, to everyone's delight, there was much more of the other Harlow—the uninhibited belles of *Red Dust, Dinner at Eight, Libelled Lady,* and *Bombshell.*

The first Harlow who came to the attention was neither of these. She was a new type of "sex symbol" —new to the era when the very word, in family newspapers, was usually spelled "s-x." The raciest thing around would be Clara Bow doing the Charleston in rolled stockings. But then came Howard Hughes, *Hell's Angels*—and Harlow.

Hell's Angels was originally a silent picture, loaded with breath-taking air scenes, but the sound revolution occurred during its production. In turning it into a talkie, Hughes scrapped all the scenes involving Greta Nissen, who spoke with a pronounced Scandinavian accent, and engaged a spectacular-looking substitute who had been playing walk-on roles under her own name, Harlean Carpentier.

Miss Harlow was a lush creature who went in for gobs of makeup on her eyes and lips and who proudly wore a head of hair the like of which we hadn't seen. It looked like cotton candy—or sometimes like vanilla ice cream—and was called "platinum blonde." Miss Harlow also wore low-cut, clinging gowns and emphasized her breasts, something very shocking for the day.

The Harlow harlot—until she took to kidding it— was a pretty hokey lady, and you'll find few performances more inept than her bits, because that's about all they were, in *Hell's Angels, Public Enemy* and others of the period. An embarrassing memory is of this same Harlow as a debutante in a picture titled after her coiffure, *Platinum Blonde.*

It was when she went to MGM and somebody decided to accent the common touch—have her drop the studied diction for the magnificent vulgarity of the Harlow voice and pronunciation, let her stop trying to be a siren and become a babe—that's when the real Harlow emerged.

Every so often, even after that, they made a mistake. There was a period (mercifully brief) when they attempted to tone her down and started by making her "brownette"—but the platinum personality couldn't be subdued. There were pictures (like *Riffraff* and *Reckless*) in which she got herself into emotional turmoils more appropriate for Kay Francis and Ann Harding. Can you imagine Miss Harlow, in an excess of mother love, sobbing "Give me back my baby—she's mine!"? Draw the veil over scenes like that. They didn't allow them to happen more than a couple of times.

For the rest, she was that conniving chippy, the *Red Headed Woman* . . . that worldly-wise dame who

JEAN HARLOW, Lee Tracy in *Bombshell*

JEAN HARLOW, Clark Gable in
Hold Your Man

JEAN HARLOW, Ben Lyon in *Hell's Angels*

JEAN HARLOW

129

JULIE HAYDEN, Noël Coward in *The Scoundrel*

LILIAN HARVEY in *I Am Suzanne*

HELEN HAYES and Ronald Colman in *Arrowsmith*

HELEN HAYES in *The Sin of Madelon Claudet*

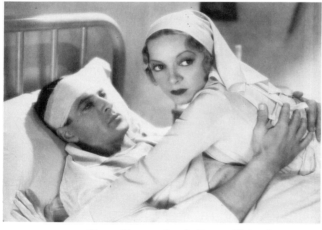

HELEN HAYES, Gary Cooper in *A Farewell to Arms*

turned up incongruously in such places as a rubber plantation in the tropics (*Red Dust*) or on the *China Seas* . . . the hot-shot *Girl from Missouri*, who knew all the angles. She was *Bombshell* (title changed to *Blonde Bombshell*, so that nobody would think it was a war film) in that barbed takeoff on the private life of a movie glamour girl. She battled and screeched as the showgirl wife with social aspirations in *Dinner at Eight* and as the long-time would-be wife in *Libeled Lady*.

In private life, she survived a series of dramas and tragedies—all documented in lurid books and films based on her life. Friends and associates say that the pictures painted of her are excessive and untrue.

After her death, her final picture, *Saratoga*, was released with her stand-in, Mary Dees, completing the Harlow role in long-shots. It wasn't a very good picture, and not representative of the Jean Harlow we cared about—the Beloved Broad.

LILIAN HARVEY

Lilian Harvey, an English girl who became known in German films, made an international splash with the lilting *Congress Dances*. Petite and delicate, she came to Fox, who already had the petite and delicate Janet Gaynor. What to do? Giver her Gaynor's cast-offs. At least, that's what they looked like.

My Weakness and *My Lips Betray* were as thin as Miss Harvey's eyebrows and her performances were as fluffy as the plots. *I Am Suzanne*, which had puppets as well, did have some grace—but not enough, and not soon enough. She made one regrettable return to Hollywood (*Let's Live Tonight*), but the German movie industry got her back.

JULIE HAYDON

Julie Haydon looked like Ann Harding, they said. RKO signed her because of it. Her publicity trumpeted it. She played Miss Harding's daughter in *The Conquerors*.

Then, because Miss Harding wasn't having any more daughters of that age, Julie Haydon was left to work out her contract in Westerns and in films like *Lucky Devils* and *Thirteen Women*. There was certainly no reason to give another thought to Julie Haydon.

But somebody did give another thought—quite a few people fortunately, and they ranged all the way from George Jean Nathan to Noël Coward. So, at least, theatre audiences saw a succession of lovely Haydon performances—in plays like *Shadow and Substance*, *The Time of Your Life*, *The Glass Menagerie*.

And movie audiences found out what the stage had seen in her when Noël Coward cast her as the ethereal, haunted girl in *The Scoundrel*. Even after that though, the best Hollywood could do was a set of sup-

SUSAN HAYWARD, with Robert Preston, Gary Cooper, Ray Milland in *Beau Geste*

porting roles—in a monotonous program picture, *A Son Comes Home*, a frantic mystery, *The Longest Night* and *A Family Affair* as the older sister of Andy Hardy, the one who was dropped from further films of the series.

HELEN HAYES

One of the roles for which Helen Hayes is best remembered is that of Maggie Wylie in Barrie's *What Every Woman Knows*, which she played on both stage and screen. Maggie Wylie was the self-effacing wife who kept directing the destinies of her politician husband without ever letting him know. She was fond of saying that she had no charm.

And that was singularly inappropriate for Helen Hayes. For if there was one thing that lady had in abundance, it was charm. Also warmth and sincerity.

There are some mannerisms that have become Helen Hayes trademarks over the years. Some find them ever-endearing, others sourly treat them as "the Helen Hayes shtick." They may have been part of her repertoire way back then but, if so, they blended so beautifully into the simplicity of her technique that even the crustiest critic wouldn't have chastised them as tricks.

For Miss Hayes, in a series of very good pictures and others that were worthy only because of what she brought to them, was one of our most vibrant screen actresses. Almost all of her roles were heavy on the emotions but she didn't suffer with the strained intensity of most of the other movie ladies. She seemed artless and unaffected and therefore almost heartbreaking.

Hollywood saw her first in *The Sin of Madelon Claudet*, a shameless ripoff that embroidered the *Madame X* plot. It's hard to think of another actress who could have played that role without becoming mired in its lachrymose swamp. But as Miss Hayes played it, strong men wept, and the Academy gave her its Oscar.

There was the brave wife of *Arrowsmith*. Everybody got very uptight when Helen Hayes reached for that plague-soaked cigarette. It was always rewarding to watch Helen Hayes die. The death scene in *A Farewell to Arms*, in which Miss Hayes played Hemingway's little war nurse, tore at your tearducts in the most untheatrical way.

She was also very down-to-earth as the independent girl who marries into a mother-dominated family in Rose Franken's *Another Language*. But there were other pictures which even the Hayes artistry could not completely salvage. *The White Sister*, for instance, still had its virtues—most of them in her performance—but it seemed hopelessly dated by 1933. *Son-Daughter* was a melodramatic flick about San Francisco's Chinatown. And *Vanessa: Her Love Story* was a plot-laden Victorian relic.

Still there were those five lovely performances—Catherine Barkley, Leora Arrowsmith, Madelon Claudet, Maggie Wylie and Stella Hallam of *Another Language*—to assure Miss Hayes' immortality as one of the important screen stars of the thirties. She wouldn't come back to the screen until she was ready for roles as a character actress. In all those intervening years, she was very busy living up to her title as one of the First Ladies of the theatre. But she was a great lady of the screen, too.

SUSAN HAYWARD

There was a little flurry of publicity when Edythe Marrener, of Brooklyn, renamed Susan Hayward for the occasion, tested for the Scarlett O'Hara role. She didn't get it, you know. She did get a bit in *Girls on Probation* and the leads in *Beau Geste* (although that was practically a bit, too), *Our Leading Citizen*, with Bob Burns, and *$1000 a Touchdown* in which the overpowering mouths of Joe E. Brown and Martha Raye won out.

If you looked closely, you might have noticed an intensity in her expression—but really there was so little reason to look closely in the kind of roles she had that one could be forgiven for not realizing the potential that became reality in the forties.

RITA HAYWORTH

Like Susan Hayward, Rita Hayworth didn't give much hint of what she would become in the forties. She made more thirties movies than Hayward but the quality, to put it charitably, was even lower. As Rita Cansino, she was the very, very Latin dancer of *Dante's Inferno* and some other films.

But even with a new name and a new hairline—not to mention a flowing auburn bob to replace the Spanish black—she didn't immediately become *Gilda* or *Cover Girl*.

Just before the decade finished, she had a part in Howard Hawks' *Only Angels Have Wings*. Cary Grant and Jean Arthur and a number of capable character actors had most of the plums in that; but you would have had to be extremely inattentive not to note Miss Hayworth. So, in that one role, she achieved more than she had in all of her other films of the thirties. And if, at that point, anybody had told you that she would turn out to be Hollywood's "Love Goddess" of the forties, you might have actually believed it.

SONJA HENIE

After we had had the taps of Eleanor Powell and Ruby Keeler and the swirling ballroom dances of Ginger Rogers and the ladies who followed in her footsteps—after that, what? The answer was Sonja Henie, who didn't dance at all and neither did she sing. But Sonja skated.

RITA HAYWORTH, Tony Martin, Joseph Crehan in *Music in My Heart*

RITA HAYWORTH in *Charlie Chan in Egypt*

SONJA HENIE

SONJA HENIE, Tyrone Power in *Thin Ice*

KATHARINE HEPBURN and Brian Aherne in *Sylvia Scarlett*

CHARLOTTE HENRY in *Alice in Wonderland* with the Gryphon (William Austin) and the Mock Turtle (Cary Grant)

And, at least at 20th Century-Fox, rinks replaced ballroom floors and skating spectacles took over from Busby Berkeley. Because everybody enjoyed watching Sonja Henie glide over ice. And Sonja, off skates, was twinkly and no hardship to watch—particularly when she was surrounded, as she usually was, by Tyrone Power-type leading men and supporting casts for comedy and song.

So the studio used her well, giving her roles that were not beyond her limited off-skates talents and lots of changes of her tiny costumes—miniskirts long before they were the fashion. Other people may have done the actual thespic performing but Sonja was there, looking like a fluffy bunny.

Someone once said of Esther Williams, "Wet she's a star—dry she ain't." And Sonja Henie's time came only when she hit the ice.

Then, swooping and pirouetting, she was truly a star—and she stayed in that category for a series of pleasant, popular pictures.

CHARLOTTE HENRY

Let's all say a word of gratitude to Charlotte Henry. If Charlotte hadn't won out, Ida Lupino would have played *Alice in Wonderland* and that wouldn't have been right at all. We needed Ida for other things.

Miss Henry was a passable Alice. But a girl can't do much when she is surrounded by W. C. Fields as Humpty Dumpty and Edna May Oliver as the Red Queen and half the hams in Hollywood in Tenniel-inspired masks—all with only a minute or two to establish their characters, and themselves. There had been a few roles before Alice for Miss Henry—she was billed as Charlotte V. Henry then. And there would be a few to follow—Bo-Peep in *Babes in Toyland* and a girl in *The Last Gentleman*. But you can't get much attention when you're playing with Laurel and Hardy or George Arliss. So she didn't linger long on the movie scene. Sorry about Charlotte—but we're glad it wasn't Ida.

KATHARINE HEPBURN

Katharine Hepburn was a coltish girl with an angular face. (Someone once referred to her cheekbones as "the greatest calcium deposit since the White Cliffs of Dover.") Her voice, with its flat New England tones, could become strident. A very unusual leading lady.

And suddenly you realized that, although John Barrymore was giving one of the performances of his life as the gentle madman in *A Bill of Divorcement* that girl was right with him all the way. It was a dazzling debut.

Her next two films were even more striking. (There was another, a trite program drama, *Christopher Strong*—but we're going to forget it ever happened.)

KATHARINE HEPBURN and Fredric March in *Mary of Scotland*

KATHARINE HEPBURN, Joan Bennett in *Little Women*

She was Eva Lovelace, the dedicated, garrulous aspirant to the theatre, in *Morning Glory*—a role that needed Hepburn, with all her eccentricity, to make it work on any level above caricature. And she was Jo, the dreamer-tomboy, in George Cukor's immaculate, sentimental but never mawkish version of *Little Women*.

133

KATHARINE HEPBURN, with Ginger Rogers, Adolph Menjou, in *Stage Door*

Such a high standard was almost impossible for any actress to maintain and Katharine Hepburn was no exception. Sometimes her own magnetism prevailed in spite of lesser material—an old fashioned mountain melodrama, *Spitfire*, for instance, or a quaint, but dated and pedestrian version of Barrie's *The Little Minister*. In *Sylvia Scarlett* she took to boy's clothes for the first such believable masquerade since Louise Brooks in *Beggars of Life*. But the picture, despite good characterizations, was a hodge-podge. She seemed much too sharp to be Lombard-zany in *Bringing Up Baby* but she managed some merriment with Howard Hawks' late entry in the screwball cycle.

There were other Hepburn thirties pictures that were complete messes—and her own performances contributed. Those eyes, always ready to well with tears, constantly overflowed in *Break of Hearts*, which only needed organ music to make it ideal for housewives on the radio. She gave a performance to match. As Maxwell Anderson wrote her for Helen Hayes, *Mary of Scotland* had to be winsome to gain sympathy—and Hepburn certainly was not that. Besides, John Ford directed it as a pageant.

Then there were the coy, artificial and mannered performances of her most terribly girly period—in *Quality Street* and *A Woman Rebels*. There was so much so wrong about Hepburn in many of her movies in the thirties.

But when she was right—oh, yes, when she was right. She was right as Linda in *Holiday*, glowing and eager and speaking those faintly archaic lines as if they were brand-new, written just for her.

She was right as Terry in *Stage Door*—not an Eva Lovelace this time, although again determined to make it in the theatre. But Terry was direct and perceptive and the match of all those other career-driven girls with whom she lived.

And she was right as *Alice Adams*—oh, how right she was! Hepburn's Alice was pretentious and silly and exasperating and eventually ridiculous. And she broke your heart.

Let *Alice Adams* remain forever the property of Katharine Hepburn—the frantic gaiety as she waits for a dancing partner who will never come . . . the tremulous enthusiasm at the disastrous dinner party . . . the desperate cheerfulness that turns to sobs in the night. Let it all be Hepburn's—forevermore.

IRENE HERVEY

When Irene Hervey had the chance, she could flash her dimples and be entertaining as well as ornamental. She had the chance in *The Girl Said No*, in which she played a taxi dancer who got involved with Gilbert and Sullivan operettas. Don't ask us how—we weren't quite sure even when we were watching the film. But she was delightful. She had such moments, also, in *Say It in French*.

She made her debut in *The Stranger's Return* in 1933 and finished out the thirties with *Destry Rides Again*. In both of them, she was attractive but considerably muted in relation to Misses Hopkins and Dietrich. And her other thirties films were Westerns and quickies.

WENDY HILLER

With all due respect to the wondrous things done by Alan Jay Lerner and Frederick Loewe in turning Shaw's *Pygmalion* into *My Fair Lady*, it is the initial exposure to the original that is an event in our theatregoing life. And of course, it wasn't the original at all —it was that incomparable film as scripted by Shaw and brought to the screen by an extraordinary company, headed by Leslie Howard, who both starred and co-directed (with Anthony Asquith).

And with fond memories of Julie Andrews and Audrey Hepburn in the Lerner version, we're just as certain that there could never have been so enchanting an Eliza as was Wendy Hiller. (We never saw such ladies of the stage versions as Lynn Fontanne, Gertrude Lawrence and Mrs. Pat Campbell play it, but we feel safe in including them, too.)

For Miss Hiller—new to America except to those who remembered her in the Broadway production of *Love on the Dole* years before—was an unqualified

KATHARINE HEPBURN

marvel as the Cockney flower girl who is transformed into a great lady under the tutelage of a waspish phonetics professor. What more can be said? You know the role. Conceive of its being played to complete and utter perfection and you may have some idea of Wendy Hiller's performance.

It was her only appearance in a movie that played in America in the thirties. There would be many more performances over three decades, which would earn her an Academy Award and international acclamation. But there was no more brilliant a performance on screen by Wendy Hiller—or by any other actress, for that matter—than her Eliza Doolittle of *Pygmalion*.

HARRIET HILLIARD

Harriet Hilliard, blonde band singer, darkened her hair and became a movie mouse with a nice voice. She played low-keyed romantic leads with some appeal and sang some good songs with even more. Among the pictures were *Follow the Fleet* and *Cocoanut Grove* and the songs included "Says My Heart," "Get Thee Behind Me, Satan," "Roses in December," and "You Leave Me Breathless." Ozzie was already in her off-screen life, Ricky and David yet to come.

ROSE HOBART

When Janet Gaynor refused to join her usual co-star, Charles Farrell, in *Liliom*—Rose Hobart got the role. Miss Hobart was an accomplished stage actress and made an affecting Julie, but the film was so harmed by the miscasting of Farrell that it was quickly forgotten.

Miss Hobart had a few more roles which she played capably enough but the films (like *A Lady Surrenders, Chances, East of Borneo*) were routine and her performance in *Dr. Jekyll and Mr. Hyde* was overshadowed by the bravura of Miriam Hopkins.

So Rose Hobart returned to the theatre in 1932, not to come back to movies until the forties, when she would play entirely different kinds of roles as a well-groomed character woman.

VALERIE HOBSON

Valerie Hobson, a slim and comely British girl, looked properly apprehensive during the melodramatics of her American films of the thirties. These included *The Mystery of Edwin Drood, The Werewolf of London, The Great Impersonation* and a session with the monster himself in *The Bride of Frankenstein*.

She returned to London and less frightening fare like the Laurence Olivier-Ralph Richardson *Clouds Over Europe* and Douglas Fairbanks, Jr.'s *When Thief Meets Thief*. She would be adornment to British films for more than a decade to follow.

In private life, she became the wife of John Profumo.

FAY HOLDEN

In a family that contained both the irrepressible Andy Hardy and his father, the gruff Judge, there wasn't much of a chance for individuality on the distaff side. So Fay Holden, who played Mother Hardy, was just the "Mom" figure whose most dramatic moments would involve something like clucking over Andrew's neglecting to wear his overshoes or fussing whether the Judge had his slippers and evening paper.

MIRIAM HOPKINS

Miriam Hopkins seemed compulsively vivacious—dashing about, constantly making little gestures and chattering endlessly. And in the rare moments when the rest of her was quiet, there would be those eyes batting away.

Yet she was much more than all flim-flam. When the role called for it, she could be very real. Of course, reality for Miss Hopkins was slightly different from reality for anyone else. There was always a prodigality to her technique even if she was playing a basically repressed girl, as in *These Three*, where she didn't flare out until the very end. This performance, as one of the two tormented teachers in Lillian Hellman's screen version of her play *The Children's Hour*, was one of Miss Hopkins' most restrained and most remarkable.

But restraint was hardly an essential for a Hopkins performance—there was very little of it in most of her work. Sometimes, of course, it all seemed too much, but you could blame that on a director who wasn't able to curb the Hopkins exuberance. And this very extravagance was what made her best work so individual.

During the thirties, there were a lot of good Hopkins performances in notable pictures. There were others in which the Hopkins style came through in spite of less-than-worthy vehicles. And there were some in which neither the star nor her films could be commended.

The latter dotted her entire screen career. She would follow a *Dr. Jekyll and Mr. Hyde* with something like *The World and the Flesh* or *Two Kinds of Women* . . . an *All of Me* would come after a *Design for Living* . . . a *Splendor* would be sandwiched between *Barbary Coast* and *These Three*. After the latter, there were several that were mishaps in every sense of the word—things like *Woman Chases Man, The Woman I Love*, and *Wise Girl*. Yet she finished the thirties playing with Bette Davis in *The Old Maid*—with Miss Davis, and right up to her. It was an experience watching the two of them—Miss Davis as the prim lady of the title, Miss Hopkins more flagrant, and neither yielding an inch.

After a movie debut in *Fast and Loose*, she won her first acclaim as the dowdy princess of *The Smiling Lieutenant*, a Lubitsch confection in which the nomi-

WENDY HILLER, Leslie Howard in *Pygmalion*

IRENE HERVEY

FAY HOLDEN, with Mickey Rooney, Lewis Stone, in *You're Only Young Once*

ROSE HOBART in *Chances* with Douglas Fairbanks, Jr.

HARRIET HILLIARD in *Follow the Fleet* flanked by Lucille Ball, Betty Grable

MIRIAM HOPKINS, with director Ernst Lubitsch. Co-stars Gary Cooper, Fredric March on set of *Design For Living*

VALERIE HOBSON, Douglas Fairbanks, Jr. in *When Thief Meets Thief* with Barbara Everest, Edward Rigby, Hindle Edgar in background

MIRIAM HOPKINS, Joel McCrea in *These Three*

137

MIRIAM HOPKINS in *The Story of Temple Drake*

MIRIAM HOPKINS, Fredric March in *Dr. Jekyll and Mr. Hyde*

HEDDA HOPPER, (center) with Patricia Wilder, Shirley Ross in *Thanks For the Memory*

nal leading lady, Claudette Colbert, taught her how to "jazz up" her personality so that she could capture Maurice Chevalier. She won Chevalier—and the picture.

In Mamoulian's *Dr. Jekyll and Mr. Hyde*, she was sexy enough to lure the latter gentleman (remember that leg swinging from under the bedclothes), and pitiful as his victim.

Lubitsch brought out her polished comedy qualities again in a vastly rewritten screen version of Noël Coward's *Design for Living* and in *Trouble in Paradise*, one of the most effervescent comedies ever put on screen.

She was a hunted chorus girl, hiding out in a fraternity house and masquerading as one of the boys in *She Loves Me Not*. And she was a sly *Becky Sharp*, although the interest in that picture was based largely on the fact that it was the first in the "new Technicolor." Add a showy role as a San Francisco gambling queen in a Howard Hawks meller, *Barbary Coast*.

Those were the Hopkins pictures in which she made her mark. But there were so many others—makeshift melodramas, feeble attempts at comedy—that the Hopkins star excitement was too frequently dissipated.

HEDDA HOPPER

Hedda Hopper made herself such a star as a columnist—with her hats, her wicked tongue and general showing-off—that it's difficult to think of her as merely a bit player. Yet, for the better part of her talkie career, that's exactly what she was. Even then, she was social and stylish—you'd never see Hedda scrubbing down the steps. But most of her roles were little better than walk-ons.

Among those in which she had more than a moment were *As You Desire Me*, *Holiday*, *The Last of Mrs. Cheyney*, *Alice Adams*, and *The Women*.

And by the forties, she had her column—then she could get back at all those upstarts in whose shadow she had once played support.

LOUISE HOVICK

You might be the Toast of New York, renowned as much for your brain as for your body. But if you were Gypsy Rose Lee from Minsky's, there was no way you were going to get into the movies in those censor-ridden days of the late thirties.

But Gypsy managed it. She reverted to her own original name, Louise Hovick, and did some pictures with all of her clothes firmly in place. It would be nice to say that what had fascinated the Gypsy fans came through in spite of all the restrictions. Nice—but not true.

So Miss Hovick walked through some pictures like

You Can't Have Everything, Sally, Irene and Mary, Ali Baba Goes to Town and *Battle of Broadway* and then, after a particularly miserable experience way down in the cast list of a Sonja Henie ice-musical, went back to being Gypsy Rose Lee, back to New York where her talents were recognized.

JOBYNA HOWLAND

Jobyna Howland was an overwhelming character comedienne—overwhelming in both size and personality. She played domineering matrons in films like *Honey* and *Once in a Lifetime* (she was the mother of the movie-struck Sidney Fox); a retired burlesque queen turned Shakespearean actress in *Stepping Sisters*; a bibulous mama in *Rockabye*; and other such roles in films like *Dixiana* and *The Cuckoos*.

ROCHELLE HUDSON

Rochelle Hudson, a slim brunette with sapphire eyes, should have had a Madge Evans kind of leading-lady career. She started out well enough as the good girl among the delinquents in *Are These Our Children*, and as an innocent victim saved from white slavery by Mae West in *She Done Him Wrong*. She worked her way through a spate of ingenue roles—including four with Will Rogers and one each with Wallace Beery and Shirley Temple—to the point where she was being seen in such important pictures as *Imitation of Life* and *Les Miserables*.

But then she had the misfortune of replacing an ill (or was it smart?) Janet Gaynor in a remake of *Way Down East*. And not Miss Gaynor—or probably even Lillian Gish—could have made the miseries of this poor-pitiful-Pearl believable at the late date of 1935. Miss Hudson was at a complete loss.

After that, it all seemed to go downhill for her. When she got into a decent picture—like *Show Them No Mercy*—it was in a minor role. She was a daughter to W. C. Fields in *Poppy* but that picture belonged to the Great Man. At her own studio, 20th Century-Fox, she was relegated to programmers, things like *Woman Wise, She Had to Eat, That I May Live, Born Reckless*, and in support of Jane Withers and Mr. Moto. And when the Fox contract was over, the pictures—like *Storm Over Bengal* and *Missing Daughters*—were even worse.

JOSEPHINE HULL

Of course, you remember dear, dumpy little Josephine Hull from *Arsenic and Old Lace* and *Harvey* and *The Solid Gold Cadillac*. But unless you were a devotee of the most minor movies in the thirties, it's doubtful if you have any memory of her in *After Tomorrow*.

It was a tiresome little item about how hard it was

JOBYNA HOWLAND, Louise Dresser in *Stepping Sisters*

LOUISE HOVICK (Gypsy Rose Lee) and Eddie Cantor in *Ali Baba Goes to Town*

ROCHELLE HUDSON, with Eric Linden, Beryl Mercer, in *Are These Our Children?*

ROCHELLE HUDSON, with John Beal, Fredric March, in *Les Miserables*

JOSEPHINE HULL with Martha Mattox and Nora Lane in *Careless Lady*

for Charles Farrell and Marian Nixon to get married. One of the main reasons was his mother, one of the deadliest of the species. Mrs. Hull was priceless in the part but the picture was hardly worth it. She is also listed as having appeared in a Joan Bennett movie called *Careless Lady*. Yes, we vaguely remember *Careless Lady*, but damned if we have any recollection at all of Josephine Hull in its cast.

BENITA HUME

Benita Hume, a well-dressed British actress, came to American films after being noticed in such imports as *Reserved for Ladies* and *Blame the Woman*. In America, she played well-dressed British ladies opposite actors who ranged from Lee Tracy (in *Clear All Wires*) to Cary Grant (in *Gambling Ship*). After a piece of claptrap called *The Worst Woman in Paris?*, she returned to London for roles in a historical drama, *Power*, and as one of the women in *The Private Life of Don Juan*, as portrayed by Douglas Fairbanks, Sr., in his last picture.

Back in America, the roles grew slimmer in films like *The Garden Murder Case*, *Moonlight Murder*, *Suzy*, *The Last of Mrs. Cheyney* and *Tarzan Escapes*, although we gratefully recall her being quite nasty to Master Bobby Breen in *Rainbow on the River*.

Miss Hume quit the movie scene to take an important position in Hollywood's off-screen society as the wife of Ronald Colman and later the wife of George Sanders, to whom she was married at the time of her own death in 1967.

MARSHA HUNT

We always thought Marsha Hunt was one of the prettiest girls in movies, with her wide, clear eyes, her fresh-faced grin and that marvelous curly nose. She was an ideal Tarkington heroine in *Gentle Julia* but most of her other thirties movies gave her only the usual roles for a pretty young actress.

Certainly you would not have expected her to develop into one of the best young character actresses. But that's exactly what happened.

She was piercingly affecting as the feverishly gay college widow, considered over the hill by the boys and a joke by the other girls in *These Glamour Girls*. And she was lovely in *Joe and Ethel Turp Call on the President*—both as the young bride and as the old lady she becomes.

She would be entering her period of greatest popularity and potential in the forties, only to be waylaid as an innocent victim of the McCarthy blacklist era.

RUTH HUSSEY

Ruth Hussey, dark-haired and blue-eyed, was the kind of efficient, no-nonsense girl that MGM kept in its stable because she could fit into just about any assignment. So she would alternate a lead in a program picture (like *Within the Law* or *Rich Man, Poor Girl*) with a secondary role in something like *Another Thin Man*.

But there were bits, too—and just because she had been the leading lady yesterday didn't mean she wouldn't have a mere walk-through today. MGM did that to a lot of girls then. Most of them stayed in their minor niche—Miss Hussey, however, was too intelligent not to be an obvious choice for better things. By the forties, she would get a few.

JOSEPHINE HUTCHINSON

Josephine Hutchinson, having by movie standards a rather plain face—by any other standards, of course, she could be the belle of the country club set—was fated to play sincere and devoted women, primarily wives. She was the wife who helped her husband struggle against the injustices of the American commercial system, represented by a great American oil company in the far East, in *Oil for the Lamps of China*. She was as fervent in her domestic duties as the wife of Paul Muni's *Louis Pasteur*.

She was also the Carol Kennicott of Sinclair Lewis' *Main Street*, fighting the ignorances and prejudices of an American midwest small town. (The movie changed the title to *I Married a Doctor* and changed Lewis' story to give it a happy ending, with everybody turning out to be pretty neighborly after all.)

Miss Hutchinson was thoughtful and believable—not only in such roles but in others which made her just a foil for a singing Dick Powell in her debut film, *Happiness Ahead*, one of those mothers whose child doesn't know her in *The Melody Lingers On* and a mistreated hillbilly in *Mountain Justice*. She even found herself as a terrified lady surrounded by such bogeymen as Rathbone, Atwill, Lugosi and Karloff's Monster in *Son of Frankenstein*.

So most of her film career was a far cry from the things for which she had been hailed when she was leading lady of Eva LeGallienne's Civic Repertory Theatre in New York. Even so—particularly in *Oil* and *Doctor*—she gave the screen some fine performances.

LEILA HYAMS

Leila Hyams had the kind of blonde good looks and unaggressive personality that made her fit in as a leading lady for just about any type of male star. John Gilbert might glower romantically at her or William Haines might wisecrack. Leila was there, not intruding at all but behaving like a leading lady should. She did three pictures with each of those gentlemen among the dozen plus she made for MGM in 1929-31. When MGM had a player under contract, they gave her little idle time.

Among her other pictures were similar roles opposite a youthful Chester Morris in *The Big House*, a young Bing Crosby in *The Big Broadcast*, and more seasoned gentlemen like Warner Baxter (in *Surrender*) and Roland Young (in *Ruggles of Red Gap*.) She was also properly frightened in *Freaks* and *Island of Lost Souls*.

But by the time she was doing such things as *$1000 a Minute* and *Yellow Dust*, her pictures weren't much more interesting than her parts. So she gave it all up for domesticity.

MARSHA HUNT, with Ann Sothern and William Gargan in *Joe and Ethel Turp Call on the President*

BENITA HUME, Cary Grant in *Gambling Ship*

RUTH HUSSEY, with Lew Ayres, Robert Young, Gordon Jones in *Rich Man, Poor Girl*

MARSHA HUNT, Leif Ericson, in *College Holiday*

MARSHA HUNT, Lana Turner in *These Glamour Girls*

JOSEPHINE HUTCHINSON, Paul Muni in *The Story of Louis Pasteur*

LEILA HYAMS, William Haines in *Way Out West*

GLORIA HOLDEN, Irving Pichel in *Dracula's Daughter*

ELEANOR HUNT

JOY HODGES, John King in *Merry Go Round of 1938*

HARRIET HOCT

MARY HEALY

NOTES ON OTHER "H" LADIES

Anyone who read the papers would know the names of *Hope Hampton* and *Eleanor Holm*—the former in society pages, Miss Holm in the sports section, both in columns. Each name appeared in a movie cast list of 1938—but it didn't make movie news. Miss Hampton, who had had some prominence in the theatre and films a generation earlier, attempted a comeback in something called *The Road to Reno*, and Miss Holm, while not Jane, was a Tarzan leading lady (*Tarzan's Revenge*) opposite Glenn Morris. (Another "H" lady, *Ula Holt*, also played opposite "Tarzan" in 1935—hers was Herman Brix—but her character wasn't Jane either.)

Let's also note a few other ladies of the "H" group. There were girls like *Mary Howard*, *Louise Henry*, *Carol Hughes* and *Mary Hart* who had a few secondary leads. There was *Bernardene Hayes*, who usually played broads, and *Esther Howard*, who played broader broads. Some other character actresses—pickle-faced *Lillian Harmer* . . . *Aggie Herring*, who got a lot of the "shanty Irish" bits . . . the fussy *Grace Hayle* . . . *Nedda Harrigan*, who would become better known in future years as the hostess-wife of Joshua Logan than as the dignified suspects in Charlie Chan and Mr. Moto cases . . . *Griselda Harvey*, a drab with whom Victor McLaglen has a moment in *The Informer* . . . *Kathleen Harrison* and *Martita Hunt*, two distinguished British actresses who would become more impressive to American moviegoers in future eras . . . *Violet Heming*, with some celebrity in the theatre, not making much of a movie ripple in *Almost Married* or as a friend of George Arliss in *The Man Who Played God*.

HOPE HAMPTON

DOLLY HAAS

PHYLLIS HAVER in *Chicago*

GRACE HAYES, with Mickey Rooney, Charles Winninger, Judy Garland in *Babes in Arms*

KATHLEEN HOWARD, with W. C. Fields, Mary Brian in *The Man on the Flying Trapeze*

Sara Haden may be best remembered as Andy Hardy's Aunt Milly, but she was one of the busiest character actresses of the thirties and forties—generally only for a scene or two but always effective . . . *Gloria Holden* ran the gamut from portraying *Dracula's Daughter* to playing the wife of Paul "Emile Zola" Muni, although most of her other roles were unimportant . . . Platinum blonde *Mary Beth Hughes* just started on the screen in the last days of the thirties . . . *Joy Hodges* sang and danced in *Merry Go Round of 1938* and a few others . . . *Kathleen Howard* nagged W. C. Fields in *It's a Gift* and *You're Telling Me* and had a few other character roles . . . *Theresa Harris* was impudent in *Baby Face* and in some other bits . . . *Victoria Hopper* played *Lorna Doone* and *The Constant Nymph*, the British versions with a very limited release here . . . *Helen Haye*, a British character actress, was most impressive in *39 Steps*—and also found herself featured on the marquee for pictures in which she had had only small parts, put there by theatre managers who couldn't resist the temptation to add an "s" to her surname . . .

And others to mention—*Gladys Hulette, Doris Hill, Juanita Hansen, Mildred Harris, Ella Hall*—all holdovers from the silent era but with only a minuscule credit or two in talkie times . . . *Verna Hillie*, with more publicity as a Panther Woman contest runner-up than for her movies . . . *Grace Hayes*, who left her "Lodge" for a role in *Babes in Arms* and *Mary Healy*—who, in real life, would eventually become Miss Hayes' daughter-in-law via son, Peter Lind Hayes—

making an impression with her "Back to Back" number in a Sonja Henie film, *Second Fiddle* . . . *Daisy* and *Violet Hilton*, the Siamese twins, doing their thing in *Freaks* . . . *Eleanor Hunt*, film debuting with the ingenue lead in Eddie Cantor's *Whoopee* but thereafter demoted to much less showy roles . . . *Fay Helm*, a good youngish character actress but without any role of note in this decade . . . *Darla Hood*, grown up from "Our Gang" to a couple of ingenue roles . . .

And a nod to a few more—*Virginia Hammond, Orien Heyward, Ruth Hall, Ruth Hiatt, Grace Hampton, Kay Hammond, Ann Hovey, Gertrude Hoffman, Jean Howard, Virginia Howell, Betty Jean Haney, Marilyn Harris, Kay Hughes, Edna May Harris, Dorothy Howe, Winifred Harris, Georgette Harvey, Linda Hayes, Muriel Hutchison, Gertrude Howard, Anne Howard, Ara Haswell, Marcia Harris, Dorothy Hall, Evelyn Hall, Gretchen Hartman, Gale Henry, Josephine Houston, Lottice Howell.* And a foursome who did specialty numbers—girl bandleader *Ina Ray Hutton* (*The Big Broadcast of 1936*), singer *Marion Harris* (*Devil May Care*) and dancers *Eunice Healy* (*Follow Your Heart*) and *Harriet Hoctor* (*Shall We Dance?*)

FRIEDA INESCORT

I ~ J

FRIEDA INESCORT

Because she was handsome, mature and gave an appearance of intelligence, Frieda Inescort became the first actress of whom producers would think when they cast a professional woman. So she appeared in *Portia on Trial*, *A Woman Is the Judge* and *Woman Doctor*, potboilers all. But Miss Inescort was imposing.

Her other roles were frequently neglected wives or snobbish socialites. The best of these was in *Call It a Day*, as a wife and mother who has a mild fling of her own, unaware that the rest of the family is also involved in closet romances.

SYBIL JASON

Hot on the heels of Shirley Temple came numerous child actresses, all hopefully box-office. Only Jane Withers came through. Warners' entry was Sybil Jason, from South Africa, who sang, danced and did impersonations.

She seemed a trifle self-conscious (Shirley certainly never was that), but it is really impossible to judge on the basis of her series of bombs. These included her own initial starring vehicle, *Little Big Shot*, and then some which pitted her against adult stars (Al Jolson, Kay Francis, Pat O'Brien).

Sybil completed the thirties—and her movie career—with supporting roles in two pictures starring Shirley Temple, still going strong (*The Little Princess*, *The Blue Bird*).

GLORIA JEAN

With Deanna Durbin all grown up and receiving her first kiss, what was poor Universal to do? One hope was to find a younger girl with as much of the Durbin appeal as possible. Gloria Jean was the answer—in the Durbin tradition, with a pleasant voice, a sunny smile.

But she seemed to lack the Durbin style, the Durbin personality, even though she certainly had the excuse that her pictures were the most pallid imitations of those of her predecessor. *The Under Pup*, her first, was nothing special, but it was perhaps a little better than any that would follow.

ISABEL JEWELL

Memories of Isabel Jewell are memories of moments —frequently furious outbursts. Right from the beginning, from *Blessed Event*, you knew she wouldn't hold back. She had a short scene but it was one of those hysterical ones, and she played it with all stops out.

She had other such roles, played as effectively, in pictures like *Evelyn Prentice*, *Ceiling Zero* and *The Crowd Roars*. There were more moments to remember in *Marked Woman*, as the terrorized B-girl; as Gloria, the prostitute, in *Lost Horizon*; in *Gone with the Wind* as Emmy Slattery; and a number of others.

But one memory, quite unlike the others, continues to stand out—her almost inarticulate little seamstress riding to the guillotine with Ronald Colman in *A Tale of Two Cities*.

ZITA JOHANN

Zita Johann had something of a reputation in the theatre but her movies didn't give her much opportunity to live up to it. She started on the screen in D. W. Griffith's last, and worst, picture, *The Struggle* (1931), as the ill-treated wife of drunkard Hal Skelly.

Horror fans will note that she was the reincarnation of the Egyptian girl loved by Boris Karloff's *Mummy* back in his reigning days. But for the rest, she gave good enough performances, but in roles and pictures (*Tiger Shark*, *The Man Who Dared* and *Luxury Liner*) of considerable unimportance. Her last was *Grand Canary*.

KAY JOHNSON

Kay Johnson was so obviously a brain that she must have felt ill at ease in the roles she was called upon to play in her early talkie career. There were two for Cecil B. DeMille (who signed her to a contract during his brief stay at MGM)—a rich girl-poor man piece called *Dynamite*, and a really ridiculous affair. *Madame Satan*, in which poor Miss J. had to impersonate the slinky title devil during an orgy in a Zeppelin, of all places. Then she had passive female leads in *Billy the Kid* and *The Spoilers*, and participated in some forgotten third-raters like *Ship From Shanghai* and *The Passion Flower*.

Her career improved when she was demoted to secondary parts. She was a neurotic victim of menace Myrna Loy's murder rampage in *Thirteen Women*, and she played some perceptive women, which she always did believably, in pictures like *Of Human Bondage*, *Eight Girls in a Boat*, *This Man Is Mine*, *Jalna* and *White Banners*.

RITA JOHNSON

She would have better parts in bigger budgeted pictures in the next decade but, during the thirties, when Rita Johnson appeared in what you might call an "A" picture (*Man Proof*, *Honolulu*, *Broadway Serenade*), she had minor roles. (The pictures may have been "A" in intent; they turned out to be somewhere below "F.") There was one comparative "A," *Letter of Introduction*, and although her role again was secondary, she was rather fetching.

She was better off in "B" pictures—*London By Night*, *They All Come Out*, *Nick Carter, Master Detective*—in all of which she was quite an acceptable leading lady.

MARCIA MAE JONES

If only for *These Three*, Marcia Mae Jones is high on our list of child actresses. She played Rosalie, the miserable and terrified victim of a dominating, psychopathic schoolmate. The role can be completely overshadowed by that of the other girl—as it has been in every other version of *The Children's Hour* we have seen.

But little Miss Jones was pitifully tormented, with one of the most expressive faces since the debut of Sylvia Sidney. Nobody used her so well again. You would see her turning up as a friend of Deanna Durbin's or Shirley Temple's or as an adolescent romance for Jackie Moran, but she never had another chance to really shine.

DOROTHY JORDAN

Although she usually played conventional leading ladies, we best recall Dorothy Jordan for two ragged waifs—the girl mothered by Marie Dressler in *Min and Bill* and a resident in a home for unwed mothers in *Bondage*.

She had started out, surprisingly enough for someone with so little hint of Latin, as lady-love to Ramon

DOROTHY JORDAN, with Joel McCrea, Richard Dix, in *The Lost Squadron*

GLORIA JEAN

FRIEDA INESCORT, with Olivia de Havilland, in *Call It a Day*

ISABEL JEWEL, with Ronald Colman, in A *Tale of Two Cities*

ZITA JOHANN, with Edward G. Robinson, in *Tiger Shark*

KAY JOHNSON with David Manners and Ian Hunter in *Jalna*

RITA JOHNSON

MARCIA MAE JONES, with Bonita Granville, in *These Three*

LEATRICE JOY

MIRIAM JORDAN

BRENDA JOYCE

ARLINE JUDGE, Kent Taylor in *College Scandal*

Novarro in *Devil May Care*, *In Gay Madrid*, and *Call of the Flesh*, as well as playing Bianca in the Pickford-Fairbanks version of *The Taming of the Shrew*. Then she had her innings with brash young men (Robert Montgomery in *Love in the Rough* and *Shipmates*; William Haines in *A Tailor Made Man*). She also was the girl in pictures like *70,000 Witnesses*, *The Lost Squadron* and *One Man's Journey*.

Only the waifs suggested that she had more to offer.

146

MIRIAM JORDAN

Miriam Jordan had the misfortune to be cast opposite Warner Baxter (three times) and Clive Brook in the dimming days of their movie careers. Both were good enough actors but past their prime, so their leading ladies made no news.

There was a publicity story that she was changing her name to "Mimi" to liven up her rather staid image but nothing ever came of it. And, although she had a moment or two in *I Loved You Wednesday*, they weren't enough to help, so nothing really came of her screen career either.

LEATRICE JOY

Why Leatrice Joy, a competent and well-known silent star, should have vanished after only two talkies is one of the movie mysteries. But then why should the same fate have overtaken Jacqueline Logan, May McAvoy, Colleen Moore—or a dozen others?

The Joy voice registered well enough and at least one of her talkies, *The Bellamy Trial*, in which she played the defendant, wasn't bad for its day. (The other, *A Most Immoral Lady*, was atrocious in any day.)

Miss Joy came back briefly at the end of the decade in a small role in Deanna Durbin's *First Love* but that didn't cause a Joy revival either.

BRENDA JOYCE

Brenda Joyce was a clean-cut blonde with good teeth (which she bared constantly, whether smiling or scowling). Although her debut film, *The Rains Came*, was a hoked-up and overblown version of Louis Bromfield's novel, Miss Joyce was personable. Nor did her other movie of the thirties, *Here I am, a Stranger*, lessen her potential.

One would have expected more in the future, would hardly have prophesied that the highlights of her career to come would be vis-à-vis Tarzan in some of his tackier exploits.

ARLINE JUDGE

Arline Judge, bold and sharp, made her movie mark as a baby vamp in such younger generation exploitation pictures as *Are These Our Children?* and *The Age of Consent*. She soon was doing the same things in comedy style with her targets the likes of Jack Oakie and Stuart Edwin. *Shoot the Works*, *College Scandal*, *King of Burlesque*, *Pigskin Parade* and *One in a Million* were among the better pictures in which she disported, and she had a straighter role in *Valiant Is the Word for Carrie*.

But she became much more familiar to tabloid readers for a marathon series of off-screen marriages to a group of well-known gentlemen, including both of the millionaire brothers Topping.

DOROTHY JANIS

JANICE JARRETT

PEGGY HOPKINS JOYCE, with W. C. Fields,
Sari Maritza, in *International House*

NOTES ON OTHER "I, J" LADIES

Among the "I" and "J" ladies were a couple who had leads in low-grade Westerns. *Phyllis Isley* appeared with John Wayne in one of his Republic oaters, *New Frontier,* and in a Dick Tracy serial, and *Laraine Johnson* was with George O'Brien in *Arizona Legion* and *The Painted Desert.* Miss Isley would fade back into obscurity, reappearing in the forties with a new name—Jennifer Jones. Miss Johnson moved away from Westerns and changed her last name. You can read about her in the "D" section of this book as Laraine Day.

Add a few other better-known names. There was *Peggy Hopkins Joyce,* Gotham's diamond-studded play-girl, opposite W. C. Fields, of all people, in a little monstrosity, *International House.* Alice Joyce, matured considerably but still striking, joined George Arliss in his talkie version of *The Green Goddess,* playing the same role she had had in his 1923 silent film.

Helen Jepson came from the Metropolitan Opera to *Goldwyn Follies* to sing *Traviata* . . . *Betty Jaynes,* a warbler of less pretension, was one of the *Babes in Arms* . . . Portly *Jane Jones* gave out with barroom ballads in *Alexander's Ragtime Band* and *East Side of Heaven* . . .

And there were *Soledad Jiminez,* the prototype Mexican mother (as for Muni in *Bordertown*) or even an Italian mama mia (for Edward G. Robinson in *Kid Galahad*) . . . *Marian Jordan,* who teamed with her husband, Jim, in *This Way Please* under the better-

URSULA JEANS

147

GLYNIS JOHNS in *South Riding*

known names of their characters, Fibber McGee and Molly . . . *Joyzelle*, who contributed some exotic dancing to *Just Imagine* and *The Sign of the Cross* . . . *Lois January*, who had some bits in major company movies and leads in quickie Westerns . . .

Dorothy Janis, who played with Novarro in his first talkie—he sang "Pagan Love Song" to her . . . *Helen Johnson*, who had leads (*Vice Squad*, *It Pays to Advertise*) and a few lesser parts . . . *Ursula Jeans*, who disappeared from the American screen after a good role in *Cavalcade*, coming back later in the decade in British imports (*Dark Journey*, *Storm in a Teacup*) . . . *Isabel Jeans* (we don't know if she was related to Ursula) who played such socialites as the mistress of the household in which Boyer and Colbert were employed in *Tovarich* . . . *Glynis Johns*, an oddly interesting youngster who stood out in small roles in *South Riding* and *Prison Without Bars*.

The usual nod to others—*Margaret Irving, Mary Jane Irving, Maxine Jennings, Carmencita Johnson, Julianne Johnston, Eulalie Jensen.*

ALICE JOYCE (right) with Jean Hersholt, ZaSu Pitts in *13 Washington Square*

HELEN KANE, Jack Oakie in *Sweetie*

K

HELEN KANE

Helen Kane's boop-a-dooping baby talk was already big on radio and records before she hit the screen. And she looked the way she sounded—exactly, one might note, like Betty Boop, who was her cartoon successor and who did hang around for quite a while longer, largely for the edification of the very, very young.

Helen booped her way through a crazy college courtship with Stuart Erwin in *Sweetie* and she taught a whole classroom full of Paramount kiddies how to boop-boop-a-doop for a sequence in *Paramount on Parade*.

But it wore thin before the vogue was over and her last pictures (*Pointed Heels, Dangerous Nan McGrew, Heads Up*) were rough going for anyone over the age of puberty.

RUBY KEELER

Now, in the seventies, when Ruby Keeler seems beyond criticism—when she has progressed from being the camp darling to the comeback queen—it seems churlish to remember that, in her thirties heyday, most of her movie performances were non-performances. Miss

Keeler, being a realistic and level-headed lady, would undoubtedly agree.

She tapped well, but her singing was, at best, adequate and her acting less than that. But she was certainly pretty enough for an aggressively boyish Dick Powell, and their innocent romances made pleasant breaks between the friskier activities of Joan Blondell, Jimmy Cagney, Aline MacMahon and the whole stable of Warners comics.

It all started with *42nd Street*. That was the one that brought back musical movies and in which a theatre curtain rose, to present a spectacle that couldn't *possibly* be contained in less than several city blocks. But you had to suspend belief when you watched a Busby Berkeley production number, take it as it came, and lose yourself in a sea of seemingly hundreds of girls all doing practically impossible things in the best Berkeley manner. *42nd Street* was the one in which Ruby took over for the incapacitated Bebe Daniels ("You're going out on that stage a nobody—but you're coming back—a Star!").

The Dubin-Warren songs were always a help, and most memories of Ruby are tied up with the songs—shuffling off to Buffalo . . . shadow-waltzing with neon violins . . . tapping down 42nd Street . . . tripping over typewriter keys ("Too Marvelous for Words") . . . going Oriental as Jimmy Cagney's "Shanghai Lil" . . . going Spanish as a "Latin from Manhattan" . . . "Pettin' in the Park" with Dick . . . and gazing fondly as he melodiously admits that he only has eyes for her.

Ruby was parted from Dick only twice in her thirties musicals—she joined her then-husband, Al Jolson, in *Go into Your Dance* and romanced with Ross Alexander in *Ready, Willing and Able*. But for the rest of her screen career (forgetting the forgettable nonmusical, *Mother Carey's Chickens*, and a forties quickie) she was Dick's girl—at West Point (*Flirtation Walk*), at Annapolis (*Shipmates Forever*) but usually in their accustomed place backstage (*Gold Diggers of 1933, Footlight Parade, Dames, Colleen*). By the end, they had become tiresome. But, before they staled, they were—and remain—something special.

And Ruby Keeler was—and remains—something special, too.

NANCY KELLY

Nancy Kelly had such poise and maturity when she made her first pictures in the thirties that it is too bad she had to wait almost twenty years (until *The Bad Seed*) to live up to her potential.

Miss Kelly didn't have very important roles in those first movies but she played them so attractively that you wished for more. For the record, they included one of those girls whom John Ford puts in his action pictures (*Submarine Patrol*); the loyal wife of Tyrone Power in *Jesse James*; an aviatrix in *Tailspin* (but Alice Faye and Constance Bennett got most of the

RUBY KEELER, Dick Powell in *Flirtation Walk*

RUBY KEELER, Lee Dixon in *Ready, Willing and Able*

RUBY KEELER in *Shipmates Forever*

NANCY KELLY, with Tyrone Power, Henry Fonda in *Jesse James*

footage in that one); an untypical heroine in a good Western, *Frontier Marshal* (later remade as the classic *My Darling Clementine*, although Cathy Downs, in the corresponding role, wasn't nearly as capable as Miss Kelly); and as a rather unnecessary feminine in-interest in Spencer Tracy's *Stanley and Livingstone*.

PATSY KELLY

Blessings on you, Patsy Kelly. How many nights at the movies have you rescued, at least for a moment or two, just because you were there. Of course, even you couldn't do anything for *Ever Since Eve* or *Private Number* or a picture or two like that. But it wasn't because you weren't trying.

. She was the toughest kid in town—nobody was more hardboiled than Patsy. But, then, there was always that big, soft, Irish Patsy heart.

A lot of the time, Patsy's salvage efforts had nothing to do with the feature picture you went to see. Because back in those dear, departed days of short comedies, it was always a guarantee that there would be laughs if the comedy starred Patsy and one of her sidekicks, Thelma Todd or Lyda Roberti.

But there were plenty of times when they took her away from the two-reelers to bolster features and it was always heartening to find Patsy Kelly in the cast.

Patsy played buddies to Harlow and Faye and Marion Davies and parts like comic maids (just like in *No, No, Nanette* thirty-odd years later) and it's impossible to pick out any one performance of hers because they were all of a piece. But some of her best were in *The Girl From Missouri, Every Night at Eight, Thanks a Million, Kelly the Second, Wake Up and Live* and *There Goes My Heart*.

PERT KELTON

Pert Kelton came from the stage to play the soubrette in Marilyn Miller's movie version of *Sally*. Though she didn't stay on, Pert was back in a few years in similar roles—playing the kind of girls who are usually called Trixie.

Most of these (in *Sing and Like It, Bed of Roses, The Bowery, Kelly the Second*, etc.) were comedy. Perhaps that's why we remember her best in a rare dramatic one—as the stool pigeon who helps Sylvia Sidney escape from prison, only to betray her, in *Mary Burns, Fugitive*.

BARBARA KENT

Admired in its day (if by only the comparative handful of people who saw it) and still occasionally mentioned by film historians was Paul Fejos' *Lonesome*. It was one of those hybrids—a silent to which distracting talking sequences had been added. A small big city love story, it was interestingly directed and had a personable girl, Barbara Kent.

Miss Kent made others of no consequence at all but she did become Harold Lloyd's leading lady in his first two talkies, *Welcome Danger* and *Feet First*. Not that a Harold Lloyd leading lady would ever have much to do, but Miss Kent did provide a comely inspiration for his antics.

DOROTHEA KENT

Dorothea Kent was a minor-league Marie Wilson—the same kind of bubble-headed blonde. It's just that Marie had a good picture or two, at least, in which to show off—poor Dorothea had nothing but low-grade "B's."

And not that many people were apt to have seen *More Than a Secretary*, not to mention such nothings as *Carnival Queen*, *As Good as Married*, *Some Blondes Are Dangerous*, etc. So, while Marie wound up playing Irma, Dorothea never got much beyond supporting parts.

DORIS KENYON

Doris Kenyon moved easily into the new medium in two of the earliest all-talkers, *The Home Towners*, opposite Richard Bennett, and *Interference*. Here she was a nervous, blackmailed heroine, but the bad ones (Evelyn Brent, William Powell) were much more interesting.

Through the thirties, she did a picture every so often —some of them being *Young America*, *Alexander Hamilton*, *Whom the Gods Destroy* and *Counsellor at Law*. She was always pleasing, never much more—even her Mme. de Pompadour in Arliss' *Voltaire* was a lady who who would have seemed more at home in the P.T.A.

EVALYN KNAPP

Evalyn Knapp was one of those utility blondes who could be cast opposite Edward G. Robinson as well as opposite David Manners, opposite George Arliss as well as Joe E. Brown. Protected by a movie contract, she had a couple of years of such roles (*The Millionaire*, *Smart Money*, *Fireman Save My Child*, *Mothers Cry*). You never noticed that she had the nominal lead in *Sinners' Holiday*, since that picture introduced James Cagney and Joan Blondell. After the Warners contract ran out, it was serials and quickies for Evalyn.

MARILYN KNOWLDEN

Marilyn Knowlden was an exquisite child. She played exquisite children (Kim in *Show Boat*, Agnes in *David Copperfield*, Cosette in *Les Miserables*) through the thirties.

We fully expected her to grow up to become as lovely as some of the ladies she played as children (Madge Evans, Ann Sheridan, Rochelle Hudson), and perhaps a better actress. But the spate of juvenile roles ceased and, maybe by her own wish (there are

DOROTHEA KENT, Robert Wilcox in *Carnival Queen*

NANCY KELLY

PATSY KELLY, Walter Winchell in *Wake Up and Live*

PATSY KELLY, Alan Mowbray in *There Goes My Heart*

PERT KELTON, Sylvia Sidney in *Mary Burns, Fugitive*

BARBARA KENT, Myrna Loy in *Vanity Fair*

DORIS KENYON (right) with George Arliss, Margaret Lindsay in *Voltaire*

MERNA KENNEDY in *The Circus*

EVALYN KNAPP, Lee Tracy in *Night Mayor*

MURIEL KIRKLAND (left) with Anna Sten, Mae Clarke, in *Nana*

MARILYN KNOWLDEN in *Show Boat*

JUNE KNIGHT, Russ Columbo in *Wake Up and Dream*

ALMA KRUGER, Lionel Barrymore in *Calling Dr. Kildare*

child actors who can hardly wait to get away from the grind), she was not to show up on the screen again after 1939.

MILIZA KORJUS

Miliza Korjus (pronounced "Gorgeous," according to the publicists) was blonde and voluptuous—a combination of very grand opera and Mae West.

In *The Great Waltz*, her gestures were sweeping, her manner relentlessly seductive. She was the toast of Vienna, and she sang the Strauss waltzes in a full-bodied soprano, fluttering her eyelashes all the time.

But after a steady diet of Jeanette MacDonald apple-pie operetta, the American public seemed not quite ready for chicken paprika. Anyway, Miss Korjus' movie day came and went with this single picture.

ALMA KRUGER

Like Marcia Mae Jones, Catharine Doucet and Bonita Granville, Alma Kruger must be principally lauded for her performance in *These Three*. As the outraged grandmother to whom a youngster whispers a venomous lie, she was formidable; as the sorrowing woman who realizes that, because of that lie, she has been the instrument of wrecking the lives of three people, she evoked pity.

There were to be no more roles like that for Alma Kruger. She had cogent moments as the aunt who tells Craig's wife that "people who live to themselves are generally left to themselves." But afterward there were just all the routine things, climaxed at the end of the thirties with appearances in the first pictures in the *Dr. Kildare* series. Miss Kruger would remain a familiar, tolerant sparring partner nurse to the irascible Dr. Gillespie for the next few years.

MILIZA KORJUS, Fernand Gravet in *The Great Waltz*

EVELYN KEYES, right, with Ann Rutherford in *Gone With the Wind*

MARJORIE "BABE" KANE, with Victor Potel, in *Border Romance*

ROSALIND KEITH, with Tom Brown, Richard Cromwell, in *Annapolis Farewell*

NOTES ON OTHER "K" LADIES

Evelyn Keyes, with bits in two DeMille specials (*The Buccaneer, Union Pacific*) and as Scarlett's sister, Suellen, in *Gone With the Wind*, would have her better days to come . . . So would *Pamela Kellino*, who with her husband, Roy Kellino, directing and their friend James Mason co-starring, appeared in a British melodrama, *I Met a Murderer*. (Offscreen, the soon-to-be-ex Mrs. Kellino would become Mrs. James Mason and then the ex Mrs. Mason.) . . .

Violet Kemble-Cooper was one of the more forbidding visitors to the life of young David Copperfield as Miss Jane Murdstone and was also, less unattractively, one of *Our Betters* . . . *Cammie King* was Bonnie Blue, daughter of Scarlett and Rhett in *Gone With the Wind* and another child, *Suzanna Kim*, made an indelible impression with a few closeups as Little Fool in *The Good Earth* . . .

And there were *Kitty Kelly*, who had the best of her comedy roles in *Too Much Harmony* and *Ladies of the Jury* . . . *Mary Kornman*, once an "Our Gang" kiddie but, in this era, a minor ingenue in minor movies . . . *Muriel Kirkland*, an excellent actress in small roles in pictures like *Nana, Little Man, What Now?* and *The Cocktail Hour* . . .

Merna Kennedy suffered the fate of most Chaplin leading ladies—"The Girl" in a Chaplin film never counted for much. Merna had some talkie opportunities—most notably in *Broadway*—but her performances were hardly hailed and her career fizzled out . . .

Worth a mention, if only for the fact that she gave

Buddy Rogers, NATALIE KINGSTON in *River of Romance*

153

KITTY KELLY (third from left) surrounded by Robert Woolsey, Eddie Quillan, Dorothy Lee, Mitzi Green, Bert Wheeler in *Girl Crazy*

undoubtedly the worst performance ever put on celluloid by an actress in a leading role—*Carlotta King*. Her Margot in *The Desert Song* could be compared only to Margaret Dumont parrying the advances of Groucho Marx—but you were supposed to take Margot seriously . . . *June Knight*, a long-limbed Broadway blonde, made a few excursions into movies (*Take a Chance*, *Broadway Melody of 1936*, etc.) as, what else, a long-limbed Broadway blonde . . . We seem to remember some confusion about an actress, *Rosalind Culli*, announced to appear in *The Glass Key*, but, during filming, her name was changed to Rosalind Culli-Keith. When the picture opened, she was *Rosalind Keith*. That's all really we remember about Miss Keith. . . .

A tip of the hat to these others—*Suzanne Kaaren*, *Nina Koshetz*, *Lorraine Kruger*, *Karol Kay*, *Gayle Kaye* and *Claudelle Kaye*, *Jane Keckley*, *Natalie Kingston*, *Margie Kane*, *Lillian Kemble-Cooper*, *Edith Kingdon*, *Helen Kaiser*, *Peggy Keys*, *Kathryn Kane*, *Suzanne Kilborn*, *Anna Kostant*, *Phyllis Kennedy*, and, playing a young reporter in *Sinner Take All*, a young reporter named *Dorothy Kilgallen*.

VIOLET KEMBLE-COOPER, as Lady Capulet, with Edna May Oliver, C. Aubrey Smith, Norma Shearer in *Romeo and Juliet*

HEDY LAMARR in *Ecstasy*

HEDY LAMARR

𝕃

HEDY LAMARR

In these *Deep Throat* days, it may seem inconceivable that such a fuss could be made over a nude female body as over that of Hedy Lamarr in a Czechoslovakian film called *Ecstasy*. Said body was merely glimpsed—in long shots running through the woods, and in a swimming sequence in which the rippling water rather effectively distorted it. The other "scandalous moment" of the picture was a close-up of the lady's face during the act of love, registering the feeling of the title.

They were enough to embroil the film in six years of censorship battles before it was finally allowed into the United States.

Actually, by the time *Ecstasy* came here, its leading lady was already an American star. Miss Lamarr (she had been known as Hedy Kiesler when she made *Ecstasy*) had been brought over to provide the luscious allure that would attract Charles "Pepe le Moko" Boyer out of the Casbah in *Algiers*.

Once in America, nobody paid much mind to the body of Hedy Lamarr. But that face! It may have possessed the most fabulous brunette beauty—with the possible exception of Dolores Del Rio and, later, Elizabeth Taylor—to have ever hit the silver screen. Holly-

HEDY LAMARR and Charles Boyer in *Algiers*

wood makeup men did their job well—the face of Hedy Kiesler was nowhere close to being as entrancing. But obviously, there must have been something there in the first place.

155

DOROTHY LAMOUR in *Her Jungle Love*

DOROTHY LAMOUR, Jon Hall in *Hurricane*

ELSA LANCHESTER, Colin Clive in *The Bride of Frankenstein*

ELSA LANCHESTER, Charles Laughton and players in *The Beachcomber*

The beauty of Hedy Lamarr should be seen in repose—you tended to be distracted from it when she smiled, spoke more than monosyllables or tried to act as she did in her only other American movie of the thirties, *Lady of the Tropics*. But in *Algiers*, she just lay about, letting Boyer do most of the talking—and looked absolutely gorgeous.

DOROTHY LAMOUR

The one thing of which nobody ever accused Dorothy Lamour in the thirties was acting. She had her own deadpan and apparently saw little reason to vary it. She'd let those masses of black hair hang down, encase herself in a sarong and she'd be *The Jungle Princess*.

Or she'd slick back the hair, wear a gown and be a sultry menace to Carole Lombard or Irene Dunne. But the expression never changed.

The glints of humor she would show as *Road*-mate to Bing and Bob would come in the next decade.

In the thirties, she stuck to her sarong in pictures like *Her Jungle Love*, which was sheer fairytale, and *The Hurricane*, which was to be taken more seriously, being a Goldwyn picture directed by John Ford and all. And there were some others—like *St. Louis Blues*, *Man About Town* and *Tropic Holiday*—in which she sang and wore dresses that, as much as possible, resembled her sarongs.

And there was even a picture in which she was forced to try to act. It was a Lloyd Douglas parable, *Disputed Passage*, and it was unspeakable. So was Dotty's performance. But cheer up!—Bing and Bob and "The Road" were waiting.

ELSA LANCHESTER

Just about all of the wives and some of the courtiers in Charles Laughton's *Private Life of Henry VIII* stood out, but nobody came off with more bravos than Elsa Lanchester who, in private life, was Mrs. Laughton. She was the Dutch princess, Anne of Cleves, and she distorted that fascinating face to make herself repulsive to the monarch whose unwilling wife she had become.

The other "wives"—Wendy and Binnie and Merle—all came to Hollywood. Miss Lanchester came, too, but as Mrs. Laughton, and it was his career that came first.

Once or twice she took a part on her own—the scowling wife of Frank Morgan in *Naughty Marietta* or the mate created for the Monster in *The Bride of Frankenstein*—those great eyes glassy and lightning streaks through the shock of her hair.

But she really came into her own again when she returned to England to play opposite her husband in two of his most powerful characterizations—*Rembrandt* and *The Beachcomber*. In the first, she was the self-effacing housemaid who becomes the model and mistress of the painter. And in *The Beachcomber* she was the schoolmistress, personification of all the forces of righteousness—the most relentless fury to torture a happy-go-lucky, sodden reprobate until Katharine Hepburn took off after Humphrey Bogart some dozen years later.

ELISSA LANDI

If you read the movie magazines, the publicity on Elissa Landi would certainly turn you off. She was, oh, so superior—so keen, so well read—and a real-life Countess to boot. If you could divorce the actress from her press, you found Miss Landi a very capable lady of parts—the parts ranging from the saintly Christian of *The Sign of the Cross* to the strident Amazon of *The Warrior's Husband.*

Actually Miss Landi proved her mettle upon her arrival in America (she had appeared in some British films) by surviving a set of old-fashioned hack melodramas (*Body and Soul, The Yellow Ticket, Wicked*) in which she was invariably a lady of shocking reputation who was, of course, not a bad girl at all.

Fortunately DeMille saw something else in her performances—which were always better than her roles—and the prestige of the DeMille assignment (*Sign of the Cross*) gave her *The Warrior's Husband.* That led to the pictures in which she played a mixture of romantic drama and comedy. But the pictures—*I Loved You Wednesday, By Candlelight, Sisters Under the Skin, The Great Flirtation* and *Enter Madame*—were mild fare, even though Miss Landi's performances were better than that.

Eventually there came roles in which she was subordinated to strong male leads—Ronald Colman in *The Masquerader,* Robert Donat in *The Count of Monte Cristo,* Francis Lederer in his American debut, *Man of Two Worlds* and Douglas Fairbanks, Jr., in *The Amateur Gentleman.* And there were a couple of pretty good mystery melodramas, *After the Thin Man* and *The Thirteenth Chair*—but Miss Landi was just one among a number of suspects.

She deserted the screen for the theatre, also doing extremely well on the lecture circuit; being that intelligent paid off after all.

LOLA LANE

Long before anybody had ever heard of Priscilla or Rosemary, Lola Lane was busy in Hollywood. Actually, Miss Lane went all the way back to the earliest Fox talkies like *Speakeasy, Fox Movietone Follies* and *The Girl from Havana*—all bombs. Before long, the Lola Lane career had foundered. You'd see her in a minor role here or there, but the only one of more than passing note was as one of the ladies of the night in *Marked Woman.*

In the meantime, Miss Lane's singing sisters were beginning to make something of a splash, and when

ELISSA LANDI, David Manners in *The Warrior's Husband*

ELISSA LANDI, Laurence Olivier in *The Yellow Ticket*

ROSEMARY LANE, John Garfield in *Blackwell's Island*

they were cast together in *Four Daughters, Daughters Courageous* and *Four Wives,* it was natural for Lola Lane to be cast as their older sister, with not too much to do except be there.

PRISCILLA LANE

Priscilla Lane looked like one of those girls on a bon-bon box come to life—masses of blonde curls, wide blue eyes, juicy lips. She sang, too, just like you'd expect a girl who looked like Betty Co-Ed to sing—and just like Betty Co-Ed, she was the ideal leading lady for rah-rah boys like Wayne Morris and Dick Powell. So you saw her with Mr. Powell in *Varsity Show* and *Cowboy From Brooklyn* and opposite Mr. Morris in some silly things like *Love, Honor and Behave* and *Men Are Such Fools.*

But she was also with Morris in *Brother Rat,* which was a movie version of the Broadway farce about cadets and their girls. (Too bad it had to be followed by *Brother Rat and a Baby,* which was a case of carrying a good thing too far.)

She was the same kind of girl in *Yes, My Darling Daughter,* which aroused the wrath of the censors by its suggestion that its heroine had in mind an illicit weekend with her young man.

157

Four Daughters took Miss Lane out of the ranks of mere bubbling sweeties. It also introduced an intense and brooding young actor, John Garfield, and was a very sentimental, but remarkably appealing movie about the tangled loves of the girls in one family. Priscilla, as the sister most put upon, had matured considerably as an actress. And she played a similar role as well in *Daughters Courageous*, which was not a sequel but used the same cast, and *Four Wives*, which was.

ROSEMARY LANE

Rosemary Lane was the third of the sisters, destined to remain in the shadow of Priscilla. Priscilla got most of the attention and Rosemary settled down to routine roles like those in *Gold Diggers in Paris* and *Hollywood Hotel*.

She and her sister often had the same leading men, but poor Rosemary caught Cagney, Garfield and even Wayne Morris in off pictures so her roles with them did nothing for her. And in *Four Daughters*, *Daughters Courageous* and *Four Wives* she was present, but all the drama went to Priscilla. We know how Olivia de Havilland and Joan Fontaine felt about each other at one stage of their careers but if ever a girl had reason for a sibling jealousy, it was Rosemary Lane. As far as we know though, it didn't occur to her.

JUNE LANG

June Lang—she worked first under the name of June Vlasek—never bothered to act very much. But she really didn't need to—it was enough to have her ornamentally around.

Most of her pictures didn't call for much more than that.

She was with Eddie Cantor and Laurel and Hardy and Shirley Temple and played in a few "B's." Her heaviest role was as the girl desired by both Fredric March and Warner Baxter in *The Road to Glory* but, again, she wisely let Messrs. March and Baxter do the acting—she was just there to be a reason for their conflict.

FRANCES LANGFORD

There were a lot of girls who sang a lot of songs in movies of the thirties but, if we had our choice, we'd take Frances Langford every time. She wasn't the best actress around—but she didn't have to be. She had a cute Pekinese kind of face but you'd never list her among Hollywood's beauties.

With Frances Langford, you got singing that caressed the lyrics and made the most of the melody. And maybe that's why she got such surefire hit songs to sing. As for example, "I'm in the Mood for Love" (Dorothy Fields, Jimmy McHugh), in *Every Night at Eight*; "Broadway Rhythm" (Arthur Freed, Nacio Herb

Brown) in *Broadway Melody of 1936*); "I Feel Like a Feather in the Breeze" and "You Hit the Spot" (Mack Gordon, Harry Revel) from *Collegiate*; Cole Porter's "Easy to Love" from *Born to Dance*; "Was It Rain?" (Lou Handman, Walter Hirsch) from *The Hit Parade*—but you see what we mean.

LAURA LA PLANTE

Laura La Plante was the very movie-starrish name for an unpretentious girl, with a distinctive blonde bob, who worked her way up through program farces to Universal's *Show Boat*. She was a non-singing Magnolia —non-talking, too, as the film was mostly silent with a musical prologue in which the songs were sung by members of the Broadway cast.

She did talk in another Universal super-special, *Captain of the Guard*, which also turned out to be a superflop, not through any fault of hers. But Universal dropped her, and after a few routine roles she faded from the screen.

GERTRUDE LAWRENCE

The superlative Gertrude Lawrence of the theatre was dreadfully misused by the movies. Blame Hollywood for only a bit of it this time. Like everyone else who could sing or dance, or even talk, in those first days of audible movies, she was brought to the Paramount sound studios to do *Battle of Paris*. It was a stupid film and Miss Lawrence didn't stick around very long.

But she still made pictures through the thirties— in London—and they didn't show her off any more effectively than had the one American start. There was the Lonsdale antique, *Aren't We All?* and something indescribable called *No Funny Business*. There was *Mimi*, which used the plot of *La Boheme* and the music of Puccini—but it wasn't much of a role for Gertrude Lawrence. *Men Are Not Gods* cast her as a Shakespearean actress playing Desdemona but it was a Miriam Hopkins movie, and a pretty incredible one at that.

That left *Rembrandt*, and here Miss Lawrence did have a chance for an impressive characterization as the shrewish, nagging mistress. But her death scene came early and, despite her fine performance, the triumph was that of Charles Laughton's.

Miss Lawrence was one of the first ladies of the theatre. But you never would have known it if you knew her only through her movies.

EVELYN LAYE

Evelyn Laye was the reigning star of the British musical theatre—and still is a star over there. But her film career was less than sensational. She was brought over here to do *One Heavenly Night* in 1931 and it

PRISCILLA LANE, John Garfield in *Four Daughters*

THE LANE SISTERS, Rosemary, Lola, Priscilla

GERTRUDE LAWRENCE, Charles Laughton in *Rembrandt*

JUNE LANG, Michael Whalen in *Wee Willie Winkie*

FRANCES LANGFORD, Dick Powell in *Hollywood Hotel*

LAURA LAPLANTE, Douglas Fairbanks, Jr. in *Man of the Moment*

EVELYN LAYE, Ramon Novarro in *The Night is Young*

was about as inane as movie operettas can get, although Miss Laye did her damnedest to lift it.

There were a couple of British musicals which had limited circulation in this country—*Waltz Time* and *Evensong*—and while not nearly as bad as *One Heavenly Night*, they were no great shakes either.

159

DOROTHY LEE, Bert Wheeler in *The Cuckoos*

GWEN LEE, with Dorothy Sebastian

LILA LEE, Richard Barthelmess in *Drag*

ANDREA LEEDS, Charlie Mc-Carthy in *The Goldwyn Follies*

GWEN LEE

Gwen Lee was a tall, seemingly vacant blonde who played tall, vacant blondes. When Carol Channing first burst upon us with her priceless impersonation of a jazz age baby doll in "The Gladiola Girl" number from *Lend an Ear*, it was of Gwen Lee that we thought.

Our most vivid picture of Miss Lee was in a scene from an early talkie, *Untamed*, when the synchronization went completely out of whack. As we remember, she was dancing with Robert Montgomery, while Joan Crawford's partner was Eddie Nugent and the sequence alternated between shots of the two couples, each mouthing words while the voices of the others emerged. Montgomery, Nugent and Miss Crawford have done enough in the interim to dim the recollection, but whenever we think of Gwen Lee, we remember her mouth moving as we heard the voices of Montgomery and Nugent.

LILA LEE

Lila Lee was one leading lady of the silents who did not nosedive when talkies came along. Demure as a young girl opposite Rudolph Valentino in *Blood and Sand* and other films of the earlier era, she bobbed her black hair and was ready for more wordly things when she began to talk. In the early thirties, she seemed to pop up in a picture, sometimes two, every month. She'd go from causing trouble between Jack Holt and Ralph Graves, to playing a pickpocket as one of Lon Chaney's wicked companions in his only talkie, *The Unholy Three*.

But she was always sympathetic—love reformed her in *The Unholy Three*, and although she was the girl with whom married Richard Barthelmess got involved in *Drag*, the audience was pulling for her against his grasping wife. She was a troubled wife in *The Sacred Flame*, frightened by *The Gorilla*, present for the first talkie excursions of Texas Guinan, Sophie Tucker and George Jessel.

Her name started to move down in the cast lists and finally, her life complicated by a long siege of illness, she dropped her career.

ANDREA LEEDS

In *Stage Door*, Andrea Leeds gave a sensitive performance as a girl who had had one critically acclaimed role and then was driven to suicide when she couldn't get another.

In her own career, things were not quite that bad. She had another fine role in *Letter of Introduction*, as a stage-struck girl meeting her father, a famous actor, for the first time. And she was an attractive, if subdued, leading lady for Gary Cooper in *The Real Glory*, Don Ameche in *Swanee River*, and Joel McCrea in *They Shall Have Music* and *Youth Takes a Fling*.

Even so, Grace Moore and Jeanette MacDonald were making music at the box office, so Hollywood sent once more for Miss Laye. Again, her appearance, her voice and performance were beyond reproach but *The Night Is Young* was old and tired. The only purpose it served was to send Miss Laye hurrying back to the West End, where she continues to appear.

DOROTHY LEE

Unlike the Marx Brothers or Laurel and Hardy, Wheeler and Woolsey were an early talkie comedy team who have faded into obscurity. They made over a dozen movies but nobody has clubs in their honor and even TV stations don't bother presenting their films. Sharing their oblivion is Dorothy Lee, who was as closely associated with them as was Margaret Dumont with the Marx boys.

Miss Lee was saucy and might have gone on to better things had she not been considered part of the team. Their earlier pictures had some mirth but, as they went on, the comedy became more and more mechanically slapstick. When Wheeler and Woolsey inevitably perished, Dorothy Lee went down, too.

But there was nothing in which she could live up to the potential she exhibited in *Stage Door*. So Miss Leeds left the screen—without regret, we understand, for a successful marriage.

VIVIEN LEIGH

Wasn't it a shock and surprise to all the Davis-Shearer-Goddard-Crawford devotees when an "unknown" English girl walked off with the Scarlett plum? Of course, if you had seen Vivien Leigh as a college vamp in *A Yank at Oxford* or as a small town girl involved in a *Storm in a Teacup* or as a spy in *Dark Journey*, you knew she was a saucy charmer. And if you saw her as a lady-in-waiting to Elizabeth in *Fire Over England*, you knew how ravishing she could look in costume.

But Scarlett O'Hara! Everybody but Garbo wanted that part. And who was this British upstart? (They found out, didn't they?)

Why attempt to describe the magic of Vivien Leigh's captivating performance? If you haven't seen it for yourself, you're one of the few. But you'll have your chance. Every several years, *Gone with the Wind* comes back. And will keep coming.

WINNIE LIGHTNER

"Subtlety" was not exactly the attribute for Winnie Lightner. Her madly mugging approach got a few snickers in *Gold Diggers of Broadway* but she did the same thing in all her movies thereafter. Let's say that *Life of the Party* was the best of them because here, at least, we had Charles Butterworth, whose droll and dry humor was in happy contrast to that of Miss Lightner. But then there was *Sit Tight* and *Hold Everything* which teamed her with Joe E. Brown. And if you though Winnie Lightner alone was too much . . .

BEATRICE LILLIE

The greats of the theatre too often didn't fare well in the cinema. Having pondered the cases of Misses Lawrence and Laye, we come to Beatrice Lillie, clown without peer. Hollywood didn't do right by our Bea. Her one silent, *Exit Smiling*, completely ignored at the time of its release, turned out to be something of a comic masterpiece when revived at the New York Film Festival in 1969.

But her talkies were a different matter. *Are You There?* was shown at the Museum of Modern Art in 1971 and it was plain to see why it had been forgotten. And in Warner's all-star revue, *Show of Shows*, she was merely a mistress of ceremonies with a minimum of clever material.

Those were early talkies and they seemed to seal her cinema doom. But in 1938, she had become a ranking radio comedienne so Hollywood beckoned again. The picture, one of Bing Crosby's flimsiest, was *Dr. Rhythm*,

and our Miss Bea was forced into some terribly trite situations. But this time, she could display her outrageous invention—in a minute or two of a rather weary spoof on gypsy operetta, and in all of one of her most famous set-pieces, the "Dozen Double Damask Dinner Napkin" routine. One can't say that Hollywood was exactly original in giving her that—she had established it in the theatre and on radio. But, at least, they were letting her use material in which she had been proven brilliant.

MARGARET LINDSAY

Not one of your namby-pamby young things was Margaret Lindsay although most of the roles she had to play would have been just that if played by someone else. But Miss Lindsay was crisp and forthright, with an engaging smile and a casual manner. You felt she could have held her own against Bette Davis if ever it had come to that in *Jezebel* or *Bordertown* or *Fog Over Frisco*. Or she could have been a match for most of the male stars opposite whom she played—Cagney or Fonda or Flynn—if they had given her more to do then wait around while the gentlemen had all the action.

She first was noticed in *Cavalcade* as the bride who sailed on the *Titanic*. It is said that she got into the all-British cast by lying about her nationality. But even after her American origins were revealed, she remained "British" for *Captured* and *Paddy the Next Best Thing*. Finally however, she reverted to being the American girl, adding a little more than was there to most of her mediocre roles.

Another studio might have seen the possibilities in her that MGM saw, for instance, in Myrna Loy and Rosalind Russell. She showed them particularly on one loanout—as Ann Harding's willful antagonist in *The Lady Consents*. But at Warners it was more of the same—leads in their program pictures, secondary roles in their major fare. And, except for an occasional item like *Garden of the Moon*, which we recall with particular pleasure, there were few roles among dozens which gave her anything at all.

MARGARET LIVINGSTON

Margaret Livingston, a svelte brunette of the silents—she briefly enticed George O'Brien away from Janet Gaynor in *Sunrise*, for example—had a few more such roles in the earlier talkies. Mary Pickford (in *Kiki*) and Gloria Swanson (in *What a Widow!*) were others to whom she lost out. Vamps like Miss L. always lose out in the movies.

She also made a few mysteries (*Seven Keys to Baldpate*, *The Last Warning*, *The Bellamy Trial*, *Tonight at Twelve*). But by 1931, Miss Livingston had packed it in and retired to her official offscreen position as Mrs. Paul Whiteman.

WINNIE LIGHTNER, with Loretta Young, in *Play Girl*

BEATRICE LILLIE and Bing Crosby in *Doctor Rhythm*

DORIS LLOYD

Doris Lloyd was one of those actresses you take for granted—may not even recall by name. Yet her career in films extended from the silent era through the mid-sixties. There are some roles she played to which old-timers can point—the spy, Mrs. Travers, in George Arliss' *Disraeli*; Nancy Sykes in the Monogram version of *Oliver Twist*; the woman who has taken the child of Ruth Chatterton in *Sarah and Son*; a companion of Mae Clarke's in *Waterloo Bridge*; a society lady in *Sisters Under the Skin*.

But mostly her parts were bits, and she did dozens of them, whenever an efficient British character actress was needed. You may not remember her in pictures like *Becky Sharp*, *Peter Ibbetson*, *Clive of India*, *Mary of Scotland* and others—but she was there. And in so many others.

MARGARET LOCKWOOD

Margaret Lockwood had been in British pictures (like *Dr. Syn*, *The Beloved Vagabond*) in the mid- and late thirties. But since she played in support of people like George Arliss and Maurice Chevalier, nobody here paid much heed to Margaret except to note in passing that she was a likely lass. Alfred Hitchcock obviously saw much more than that, and we suddenly found Miss Lockwood carrying the intricate plot of one of Hitchcock's most intriguing pictures, *The Lady Vanishes*.

She was the girl on the train who discovers that an old lady has disappeared. Growing more and more frantic in her search, as everyone she approaches stoutly denies knowledge and hints that the lady may exist only in her imagination, Miss Lockwood gave a taut performance.

VIVIEN LEIGH, Hattie McDaniel in *Gone With the Wind*

VIVIEN LEIGH, Laurence Olivier in *Fire Over England*

BEATRICE LILLIE and player in *Doctor Rhythm*

MARGARET LINDSAY

MARGARET LINDSAY, John Warburton in *Cavalcade*

DORIS LLOYD (right) with Ruth Chatterton (center), Ethel Griffies, Geoffrey Kerr, Stella Moore in *Once a Lady*

MARGARET LOCKWOOD in *Rulers of the Sea*, with Douglas Fairbanks, Jr., Will Fyffe

With *The Lady Vanishes* an international hit, the next move was to Hollywood. But she had to play in support of Shirley Temple in one of that young lady's most boring movies, *Susannah of the Mounties*. She followed with a ho-hum role in a would-be epic, *Rulers of the Sea*. Small wonder that she seemed glad to shake the dust of Hollywood from her feet and return to London where roles for her had more substance.

JACQUELINE LOGAN

Jacqueline Logan was one of Hollywood's real beauties—and a Ziegfeld girl before that. She was a popular leading woman in the silent era. Why her talkies should have been limited to a minor role in John Barrymore's *General Crack*, a couple of quick flashes in *The Show of Shows* and one or two quickies, we'll never know.

Her voice was good enough for the theatre, to which she turned briefly after a few non-movie years. She didn't suddenly lose her red-haired, green-eyed good looks. Why didn't she continue?

It's a question that must have haunted so many actresses who had been doing well in movies and then, with talkies, were out in the cold.

CAROLE LOMBARD

Carole Lombard looked as if she sucked in her cheeks. That she didn't became obvious when you watched her cavort through some of her slambang comedy scenes. Nobody could outdo Lombard when it came to that kind of carrying on, and it was patently impossible with sucked-in cheeks. So let's say she had great bone structure and interesting hollows.

She also had a square jaw which detracted not one whit from her femininity. The best comediennes have been very feminine, which may be a reason why they are so effective when they do such outlandish things.

Actually comedy came late to the career of Carole Lombard. She appeared in a Mack Sennett short but she was just a girl there to be pretty while Daphne Pollard did all the pratfalls.

Promoted to features, Carole was first an ingenue, then a leading lady. But she really gave little hint of the hilarity she would eventually provoke. More often than not, she was taking everything very seriously in pictures like *I Take This Woman*, *Sinners in the Sun* and *Bolero*. Not to mention *Supernatural* and *White Woman*, so supernaturally dreadful that they can be counted among Miss Lombard's funniest films.

The real Lombard comedy touch—it was usually more of a wallop—came to the fore with *Twentieth Century*. In the screen version of Hecht and Mac-Arthur's wild farce about the transcontinental train trip involving a mad genius of the theatre and one of the most temperamental stars since the palmy days of Pola Negri, John Barrymore was in his element as the producer. But right with him, snarling and screeching in good old high style, was our Miss Lombard.

It didn't seem to be enough for her home studio (*Century* was a loanout to Columbia), because back at Paramount, she was being a good companion to Shirley Temple in *Now and Forever* and to George Raft in *Rumba*.

But the other studios kept borrowing her to take advantage of those inimitable comic talents and, although some of those borrowings (*Love Before Breakfast, Fools For Scandal*) were not exactly fortunate for anybody involved, they had the right idea.

But some others had the right material, and so we had a series of delicious Lombard comedy characterizations. Some of these were not an unmixed blessing. *Gay Bride*, for instance, ran out of steam about halfway through after a promising beginning about a dumb-belle whose ambition was to make lots of money by marrying gangsters who then, of course, would be killed off.

Back at the home studio, *The Princess Comes Across* had Miss L. as a Brooklyn girl masquerading as Garboesque royalty, but degenerated into an ordinary murder yarn. *True Confession* was much more successful in its story about a congenital liar who gets into all kinds of trouble—but either Miss Lombard or her director rather spoiled things by resorting to the distressingly obvious tactic of her planting her tongue too deliberately in her cheek before each and every lie.

But you couldn't fault three other Lombard comedies. In *Hands Across the Table*, she was a cynical manicurist who was straightforwardly out to marry money and who fell in love with a handsome gentleman with the same idea, just because she thought he had money, too. In *My Man Godfrey*, she was the most adorable screwball in a family of screwballs in the picture that launched the whole series of screwball comedies. And *Nothing Sacred* cast her as Hazel Flagg, the girl who becomes a national heroine when it is believed (mistakenly) that she is dying of radium poisoning. As written by Ben Hecht, directed by William Wellman, produced by David O. Selznick and with Fredric March heading a top cast, it was one of the most brilliantly satiric films ever made. The credits for the other two pictures are almost equally distinguished. But Miss Lombard was the bright, particularly shining star of all three.

She ended the thirties with a couple of films that showed she could also be an exceptionally capable dramatic actress. *In Name Only*, her final picture of the decade, was a predictable triangle piece but Miss Lombard was believable. And *Made For Each Other* was just one of those things that had been done dozens of times—the first year or so in a young married life—but it avoided sloppy sentimentality and Miss Lombard, along with Jimmy Stewart, made it human and funny and touching.

MARGARET LOCKWOOD, (second from left), with Michael Redgrave, Linden Travers, Paul Lukas in *The Lady Vanishes*

JACQUELINE LOGAN and William Boyd in *The Cop*

CAROLE LOMBARD, Charles Laughton in *White Woman*

There would be more Lombard in the following decade. And then would come the wartime tragedy—the airplane crash at the end of a war bond tour which took her from all of us who had loved her so much.

PAULINE LORD

Unquestionably one of the supreme actresses of the theatre, Pauline Lord was treated with nowhere near the respect she deserved when she went to Hollywood. First she was given *Mrs. Wiggs of the Cabbage Patch*, in which she had to play straight while comics who ranged from W. C. Fields through ZaSu Pitts to an impish Virginia Weidler dominated the activities.

A year later, she became one of those self-sacrificing movie mums whose son doesn't know her in a sobby thing called *A Feather in Her Hat*. Miss Lord gave quietly compelling characterizations in both pictures but neither was worth her while. She returned to the theatre.

ANITA LOUISE

If you are casting Titania in *A Midsummer Night's Dream*, chances are that you'll go for the most airy and fragile blonde you can find. (There's something

CAROLE LOMBARD in her only film with Clark Gable, *No Man of Her Own*

CAROLE LOMBARD, John Barrymore in *Twentieth Century*

blonde about Titania.) In 1935, at Warners, there could have been no other choice than Anita Louise.

A beauty she was—and had been since the silent era when she was playing Garbo as a child in *Woman of Affairs*. She probably wasn't a very good actress—her performance in *Green Light*, for instance, was stilted, although it's doubtful if even Bette Davis could have made much more of that insipid role. Even so, we remember Anita being nasty to Lana Turner and Marsha Hunt in *These Glamour Girls*. She did that well, and she did nicely enough as the worldliest of *The Sisters* and in various ingenue roles.

But mostly Anita existed on the screen to decorate it. She managed that extremely well—as the mother of *Anthony Adverse*; a princess in *Marie Antoinette* (she had once played the queen herself, in Del Rio's *Madame DuBarry*); and a number of other pictures. When you looked like Anita Louise, acting was hardly a prime consideration.

BESSIE LOVE

Bessie Love had passed her peak in silent films, but she had another shot at it when talkies came and she was given a role in a picture released without fanfare. The fact that the picture was *Broadway Melody*, first of the "All Talking-All Singing-All Dancing" backstagers, gave it stature. And it looked as if Bessie Love, a good little trouper, was on her way back up.

But MGM rewarded her by casting her in films of no merit at all (*Idle Rich*, *Chasing Rainbows*, etc.).

166

CAROLE LOMBARD

PAULINE LORD in *Mrs. Wiggs of the Cabbage Patch*, with Kent Taylor, Carmencita Johnson, Edith Fellows and (partially hidden) Virginia Weidler

ANITA LOUISE

ANITA LOUISE, as a child actress, with J. Farrell MacDonald in *Four Devils*

BESSIE LOVE and Charles King in *Broadway Melody*

So Miss Love vanished into obscurity from which she did not emerge until she began showing up in British pictures a couple of decades later.

MYRNA LOY

Myrna Loy was hip twenty-five years before "hip" became an adjective. She was the original cool cat. They called her "the perfect wife." And she was just the right marital companion—completely unflappable, never perturbed—for a gentleman of such unrestrained whimsy as William Powell. Yet she was the ideal mate for a fiercely masculine Gable, too—feminine and warm. (Yes, you could be warm and cool all at once—at least, Myrna Loy could.)

It's hard to think of that Loy as a sinuous and sensuous Oriental siren—but that's what she was for her first talkie years. (She had been around in the silent era, back to a bit in the first *Ben-Hur*, and in *Pretty Ladies*, which also introduced Joan Crawford.) She was in the early sound film *Don Juan*; and if you looked quickly, you could spot her in the pioneer talkie, *The Jazz Singer*. Incidentally, she is the only actress who has had leads in movies of all of the last six decades. (Joan Crawford, who also began in the twenties, hasn't had a seventies film at this writing.)

Red hair, freckles, tip tilted nose (the Loy nose is one of the world's treasures) and all, she still had eyes that, with a little help from the makeup man, could slant. And, with lots of help from the makeup man, her face could become exotic. Presto—a series of lissome Azuris, Nubis and Yasminis. (She played those ladies in three pictures all released in the same month back in 1929.) And there were many more—gypsies, Creoles, half-castes—all in pictures of the 1929-1930 period. Even when Warners did their all-star, all-bore revue, *Show of Shows*, Miss Loy was introduced as Li-Po-Li, a Chinese dancing doll.

Finally she became a full-fledged Occidental, but her roles remained minor. She was usually fairly evil, even with Will Rogers—as Morgan Le Fay in *A Connecticut Yankee*. She had a less unsympathetic bit—but only a bit—with Ronald Colman in *Arrowsmith*, and displayed her shining comic talents first as a man-crazy countess in Mamoulian's *Love Me Tonight*.

But even after these, she returned to the Oriental roles—two of the wildest. In *Thirteen Women* she was a Javanese half-caste who methodically planned the violent deaths of twelve former sorority sisters who had snubbed her in college. And she was the daughter of nobody less than the dreaded doctor himself in *The Mask of Fu Manchu*.

The turning point in her career was *The Animal Kingdom*. In this film version of the Philip Barry play, Leslie Howard repeated his stage role and Ann Harding was his upstanding mistress. Miss Loy played the woman he married but, in one of those twists of thir-

The intriguing MYRNA LOY profile, with Cary Grant in *Wings in the Dark*

MYRNA LOY, Ramon Novarro in *The Barbarian*

ties drawing room comedy, the wife was the calculating seductress. Loy lost her man in the movie—but she won the principal recognition.

Better still, she had proved ability to speak dialogue with wit and grace. No more Nubis for Myrna. In the pictures that followed—*Topaze*, opposite John Barrymore, *The Barbarian*, with Ramon Novarro, *When Ladies Meet*, with Robert Montgomery, *The Prizefighter and the Lady*, with Max Baer, an entertaining minor mystery, *Penthouse*, and *Manhattan Melodrama*, with Gable and Powell—she continued to rack up points as one of the most attractive and capable leading ladies around.

Even all this didn't prepare audiences for *The Thin Man*. It was the film version of a popular Dashiell Hammett novel, but it starred William Powell as the detective and, after many movies as Philo Vance, Powell as a detective was hardly news.

But Powell as *this* detective certainly was. His Nick Charles was a movie original, and not the least of his virtues was his wife. Myrna Loy's Nora remains one of the most delightful of all movie wives—even seen today, decades after the breed has become commonplace. Miss Loy credits W. S. Van Dyke for realizing her potential and for giving her the role. And she be-

moans the injustice of his having become virtually a forgotten name among directors.

From there on, Myrna Loy could do no wrong on the screen. Occasionally some of her roles did her wrong—*Parnell*, for instance, or ridiculous excuses for comedy like *Petticoat Fever* and *Lucky Night* which even her talents couldn't help. Not all of the others were great either—*Wings in the Dark* had a silly story line, *Whipsaw* was routine melodrama and so was *Evelyn Prentice*, while *The Great Ziegfeld* unaccountably didn't allow her to use her own effervescence as the undeniably effervescent Billie Burke.

But she was lovely in them all, and in all the others. She was Nora Charles again in more *Thin Man* pictures—not, of course, as unexpectedly hilarious as the first but a series that held up remarkably well, due in no small part to Miss Loy and Mr. Powell. She was "the perfect wife" again—she gave the married women of the world so much to live up to—in dramas like *Wife Versus Secretary* and a nostalgic study of marriage in the twenties, *To Mary with Love*. She worried when Clark Gable was in the clouds in *Test Pilot* and shared his exploits as a daredevil newsreel cameraman in *Too Hot to Handle*. She reverted briefly, as a spy in *Stamboul Quest* and a snobbish, adultery-

MYRNA LOY, William Powell and Asta in *After the Thin Man*

IDA LUPINO, Ronald Colman in *The Light That Failed*

IDA LUPINO as a blonde starlet

minded lady in *The Rains Came*—but continued to excel in comedy, sentimental Capra comedy like *Broadway Bill* and riotous farce like *Libeled Lady* . . . comedy mixed with soap opera like *Man Proof* and comedy mixed with slapstick like *Double Wedding*. All of those roles became so very special because she was playing them.

That was the Myrna Loy of the thirties. What a lot was to come! There would be the *Best Years*, but they've all been best years for Myrna Loy who started in the twenties and still—in the seventies—is a rare and lovely star.

IDA LUPINO

Ida Lupino started as a vanilla ingenue in *Search for Beauty* and kept playing vanilla parts in things like *Ready For Love, Come on Marines, Paris in Spring* and *Anything Goes*. But something about her—a glint in the eye, a brusque quality in her speech, a touch of intensity—would make you realize that this girl had more to offer than the roles given her.

A bit in *Peter Ibbetson*, some merriment beyond the call of duty in *One Rainy Afternoon* and *The Gay Desperado*—they gave you pause. And then, right at the end of the thirties, she played that vengeful cockney strumpet in *The Light That Failed*, and the way she treated poor blind Ronald Colman reminded you of the way Bette Davis had treated poor lame Leslie Howard in *Of Human Bondage*. Not that Lupino was any slavish imitation of Davis, but you could see the development of the same kind of forceful acting personality.

The forties proved it.

SHARON LYNN

Sharon Lynn was the rich bitch who made Janet Gaynor lose her *Sunny Side Up* ever so briefly. She also had roles in a few other Fox pictures in 1929 and 1930—*Let's Go Places, Wild Company, Up the River* and *Lightnin'*—but when she finished at Fox, she just seemed to drop out. Adding an "e," she reappeared as Sharon Lynne in a few widely spaced pictures (*The Big Broadcast* in 1932, *Enter Madame* in 1935, *Way Out West* in 1936 and a couple of others). And that was it for Sharon Lynn—and also for Sharon Lynne.

MYRNA LOY, Leslie Howard in *The Animal Kingdom*

CLAIRE LUCE with newcomers, Humphrey Bogart, Spencer Tracy, Warren Hymer in *Up the River*

FLORENCE LAKE and a very young Sylvia Sidney in *Thru Different Eyes*

LUCILLE LA VERNE, Edward G. Robinson in *Little Caesar*

MARY LIVINGSTONE (right) with Lee Bowman, Betty Grable, Buddy Rogers in *This Way Please*

NOTES ON OTHER "L" LADIES

Francine Larrimore was John Meade's Woman and *John Meade's Woman* was a drag. She gave a condescending "Broadway-Star-Slumming" kind of performance and Hollywood didn't see her again.

On the other hand, *Ella Logan*—also a Broadway name—brought her burr and vigor to a few movies (*Goldwyn Follies*, *42nd Street*, *Woman Chases Man*) and tried her best with roles she would have spurned on Broadway. *Mary Livingston* was another who decided she was better off with Jack Benny in radio—a humdrum little programmer, *This Way Please*, giving her a humdrum little role. And, from stage musicals, came *Collette Lyons* for a few forgettable film bits.

Tilly Losch, "toast," as they say, "of two continents," did two American pictures—the first, one of those dancing girls in *Garden of Allah*. The other was the renowned *Good Earth*, in which she was the second wife. *Jessie Royce Landis*, a Broadway name of note, got into movie character roles in the fifties, but, in 1930, she had a film lead opposite George Bancroft in *Derelict*. Forget it. Her one American film role (in *Up the River*) sent *Claire Luce* right back to Broadway and better things (like *Gay Divorce* and *Of Mice and Men*). And *Mary Lawlor* must have had better days in the theatre than in the movie *Good News*, in which she made hardly any impression at all.

Among character actresses, you saw films with *Kathleen Lockhart* and *Helen Lowell* in the casts. Miss Lockhart usually played the wife of her real-life

MARGARET LIVINGSTON (center) with Maurice Chevalier, Sylvia Beecher in *Innocents of Paris*

172

SHARON LYNNE with Elissa Landi, Cary Grant in *Enter Madame*

CAROLE LANDIS as a starlet

JESSIE ROYCE LANDIS, George Bancroft in *Derelict*

ANNA LEE, John Loder in *Non Stop New York*

FRANCINE LARRIMORE

BETTY LAWFORD (left) with Otto Kruger, Dickie Moore, Ann Harding in *Gallant Lady*

husband, Gene Lockhart, but he had the meaty characterizations—she was generally just an also-ran. Miss Lowell played a lot of old lady parts—for a while it seemed that, whenever there was an old lady in a Warners movie, it would be Helen Lowell. But there wasn't much notable about her work. *Cecilia Loftus*, better known to the theatre, was the most black-hearted of Ann Harding's persecutors in *East Lynne* but her other movie roles were inconsequential. And there was *Lucille LaVerne*—ever the hag—who looked as hideous as possible in the background of movies like *Tale of Two Cities* and *Little Caesar*. And *Vera Lewis*, the dragon-faced bit player in so many movies.

Katherine Locke did something called *Straight From the Shoulder* but nobody noticed. Her attention came when she went to the stage for *Having Wonderful Time*. *Eleanor Lynn* was the object of the affections of Andy Hardy (*You're Only Young Once*) and looked promising in a quickie, *Fugitives for a Night*. But she, too, had her better days with the Group Theatre on Broadway. Other young actresses included *Molly Lamont*, who was affecting in a minor *Jalna* role, but whose other appearances were typfied by the role she had in *Mary of Scotland* as one of the ladies in waiting who had not even a closeup to differentiate them. (Some of her other roles were bigger but not necessarily better) . . . *Leni Lynn* and *Della Lind* sang in, respectively, *Babes in Arms* and *Swiss Miss* and a cute girl, *Jeni Le Gon*, had dance specialties in a few

JEANETTE LOFF (blonde) with Eddie Quillan, Sally O'Neil, Stanley Smith in *The Sophomore*

ELLA LOGAN   DIXIE LEE, John Boles in *Redheads on Parade*   ELEANOR LYNN, Mickey Rooney in *You're Only Young Once*

movies . . . *Carolyn Lee*, a mite who enlivened *Honeymoon in Bali*, and *Jacqui Lynn*, who did the same for *Pack Up Your Troubles* . . . *Vicki Lester* stole Janet Gaynor's *Star Is Born* name—but no star was born with this Vicki . . . You had to look fast to spot *Carole Landis* in *Gold Diggers in Paris* and *Four's a Crowd* but her beauty was worth the effort. She moved to leads in Republic Westerns but her pinup days were to be in the decade to follow . . .

Rita La Roy was a sort of brunette Natalie Moorhead in the early thirties—but Natalie's roles were bigger and better . . . *Florence Lake* had a few tiny parts in features but she was better recognized from her short comedies as Edgar Kennedy's wife . . . *Dixie Lee* was pert and pretty, but soon quit movies for family life with Bing Crosby . . . *Jeanette Loff* was best known for her blonde waist-length hair . . . *Joan Lowell*, who wrote a book, and *Joan Marie Laws*, whose father (Warden Lewis Lawes of Sing Sing) wrote one, too, both had a moment in movies as a result—but just a moment.

A whole flock of "L" girls had leading lady status in a picture or two or, in some cases, even more—*Janice Logan, Laura Lee, Dorothy Lovett, Lotti Loder, Kay Linaker, Alma Lloyd, Ann Loring, Louise Latimer,* *Rosina Lawrence, Nora Lane, Anna Lee, Donrue Leighton, Drue Leyton, Marjorie Lord, Jacqueline Laurent, Corinne Luchaire, Priscilla Lawson, Diana Lewis, Dorothy Libaire, Marion Lessing, Lenita Lane, Lucille Lund.* One or two of them might make a little more of a splash in succeeding eras but, in this one, their combined excitement was near zero.

There was also *Alison Loyd*, who played in *Corsair* as a "new dramatic leading lady" but who took back her established name of Thelma Todd when drama didn't seem to work.

And a nod to still some more "L" ladies—*Barbara Leonard* and *Etheldra Leopold, Lotus Liu* and *Lotus Long, Lya Lys, Betty Lawford, Lillian Leighton, Alice Lake, Maxine Leslie, Ada Leonard, Mary Lou Lender, Lorena Layson, Caryl Lincoln, Connie Leon, Helen Lynch, Grace LaRue, Jocelyn Lee, Nola Luxford, Erin LaBissoniere, Barbara Luddy, Flora Le Breton, Ellen Lowe, Frances Lee, Blanche LeClair, Ruby Lafayette, Gwendolen Logan, Gladys Lloyd.* Some of those names may be familiar—many of them are the kind of "movie" names that, once heard or read, remain in the memory. But, quick, name a role in a thirties movie played by any of them.

JEANETTE MAC DONALD, Maurice Chevalier in *The Merry Widow*

M

JEANETTE MacDONALD

Jeannette MacDonald: Red-gold of hair, sea-green of eyes, firm of chin, singing with gay abandon.

Oh, sure, we know that your pictures had become "camp" even before Susan Sontag was heard from. But they—and you—were so right for your day.

Woody Allen has conceived a torture in which the victim is strapped down and forced to listen to the entire score of *Naughty Marietta*. Well, call us corn-ball—but welcome, torture!

We don't mind admitting it, we loved—and love—that score. Jeanette trilling "Chansonette" and "Italian Street Song" and the lovely "Boat Departure Song" . . . Nelson, never so doughty, leading his hearties to "Tramp, Tramp, Tramp" and singing probably better than ever since, the throbbing "'Neath the Southern Moon" . . . and the two, united on a staircase in a billowing "Ah, Sweet Mystery of Life"—ah, the ecstasy!

Does it matter that she was coy as an Iowa high school virgin, that Nelson Eddy was wooden, that their dialogue was stilted and its wit straight from sixth grade? *Naughty Marietta* was the very essence of operetta. And Jeanette was the prima donna of anybody's dreams.

It may have been chic to deride her vocal pre-

JEANETTE MAC DONALD and Nelson Eddy in *Rose Marie*

tensions, and perhaps in an occasional operatic aria her singing wasn't quite up to Moore and Pons. But when Jeanette sang Herbert and Romberg and Friml, she sang them just the way they must have been meant to be sung.

As their movies went on—she playing the haughty lady eventually romanced into a duet by the virile Mr. Eddy—they became boringly predictable. And she, ever more arch, became, sad to say, something of a bore, too. Not in *Rose Marie*, which had its "Indian Love Call" resounding from the mountains. But that Lacy Valentine *Maytime*, with its hearts-and-flowers story line, was a little wearing. And the entertainment value of those operettas—*The Firefly, The Girl of the Golden West, Sweethearts* and most of what followed in the forties—went down and down, with plots becoming more sophomoric and the lady herself ever more insipid.

Still, while you could stand them, MacDonald and Eddy made a very real contribution to the musical movie. And she, at least, was capable of real humor in her performances. Consider moments in *Monte Carlo, One Hour With You* and *The Merry Widow*, when Lubitsch didn't let her go beyond bounds. Sometimes, indeed, she was quite sparkling. That was true in Mamoulian's *Love Me Tonight*, as well.

JEANETTE MAC DONALD in *Let's Go Native*

JEANETTE MAC DONALD and husband, Gene Raymond

HELEN MACK, George Raft in *All of Me*

DOROTHY MACKAILL in *Bright Lights*

ALINE MAC MAHON, Edward G. Robinson in *Silver Dollar*

MARJORIE MAIN in her down-trodden mother era (in *Stella Dallas* with Edward Elton)

ALINE MAC MAHON in *Ah Wilderness*

BOOTS MALLORY, James Dunn in *Hello Sister*

MARJORIE MAIN

MARGO, Claude Rains in *Crime Without Passion*

176

Of course, even at her raciest, you were aware that it was a put on, that under the sheer negligees of those sexy Lubitsch ladies beat the heart of a true-blue Girl Scout leader. But she was so nice to see and pleasant to hear that it's churlish to carp.

So let's leave Jeanette, remembering the inspired things—"Beyond the Blue Horizon" with Jeanette lifting her voice in song from the window of a hurtling train to the accompaniment of engine chugs, clattering wheels and peasants on a hillside . . . "the brave Jeanette" as Judy Garland called her, warbling in the ruins of San Francisco . . . "Vilia" and "Sweethearts" and "Dream Lover" and "Lover"—all those musical moments that made her so endearing.

HELEN MACK

Helen Mack was one of movies' best criers. She sobbed up a storm in the first picture in which we remember her, *Sweepings*, and by the end of the thirties she was playing one of the best hysterical roles —the streetwalker, Mollie Malloy, in Howard Hawks' *His Girl Friday*. And playing it very capably, too.

In between, she had all kinds of leading lady roles, serving in that capacity opposite all manner of leading men—Lee Tracy, George Raft, Harold Lloyd, Joe E. Brown and *Son of Kong*. But even in the comedies, you usually got to see those pretty dark eyes well up and that pointed chin begin to quiver.

DOROTHY MACKAILL

Dorothy Mackaill, with her blonde bob and generous lower lip, had been doing all right in the silents as a breezy leading lady in a series of program comedies. She made the transition to talkies easily, too—first in several which were predominantly silents with talking sequences, then all-talking films. But of them all— she did over a dozen in the first three years—only her first part-talkie, *The Barker*, had any particular merit. Miss Mackaill played the angry carnival girl who set out to seduce the naive son of the title character and wound up falling in love with him.

You could also mention *The Office Wife*, with Miss Mackaill in the title role—an early example of the "wife vs. secretary" theme. But she had the misfortune of being trapped in a whole series of films like *Party Husbands, Kept Husbands, Flirting Widow,* and *Once a Sinner*. And when her Warners contract was up, she was abruptly finished as a leading lady, at the end of 1931.

She did come back for a few more pictures—as a girl from whose clutches Gable escaped to Carole Lombard in *No Man of Her Own*, in support of Ed Wynn in *The Chief* and in a couple of quickies—before she packed it all in for marriage and the New York social world.

SARI MARITZA, Herbert Marshall in *Evenings For Sale*

ALINE MacMAHON

Aline MacMahon had a face like a tragic mask—heavy-lidded eyes under arched, thick brows, full lips. Perhaps that was why she was so unexpected as a comedienne, and why she was so good at it. Her secretaries of *Five Star Final* and *The Mouthpiece* were adept at the quick rejoinder—but there was melancholy in those ladies, too, as in most of the women Aline MacMahon played.

Of course, her May Daniels of *Once in a Lifetime* was sheer comedy—and sheer comedy genius, as played by Miss MacMahon. And she had a field day as the most acidulous of the *Gold Diggers of 1933*.

But most of her roles were dramatic and a listing of her best ones is a list of some distinguished screen characterizations—the forgotten first wife of *Silver Dollar*; the matriarch of *The World Changes*; the understanding helpmates of *Babbitt* and *Big-Hearted Herbert*; the menaced *Kind Lady*; the gentle spinster aunt of O'Neill's *Ah, Wilderness*. One might also put in a word for her performances in *I Live My Life*, *One Way Passage*, *Back Door to Heaven* and *Life Begins*, all pretty good pictures, and in *Heat Lightning*, *Side Streets*, *The Merry Frinks* and *Heroes For Sale*, pretty bad ones.

MARJORIE MAIN

The hardbitten Marjorie Main that we know began to make her appearance at the end of the thirties—in pictures like *The Women*, *Test Pilot* and *Another Thin Man*. But before that, she had several dramatic roles as a flat-voiced slattern, most notably in *Dead End*, where she played the mother who cursed out her gangster son. Miss Main won a great deal of acclaim for that scene but this minority report found her miscast as a New York slum dweller and felt that her dreary, whining voice robbed the moment of dramatic validity.

For us, she was more acceptable when she was funny.

BOOTS MALLORY

Boots Mallory, who had played ingenues, was the girl picked by Erich von Stroheim for his comeback picture, *Walking Down Broadway*, which would have been a dramatic study of New York life. But the director and the studio disagreed violently and another director took over, discarding, it is said, most of the von Stroheim conception and turning it into a terribly ordinary program picture. It was retitled *Hello, Sister*, but for her screen career it was "Goodbye, Boots."

MARGO

Margo used her dancing talent in a couple of films, but it was as an actress that she primarily scored. Of but five films of the thirties, she was dramatically effective in three.

There was her emotional performance in her film debut, *Crime Without Passion*, as the discarded sweetheart and murder victim of Claude Rains. There was Miriamne, the agonized slum girl of *Winterset*, a role she had created on stage. And there was the restless resident of Shangri-la in *Lost Horizon*, who escapes with her love—and exposed to the outer world, becomes an aged, wrinkled hag.

Margo played a few other roles in the forties and fifties but she seems not to have cared too much about her career, content to be the wife of Eddie Albert and mother of young screen personality Edward Albert, Jr.

SARI MARITZA

Sari Maritza came to American movies in a period when every import had hopes of being another Garbo or Dietrich. Sari didn't make it—not by a long shot. She was a rather ridiculous *femme-fatale* in a very ridiculous movie, *Forgotten Commandments*, seemingly put together in order to use the Biblical footage from DeMille's silent spectacle *The Ten Commandments* over again.

When it became apparent that Sari was no threat to Marlene, they let the word slip that she wasn't even Continental but, in actuality, was a British girl whose real name was Patricia Detering. She played a few more roles—in *Evenings For Sale*, *International House*, *A Lady's Profession*, *Right to Romance* and *Crimson Romance*—and then disappeared quietly back into the professional limbo from whence she had come.

JOAN MARSH

What can you say about a girl like Joan Marsh? She was of the Anita Page type, but much lower on the scale. And that's getting down there. She made a

MAE MARSH, with Sally Eilers, James Dunn in *Over the Hill*

MARIAN MARSH

MARIAN MARSH, John Barrymore in *Svengali*

ILONA MASSEY, Nelson Eddy in *Rosalie*

JESSIE MATTHEWS

JESSIE MATTHEWS

JESSIE MATTHEWS (right) in *First a Girl* with Sonnie Hale, Griffith Jones

stab at being a sort of baby Jean Harlow, but one Harlow was quite enough. So you end up saying she was a glossy blonde and that wasn't much of a distinction in the movies of the thirties. Even so, her career spanned the entire decade.

MAE MARSH

Mae Marsh, who was the Little Sister in D. W. Griffith's *The Birth of a Nation* and the Little Dear One in his *Intolerance*, had been absent from the screen for years before she came back to play the mother in a remake of *Over the Hill*. Miss Marsh was competent enough, but by 1931 there could be only jeers for that tear-drenched old chestnut. She had a few other small roles (in *Rebecca of Sunnybrook Farm*, *Little Man, What Now? Black Fury*, etc.) before descending to the ranks of unbilled bit and extra players.

MARIAN MARSH

Marian Marsh, batting big blue eyes, was expressionless enough to make you believe that her Trilby was really an automaton controlled by Svengali. The trouble was that her doll face carried scarcely more expression in any of her other pictures. *The Mad Genius* was practically a reprise of *Svengali* with Miss Marsh again stalked by a sinister Barrymore. It was frequently said that Josef von Sternberg was a sort of Svengali to the ladies he directed. Svengali or not, he got nothing much from Miss Marsh in *Crime and Punishment*.

You probably couldn't have expected much more in the way of acting from the roles she was given in things like *Under 18, Beauty and the Boss, Daring Daughters* and the like. So maybe Miss Marsh was less cloying and vacuous than she usually seemed. But you couldn't prove it by her pictures.

ILONA MASSEY

Ilona Massey was the very picture of a Mittel-European prima donna. She was blonde, Hungarian, and while maybe not as endowed as Miliza Korjus, she was ample of figure and voice. She had her thirties day with Nelson Eddy in *Balalaika* and *Rosalie*. But having joined Eddy and Jeanette MacDonald together in their hearts, the public really never took to another singing teammate for either.

JESSIE MATTHEWS

"The Dancing Divinity" was the publicity catch-phrase for Jessie Matthews and, as catch-phrases go, it wasn't inappropriate. Miss Jessie's dancing was indeed out of this world. Fluid and graceful, she had no peer among the other screen dancing ladies. (A union with Fred Astaire was frequently suggested but, alas, it never came to pass.)

MAY MC AVOY, Lionel Barrymore in *The Lion and the Mouse*

Miss Matthews also had an adequate singing voice and a joyous sense of comedy. Unfortunately, she usually needed all of her attributes to rise above the material she was given, and even they were no match for the leaden humor of her later films.

At first, all was well. British light-comedy movies of the era were not notable for wit, but the first few provided a pleasant framework for the Matthews songs and dances. Their plots were predictable. Jessie was always a stage-struck girl pretending to be someone else—a Mrs. Smythe-Smythe, big game hunter . . . a boy with a knack for female impersonation ("First a girl, then a boy, always a joy!" cried the blurbs) . . . or even her own mother. Having won acceptance in her masquerade, Jessie was always unmasked, but triumphant on her own.

She was piquant and bright-eyed and the silly plots were not too much of a hurdle. Even the frequent presence of Sonnie Hale, that most deadly of English "funnymen," didn't hurt. So she danced and sang and clowned merrily through *Evergreen*, *It's Love Again* and *First a Girl*.

But then came *Head over Heels in Love*, in which she sang more than she danced—and how we missed her dancing. *Gangway*, *Sailing Along* and *Climbing High* gave her progressively fewer chances to do things she did well, and were even more witless as vehicles.

MAY McAVOY

Why was May McAvoy reduced to extra roles only a few years after she had been a star? She was given a publicized contract for unbilled appearances after she was reported destitute. She was a blue-eyed, dark beauty who had scored in such diverse silents as *Ben-Hur*, *Sentimental Tommy*, *Enchanted Cottage* and *Lady Windermere's Fan*. What's more, she had had the lead in *The Jazz Singer*. Although she didn't talk in that, she was one of the earliest talkie leading ladies in pictures like *The Lion and the Mouse*, *The Terror* and *Caught in the Fog*.

So it wasn't her voice, which didn't seem too bad for those tinny days of early talkies. And although the pictures were bad, they didn't scuttle the careers of other actors who appeared in them (Lionel Barrymore, Edward Everett Horton, Conrad Nagel, Louise Fazenda, for instance). But Miss McAvoy was washed up by the end of 1928. We always wondered why.

HATTIE McDANIEL

Probably Hattie McDaniel would be barred from today's screen as a symbol of everything the Blacks deplore. Maybe she was that—but what pleasure she gave us back in those days before we knew better.

She was priceless as the inept hired maid at the disastrous dinner party given by *Alice Adams*. But mostly we remember her broad black face shining, as she growled fondly at her charges. There were *Valiant Is the Word for Carrie*, *Show Boat*, *Judge Priest*, *Gentle Julia* and many more.

And there was *Gone with the Wind*. Nobody—not Scarlett, nor Rhett nor Melaine—was stronger or more loving than Mammy in *Gone with the Wind*. And Hattie McDaniel *was* the eternal, wonderful Mammy. She won an Academy Award for her performance and no Oscar has ever been more popular.

NINA MAE McKINNEY

In a later era, Nina Mae McKinney might have found more movie work. But there seemed to be little for movies of the thirties to offer a black girl, no matter how vivid. She had made an immediate impression as the dusky temptress in King Vidor's *Hallelujah!* but that was in 1929. And there wouldn't be another major role for her until the British *Sanders of the River* some six years later. She was active in night clubs and revues, but it would have been nice to have her in the movies more often.

BUTTERFLY McQUEEN

Butterfly McQueen was Prissy in *Gone with the Wind*—her chirpy little voice squeaking in terror as she confesses that she "don't know nuthin' 'bout birthin' babies." Like Stepin Fetchit, she wouldn't be allowed to play such a racial stereotype in a film of today. But we're guiltily glad that Butterfly McQueen played Prissy in *Gone with the Wind*—just the way she played it.

BERYL MERCER

Beryl Mercer was an absolute darling, with her great mournful eyes, her shy smile, and her fetching little waddle of a walk. She was very capable of pouring on lots of extra syrup—Mercer mothers could be as gooey as a caramel-fudge sundae smothered in whipped cream.

But when she didn't go too far, her Cockney mums were a joy. We would single out Mrs. Gubbins, the greedy old girl of *Three Live Ghosts*, and Mrs. Dowey, the scrubwoman with an unexpected soldier son to show off to her cronies, in *Seven Days' Leave* (movie title for Barrie's *The Old Lady Shows Her Medals*). She was also a very humble and touching Mrs. Midget in *Outward Bound*, and did her bit beautifully in such other pictures as *East Lynne*, *Lovers Courageous*, *Merely Mary Ann* and *The Little Minister*. At the other extreme were those saccharine mamas in pictures like, we're sorry to say, *The Public Enemy* and *All Quiet on the Western Front*.

UNA MERKEL

D. W. Griffith saw in Una Merkel the Lillian Gish quality that made her right for his Ann Rutledge in

HATTIE MC DANIEL, with Vivien Leigh, in *Gone With the Wind*

HATTIE MC DANIEL, with Ann Shoemaker, Fred MacMurray, Katharine Hepburn, Fred Stone in *Alice Adams*

NINA MAE MC KINNEY, (right) with Fannie De Knight, Daniel Haynes in *Hallelujah*

BUTTERFLY MC QUEEN in *Gone With the Wind* with Clark Gable, Vivien Leigh

BERYL MERCER, with Robert Montgomery, Charles McNaughton in *Three Live Ghosts*

Abraham Lincoln. She had a similar kind of role in *Eyes of the World* and was a nervous ingenue in *The Bat Whispers*.

Then—and not a moment too soon—somebody saw her comedy potential and let her use her down-South speech effect in a Jeanette MacDonald vehicle, *Don't Bet on Women*. From that point on, there was no turning back. Una Merkel was for laughs. And, as she put on a pound or two, she didn't even look Gish-y any more.

Although she could be disarmingly scatterbrained (as Sybil, the second wife in *Private Lives*, or in the mystery romp, *Whistling in the Dark*), the Merkel forte was as the wise-guy associate of the heroine, always ready with a nifty retort, delivered deadpan in her best Merkel drawl. She played such buddies to Ruby Keeler in *42nd Street*; Janet Gaynor in *Daddy Long Legs*; Myrna Loy in *Evelyn Prentice*; to Carole Lombard in *True Confession*; and to Jean Harlow in several pictures. One might also cite her contributions to the cause of mirth in *The Cat's Paw*, with Harold Lloyd, *The Merry Widow*, with Maurice Chevalier, and *Bulldog Drummond Strikes Back*, with Charles Butterworth.

To finish off the thirties, she engaged none other than Miss Marlene Dietrich, in the most all-out no-holds-barred battle since *The Spoilers*, in *Destry Rides Again*.

ETHEL MERMAN

Ethel Merman might have been First Lady of Musical Comedy and the Belter of Broadway, but you'd never guess it from most of her movies. Hollywood had sense enough to let her repeat her role of Reno Sweeney in *Anything Goes*, so she got to reprise some of her great stage numbers for the soundtrack, although for some reason the movie cut out some of the best numbers of the Cole Porter score.

But otherwise it was a shame what the movies did to Ethel Merman—gave her second banana roles and worse to Eddie Cantor (*Kid Millions*, *Strike Me Pink*), Ed Wynn (*Follow the Leader*), a whole shipload of comics (*We're Not Dressing*), Sonja Henie (*Happy Landing*), Alice Faye and Tyrone Power (*Alexander's Ragtime Band*) and worst of all, the Ritz Brothers in *Straight, Place and Show*.

And, except for "My Walking Stick" and a few other Irving Berlin standards in *Alexander's*, the songs they provided for that matchless Merman voice would have been thrown out of any Merman legitimate show in New Haven.

MAYO METHOT

Mayo Methot could look meaner and talk tougher than Iris Adrian and Wynne Gibson combined. But other than *Night Club Lady*, in which she had a lead, her screen roles were minor. And although she always

BERYL MERCER in *Outward Bound*

made an impression, she usually had to do it in a few moments of screen time. Among her movies—*Afraid to Talk, The Mind Reader, Lilly Turner, Dr. Socrates* and *Marked Woman*, in which she was one of Bette Davis' prostitute chums. She was much better known to the tabloids for her pugnacious off-screen antics. As Humphrey Bogart's battling wife, known as Sluggy, her escapades enlivened the news of the day.

GERTRUDE MICHAEL

Gertrude Michael was so tall and elegant that she might have seemed like strange casting for *The Notorious Sophie Lang*, a lady on the wrong side of the law. But of course, Sophie was elegant, too—that's why you wouldn't suspect her as a jewel thief.

Miss Michael had played so many parts before she got Sophie—*I'm No Angel, Murder at the Vanities* and *Murder on the Blackboard* were three, but there were many more of little note—that it must have been cause for celebration when she got the meaty Sophie Lang role. But her troubles were not over.

She was in *Menace* and *It Happened in New York*—both entertaining but strictly program fare. And she gained no personal points in pictures that followed—*The Last Outpost, Four Hours to Kill, Till We Meet Again* and *Forgotten Faces* were some of them. She was Sophie Lang again in sequels but neither of them could approach the amusing first version.

So, before the end of the thirties, she was heading back to where she had been—pictures less frequent and of lower quality, and her name sliding down the line in the cast lists.

But she had had something to remember with *The Notorious Sophie Lang*.

ANN MILLER

Who would have ever guessed that Ann Miller was just a kid back there in the late thirties? Seeing her lithe body and long legs, coal black hair, snapping eyes and apple cheeks, the gentlemen of the era could be pardoned for thinking of her more as a "babe" than a baby.

As a very young teenager, she played post-teen roles but most of them were sexless enough—in *Stage Door* and *Having Wonderful Time*, a foil for the Brothers Marx in *Room Service*, the ballet-aspiring member of the nutty Sycamore family in *You Can't Take It With You*.

Her heyday, when she was finally ready to really show off her sexiness and her dancing and comedy gifts, wouldn't be coming up until the forties and fifties. And right on into the seventies via Broadway and TV.

MARILYN MILLER

Marilyn Miller, the golden girl of New York musicals, transferred two of her biggest stage hits to film.

UNA MERKEL, Marlene Dietrich, James Stewart (pouring) in *Destry Rides Again*

ETHEL MERMAN, Eddie Cantor in *Kid Millions*

MAYO METHOT (offscreen) with husband, Humphrey Bogart

MARILYN MILLER

GERTRUDE MICHAEL (2nd right) with Arthur Byron, Alison Skipworth, Paul Cavanagh in *The Notorious Sophie Lang*

ANN MILLER

181

PATSY RUTH MILLER (left) with Alice White in *The Show of Shows*

COLLEEN MOORE in *Smiling Irish Eyes*

GRACE MOORE, Franchot Tone in *The King Steps Out*

GRACE MOORE in *When You're in Love*

NATALIE MOORHEAD

LOIS MORAN, Jean Hersholt in *Transatlantic*

But *Sally* and *Sunny* were both made in the primitive days of early talkies and, except for a couple of their popular musical numbers, they were minus most of their original charms.

So, unhappily, was Miss Miller. Neither the camera nor the microphone did her justice. After one more feeble romantic comedy, *Her Majesty, Love*, she returned to the Main Stem.

PATSY RUTH MILLER

Patsy Ruth Miller, dark and comely, had been working steadily in silent movies. But when talkies came, there were only a few last gasps for Patsy in some of those moronic farces that turned up so frequently in the early days. She was in *The Fall of Eve* and *Twin Beds* and then joined Edward Everett Horton for a trio—*The Hottentot*, *The Aviator* and *Lonely Wives*.

Then she went the way of all silent screen names in that unhappy era, which seemed to have no place for the ladies who had been around before they had to open their mouths. It was a new time in Hollywood and the idea seemed to be to sweep away all the remnants of the past one, whether or not they could talk.

COLLEEN MOORE

Colleen Moore, who had played all those Dutch-bobbed comic flappers in the silents, tried to change her image when talkies came. So we saw her as a lass from the Emerald Isle in *Smiling Irish Eyes* and as a stage star in the throes of an unblissful love affair in *Footlights and Fools*. The image change didn't work—but at least she tried. But it wasn't the Colleen the public knew, and she quickly tumbled from eminence.

She did come back some five years later and gave a subdued performance in support of Spencer Tracy in *The Power and the Glory*. A year later, she attempted another return in *Success at Any Price*. And there was a small-time version of *The Scarlet Letter*. But they were not enough to re-establish her.

GRACE MOORE

Grace Moore certainly has a place in movie history if only for the fact that she brought opera to the screen—and made her audiences enjoy it. She was responsible for an influx of rivals as well. None of them ever made it as importantly as Miss Moore, but it was worth sitting through some bad pictures to hear the voices of Lily Pons, Gladys Swarthout, Risë Stevens and others.

Grace Moore entertained audiences with some romantic meringues, dotted with her arias. She was *Miss* Grace Moore—and her studio never let you forget the "Miss." Nor did the lady herself, who sometimes gave you the impression that she was playing down to the peasants, particularly in moments designed to show

POLLY MORAN (right) and Marie Dressler in *Dangerous Females*

off what a regular feller she really was. These would include her rendition of "Minnie the Moocher," which, with for all her best intentions, never got very low-down.

Miss Moore had come to the screen in 1930—to play Jenny Lind in *A Lady's Morals* and to sing opposite Lawrence Tibbett in *New Moon*. But she was stolid then, severely coiffed and very much the slumming prima donna.

Things were different upon her return in 1934. She was blonder, slimmer, had developed comedy talent and the voice seemed more golden than ever. Her first picture, *One Night of Love*, cast her as an ordinary girl—could Miss Grace ever be ordinary?—going through the rigors of training for opera.

Each year thereafter, she did another—*Love Me Forever*, *The King Steps Out*, *When You're in Love*, *I'll Take Romance*—but, although the voice retained its splendor, the story lines grew wispier and Miss Moore seemed to grow ever more the prima donna. Her last couple of pictures didn't make it with the public and she returned to opera, where a singer doesn't have to be just one of the girls.

NATALIE MOORHEAD

Natalie Moorhead, a clotheshorse with a marcelled blonde bob, was all over the place in 1930 and 1931. Whenever a cold, calculating type was needed, chances were better than even that it would be Miss Moorhead. She had such parts in *Shadow of the Law*, *My Past*, *Office Wife*, *Illicit*, *The Unholy Night*, *The Benson Murder Case*, to name only a few.

By 1932, those roles were falling off, and after 1933 she had only a few spots. But one of them was as the faithless mistress-secretary who knows all about the murder of *The Thin Man* in the only one of her pictures which is still shown, or even remembered. So it's the one for which she is best known.

LOIS MORAN

Lois Moran's movie high spot was as Laurel in the silent *Stella Dallas*. She will be remembered for that; for her appearance in the Broadway musical *Of Thee I Sing*; and, in private life, as the inspiration for F. Scott Fitzgerald's Rosemary in *Tender Is the Night*. But she won't be remembered for any of her talkies—mere ingenue roles in pictures like *The Spider*, *Behind That Curtain*, *The Dancers* and *Transatlantic*.

POLLY MORAN

Polly Moran was raucous, had buck teeth, and was lucky enough to be teamed with the vastly popular Marie Dressler. They appeared together in silent pictures and then, after Miss Dressler had reached screen eminence, Miss Moran was brought back as her foil in a series of topical funny-paper movies. Together they were involved in *Politics*, *Prosperity*, *Caught Short* and *Reducing*. But, on her own, Polly did only a few bits.

HELEN MORGAN

Helen Morgan, sad-eyed, tousle-haired, smoky-voiced star of Broadway, made infrequent appearances on the screen and only two of them are worth mention. But these were as notable as anything for which she was appreciated in the theatre.

As a matter of fact, one of them was a filmed repeat of a theatre role in which she had triumphed. This was Julie in *Show Boat*, with her songs, "Bill" and "Can't Help Lovin' That Man," remaining completely her own.

In the earliest days of talkies, she had been brought to the screen by the brilliant Rouben Mamoulian for his innovative *Applause*. As the over-the-hill burlesque queen, she gave an absolutely unforgettable performance. But outside of these, there was nothing much in movies for one of the great stars.

PATRICIA MORISON

Patricia Morison, with her cultured voice, chignoned black hair, sky-blue eyes and lush mouth, was such an aristocratic beauty that it seemed strange for her to be cast as a wanted criminal in her first picture, *Persons in Hiding*. They then gave her thankless parts in Bob Burns' *I'm From Missouri* and in Akim Tamiroff's *Magnificent Fraud*.

Even so, she showed so much promise that you knew movies would latch on to it and use her effectively. Alas, it wasn't until she deserted the screen for Broadway's *Kiss Me Kate* that the promise was fulfilled. Hollywood never made the right move.

HELEN MORGAN (right), Joan Peers in *Applause*

PATRICIA MORISON

PATRICIA MORISON, Ray Milland in *Untamed*

KAREN MORLEY, Paul Muni in *Black Fury*

KAREN MORLEY

Karen Morley had a small role, but gave an interesting performance, in her screen debut in Garbo's *Inspiration*. And although she continued to play young contract players' parts, she almost completely avoided the starlet snare.

She wasn't conventionally pretty. She had high cheekbones, hooded eyes, a deep, liquid voice. Not easy to cast, she broke into prominence with three varied but compelling performances—as the disagreeable wife of William Haines in *Are You Listening?*, a sophisticated sparring partner for John Barrymore in *Arsene Lupin* and a glistening gun-moll in *Scarface*.

Her career should have gone onward and upward from there but good roles weren't that plentiful for a Morley type, so she had to make do with a preponderance of poor ones. On the better side, list the mother struggling vainly to regain her son's love in *Wednesday's Child*, a "back-to-the-earth" advocate in King Vidor's *Our Daily Bread*, and the faithless sweetheart of Paul Muni in *Black Fury*. She handled other roles intelligently enough, but there wasn't much to them.

JEAN MUIR

Jean Muir, a tall, large-boned girl, could play awkward and ungraceful youngsters so realistically it hurt. Then you'd see the rare beauty of her face and you'd know, for instance, why a suave gent like George Brent could pass up the svelte Verree Teasdale for Jean.

She could be graceful and quite conventionally pretty—as Helena in *A Midsummer Night's Dream*, or as the one who "was" in *And One Was Beautiful* (released a few months into 1940). But the thing that came through in her best roles was her sincerity. She seemed to care about everything.

Jean Muir's movie career suffered—like those of Margaret Lindsay, Josephine Hutchinson and other talented actresses—because she was under contract to Warners, a studio that had no conception of how to use an actress most effectively. Even Bette Davis, who fought all the way, had a number of dogs for every worthwhile picture the studio gave her.

In her first year under contract, Miss Muir gave three glowing performances—as a suffering young girl in a Kay Francis soap opera, *Dr. Monica*; as a plain but idealistic farm girl in *As the Earth Turns*; and as the lonely, hidden adolescent daughter of a glamorous stage star in *Desirable*. Another studio might have thought of her in Hepburn terms.

But Warners threw her into everything that came along—program pot-boilers, "B" mysteries, undemanding supporting roles, even a stint opposite Joe E. Brown. On one loanout (playing a lovelorn florist in Fox's *Orchids to You*) she did manage to make an impression. But for the rest of it, you would go to a Jean Muir film, however humble, with high hopes that per-

184

KAREN MORLEY, William Haines in *Are You Listening?*

haps *this* time they would have given her a role in which she could make some use of her expressive gifts. Those hopes were always dashed.

ONA MUNSON

Ona Munson, better known to the stage, had been around Hollywood briefly in 1931. But her pictures—Joe E. Brown vehicles, and a dismal thing called *Hot Heiress*—weren't enough to encourage her staying on.

When she returned in 1939, it was for something far different. By this time she could be called a character actress, and she nabbed the plum role of Belle Watling in *Gone with the Wind*—a part coveted almost as much by character actresses as was Scarlett O'Hara by leading ladies. Belle was *the* "heart-of-gold" prostitute, and Miss Munson did well by her. But her success meant that Miss Munson would be condemned to playing whores, good hearted and otherwise, forever—with one side excursion as the ludicrous Mother Gin Sling, Hollywood's a more genteel name for the lady known on stage as Mother Goddam, in *The Shanghai Gesture*.

MAE MURRAY

Mae Murray might have been "Miss Itsy-Poo of 1922" but she was a little long in the tooth to be so coy and cutesie by 1931, when she made a "comeback" in a talkie, *Bachelor Apartment*. She seemed ridiculous by this time and was one silent star whose talkie demise was evident the minute she opened those bee-stung lips.

CARMEL MYERS

Carmel Myers who, as Iras in *Ben-Hur*, had been the vampiest vamp since Theda Bara and had shown up well in other silents, was another casualty of the talkies. After a few very early ones (*The Ghost Talks, Careless Age, Ship from Shanghai*, etc.) she was brought back by none other than John Barrymore, with whom she had appeared before sound. But her roles in *Svengali* and *The Mad Genius* gave her little opportunity. Besides, they were two of Barrymore's poorest pictures.

So Carmel Myers soon dropped out of the Hollywood hurly-burly.

JEAN MUIR

ONA MUNSON

MAE MURRAY

JEAN MUIR, John Boles·in *Orchids to You*

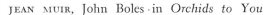

CARMEL MYERS, with John Barrymore, in *Svengali*

JUNE MAC CLOY   MARIAN MARTIN   HELEN MAC KELLAR

NOTES ON OTHER "M" LADIES

Probably our favorite of the "Other 'M' Ladies"—those whose contribution to cinema was minimal—is *June MacCloy*, a tall blonde with a wide grin and a contralto voice who appeared in alas, only a couple of films (*June Moon, Reaching for the Moon*). Bigger and blonder was *Marian Martin*, just starting at the end of the decade with her best dumb-moll days still before her.

We were fond, too, of *Eily Malyon*, best remembered as the grim spinster ("Aunt Demetria is a pismire!") of *On Borrowed Time* but around all through the thirties in bits. Even more harsh was the visage of *Martha Mattox*, known from the silent era as the sinister housekeeper of *The Cat and the Canary*, but with only a few similar bits in the talkies. Other character ladies would include *Norma Mitchell*, who gave a little gem of a performance as Nancy Carroll's maid in *Woman Accused*, *Odette Myrtil*, the titled Frenchwoman who fell in with Ruth Chatterton in *Dodsworth* and *Doro Merande*, whose quavery voice would be heard to better advantage in movies of succeeding eras than in her bit in *The Star Maker*. There was also *Helen MacKellar*, a particularly leaden actress who played without restraint in *The Past of Mary Holmes* and was thereafter demoted to bits. Others would include *Claire McDowell* who had the same mother roles in talking movies that she had played in the silent days . . . *Eva Moore*, the gargoyle ancient of *The Old Dark House* . . . *Margaret McWade*, who, with Margaret Seddon, brought chuckles as "the pixi-

lated sisters," to a few moments of *Mr. Deeds Goes to Town* but then was stuck in the same role for her other film appearances . . . *Mary Morris*, who repeated her stage role in the movie version of *Double Door*—but it seemed more ludicrous than chilling this time . . . There was also a British *Mary Morris* . . . *Dennie Moore*, who enlivened such pictures as *The Perfect Specimen* in bits as a rattlebrained blonde . . . *Esther Muir*, a minor league Iris Adrian (although Iris was just beginning to be around herself), who was a foil to such as the Marx Brothers and Wheeler and Woolsey and snapped her gum for a moment or two in an occasional big picture, like *The Great Ziegfeld* . . . *Lucie Mannheim*, who had moments in British films, most particularly in *The 39 Steps* . . . *Dorothy Mathews*, Lew Ayres' leading woman in *Doorway to Hell* . . . *Margaret Matzenauer*, the opera star, playing an opera star in *Mr. Deeds* . . . *Elsa Maxwell*, chattering away and taking it all very big in *Hotel for Women* . . . and still others . . . like *Leila McIntyre, Margaret Mann, Kitty McHugh, Etta McDaniels, Lulu McConnell* (better known to radio), *Alice Duer Miller* (playing a small part in *Soak the Rich* for her friends Hecht and MacArthur) *Renate Muller, Ada May, Mary McLaren, Adrienne Marden, Helene Millard, Gertrude Messinger, Zita Moulton* and, of course, *Greta Meyer* who was on call whenever a stout Frau was needed . . .

There were others, whose even better days were still ahead. *Mary Martin*, already established on Broadway,

ISA MIRANDA, Ray Milland in *Hotel Imperial*

CONSTANCE MOORE

MARY MARTIN, with Jerome Cowan, Allan Jones, in *The Great Victor Herbert*

had merely started her movie career in 1939 as the singing leading lady of *The Great Victor Herbert*. *Brenda Marshall* had only limited opportunity to display her dark beauty and dimples in her one thirties film, *Espionage Agent*. *Constance Moore* did some ten pictures, most of them made for the lower halves of double bills and none giving her much chance to shine as she would occasionally in the next decade.

Then there were the lesser leading ladies, heavies and ingenues ranging from *Toshia Mori*, the luscious Oriental bad girl of *The Bitter Tea of General Yen*, to *Isa Miranda*, distinguished in Italy but disappointing in her American debut, *Hotel Imperial*. And there were others, more notable for their echoes of the past—a player in a few sleazy Westerns, named *Ruth Mix*, who was the daughter of the great Tom, and a girl, named *Peggy Montgomery*, whom you would only notice in a picture like *Eight Girls in a Boat* if you were aware that she was the grown-up Baby Peggy, who had been the most popular child actress up to the time of Shirley Temple. *Goodee Montgomery*, too, got more press attention as the daughter of the old-time musical comedy man Dave Montgomery (and Stone), than for any of her few movie bits. *Shirley Mason* had been popular in silents but had only a nondescript part or two in the audible screen. *Florine McKinney* had secondary leads—most famous role being Little Em'ly in *David Copperfield*, although that role was only a bit . . . *Pauline Moore's* Constance in the Ritz Brothers' desecration of *The*

Three Musketeers was little more than a walk-on, also, and her other roles were minor . . . brunette *Dorothy McNulty*, who would become blonde Penny Singleton . . . *Jeanne Madden*, who played the Ruby Keeler role —but with even less apparent talent—in *Stage Struck*, a last gasp Warners backstage musical for Dick Powell . . . Scandinavian *Osa Massen* starting out at the end of the era in *Honeymoon in Bali*—her attention was primarily because of confusion with *Ona Munson*.

And more—dark-eyed *Mary Maguire*, in such small-time pictures as *Sergeant Murphy* and *That Man's Here Again* . . . *Rosalind Marquis*, the "other one" of the "Marked Women"—always with Bette, Mayo and the girls but with little extra to do . . . *Joyce Mathews*, who would become more familiar through her marriages than her movies . . . *Conchita Montenegro*, who played a few of the "chile con carne" roles that were probably turned down by Lupe Velez; *Mona Maris*, another Latin type but a more sultry one, and still another, *Rosita Moreno*, who may have been considered something of a cross between the other two . . . *Peggy Moran*, whose more successful leading lady days would come in the forties . . . and *Ann Morriss, Milli Monti, Frances Mercer, Dorothy Moore, Iris Meredith, Shirley Mills, Fay McKenzie, Addie McPhail, Leona Maricle, June Martel, Jill Martin, Mary Mason, Lillian Miles, Geneva Mitchell, Frances Moffet, Claudia Morgan, Edna Murphy, Charlotte Merriam, Joan Marion, June Marlowe, Betty Mack, Helen Mann, Sheila Mannors, Mae Madison, Doreen McKay, Louise Mackintosh,*

TOSHIA MORI

EDNA MURPHY

MONA MARIS, Warner Baxter in *The Arizona Kid*

BRENDA MARSHALL

MARTHA MATTOX, Laura La Plante in *The Cat and the Canary*

Helene Madison, Sheila MacGill, Lucila Mendez, Renee Macready, Christine McIntyre, Christine Maple, Catherine Moylan, Claire Maynard, Aileen Manning, Marcia Manon, Florence Midgely, Rosita Marstini, Nita Martone and *Blanche Mehaffey*, who complained bitterly at the rerun of her thirties movies in the early days of television. But she didn't need to fret for long—TV soon acquired more important movies and it was bye, bye, Blanche.

One more "M" girl—down at the bottom of cast lists in which Shirley Temple and Jane Withers were on top and without the slightest chance to show any hint that she would eventually become one of Broadway's brightest. She was *Mary McCarty*.

188

ANNA NEAGLE, Anton Walbrook in *Sixty Glorious Years*

N~O

ANNA NEAGLE

She would be best known to America for her musical comedies of the forties but the most impressive work of Anna Neagle came in her British films imported in the thirties. Her director-producer husband, Herbert Wilcox, saw to it that she played, for the most part, ladies out of British history. Miss Neagle played them, until they became too regal, with a nice touch of vulgar humor.

Especially was this true of her characterizations of *Nell Gwyn* and *Peg of Old Drury*, both spirited wenches. That bit of bawdiness was gone, never to return, when she became *Victoria the Great*. She gave an affectionate characterization and was as accomplished, if even a trifle more reverent, in a sequel, *Sixty Glorious Years*. But this just went over the same ground and was really only a tiresome attempt to repeat a success.

She ended the thirties in her first American picture but again as a figure of British history. This was *Nurse Edith Cavell* and, except for the cast presence of such notably non-British types as ZaSu Pitts and Edna May Oliver, it was very much in the style of the British Wilcox-Neagle collaborations that had preceded.

It was the last of them, though. The forties would see her trying to breathe new life into film versions of passé musical comedies and then returning to London.

POLA NEGRI

Pola Negri seethed darkly through a decade of silents, but waited too long to make her talkie debut. By the time she did in 1932 (in *A Woman Commands*), nobody cared. She was terrible too, even though she had one of the most sensual songs of the time ("Paradise") to sing. But Pola, breasts heaving and nostrils dilated, piled on the drah-ma in what was merely Continental fluff.

GRETA NISSEN

Greta Nissen is in the odd position of being probably most noted for a movie in which she was never seen. She had played the blonde nymph in Howard Hughes' big air spectacle, *Hell's Angels*. But talkies came in before it was released, and Greta's performance became obsolete. Instead of letting Greta talk for herself, Norwegian accent and all (she later proved she could make her lines intelligible in *Transatlantic, Ambassador Bill, Circus Queen Murder*), they remade her sequences with a replacement. That girl's name was Jean Harlow.

MARIAN NIXON

A sort of minor league Janet Gaynor, Marian Nixon played very sweet young things—unfortunately long beyond the point where she believed them herself. Although she played demure leading ladies to actors who ranged from Al Jolson to John Barrymore, one among her early talkies stands out. This was *Young Nowheres*, a simple drama about an elevator operator (Richard Barthelmess) and a chambermaid (Miss Nixon) and their tentative gropings at love.

But she seemed to have outgrown such things by the time Fox signed her as a standby, so to speak, for their own Miss Gaynor. Here she had to play a series of innocent heroines in movies not strong enough for Janet—like *Amateur Daddy, Face in the Sky, After Tomorrow* and, as a replacement for the star herself, in *Rebecca of Sunnybrook Farm*.

She was much more at home as a spoiled and silly rich girl who temporarily took Joel McCrea away from Ginger Rogers in *A Chance at Heaven*. But that was close to the end of her career and it only served to get her cast as another scatterbrain—this one in a boring and overboard comedy, *We're Rich Again*.

DORIS NOLAN

In *Holiday*, Julia must be warm and feminine and everything a Johnny Case would want in a girl. If she is not, there is no reason for Johnny not to pick Linda in the first place. Mary Astor was all a Julia should be in the first movie version of *Holiday*, even with such a vibrant Linda as Ann Harding. But as the 1938 Julia, Doris Nolan was no match for Katharine Hepburn. Miss Nolan had other pictures, like *As Good as Married*, *The Man I Marry* and *Top of the Town*. They weren't enough to make her a star.

MERLE OBERON

When she arrived in Hollywood, Merle Oberon resembled an animated Benda mask, with lacquered hair and an expressionless, vaguely Eurasian face that seemed to have been painted on. Devotees of the British film were already aware that Miss Oberon was exotic and unusual—lovingly photographed in such films as *The Private Life of Henry VIII*, in which she had only a moment as the doomed Anne Boleyn; the roistering *Scarlet Pimpernel*; in Douglas Fairbanks, Sr.'s last film, *The Private Life of Don Juan*; and in *The Battle* (also titled *Thunder in the East*) in which she was particularly telling as the Japanese wife betrayed by her husband (Charles Boyer).

But her American debut in *Folies Bergere* carried the exoticism to an almost foolish degree. Smart Sam Goldwyn saved her from a possible fate of playing Anna May Wong rejects.

The goo was wiped from her eyes and lips, the lacquer was taken from her hair and she was given what they called a "natural look." Not that Merle Oberon ever really looked "natural," not in normal terms. But with hair soft and casual, sloe eyes unadorned by makeup, she looked more the British belle she would portray.

She was admirable, even in relatively passive roles in films like *The Dark Angel* and *These Three*. *Beloved Enemy*, an excellent drama about a love between a high-born British lady and an Irish revolutionary, was the third of these American films which presented her well.

She returned to England for inconsequential comedies, *Over the Moon* and *Divorce of Lady X*, but it was back to America for the role most closely associated with her—that of Cathy in *Wuthering Heights*.

Wuthering Heights was one of the classic romantic dramas and remains so. Every element—the screenplay by Ben Hecht and Charles MacArthur, the direction of William Wyler, the performances of an extraordinary cast—contributed.

Miss Oberon's Cathy was tempestuous in her early stages and poignant in her death scenes. Perhaps her passion was not a match for that of Laurence Olivier's tormented Heathcliff but her performance was always vivid.

It was the high point of her film career, never to be approached by her again.

ERIN O'BRIEN-MOORE

Although Erin O'Brien-Moore was a well-known stage actress, there were small pickings for her in Hollywood. She gave a quietly effective performance as the wife of Humphrey Bogart in *The Black Legion*, a strong study of a man who joins that infamous group. Then in a mere few moments, she sketched the woman of the streets who was the inspiration of Zola's "Nana," in Muni's *Life of Emile Zola*. Her performance had more depth than the entire Anna Sten movie. For the rest of it though, there were just minor roles in pictures like *The Plough and the Stars*, *The Ex Mrs. Bradford* and *Seven Keys to Baldpate*.

UNA O'CONNOR

The first thing you recall when you think about Una O'Connor is her shriek. Piercing it was, usually accompanied by loud wails and keening. Sometimes the directors used it for laughs, but usually it was the real thing. The ear-splitting screech of fright in *The Invisible Man* or *The Bride of Frankenstein* was related to the cry of anguish in *Cavalcade* or *Informer* only by virtue of its volume.

Pinch-faced, round-eyed, purse-mouthed, Una O'Connor first came to American attention as the maid in *Cavalcade*, and then showed up whenever the locale was English or Irish as a variety of biddies and gossips. She even turned up, incongruously, in the middle-European atmosphere of the Frankenstein castle. Some of her best roles—the loyal maid of *The Barretts of Wimpole Street*; the "lone, lorn" Mrs. Gummidge of *David Copperfield*; the mourning mother of *The Informer*; the tippling crone of *The Plough and the Stars*; and the scandal-monger of *We Are Not Alone*.

MAUREEN O'HARA

Thank Alfred Hitchcock for Maureen O'Hara. (In years to come, we'd also thank John Ford.) It was later that Technicolor let us know that her hair was flaming, but her beauty, even in black and white, was special indeed.

In the two pictures that introduced her in 1939, her beauty was the most important thing. Her role in the Hitchcock film *Jamaica Inn* consisted largely of looking alternately worried and terrified; that of the gypsy, Esmeralda, in *The Hunchback of Notre Dame* was only moderately more demanding. Both were Charles Laughton pictures and featured him at his most outrageously hammy.

But once you moved past his scenery chewing, which monopolized the screen, you came to Maureen O'Hara, one of our all-time most welcome imports from Erin.

EDNA MAY OLIVER

Edna May Oliver was triumphantly herself among character actresses—inimitable, if occasionally imitated.

ANNA NEAGLE in *Peg of Old Drury*

POLA NEGRI

GRETA NISSEN, Donald Cook in *The Circus Queen Murder*

MARIAN NIXON, James Cagney in *Winner Take All*

MARIAN NIXON in *Rebecca of Sunnybrook Farm*

DORIS NOLAN, Cary Grant, Katharine Hepburn in *Holiday*

MERLE OBERON, Maurice Chevalier in *Folies Bergere*

MERLE OBERON, Laurence Olivier in *Wuthering Heights*

MERLE OBERON, Leslie Howard in *The Scarlet Pimpernel*

MERLE OBERON, Fredric March in *The Dark Angel*

ERIN O'BRIEN MOORE, Paul Muni in *The Life of Emile Zola*

UNA O'CONNOR in *The Bride of Frankenstein*

MAUREEN O'HARA, Charles Laughton in *The Hunchback of Notre Dame*

EDNA MAY OLIVER in *Pride and Prejudice*

Her appearance was unique—the spare, ramrod-straight frame . . . the great horse-face with its incomparable sniff . . . the owlish, watchful eyes. And above all, that voice—the ultimate aristocratic rasp.

She played an occasional wife or mother, but primarily she was the ideal spinster—nothing so watery as a "maiden lady," mind you—just a good strong spinster. Sometimes she showed up only because a picture needed her acidulous wit. But more often than not, she was much more important to a film than to just add vinegar.

In her gallery of eccentrics, let's list these as particularly notable—Aunt Betsy Trotwood in *David Copperfield*; Miss Pross in *A Tale of Two Cities*; the Nurse of *Romeo and Juliet*; Aunt March of *Little Women*; the Red Queen of *Alice in Wonderland*; the pioneer women in *Cimarron* and *Drums Along the Mohawk*. And don't forget that intrepid schoolmistress-sleuth, Miss Hildegarde Withers, who shrewdly solved such crimes as *The Penguin Pool Murder*, *Murder on the Blackboard* and *Murder on a Honeymoon*.

In a group like that, who is going to worry about such lapses as *Laugh and Get Rich*, *We're Rich Again*, *Paradise for Three* and *Little Miss Broadway*. To be fair, they weren't Miss Oliver's lapses at all—she was trapped.

BARBARA O'NEIL

Barbara O'Neil, mature and brunette, will be most immediately remembered as Scarlett O'Hara's mother in *Gone with the Wind*. But although her best role (the neurotic wife in *All This and Heaven Too*) was still to come, she played gracefully in other films of the thirties—as the compassionate second wife in *Stella Dallas*; the queen in *Tower of London*; as one of those handy mad wives who exist to keep lovers apart (*When Tomorrow Comes*); and as a relentlessly "good sport" mother in *Love, Honor and Behave*.

SALLY O'NEIL

Sally O'Neil was pert and Irish, but by talkie time she had outgrown the urchin roles in which she specialized. *On With the Show* gave her the part of the girl who is snatched from obscurity when she replaces the ailing leading lady. Yes, *42nd Street* was its uncredited remake.

But there was to be no Ruby Keeler rise-to-renewed-fame for Sally. There were routine musicals in which she sang a little (not very well) . . . an unhappy return in *The Brat* to the kind of role in which she sparkled in silents . . . and, a half dozen years after she was washed up, an attempt at a comeback in an Irish-made film, *Kathleen*. She and her sister, Molly O'Day, sang and danced in the "Sisters" number in *Show of Shows*. Too bad there was no place left for either of them in the talkie era.

EDNA MAY OLIVER in *David Copperfield*

BARBARA O'NEIL in *Toy Wife*

SALLY O'NEIL, William Bakewell in *On With the Show*

VIVIENNE OSBORNE

Vivienne Osborne was one of those thorns in the sides of proper wives seeking to hold their husbands. Plump and dark-eyed as she was, Miss Osborne's appeal was largely to such senior citizens of the screen as Clive Brook, Warren William, Paul Lukas and the like. But she also had such sidelines as vamping Jack Oakie (*Sailor Be Good*), giving birth in a maternity ward (*Life Begins*) and as an executed murderess, inhabiting the body of Carole Lombard (*Supernatural*).

MAUREEN O'SULLIVAN

An Irish brunette has a very special kind of beauty —fresh skinned, dark haired, with the bluest eyes behind sooty lashes. (The Irish also produce a red-haired species—Miss O'Hara being an example.) But Maureen O'Sullivan must certainly have been the most beauteous of all colleens.

Although she started out playing just disturbingly decorative girls, it wasn't long before they discovered the dividend—she could act, too. She could be stormy and defiant as the rebellious young sister in *The Barretts of Wimpole Street* . . . happily naive as the child bride, Dora, in *David Copperfield* . . . gentle as a country girl in love with a runaway gangster in *Hideout* . . . touching as a deserted sweetheart in *Port of Seven Seas* . . . straightforward as a girl fighting injustice in *Let Us Live*.

If you looked like that, you couldn't censure the producers for frequently using you just to dress up their pictures. Maureen played many such roles, but always winningly. Among others we wouldn't want to forget would be the girl living in that faraway futuristic world of 1980 in *Just Imagine*; as well as others, all well played, in such pictures as *The Flame Within*, *The Thin Man*, *Stage Mother*, *Hold That Kiss*, *A Yank at Oxford*, *The Crowd Roars*.

And there was Tarzan's Jane, swinging through the trees in the skimpiest of outfits, teaching Tarzan the niceties of civilization and romance. Come to

VIVIENNE OSBORNE, Chester Morris in
Tomorrow at 7

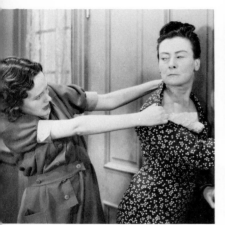

RAFAELA OTTIANO (right),
Dorothy Jordan in *Bondage*

MAUREEN O'SULLIVAN, Johnny
Weissmuller in *Tarzan's New York
Adventure*

CATHERINE DALE OWEN, John
Gilbert in *His Glorious
Night*

194

MAUREEN O'SULLIVAN, with Norma
Shearer, Charles Laughton, in *The
Barretts of Wimpole Street*

think of it, perhaps she had to act more in that role
than anybody realized.

RAFAELA OTTIANO

Small, birdlike Rafaela Ottiano was an indelible part
of the thirties, although usually in roles that required
only atmosphere. Even so you were always aware of
her—black eyes snapping, head cocked—somewhere in
the background. Occasionally she would be witchlike,
as in *Bondage*, where she ran that horrible home for
unwed mothers; or as a vicious white slaver, antagonist
for Mae West in *She Done Him Wrong*. But she was
most in her element as the kind of devoted maid she
played to Garbo's ballerina in *Grand Hotel*.

MARIA OUSPENSKAYA

If you had seen one Maria Ouspenskaya performance, you had seen them all. Her ancient monkey
face, tiny, gnarled body, sometimes incomprehensible
accent were unchanged whether she was playing a
Viennese Baroness (*Dodsworth*) or an imperious Ma-
harani (*The Rains Came*); a loving *grandmere* (*Love
Affair*) or a crazed Polish countess (*Conquest*). She
was always exactly the same—but wasn't she a treat!

CATHERINE DALE OWEN

Perhaps it wasn't all John Gilbert's fault that he
seemed ludicrous in his first talking picture love scenes.
We were used to Gilbert with Garbo or Crawford or,
at the very least, Renee Adoree. But *His Glorious
Night* gave him Catherine Dale Owen, an unbending
blonde, and his protestations of love provoked little
response. She was similarly icy in *The Rogue Song*,
but Tibbett was singing so forcefully that it didn't
bother him. A few more such grand ladies and we had
no more of Miss Owen on the screen.

MARIA OUSPENSKAYA (right), Ruth Chatterton in *Dodsworth*

MARY NOLAN

GERTRUDE NIESEN, musicians, in *Top of the Town*

MOLLY O'DAY, Sally O'Neil in *Show of Shows*

NOTES ON OTHER "N, O" LADIES

Mary Nolan, a blonde beauty of silent films—she had changed her name from Imogene Wilson after being involved in a Broadway scandal—had only a few thankless roles in talkies . . . *Molly O'Day* and *Gertrude Olmstead* were others who lasted only briefly when the microphone came . . . *Zelma O'Neal* arrived to play soubrettes in *Follow Through* and *Peach o' Reno*, just about the time that such musicals had fallen out of favor . . .

There were *Mary Nash*, a good actress whose main movie function was being harsh to people like Shirley Temple . . . *Florence Nash*, one of the more mature of *The Women*, and *Jacqueline Nash*, one of the younger of *They* who *Shall Have Music* . . . *Anna Q. Nilsson*, past her *Ponjola* prime and down to a few character bits in talkies, and *Gertrude Niesen*, singing "Where Are You?" and "Blame It on the Rhumba" and making them the only highlights of *Top of the Town*—but looking as if she had decided that the movie camera called for an extra-extra dose of makeup . . . *Anne Nagel*, who played lesser leads . . . *Jane Novak*, making an old-timer's return in *Hollywood Boulevard*, and *Seena Owen*, also with only a couple of talkie roles to remind you that she had once been a silent star . . . *Sunnie O'Dea*, who sang and danced in *Show Boat* and *Strike Me Pink*, and *Dawn O'Day*, a lovely child covered more thoroughly under her later name, Anne Shirley . . . there was *Vivien Oakland*, playing rowdy ladies in small parts in Joe E. Brown and Slim Sum-

NANCE O'NEIL in *The Royal Bed*

ZELMA O'NEAL, Nancy Carroll in *Follow Through*

merville features and in any number of comedy shorts
. . . And a nod to a few more—*Ottola Nesmith, June Nash, Marguerite Namara, Gertrude Norman, Hattie Noel, Patsy O'Byrne, Nell O'Day, Shirley O'Hara, Patsy O'Connor, Maureen O'Connor.*

JANE NOVAK

ANNA Q. NILSSON, Babe Ruth in *Babe Comes Home*

ANNE NAGEL, Ross Alexander in *Here Comes Carter*

ANITA PAGE

a great deal to do except to cluck sympathetically when something happened to one of her sisters.

Miss Page came to the screen from radio, where her well-modulated voice was familiar. Besides the "Daughters" pictures, she had film roles in several other movies, but there was always an Ann Sheridan or Claire Trevor to take the attention while Miss Page performed capably in the background. Still, it was always good to see her dark eyes smiling in a heart-shaped face.

CECILIA PARKER

You were apt to see Cecilia Parker carrying on adolescent romances with Eric Linden, most notably in *Ah, Wilderness.* She and Linden, who must have been the most unexciting romantic team of the period, went into other pictures—*In His Steps, Old Hutch* and *A Family Affair.* The latter was the first film in what became the Hardy Family series. Linden did not return for future installments, but Miss Parker found a home with the Hardys.

She was Andy Hardy's sister, Marion, a thankless part. Cecilia just had to sort of hang around while Andy had all those big-time love bouts, and all those heart-to-heart talks with Judge Hardy.

JEAN PARKER

Jean Parker seemed made to order for the most sentimental—sometimes maudlin—movie yarns. Does Apple Annie have a daughter who thinks her mother is in society? She does—and it's Jean. Is there an orphan to be helped by some Runyon characters? A high school girl whose mother doesn't tell her? A cripple having a sterile romance with a Good Humor man? Parker parts, all of them (in *Lady for a Day, Princess O'Hara, What Price Innocence?, Have a Heart,* respectively). And of the four *Little Women,* she would be Beth, wasting away to a sweet, sad death.

There were some healthy, happy times. She was an American heiress in Scotland to buy an old castle and romantically involved with its dour owner and the dashing ghost of his great grandparent, both delightfully Robert Donat, in *The Ghost Goes West.* Nor was she her usual pinch-cheeked self when she romped with a puma and a deer in the beautiful nature film, *Sequoia.* But by the end of the decade, she had slipped into action programmers and Laurel and Hardy comedies.

HELEN PARRISH

Helen Parrish had child and adolescent bits all through the thirties but it wasn't until the end of the decade that she won more than passing notice. Then it was for playing disagreeable types—as a socialite with Deanna Durbin in *First Love* and as the spoiled sister of Ann Sheridan in *Winter Carnival.* Thereafter, only unimportant films for Miss Parrish, although

ANITA PAGE

Anita Page, with wide eyes under slanted straight-line eyebrows, played most of the standard roles for a blonde romantic interest that were not already taken at her studio by Leila Hyams (Miss Page was a considerably gaudier blonde than Miss Hyams, but not as competent an actress).

After her first splash in the silent *Our Dancing Daughters* we saw her as one of *Our Modern Maidens* and *Our Blushing Brides.* She was the naughty sister in *Broadway Melody* and the naughty nurse in *War Nurse* . . . the daughter of either Marie Dressler or Polly Moran in several of their sagas . . . the sweetheart of such diverse types as John Gilbert, William Haines and Buster Keaton. Finally, becoming inclined toward plumpness, she was supporting fresher blondes —Constance Bennett and Marian Marsh.

GALE PAGE

You know Gale Page—she's the one who wasn't a Lane sister. Miss Page was Emma Lemp in *Four Daughters* (the other Lemps were Lanes) and she joined the group again in *Daughters Courageous* and *Four Wives.* Emma Lemp, unfortunately, didn't have

GALE PAGE, with Gladys George, in *A Child is Born*

CECILIA PARKER (right) with the other members of the Hardy Family, Fay Holden, Mickey Rooney, Lewis Stone

JEAN PARKER, Tom Brown in *Two Alone*

HELEN PARRISH, Ann Sheridan in *Winter Carnival*

JEAN PARKER in *Sequoia*

she was a competent, pretty brunette. But when you're snotty to Deanna Durbin, what can you expect?

PAT PATERSON

Pat Paterson was a brisk British blonde whose initial American picture, *Bottoms Up*, received thumbs down. Not through any fault of Pat's, let's quickly say—even Spencer Tracy couldn't save it. Even less worthy, believe it or not, were her others—*Call It Luck, Lottery Lover, Love Time, Spendthrift, 52nd Street* and *Charlie Chan in Egypt*. And in *Idiot's Delight*, Pat only had a bit.

Her American movie career was somewhat less than spectacular; still, millions of movie-struck girls envied her. For offscreen, you see, she married Charles Boyer.

GAIL PATRICK

Gale Page was the dark and comely nice girl, Gail Patrick the dark and vivid not-so-nice one. Although Miss Patrick had her occasional innings as a leading woman, you were much more apt to find her as a vampish type—although with too much humor to be sultry.

If Miss Patrick were pitted against a blonde like Joan Bennett or Ida Lupino or Carole Lombard, you just knew that the blonde would win out every time. But not before Gail gave them some anxious moments. (And we always pulled for her.)

Miss Patrick came to the movies as a finalist in "The Panther Woman" contest. She didn't play "The Panther Woman"—Kathleen Burke did that—but Gail did very well on her own, as she moved through roles being downright vicious to the blondes who crossed her path.

Actually she could not have been more charming in the role for which we best remember her—as the Hollywood glamour girl who has an adolescent daughter (Deanna Durbin) hidden away in a school in Switzerland, in *Mad About Music*. But in her other best roles—Carole Lombard's snobbish sister in *My Man Godfrey* and the opportunistic actress in *Stage Door*—she was her usual unpleasant self.

ELIZABETH PATTERSON

That dearest of crotchety old ladies, Elizabeth Patterson, fussed her way through several dozen pictures in the thirties. Usually she turned up as Aunt Somebody or Grandma Somebodyelse. Occasionally, she had a role to remember. Our favorite was as the worried mother of shiftless Bing Crosby in *Sing, You Sinners*; but you may select the frightened lady of Bob Hope's *The Cat and the Canary* or its earlier talkie version, *The Cat Creeps* . . . Wallace Beery's long-suffering wife in *Old Hutch* . . . or one of the aunts—a regular character, in the *Bulldog Drummond* series . . . or the

PAT PATERSON, with Nils Asther, in *Love Time*

lovable one in *Remember the Night* . . . the righteous one—a departure from her comfortable small town types—in *A Bill of Divorcement* (we felt her badly miscast in that) . . . or more routine Patterson roles, as in *So Red the Rose*, *Small Town Girl* or *Go West, Young Man.*

JOAN PEERS

We never understood why the career of Joan Peers went nowhere. She seemed to have had at least the potential of someone like Jean Parker or Dorothy Jordan. She was their type, and was lovely as the convent-bred daughter of the frowsy burlesque belle in *Applause.* Her hillbilly girl in *Tol'able David* was nicely played, too. But, for the rest, she had only secondary roles in comedies with Buster Keaton, Joe Cook and the team known as the Two Black Crows. And that was about it for Joan Peers.

BARBARA PEPPER

King Vidor's *Our Daily Bread* was a striking film, badly flawed by a heavy-handed and gratuitous subplot, involving Barbara Pepper as a rather seedy sex object. Miss Pepper, a voluptuous blonde, subsequently showed up in the kind of bits in which she was billed down toward the bottom of the cast as "Blonde" or "Girl in Bar." By the end, Miss Pepper was still showing up in bits, finally identified as "Fat Lady."

DOROTHY PETERSON

Dorothy Peterson made her bow as one of the most miserable mothers in movie history. In *Mothers Cry*, she had four children—all of whom turned out badly. Miss Peterson was the most stolid of sufferers and she had plenty of chance to prove it over the next many years. Only occasionally would she vary the pattern, to play an efficient nurse for example (she took care of the Dionne Quintuplets in their movies).

She was one of the most familiar character actresses of the whole period. When you saw Dorothy Peterson coming on the screen, you were fairly sure of heavy going ahead. Probably her strangest role was that of the psychopathic patient who keeps wandering into the maternity ward in *Life Begins.*

MARY PICKFORD

Mary Pickford, shorn of the famous ringlets for the occasion, entered talking pictures with a screen version of *Coquette*, which had served Helen Hayes so well on the stage. Miss Pickford was admirable in a different role but the production was not, being alternately static and, particularly in the performance of John Sainpolis, who hammed atrociously, melodramatic. Even so, Miss Pickford won an Academy Award.

MARY PICKFORD, in *Taming of the Shrew*

GAIL PATRICK, with Jack Benny, in *Artists and Models*

GAIL PATRICK, with Ricardo Cortez, in *Her Husband Lies*

ELIZABETH PATTERSON, with Fred MacMurray, Bing Crosby, Donald O'Connor in *Sing You Sinners*

JOAN PEERS, with Richard Cromwell, in *Tol'able David*

BARBARA PEPPER

DOROTHY PETERSON, Charles Laughton in *Payment Deferred*

199

MARY PICKFORD, with Leslie Howard, Russell Simpson, in *Secrets*

ZASU PITTS, Charles Laughton in *Ruggles of Red Gap*

She was more the Mary we had known and loved in her next, even if it was a Shakespearean role, *The Taming of the Shrew*, "by William Shakespeare. Additional dialogue by Sam Taylor." Whether speaking the lines of Mr. Shakespeare or Mr. Taylor, Miss Pickford was animated and a worthy match for the Petruchio of Douglas Fairbanks.

Kiki presented Our Mary as a gamine of Paris, and while she was thoroughly winsome, the picture was pretty bad. Bad enough that she waited two years before her next, *Secrets*, one of those episodic dramas which had echoes of *Cimarron* and other such pictures, in which a well-born Eastern girl must face the hardships of life in the pioneer West.

That was the end of Mary Pickford's career as a screen star (she then turned to production) but she remains one of the Greats—"America's Sweetheart," the little girl who brought such joy to the screen—the first real international superstar.

NOVA PILBEAM

With apologies to every child actress who ever stepped onto the screen, we hereby state that the best performance ever given by one was that of a now virtually forgotten British youngster, Nova Pilbeam. The picture was *Little Friend*, and that film and most of her others have been long unavailable.

Americans saw Nova Pilbeam only three times as a child. Of the few pictures she made as a young leading woman, only one—Hitchcock's *The Girl Was Young*—is worth mentioning in any review of her performances.

She was fourteen when she played Felicity in *Little Friend*. It was a story of divorce told through the eyes of a youngster, old enough to grasp what is happening, too young to comprehend the circumstances. She was a remarkably plain little girl in an era when screen children were all curls and dimples. But in her desperate anguish which drove her to the brink of suicide, she was almost beautiful.

She gave another superb performance two years later as Lady Jane Grey, the pawn of royal intrigue, in *Nine Days a Queen*, certainly one of the most distinguished historical dramas ever filmed. And she appeared for Hitchcock twice—as the kidnaped child in the first version of *The Man Who Knew Too Much* and in *The Girl Was Young*, the most underrated of his British thrillers.

Nova Pilbeam is just an odd name to movie fans today, but we'll wager that nobody who saw *Little Friend* or *Nine Days a Queen* has ever forgotten her.

ZASU PITTS

ZaSu Pitts was one of the superlative dramatic actresses of the silent screen. Erich von Stroheim, for whom she created her stunning *Greed* characterization

200

ZASU PITTS, Roy D'Arcy in *Sing and Like It*

NOVA PILBEAM in *Little Friend*

NOVA PILBEAM in *Nine Days a Queen*

201

ZASU PITTS, Lew Ayres in the unreleased (it was refilmed) sequence of *All Quiet on the Western Front*

LOUISE PLATT (foreground) in *Stagecoach* with (from left) Andy Devine, George Bancroft, John Carradine, Donald Meek, Claire Trevor, John Wayne

LILY PONS, with Gene Raymond, Lucille Ball, in *That Girl From Paris*

MARIE PREVOST (right) with Helen Hayes in *The Sin of Madelon Claudet*

ELEANOR POWELL, Nelson Eddy in *Rosalie*

and another in *The Wedding March*, was only one authority who felt that.

Then came the talkies. And the flat, woebegone accents of ZaSu's voice plus the already established mournful face added up to laughter, not tears. This new ZaSu Pitts image was quickly set in such early talkies as *Honey* and *The Dummy* and she added to it. The eyes grew wider, the voice more doleful, the hands ever more aimlessly waving.

There were tries at re-establishing her dramatic potential. But at the first screening of *All Quiet on the Western Front*, audiences hooted at her deathbed scene and her scenes were re-shot with Beryl Mercer, more the conventional old mother. And von Stroheim cast ZaSu as a psychopathic girl in *Walking Down Broadway*, but he was fired from the film. In the process, the Pitts role was converted into just another of her comedy spinsters.

So it became total commitment to people like Thelma Todd in short comedies and Slim Summerville in features. There was an unending stream of Pitts movies—up to the end of the thirties alone, she made around seventy talking pictures, not counting the short comedies. Sometimes it seemed like too much of a good thing.

Even so, she usually could stir up amusement even in her most thankless roles. There are several that still remain in the memory. Among them we'd list the super genteel receptionist of *Once in a Lifetime*, the dotty Miss Hazy in a frantic romance with W. C. Fields (*Mrs. Wiggs of the Cabbage Patch*), the lady love of Charles Laughton in *Ruggles of Red Gap*, a dreadfully inept singing lady in *Sing and Like It*, and any number of other maids and maiden ladies.

LOUISE PLATT

For all we know, Louise Platt may have been a teenager when she played the role, but she seemed neither young nor volatile enough to be a college girl with a crush on her professor in *I Met My Love Again*. She was more satisfactorily cast in *Spawn of the North*, *Tell No Tales* and *Stagecoach*, in which she was the pregnant wife.

LILY PONS

With Miss Grace Moore having proved that movie audiences would sit still and listen to operatic arias, the influx was on. Most prestigious import from the Met was Lily Pons. She was also petite, with oversized brown eyes and a fresh-from-Paree accent.

Her first film, *I Dream Too Much*, wasn't bad at all —well, it was "cute," with romantic comedy scenes for tiny Lily and tall Henry Fonda. But *That Girl From Paris* was trivial farce, and by the time she got to *Hitting a New High*, it was a low for Lily and quite a good reason for her to shake the sands of Hollywood

AILEEN PRINGLE

from her shoes and travel back to her own world.

By that time, Hollywood had decided that divas must be "humanized." So they had Grace Moore belting out "Minnie the Moocher" and they plunged poor Miss Pons into stupid slapstick, making her pretend to be some kind of tweet-tweeting bird girl.

But the songs she gave us—from Jerome Kern to *Lakme* and *Lucia*—made the movies almost worth it.

ELEANOR POWELL

Eleanor Powell had a big, wide smile with lots and lots of teeth. She also had long, extremely functional legs. Those legs were made for dancing.

Her acting was somewhere in between the abilities of Dixie Dunbar and Ruby Keeler. She sang a little but not so you'd remember it. But how that girl could tap dance!

The story lines in her pictures were just that—story lines on which to hang a profusion of musical numbers. There were talented back-up people in her casts—Frances Langford, Judy Garland, Sophie Tucker, Jack Benny, Buddy Ebsen, Gracie Allen. There were leading men like Jimmy Stewart, Robert Taylor and Nelson Eddy. And there were songs by Cole Porter or Arthur Freed and Nacio Herb Brown—songs like "Easy to Love," "I've Got You Under My Skin," "In the Still of the Night," "You Are My Lucky Star." And Eleanor would sit by while Frances or Nelson or Judy sang them. And eventually it would be her turn.

And then it would be "Broadway Rhythm" or "Rap Tap on Wood" or something like that. And Eleanor would smile her big smile, shake her shapely legs and beat out her amazing percussion. Then—whether it was in her *Broadway Melody* pictures or *Born to Dance*, where it was all enjoyment, or in something like *Rosalie* or *Honolulu*, where it was anything but—during the Eleanor Powell tap times, all was right with the movie.

MARIE PREVOST

Marie Prevost moved from the beaches of the Sennett bathing beauties to the boudoirs of a cute French maid in the silents. By talkie time, with some extra weight, she became one of the earlier talkie toughies—usually one with a heart of mush (as distinguished from such girls as Wynne Gibson and Marjorie Rambeau whose hearts were more apt to be flint). Miss Prevost was a buddy of Joan Crawford's in *Paid*, Barbara Stanwyck's in *Ladies of Leisure*, Helen Hayes' in *Sin of Madelon Claudet*, Carole Lombard's in *Hands Across the Table* and performed similarly with several other actresses.

AILEEN PRINGLE

Aileen Pringle lolled on tigerskins in *Three Weeks* and shared some domestic farces with Lew Cody before movies talked. Publicity on her private life always dealt with her wit and intelligence. Unfortunately little of either showed in her few talkies. They were shoddy mysteries for the most part, with Miss Pringle such an obvious suspect (*Subway Express, Murder at Midnight, Phantom of Crestwood,* etc.) that you knew she couldn't be guilty. She also played a few social "other women" (*Puttin' on the Ritz, Unguarded Hour*), but by the end of the thirties, her roles were the kind that are designated in the character list merely as "Saleslady."

ELEANOR POWELL in *Born to Dance* publicity still

KATE PRICE   ANN PENNINGTON   LILLI PALMER, Peter Lorre in *Secret Agent*

JUNE PREISSER, Mickey Rooney in *Strike Up the Band*

NOTES ON OTHER "P" LADIES

There are some other "P" ladies who rate a note in passing. *Lilli Palmer*, a late bloomer, was in *Secret Agent* and *Silent Barriers* with no more than a flicker of notice. *Lee Patrick* would have more to do in the forties, too. She did have a good moment in *The Sisters* as a kind-hearted prostitute but her other movie roles of the thirties were bits.

Mary Phillips was Helen Hayes' stern nurse friend in *A Farewell to Arms* and *Irene Purcell* was Robert Montgomery's leading lady in *The Man in Possession* but their few other movie roles were unremarkable.

Tempe Piggott had only minutes as the guzzling charwoman of *Seven Days' Leave* (screen version of Barrie's *Old Lady Shows Her Medals*), but they tickled you. She turned up all through the thirties whenever a cockney bit was needed.

And *Kate Price* carciatured stout Irish ladies as she had much more frequently in the silent era. *Daphne Pollard*, the pint-size comic, was another holdover from the silents, less active in talkies but still showing up in short comedies.

Also from the silents, where they had played leads, were *Mary Philbin* and *Eileen Percy*, but each had only minor talking picture appearances.

Phyllis Povah repeated her stage supporting role as the perpetually pregnant member of *The Women*. And *June Preisser* also came in from the stage for a perky supporting part in *Babes in Arms*.

Ann Pennington still had the famous dimpled knees

IRENE PURCELL, with William Haines, in *Just a Gigolo*

DAPHNE POLLARD, Kathryn Stanley in *The Girl From Everywhere*

LEE PATRICK (right) with Bette Davis in *The Sisters*

PHYLLIS POVAH (right) with Rosalind Russell, Norma Shearer in *The Women*

but, by the time she made such talkies as *Tanned Legs* and *Gold Diggers of Broadway* her day was pretty well over. Also better known to Broadway was *Margaret Perry*, who had the lead in *New Morals For Old*. *Joan Perry* was another in later thirties films like *Good Girls Go to Paris* and *Meet Nero Wolfe*.

There were *Sarah Padden*, a particularly ponderous character woman . . . *Rosamond Pinchot*, who was very grand indeed as the Queen in the Walter Abel *Three Musketeers* . . . *The Peters Sisters*, three bulky singing ladies who contributed a great deal to *Ali Baba Goes To Town* and *Love and Hisses* . . .

As she had in the theatre, *Marguerita Padula* sang "Hallelujah" in the first movie version of *Hit the Deck* . . . *Dorothy Page* was rather a routine leading lady in *King Solomon of Broadway* . . . and a nod to *Inez Palange, Mary Parker, Gigi Parrish, Patsy Lee Parsons, Sally Payne, Adele Pearce, Lillian Porter, Linda Perry, Ann Preston, Natalie Paley, Virginia Pine, Grace Poggi, Nanci Price, Shirley Palmer, Lucille Powers, Helena Phillips, Yvonne Pelletier, Kathryn Perry, Virginia Pearson* and *Elsa Petersen*.

MARY PHILLIPS, Adolphe Menjou, Blanche Frederici in *A Farewell to Arms*

LUISE RAINER, with Suzanna Kim, Paul Muni in *The Good Earth*

Q~R

JUANITA QUIGLEY

What ever happened to Baby Jane? No, she didn't grow up to be Bette Davis—at least, the Baby Jane of the thirties didn't. She did continue in films as a child and adolescent, under her real name, Juanita Quigley. But Baby Jane she was, as Claudette Colbert's child in *Imitation of Life* and in *The Man Who Reclaimed His Head* and *Straight From the Heart*. Far from ending up like Bette's Jane, she left films to enter a convent and became a nun. She later left the convent to marry.

LUISE RAINER

Luise Rainer just about broke your heart as the inarticulate O-lan in *The Good Earth*. As the Chinese peasant in the extraordinarily impressive film version of Pearl Buck's novel, she was pathetic, even tragic. "Inarticulate" may be the key word. There was only slight hint of the copyrighted Rainer mannerisms here, and it was a beautiful performance.

It gave her no chance for the usual tricks—the choke, ever ready in her voice . . . the little tearful giggle . . . the ever-rolling eyes with their instant tears. They were rather winning the first time you saw them (in *Escapade*) and even when she was sobbing and

sniggering through her "Hello, Flo" telephone scene in *The Great Ziegfeld*.

But what a bore they would become in her succession of following pictures—*Big City, The Emperor's Candlesticks, The Toy Wife, The Great Waltz* and *Dramatic School*. She played different roles in these—an immigrant in New York or an international spy or a dedicated drama student. She was Poldi, a Viennese sweetheart, and Frou-Frou, a New Orleans coquette. Different roles—but, as played by Miss Rainer, all exactly the same. Even with two Academy Awards, her screen career evaporated within four years.

Yet never forget that she was a perfect O-lan—and O-lan has a high spot in the gallery of never-to-be-forgotten characters brought to the world by the movies.

JESSIE RALPH

Jessie Ralph was an actress who specialized in roles, mostly small, which ran the gamut from charwomen to charter members of the Four Hundred. They had one thing in common—they were all hearty old girls.

Probably because the pictures are the best remembered, you'll identify her immediately as Garbo's faithful maid, Nanine, in *Camille* . . . as Nurse Peggotty, fiercely devoted to *David Copperfield* . . . as the Nob Hill social leader who hadn't lost the common touch, in *San Francisco*. She was also the century-old matriarch of the Whiteoak family in *Jalna* and contributed to such other films as *The Good Earth, After the Thin Man, Drums Along the Mohawk, The Last of Mrs. Cheyney* and a few dozen others.

ESTHER RALSTON

Esther Ralston was a wholesome golden blonde in silents. But after a couple of routine leading-lady roles in talkies, Paramount let her go in the purge that dropped most of their silent contract players.

Miss Ralston then decided to go in for platinum glamour. She got a few roles that fitted the new look, went to England for *Rome Express*, returned to briefly steal Gene Raymond away from Joan Crawford in *Sadie McKee* and had a few others. The "new look" didn't change her personality, which remained overwhelmingly wholesome.

MARJORIE RAMBEAU

Marjorie Rambeau still had vestiges of her famous beauty when she came to the screen in 1930. But by then she was a character actress, specializing in the blowsiest of aging harlots and alcoholics in pictures like *Her Man, The Secret Six* and especially *Min and Bill*, in which she was a vicious waterfront slut eventually killed by Marie Dressler.

MGM used its contract players all the time in those days, so you would see Miss Rambeau in and out of a

JUANITA QUIGLEY, with Freddie Bartholomew

LUISE RAINER, Robert Young in *The Toy Wife*

LUISE RAINER, William Powell in *The Great Zieg-feld*

ESTHER RALSTON

JESSIE RALPH, Freddie Bartholomew in *David Copperfield*

MARJORIE RAMBEAU, Marie Dressler in *Min and Bill*

great many movies—unrewarding roles in support of Garbo, Shearer, Crawford, Beery.

Pickings were better when she left the studio. She was a commanding Queen of the Amazons in *The Warrior's Husband* and was particularly touching as a derelict in *A Man's Castle*. There were other good roles in the thirties—in films like *Strictly Personal*, *Grand Canary* and *First Lady*.

But the best Rambeau screen roles were still to come, with almost two decades of movie work left to go.

MARJORIE RAMBEAU, with Loretta Young, Spencer Tracy, in *A Man's Castle*

MARTHA RAYE and Bob Hope in
College Swing

MARTHA RAYE and friend

DOROTHY REVIER, with Walter Huston, in *The Bad Man*

IRENE RICH, Will Rogers in
They Had to See Paris

FLORENCE RICE, Alan Marshal in
Four Girls in White

IRENE RICH, Deanna Durbin in
That Certain Age

MARTHA RAYE

Martha Raye parlayed an elastic mouth and a pair of bellows-like lungs into a career. But there was more to it than that. She was a boisterous comic who all too rarely had anything worthy of her abilities. Like all true clowns she could move you; but outside of a second or two in something like *Give Me a Sailor*, she didn't have much chance for that either.

Which left her singing—something for which she never got nearly enough credit, due principally to the fact that they gave her such terrible songs to sing. She'd have a tuneful number like "What Goes on Here in My Heart" occasionally, but usually they gave her novelty songs in a futile attempt to repeat her initial singing movie triumph. That was in her first picture, *Rhythm on the Range*, and Martha blasted out "Mr. Paganini." You can probably still hear its echoes.

Her pictures were enjoyable for their times—things like *College Holiday*, *College Swing*, and a couple of *Big Broadcasts*. She romped with Hope, Crosby, W. C. Fields, Bob Burns, Burns and Allen, and even matched mouths with Joe E. Brown. And not a one of them overshadowed her. How could they? Martha was the noisiest of them all.

DOROTHY REVIER

Dorothy Revier was a faithless blonde (faithless generally to Jack Holt) who showed up in quite a few pictures of the early thirties. She had the leading-lady role in *The Bad Man*, with Walter Huston, a not very good movie version of a popular play. Other than that, her pictures were mostly low-grade programmers. When she had a part in a movie you might remember (*Dance of Life*, *The Mighty*) the role was one to forget.

FLORENCE RICE

Florence Rice was the kind of serviceable leading lady who worked a lot but seldom in anything above the "B" level. She looked the way a leading lady should look, she was competent in the roles they gave her to do, but she never got out of the rut.

There was a moment where it looked as if it might happen. She and Melvyn Douglas played amateur detectives, Joel and Garda Sloane, in a comedy thriller, *Fast Company*. It was something of a "sleeper," a surprise hit, and it would seem that they had a chance of becoming a minor-league Powell and Loy. But with Joel and Garda looking so promising, MGM took the parts away from its "B" players and gave them to better established names, Robert Montgomery and Rosalind Russell. Miss Rice went back to her routine.

IRENE RICH

Svelte Irene Rich was a favorite in so-called "woman's pictures" through the twienties. Always given mature roles, she had graduated to maternal ones by the beginning of talkies. They were pretty ordinary—nothing so interesting as parts she had played in silents like *A Lost Lady*, *Craig's Wife* or *Lady Windermere's Fan*. Instead she was a typical nagging wife for Will Rogers in several of his pictures and played other mothers in pictures like *Five and Ten* and *The Champ*.

But if movies didn't appreciate her, another medium would. She became a very popular radio name—remember all those years when she was the Grape Juice Lady? At the end of the thirties, she returned to the screen to play Deanna Durbin's mother in *That Certain Age*. There would still be another decade of occasional appearances before her final retirement in the late forties.

ELISABETH RISDON

Elisabeth Risdon had one of those small half-smiles (Joan Fontaine has one—and Frieda Inescort) that stay on the face even during an emotional scene. With Miss Risdon, the smile was on when she was at her crankiest—and she could be very cranky, indeed. Witness her treatment of Victor Moore in *Make Way for Tomorrow*—not heartless, just harassed and unaware.

That was her best thirties role, although she may be remembered for *Crime and Punishment*, *Five Came Back*, *Theodora Goes Wild*, *Craig's Wife*, *Mad About Music* and *Huckleberry Finn*.

LYDA ROBERTI

Lyda Roberti, with her mop of blonde hair, was shapely, leggy and—if a role gave her half a chance—hilarious. She had a language-mangling voice that could raucously shout out a song like "Take a Number From One to Ten." She also had a thoroughly uninhibited approach to sexy comedy.

Most marvelously, she was Mata Machree, the international spy, in a delicious Garbo/Dietrich parody in *Million Dollar Legs*. But she was similarly unrestrained in *The Kid From Spain*, *College Rhythm*, *The Big Broadcast of 1936* and in some low-comedy Hal Roach romps with Patsy Kelly.

BEVERLY ROBERTS

Beverly Roberts, with short blonde hair and a peaches-and-cream complexion, was one of those efficient actresses that every studio kept around in the thirties. Sturdy enough to be believable as a logging-camp boss in an early Technicolor action melodrama, *God's Country and the Woman*, she also had good looks enough to serve as leading ladies for leading men who ranged from Errol Flynn to Boris Karloff. Most of her pictures were program melodramas is which she was frequently the most pleasing element.

FLORA ROBSON

Flora Robson, one of Britain's most distinguished actresses, was seen only five times on the screens of American theatres during the thirties. But each performance was flawless. We saw her as the violent Empress Elizabeth in *Catherine the Great*. She was the compassionate Ellen, the servant, through whose eyes the stormy love story of Heathcliff and Cathy is witnessed, in *Wuthering Heights*. She played a devoted wife in *Troopship*, one of those superpatriotic epics to which the British were partial.

There were two more towering portrayals. As Queen Elizabeth I in *Fire Over England*, she eloquently developed this most complex character—revealing all the vanity and frailty of the woman, never losing the great dignity of the queen.

And in *We Are Not Alone*, as the harsh, forbidding wife of Paul Muni, she presented a full-bodied characterization, even winning some understanding for the basically unsympathetic domestic tyrant.

MAY ROBSON

May Robson used to huff and puff and pretend to be gruff—but nobody was fooled for a minute. She was always first choice when the part called for an old curmudgeon, but even on those occasions when she played a crusty skinflint, you knew she was really a pussycat.

Her number one picture was Capra's *Lady for a Day*, in which she was Apple Annie, turned into a grande dame by a group of Runyon types. It could have been maudlin beyond belief, but Capra's touch and particularly Miss Robson's gritty performance made it one of the most entertaining fairy-tales of the day.

Lady by Choice was a shameless attempt to capitalize on the success of the Capra film and it wasn't nearly as good. But Miss Robson was, if possible, even better as an unregenerate aged reprobate.

Her other pictures—and there were a lot of them—ranged from such conventional parts as the Grandma in the *Four Daughters* series, the Gaynor *Star Is Born*, and *They Made Me a Criminal*; through her Aunt Polly in *The Adventures of Tom Sawyer*; to such pieces of miscastings as those which had her playing a farcical crone (in *The Kid From Kokomo*) and a Jewish mama (in *Straight Is the Way*).

ELIZABETH RISDON, with Marsia Mae Jones, Deanna Durbin, in *Mad About Music*

LYDA ROBERTI, Patsy Kelly in *Nobody's Baby*

BEVERLY ROBERTS

FLORA ROBSON, Clifford Jones in *Catherine the Great*

FLORA ROBSON, with Vivien Leigh, Laurence Olivier, in *Fire Over England*

GINGER ROGERS

Ginger Rogers came in two variations in the thirties—the flip redhead and the bubbling blonde. (A third brunette Miss Rogers—she who played dramatic girls like Kitty Foyle—wouldn't be along until the following decade.)

The first Ginger we knew—the redhead—was a good-time girl, perhaps a chorus girl (as in *42nd Street* or *Gold Diggers of 1933*) or the kind of willful flapper who might be named "Puff" and say things like "Cigarette me, big boy" (in her first movie, *Young Man of Manhattan*). She did a lot of pictures, even as leads (although her leading men were apt to be no more heart-throbby than Jack Oakie or Joe E. Brown). There was even one, *Professional Sweetheart*, in which she burlesqued the kind of dreamboat she herself would eventually become.

It was the second Ginger—blonde, gowned elaborately and fluffily coiffed and the pin-up of several million fraternity boys—over whom we flipped. She was gay and cheerful with a sugar-and-spice personality, a knowing way with a quip and an ever-increasing ability at comic characterization.

Flying Down to Rio was the film in which the two Gingers met. Still reddish of hair and secondary of role (Dolores Del Rio had the nominal lead), Ginger joined another lesser player—new boy for movies named Fred Astaire—in a dance called the Carioca. And they rollicked away with the picture.

From that point on, it was a movie team made in heaven. Forget the churls—hints from Mr. A., himself, among them—that Ginger's twinkletoes were perhaps no match for the nimble dancing feet of the gentleman. He may have been the genius of the duo, but we would not have traded in Ginger as his partner for Pavlova or Plisitskaya.

They played out their merry little mistaken-identity comedies with a blithe and airy ease. They sang, winningly, some of the best songs ever written by George Gershwin, Jerome Kern, Cole Porter, Vincent Youmans and Irving Berlin.

And they danced. How they danced! The Carioca and Continental and Yam. "Cheek to Cheek" . . . "Change Partners" . . . "Isn't This a Lovely Day" . . . "Lovely to Look At" . . . "Let's Face the Music and Dance" . . . "Let Yourself Go" . . . The Maxixe and Castle Walk, as invented by Vernon and Irene, and polished up by Fred and Ginger . . . "Waltz in Swing Time" . . . "Shall We Dance?" . . . "I Won't Dance," "Never Gonna Dance," "Let's Call the Whole Thing Off." But they didn't call it off, praise be—not until the thirties were almost over. And by that time, Ginger was heading toward the third phase of her career—and we could go along with others for Fred.

If Astaire was almost completely tied to Ginger then, it didn't work that way with her. She was forever stepping out on her own—to play opposite William Powell in *Star of Midnight*, say, or Dick Powell in *20 Million Sweethearts*.

There was always a slightly abrasive edge to Ginger's personality and she used it in *Stage Door*, definitely holding her own against the competition of such caustic types as Misses Hepburn, Arden and Ball. Again, with the considerable assistance of director George Stevens, Jimmy Stewart, Beulah Bondi, and Charles Coburn, she took that cliché about the show girl marrying the professor and antagonizing his community and turned it into the vivacious *Vivacious Lady*.

Let's admit that *Having Wonderful Time* was a disaster—but not Ginger's disaster. And *Fifth Avenue Girl* came too long after *My Man Godfrey* to make any dent.

But for Ginger, to see out the thirties, there was still another absolutely irresistible performance. In Garson Kanin's *Bachelor Mother*, she was the carefree shopgirl who finds a baby and can't convince anybody it isn't hers. And if you think that sounds shopworn and contrived, you can't imagine the inventive treatment it got from Ginger—and Kanin, David Niven, Charles Coburn, Frank Albertson and the rest. It was Ginger, without her dancing shoes, entering the next decade as a full-fledged star—already up to the *Primrose Paths* and *Kitty Foyles* in her future. But that's another era, another Ginger.

MAY ROBSON, with Carol Lombard, Walter Connolly, in *Lady By Choice*

MAY ROBSON in *The Perfect Specimen*

SHIRLEY ROSS

Shirley Ross had made a few movies (she was the girl who lost her saloon job to Jeanette MacDonald in *San Francisco*, for instance) before she joined the Paramount musical stock company. Here she was much more in evidence, sharing duets and romances with Bing Crosby in *Waikiki Wedding* and *Paris Honeymoon*, and appearing in other fluffs.

Most pleasantly, she teamed with Bob Hope in her second *Big Broadcast* musical, the '38 version. They sang a ditty, "Thanks for the Memory," so successfully that they were immediately re-teamed for an enjoyable comedy titled, what else, *Thanks for the Memory*. They sang "Two Sleepy People" in that one. That meant a third teaming—in something called *Some Like It Hot* (no relation, unfortunately, to the Billy Wilder hit with Marilyn Monroe). After that, Miss Ross' movie career rather faded away, but she had been nice to have around for those few years.

LILLIAN ROTH

Lillian Roth had snapping black eyes and dimples and she added a great deal to such early movie musicals as *The Love Parade*, *Honey* and *The Vagabond King*. She had her time with the Marx Brothers, too (in *Animal Crackers*), and with Jack Oakie in *Sea Legs*.

But the first wave of movie musicals washed away

211

GINGER ROGERS, Norman Foster in *Young Man of Manhattan*

many of the players who appeared in them, Miss Roth among them, and nobody was thinking about her any more when musicals came back. She did get to sing Ethel Merman's old hit "Eadie Was a Lady," in the movie version of *Take a Chance*. Sang it very nicely, too—as she had sung such songs as "Sing You Sinners" and "Waltz Huguette" in earlier films. But *Take a Chance* was a shoestring musical which did nothing for her movie career.

So Miss Roth disappeared from the screen, not to be seen again for some twenty-odd years. Then, as played by Susan Hayward in *I'll Cry Tomorrow*, she let us know what had happened to her in that long intervening period.

ROSALIND RUSSELL

It took a long time for Rosalind Russell to become "Our Roz." Look through a list of her earliest movies and she was always some kind of willowy socialite with designs on Myrna's man, or Harlow's, or Colbert's.

Then came drama time, and Rosalind did some of the best. Varied, too. A glacial, fastidious *Craig's Wife* . . . another wife, devoted and idealistic, of Dr. Donat in *The Citadel* . . . a girl filled with loathing for, yet strangely fascinated by, the Irish charm boy she suspects may be a murderer in *Night Must Fall*. Fine performances—but funny? Not a bit.

GINGER ROGERS, James Stewart in *Vivacious Lady*

GINGER ROGERS in *Sitting Pretty*

212

GINGER ROGERS, Fred Astaire in *Top Hat*

LILLIAN ROTH, Dennis King in *The Vagabond King*

SHIRLEY ROSS, Bob Hope in *Some Like It Hot*

LILLIAN ROTH (right) with her sister, Ann, in *Sea Legs*

ROSALIND RUSSELL, Ronald Colman in *Under Two Flags*

Oh, she had traded cracks with William Powell in *Rendezvous* and everybody said she could be a threat to Myrna Loy. But Powell went right back to Myrna. And Rosalind got George Raft. It didn't seem quite fair. She was a good sparring partner for Robert Montgomery in a couple of his typical, lesser comedies—*Live, Love and Learn* and *Fast and Loose*, and there were glints of the Roz to come in supporting performances in *Man Proof* and *Four's a Crowd*. By that time, she was already noted for her off-screen nifties. For instance, in referring to a Beverly Hills church whose congregation was composed of upper-echelon Catholics, Miss R. named it "Our Lady of the Cadillacs."

But it was the great witch role of them all that turned the tide. Credit George Cukor for casting cool, calm Rosalind Russell as flamboyant, shrill Sylvia Fowler in *The Women*. Roz was devastating as she spun her poisonous little stories, casually and evilly wrecking a marriage here, a reputation there. Steel would melt in her mouth. And you wouldn't recognize well-bred Rosalind Russell in the screaming, hair-pulling fishwife brawl with Paulette Goddard, into which she entered wholeheartedly.

Then came *His Girl Friday* where she became the definitive Roz—a match for any man. It was *The Front Page* all over again, but because Hildy Johnson became a woman and because Walter Burns became Cary Grant, didn't mean they softened it. It was, if anything, even more impudent and irreverent than the original. And wasn't Roz a riot? And isn't she still?

ANN RUTHERFORD

Ann Rutherford had almost as little to do in the Hardy pictures as Cecilia Parker. Miss Rutherford was around to stamp her foot and look aggrieved while Andy pursued his current love. And she would kiss him chastely when he returned, disillusioned once again. Polly Benedict (that was Ann) never failed Andy, but she did grow a little petulant with him.

Other than as Polly, Miss Rutherford showed up here and there in small parts in pictures like *Of Human Hearts*, *Dramatic School*, *These Glamour Girls* and *Gone with the Wind*, in which she was one of Scarlett's selfish sisters.

214

ROSALIND RUSSELL, with Robert Montgomery, in *Night Must Fall*

ROSALIND RUSSELL, John Boles in *Craig's Wife*

ROSALIND RUSSELL, with Cary Grant, in *His Girl Friday*

ANN RUTHERFORD, with Mickey Rooney, in *Love Finds Andy Hardy*

215

RUTH ROLAND

VERA REYNOLDS

RENE RAY, Conrad Veidt in *The Passing of the Third Floor Back*

JOBYNA RALSTON, with Harold Lloyd, in *The Kid Brother*

JEAN ROGERS, with Buster Crabbe, Frank Shannon, in a *Flash Gordon* serial

FLORENCE REED, with Phillips Holmes, in *Great Expectations*

NOTES ON OTHER "Q, R" LADIES

Pleasant memory—a slim, dark beauty singing "Who's Afraid of Love?" and other songs in movies like *One in a Million*, *Wake Up and Live* and *Thin Ice*. *Leah Ray* had a few minor speaking parts, too (In *Holy Terror*, *Walking Down Broadway*, etc.) but it's the singing Leah who sticks in the mind.

Not such a pleasant memory—*Florence Reed*, a rather distinguished lady of the theatre, chewing scenery shamelessly as a frenzied Miss Havisham in the first talking picture version of *Great Expectations*.

Good memories, too, of *Jean Rouverol* as the insane girl ("I'm Carrie Flint—I've Come to Tea") in *Private Worlds* . . . of *Peggy Ryan*, a tap-dancing child in *Top of the Town*, who would become more prominent in the forties as a tap-dancing adolescent . . . of a girl we all liked in a number of films, although her roles were secondary, the pictures low-grade—*Jean Rogers* . . . of *Leona Roberts*, as a country crone in *Of Human Hearts* . . . of *Anne Revere*, moving in *Double Door*, although her best days would come in the next decade . . . of *Bodil Rosing*, as all of those bit-part Scandinavian and Teutonic mamas and nanas.

Not so good memories of some others—*Florence Roberts*, who was treacly, doddering granny in that dreadful *Jones Family* series . . . *Renie Riano*, a cartoon-type "comedienne" . . . *Tutta Rolf*, one of those imports who gave Garbo and Dietrich nary a worry in her bid, *Dressed to Thrill* . . . some silent actresses of minor note—*Vera Reynolds*, *Lillian Rich*, *Mona Rico*, *Fritzi Ridgeway*, *Nena Quartaro*—down to bits and

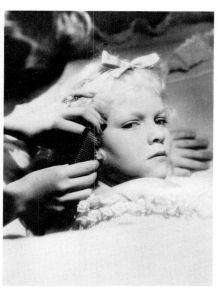

LLY RAND, with George Raft, in *blero*

MARIA RIVA (then Maria Sieber) as a child in her mother's (Marlene Dietrich) *Scarlet Empress*

LEAH RAY

FRANCOISE ROSAY, with Micheline Cheirel, in *Carnival in Flanders*

quickies in their few talkies . . . nor did *Ruth Roland, Jobyna Ralston, Alma Rubens* fare much better—each with only one or two dull talkie leads.

Others in the roundup—*Barbara Read,* the third of the *Three Smart Girls* (but overshadowed by Deanna) and a rebellious grand-daughter in *Make Way for Tomorrow* (but overshadowed by the old folks) . . . *Francoise Rosay,* whose one American film of the thirties, *The Magnificent Lie,* is noted only so that we can pay tribute to her brilliance in such French classics as *Carnival in Flanders, Un Carnet de Bal* and *Bizarre, Bizarre* . . . *Rene Ray,* of *The Passing of the Third Floor Back* . . . *Selena Royle,* only in one minor role (*Misleading Lady*) in this period but with many to come in the succeeding decade . . . *Eunice Quedens,* who had a part in a terrible picture, *Song of Love,* but would do better when she changed her name to Eve Arden . . . *Sally Rand,* waving her fans and speaking a few lines in *Bolero* . . . *Barbara Robbins* and *Polly Rowles,* good stage actresses but with little chance to show it on screen . . . *Marcia Ralston,* a brunette minor menace, and *Marjorie Reynolds,* a brunette minor lead—who would do a little better as a blonde in the forties . . . and *Marie Quillan, Lillian Randolph, Jayne Regan, Alicia Rhett* (a bit in *GWTW*), *Margaret Roach, Hedwig Reicher, Betty Jane Rhodes, Mary Alice Rice, Beatrice Roberts, Gloria Roy, Elizabeth Russell, Frances Rich, Margaret Quimby, Sandra Ravel, Manya Roberti, Rosalie Roy, Lynne Roberts, Frances Robinson, Mary Russell, Elsie Randolph.*

ALMA RUBENS

POLLY ROWLES

JEAN ROUVEROL in *Private Worlds* with Joan Bennett

217

DOROTHY SEBASTIAN, with Jack Benny, in *The Rounder*

DOROTHY SEBASTIAN

Dorothy Sebastian was just beginning to make it in silent pictures when talkies came along and spoiled it all. Not that Dorothy couldn't talk. But because she wasn't really yet established, she had to take what she could get in the new medium.

And what she could get were a couple of "friend" roles of a dominating Joan Crawford (in *Montana Moon, Our Blushing Brides*), several quickies with Bill Boyd, a couple more with Bert Lytell and Lloyd Hughes and finally something called *They Never Come Back*, a sadly prophetic title.

VIVIENNE SEGAL

Vivienne Segal was one of the reigning prima donnas of Broadway, but by the time she made it to the movies, operetta was a dirty word. Two of hers—*Golden Dawn* and *Song of the West*—would have been failures under any circumstances. You couldn't fault Miss Segal's looks or voice, but she couldn't do much for either of them, or for *Bride of the Regiment* and *Viennese Nights* which, if not very good either, were at least bearable.

Four years later, she returned for another movie

operetta, *The Cat and the Fiddle*, but this was before MacDonald and Eddy started the vogue again. Besides, the picture was poor and Miss Segal's role was unimportant. So she went back to the theatre, where before too long she would be "Bewitched" by "Pal Joey." That was more like it.

PEGGY SHANNON

Peggy Shannon was one of the girls (Sylvia Sidney was the other) who were introduced to the screen as replacements for an ailing Clara Bow. Miss Shannon had the beauty of a Follies girl, which she had been— shapely, with red hair, large brown eyes and a tip- tilted nose. Unfortunately, her personality and acting ability remained those of a showgirl.

Still she was extremely easy to look at, and as long as she didn't have to worry about performance, she decorated pictures like *The Secret Call, Touchdown, Society Girl*, and *Night Life of the Gods* very prettily indeed. But she was down to bits by the end of the thirties.

WINIFRED SHAW

Winifred Shaw, sometimes known as Wini, was a voluptuous brunette with a torchy voice. And, although she got quite a few acting roles (*Satan Met a Lady, Broadway Hostess, Case of the Velvet Claws*, etc.) it was really for that voice that she was known.

And that voice got her three very special songs— "Lullaby of Broadway," "The Lady in Red" and "Too Marvelous for Words," all from pictures (*Gold Diggers of 1935, In Caliente, Ready, Willing and Able*) in which the songs were the only worthy elements.

The girl who sang those songs—that's the Wini Shaw for our memory book.

NORMA SHEARER

She was a dandy Norma Shearer, but why did she have to be Lynn Fontanne, Katharine Cornell and Gertrude Lawrence, too? Miss Shearer, who had been an intelligent ingenue in the silent days, moved into other fields with talkies. With her patrician profile, she was hardly the type for flapper roles—and besides Miss Crawford had those sewed up at MGM. So Shearer pushed back her hair in a distinctive coiffure, got herself a wardrobe of rather daring Adrian gowns, added a little shady to the lady, and moved into a series of dramas about adultery, and such diversions, among the upper-crust. There were *The Divorcee, A Free Soul, Strangers May Kiss, Riptide, Their Own Desires* and *Let Us Be Gay*. In all of them, Miss Shearer played the typical Norma Shearer character— the emancipated woman, disillusioned by love or marriage and turning to all manner of hi-jinks, usually in the company of a cocktail-shaking playboy like Robert Montgomery.

She also reverted to the kind of role she used to play in silents in the famous old tearjerker *Smilin' Through*, and was quite lovely as both the modern Kathleen and the shimmering ghost of Moonyeen Claire.

Just about everybody has played *Private Lives*, most of them less than adequately. Let's say Miss Shearer was adequate, if temperamentally unsuited for all of her pretty rough-housing with Robert Montgomery, who was so blithe and smooth that he only pointed up the fact that comedy was not Miss Shearer's bag.

The "First Lady" roles were starting. You could discount the failure of *Strange Interlude* because, with several hours trimmed from the Eugene O'Neill original, it became just another Norma Shearer problem drama.

But then there was *The Barretts of Wimpole Street*, in which Miss Shearer was only sickly, without any hint of strong emotion, reciting her lines while everybody from Charles Laughton and Fredric March to Maureen O'Sullivan and Una O'Connor acted rings around her.

And there was *Romeo and Juliet*. Miss Shearer had once done the balcony scene with John Gilbert in *Hollywood Revue*, and their hopeless attempts to master the Bard were excused by the knowledge that the whole picture was meant to be just like a high school senior play.

But *Romeo and Juliet* was a worthy project, hand-

PEGGY SHANNON

WINI SHAW

NORMA SHEARER, with Tyrone Power, in *Marie Antoinette*

VIVIENNE SEGAL in *Golden Dawn*

somely mounted and with people like John Barrymore and Edna May Oliver quite satisfactorily Shakespearean. Leslie Howard may have been a bit mature for Romeo, which could be forgiven, but his performance was unutterably strained and theatrical. Miss Shearer, however, looked remarkably girlish and, if her performance lacked inspiration, she managed to get through it all very well.

But in *Marie Antoinette*, she was back playing the same old Norma Shearer role except that she wore a powdered wig, and high society was Versailles.

There are actresses who could have played the mysterious lady of *Idiot's Delight* with something approaching the mocking sophistication of Lynn Fontanne—but Miss Shearer wasn't one of them. She was land-locked in a role that called for the airiest of approaches. Clark Gable managed more successfully—no Lunt he, but not afraid to be himself.

Finally, finishing out the thirties, there was a Shearer to please everyone. She was the good, respect-

219

NORMA SHEARER, with Fredric March, in *The Barretts of Wimpole Street*

NORMA SHEARER, with Clark Gable, in *Idiot's Delight*

NORMA SHEARER, with Leslie Howard, in *Romeo and Juliet*

220

able woman of *The Women* to start out with—which is the way those Shearer characters always started. But she turned quite satisfactorily savage when exposed to the bitchery of such past mistresses as Joan Crawford and Rosalind Russell.

ANN SHERIDAN

Ann Sheridan was around the movie world from 1933, and here are samples of roles she played—a minute in *Behold My Wife*, a bit in *The Crusades*, minor parts in pictures like *The Black Legion, Cowboy from Brooklyn, Letter of Introduction, They Made Me a Criminal* and bigger ones in others. But try and remember those others—*She Loved a Fireman, Footloose Heiress, Alcatraz Island, Patient in Room 18*, for some for instances.

She did have leading-lady credit in *Angels With Dirty Faces*, but with James Cagney, Pat O'Brien, Humphrey Bogart and the Dead End Kids also there, there wasn't much footage for Ann. And it went on that way—*Dodge City, Naughty But Nice, Indianapolis Speedway*.

Then some clever publicist—probably Charlie Einfeld, or maybe it was Robert Taplinger—saw some gallery stills taken of her. They had "oomph," he decided, and, presto, "The Oomph Girl" was born.

"The Oomph Girl" was still being brushed off in the movies, but what a commotion those pictures caused in the newspapers and magazines! So, canny Walter Wanger borrowed her from Warners, latching on to the label, and cast her in a part to correspond. The picture was *Winter Carnival*—yes, the same one that you know about if you are students of F. Scott Fitzgerald and Budd Schulberg. It was pretty terrible, too, but it did show off Ann Sheridan as the kind of glamour girl her publicity had been insisting she was.

And it opened the doors for better Sheridan roles in the 1940s.

ANNE SHIRLEY

Anne Shirley received her screen name from that of the character she played in *Anne of Green Gables*. Previously, she had been Dawn O'Day, a dark-eyed youngster who had small roles in several pictures. The name switch was a good move because Anne Shirley, the actress, was so tender and true as Anne Shirley, the character, that they really became one.

Miss Shirley was a whimsical and winsome Anne, the orphan with an overdeveloped sense of the romantic and dramatic who comes to be adopted by a crabby, childless couple who had expected a boy who could help on the farm. Unlike most of its type, neither the picture nor Miss Shirley's performance were ever cloying or coy.

But RKO, which is to be thanked for bringing us Miss Shirley, must be censured for what they did to

ANN SHERIDAN, Humphrey Bogart in *It All Came True*

ANN SHERIDAN, with James Cagney, Pat O'Brien, in *Angels With Dirty Faces*

ANNE SHIRLEY

her after that. What they did was cast her as a series of similar adolescents in program quickies (*Chatterbox, M'liss, Make Way For a Lady,* etc.) and as a leading lady in claptrap like *Meet the Missus* and *Law of the Underworld.*

There was one exception. RKO loaned out Miss Shirley to Samuel Goldwyn to play Laurel, the sensitive daughter of the slatternly Stella Dallas. This was a beautifully gentle study of a greatly loving daughter struggling to control her aversion to her mother's crudities. One shot of the terrible concern in her eyes as she hears girls making fun of her mother, knowing that her mother is in the next Pullman berth and must be hearing it, too, is as piercing as anything in that venerable tear-jerker.

Anne Shirley would have some more good moments before she finished her screen career in the forties. But they never gave her any chance to live up to the potential she exhibited in *Anne of Green Gables* and *Stella Dallas.*

ANN SHOEMAKER

If only for that priceless performance as Alice Adams' worried mother, the name of Ann Shoemaker must go into the annals. Miss Shoemaker appeared in quite a number of other movies, but with nothing to do worth mentioning. But how affectionate, how eager she was in *Alice Adams,* and how perceptive of George Stevens to realize how, rather than a better-known actress, she would be so absolutely right.

SYLVIA SIDNEY

Sylvia Sidney was doomed to suffer in the slums. Or in prison. Or, perhaps, in the backwoods. Let others walk their rocky road in penthouses—despairing in their Adrian negligees because they were only mistresses and not wives. When Sidney was afflicted, there were no glamour gowns—she was hungry, unjustly accused, physically deprived. Her man was gone, her brother was wild on the streets, her baby would be born in misery.

Not for her the trembling chin, the glycerine-brimming eye. When Sidney had troubles, you knew it. Nobody had a more expressive face. She didn't hold back. The cries, the tears were authentic.

Every so often, that exquisite heart that was her face would light up with the most sudden and the most captivating smile in the world. Nothing was more joyous than the smile of Sylvia Sidney.

She was probably the screen's finest emotional actress—vibrant, earthy, poignant, passionate. (Nobody kissed quite as passionately but, of course, she had those lips, full and soft.)

She had a delicious comic touch, too, but they almost never let you experience it. In *Thirty Day Princess* perhaps and an occasional moment or two in *Merrily We Go to Hell* and *Accent on Youth.* These, concidentially, were also the only pictures of the era that showed her off on the screen as she was known in real life—as a modish "best-dressed woman," who later discovered her own designer (Michael Woulfe) and loaned him out to other stars.

But mostly she played truly tragic girls—even to such cliché characters as poor little Cio Cio San, yearning for her lost American, in *Madame Butterfly* . . . the Indian bride snooted by her rich in-laws in *Behold My Wife* . . . Dreiser's *Jennie Gerhardt,* coming so late in the cycle that she became just another "back street" sweetheart . . . the girl who loves the campus Casanova (*Confessions of a Coed*) . . . the cynical crook converted by *The Miracle Man.* These —along with such as *Pick Up* and *Good Dame*—were pretty bad movies. But nobody faulted the sincerity of a Sidney performance even when the roles seemed hardly worth playing.

Many of them were made by hack directors, too, but, when the right man was at the helm, the experience was significant. For Alfred Hitchcock, in *The Woman Alone* she was the numbed, dazed wife exploding into violence . . . for Fritz Lang, the heartbreaking young girl fleeing desperately from the law (*You Only Live Once*) or the girl who can only look on in uncomprehending horror as a lynch mob fires a jail in which her sweetheart is held (*Fury*) . . . for William K. Howard, an escaped prisoner, trying to build a new life (*Mary Burns, Fugitive*) . . . for King Vidor and William Wyler, Rouben Mamoulian and Josef von Sternberg, she was the brave tenement girls of *Street Scene* and *Dead End,* mixed up in the rackets in *City Streets* and the pregnant factory worker of *An American Tragedy.* For Henry Hathaway, in *Trail of the Lonesome Pine* she was a mountain girl, sent away to be educated but reverting to a savage demand for revenge when her young brother is killed in a feud.

Her movie career in the thirties was stormy—punctuated by walk-outs from pictures and returns to the theatre, culminating in a final departure when a picture she had been promised was sold to another studio for another star. (It was *Wuthering Heights*—and what a Cathy she would have made!)

She didn't have the variety of scripts that were given to her contemporaries. She missed out on the chic gowns. She didn't make "women's pictures" in which the men were just ornamental. Her comedy gifts went largely unused. What she had was superb emotional talent and an individual, unforgettable beauty. It was enough to place her with the greats of film history.

SIMONE SIMON

Simone Simon arrived in Hollywood on the heels of a publicity campaign that exhorted you to pronounce her name "See-moan See-moan."

ANNE SHIRLEY, with John Beal, in *M'liss*

ANN SHOEMAKER, with Frank Albertson, in *Alice Adams*

SYLVIA SIDNEY, Henry Fonda in *Trail of the Lonesome Pine*

SYLVIA SIDNEY in *Behold My Wife*

SYLVIA SIDNEY, Herbert Marshall in *Accent on Youth*

In spite of this, she turned out to be an actress of some conviction in her first American picture, *Girls' Dormitory*. She was a joyless adolescent, in love with her teacher, and up to the time that the simple story took a melodramatic turn of plot and then another turn for a conventional happy ending, it was quite moving. And so was Miss Simon. But Fox threw her away after that.

She was just another Parisian sex kitten in *Ladies in Love*, and although *Seventh Heaven* probably seemed like a good idea, it had lost its lyrical appeal and looked as dated as *Broken Blossoms*. And Miss Simon, who did her best to be mousey, had to contend with a very unlikely Chico in the drawling Yankee person of Jimmy Stewart.

SYLVIA SIDNEY

224

After that, there was another publicity campaign—"Simone Simon Sings Sings" and she did, she did, but not any too well. "Sing-Sing" pictures, for the record, were titled *Love and Hisses* and *Josette*.

It was enough to send the lady scuttling back to France and, thank heaven, it did. Before the end of the thirties, she was being seen on Parisian screens in a compelling characterization opposite Jean Gabin in *La Bete Humaine*—enough to erase the memory of *Josette* for good and all.

PENNY SINGLETON

Since a brunette soubrette named Dorothy Mc-Nulty was getting nowhere at all in movies, she is hardly to be criticized for changing her name and hair and blossoming out as blonde Penny Singleton. Miss Singleton didn't get any better parts than Miss Mc-Nulty had received, just more of them, in pictures like *Men Are Such Fools*, *Swing Your Lady*, *Garden of the Moon* and *The Mad Miss Manton*.

But then Penny Singleton became *Blondie*—out of the comic strips onto the screen. And, for a while there, Blondie was apt to turn up on the bottom half of the bill just about every other time you went to the movies. And wasn't that a break for Penny Singleton? Dorothy McNulty would never have gotten the part.

ALISON SKIPWORTH

Alison Skipworth, large, theatrical and wise in the ways of ham, was just the person to seek out if you were casting one of those indomitable ladies. Better make sure your character had humor, too—Miss Skipworth had it.

Starting with that lofty matron who found herself among the common folk on that ship that was *Outward Bound*, you saw her playing all manner of the gentility—frequently with a little larceny in their hearts. There wasn't much variance in the Skipworth repertoire but she was agreeable addition to almost any cast.

She may be best remembered now as the one W.C. Fields foil who could stand right up to him (in *Tillie and Gus*, *Six of a Kind* and in the riotous road hog sequence of *If I Had a Million*). But let's not forget her as the slightly seedy grande dame of the theatre staging an amateur play in Will Rogers' *Doubting Thomas* (she had played the same part in the play on which that movie was based, *The Torch Bearers*). Let's remember also her Miss Jellyman, who gave George Raft diction lessons in *Night After Night* and

SYLVIA SIDNEY in *Mary Burns, Fugitive*

SIMONE SIMON, James Stewart in *Seventh Heaven*

PENNY SINGLETON, with Arthur Lake, in *Blondie*

ALISON SKIPWORTH (center) with W. C. Fields, Cecil Cunningham in *If I Had a Million*

ALISON SKIPWORTH, with Bette Davis, in *The Girl From 10th Avenue*

had an alcoholic confrontation with Mae West. Her role in the abysmal *Satan Met a Lady*, which was based on *The Maltese Falcon*, corresponded to the part played in the later version by Sydney Greenstreet. And to pick just a few more, we'd list *Madame Racketeer*, *A Lady's Profession*, *The Casino Murder Case* and *Here Is My Heart* as other films in which the Skipworth authority was imposing.

KATE SMITH

Even if you liked Kate Smith and her full, fruity voice—and most people did—you would have to deplore her movie. The picture was titled after her radio greeting, *Hello, Everybody*, and Miss Kate played a jolly farmerette who finds fame and fortune in the city as a radio singer. But her heart is still with the pigs and chicks, particularly when she gets a crush on a city slicker (Randolph Scott) but finds that he goes for her sister instead. Kate sang a lot, which is what everybody wanted, and the songs—ranging from her standard "When the Moon Comes Over the Mountain" to a lovely new ballad, "Moon Song"—were much more welcome than the sight of Kate mooning over the fact that nobody loves a fat girl.

GALE SONDERGAARD

Gale Sondergaard won an Academy Award for her very first picture. As Faith Paleologus in *Anthony Adverse*, the faintly reptilian quality she assumed and the smile that could be almost a sneer so successfully conveyed sheer evil that it wasn't easy to do a turnabout and accept her as an upstanding type. Yet, with the exception of the sadistic sister in *Seventh Heaven*, her other thirties movies presented her that way.

Of course, she wasn't too lovable to those girls she trained in *Dramatic School*, an interesting characterization of a one-time star, reduced to coaching newcomers and jealous of their successes. And there was something sinister about her in *The Cat and the Canary*—enough to make her a logical suspect. Nobody could tell just where she stood in *Maid of Salem*. (Miss Sondergaard claims—as does Beulah Bondi for the same film—that most of her role wound up on the cutting-room floor.)

But definitely on the righteous side were the wife of the accused Dreyfus in *The Life of Emile Zola* and the Empress Eugenie in *Juarez*.

Miss Sondergaard was an always striking personality, an always capable actress.

ANN SOTHERN

When Ann Sothern showed up in *Trade Winds* in a supporting part, everybody made surprised comments about her comedy abilities. Certainly they were very much in evidence, but there was no reason for astonishment. Miss Sothern had always had them.

ANN SOTHERN as Maisie

KATE SMITH, with players, in *Hello Everybody*

GALE SONDERGAARD, with Claude Rains, in
Anthony Adverse

ANN SOTHERN, Edmund Lowe
in *Let's Fall in Love*

GALE SONDERGAARD (left) with Luise Rainer,
Virginia Grey in *Dramatic School*

BARBARA STANWYCK, with Beulah Bondi, Fred MacMurray in *Remember the Night*

BARBARA STANWYCK, Anne Shirley in *Stella Dallas*

BARBARA STANWYCK, Dickie Moore in *So Big*

Not many people noticed when she was squandering them on a series of program pictures. She had started out well enough on the screen in *Let's Fall in Love*, a doll-faced blonde with a new name (she had been known on the stage as Harriette Lake). But except for Eddie Cantor's *Kid Millions* and Maurice Chevalier's *Folies Bergere*, in which she had good parts, you were apt to miss her unless you stayed for all the second features on double bills.

So she did pictures with Gene Raymond and pictures with Bruce Cabot, like *Hooray For Love*, *There Goes My Girl*, *There Goes the Groom*, *She's Got Everything*, *Walking on Air* and *You May Be Next*. She was bonnie and flippant and, when she got a chance, an adroit performer. But nobody threw any hats in the air.

After *Trade Winds* came *Maisie*, a friendly chippie with a soft heart and a fast tongue, and Miss Sothern played her with a crackling individuality. She would keep bringing Maisie back for further adventures well into the forties. By that time, she would be established as a star in her own right, not just one of those quick-witted blondes who made pictures you never even heard about.

BARBARA STANWYCK

Take it as a tribute to the honest acting and forceful presence of Barbara Stanwyck that she established herself as a major screen personality at the beginning of the thirties, and remained so, with almost no help from her pictures and roles. As a matter of fact, a good many of them would have permanently scuttled the careers of anyone less than a Stanwyck.

All of these Stanwyck performances you cherish— *The Lady Eve*, *Double Indemnity*, *Martha Ivers* and the rest—came later. In close to three dozen movies of the thirties, you might list three as top drawer and add another handful as worth noting, if hardly up to the standard of a top star. For the rest of them, it was only the fact that Barbara Stanwyck was playing the roles that make them worthy of even passing mention.

Stanwyck was always a rare type for the screen, straightforward and gritty, without a suggestion of the Hollywood pretty-prettiness and coquettery that were regulation equipment for most stars. But when the role called for it—and hers usually did—nobody was more uninhibited in the sobbing and snarling departments.

Yet her best role of the thirties was the very antithesis of the usual smart Stanwyck. As that famous slob Stella Dallas she was flashy, basically stupid and slovenly, but fond and generous, coarsening as she moves into middle age, but remaining somehow pathetic.

The other particularly notable Stanwyck roles of the thirties were closer to the norm. The Mitchell Leisen-Preston Sturges picture, *Remember the Night*, was a mixture of sophistication and sentiment, and Miss Stanwyck excelled as the callous prisoner who is brought into a family atmosphere at Christmastime. And the role of the sardonic, bitter Lorna Moon in Odets' *Golden Boy* might have been written for her.

On a lower level, but worth mentioning, were her tomboys in George Stevens' *Annie Oakley* and in Cecil B. DeMille's *Union Pacific*. After that, you search through the typical melodramas generally given her, to come up with a few more or less superior examples of the species—*Ladies of Leisure, His Brother's Wife, The Bitter Tea of General Yen* (although her role in that was subordinated to that of Nils Asther), as well as some movies which did not live up to their promising sources—*A Lost Lady, So Big, The Plough and the Stars*. There was also an unsuccessful attempt to play a role better suited to Harlow, with a dash of Mae West, a lurid item called *Baby Face*.

Really a sorry selection for a star of Stanwyck's calibre—and we haven't even mentioned the long list of things like *Secret Bride* and *Red Salute* and *Purchase Price* and *Shopworn*.

But Stanwyck survived, ready to face a new decade and roles that would be more appropriate for her peculiar gifts.

BARBARA STANWYCK and Robert Taylor

FRANCES STARR

Frances Starr, of the theatre, made three talkies. And only one of these, *Five Star Final*, gave her a role of any value. Here she played a victim of yellow journalism—a woman who has lived down a youthful indiscretion and who is driven to suicide when it is raked up again for a circulation-building sensation. Her other film roles—well-played, of course, but inconsequential—were mother parts in *The Star Witness*, and in a film version of *The Goose Hangs High*, retitled *This Reckless Age*.

ANNA STEN

Anna Sten came to the American screen with a million-dollar publicity campaign designed to build her a pedestal on a level with those of Garbo and Dietrich. One can understand the Goldwyn reasoning. She was already noted as an actress of the Russian and German cinema and theatre. Her wide-faced Slavic beauty, enhanced by Hollywood artistry, was unquestioned. So Mr. Goldwyn cast her in a version of Zola's *Nana* (a classic is always good, particularly a classic about a girl without morals). He set his publicity mills to grinding and waited for the bonanza.

It was probably the most crashingly disastrous debut in movie history. The film was a sketchy romantic drama which lacked any semblance of vitality. Miss Sten was directed to move through it lifelessly, like a mannequin, with no flicker of feeling to disturb the newly manufactured mask of her face.

FRANCES STARR (right) with Frances Dee, Richard Bennett in *This Reckless Age*

ANNA STEN in *Nana*

ANNA STEN in *We Live Again*

229

ANNA STEN, Gary Cooper in *The Wedding Night*

GLORIA STUART, Michael Whalen
in *Time Out For Murder*

GLORIA STUART

She was given musicals like *Roman Scandals* and *Gold Diggers of 1935* because she looked like a musical heroine should look, even if she didn't sing. She had pretty blue eyes which she could widen in terror when confronted with *The Invisible Man, The Secret of the Blue Room* or *The Old Dark House*. She was regal in *The Three Musketeers*, and homey—but never homely —as those considerate wives who stay mostly on the fringes in *The Prisoner of Shark Island* and *Beloved*.

Her blonde pulchritude complemented the dark handsomeness of Michael Whalen, so she did a lot of pictures with him. But she played opposite Jimmy Cagney too, and Pat O'Brien, Lee Tracy, John Beal and Ross Alexander. And she was always exactly the way you'd want a movie heroine to be.

MARGARET SULLAVAN

Margaret Sullavan was a very special screen personality and a very special actress. Her radiance illuminated every role she played—the routine and unrewarding ones (and she had her share of those) as well as the few, very few, that were worthy of her.

She easily avoided all the movie conventions. Could you call her plain? In Hollywood terms, you could. Should you call her beautiful? How could you not?

Someone once described her voice as "liquid gravel." "Liquid diamonds," we'd say. But the voice was really indescribable except to say that once you had heard it, you could never mistake it—or forget it.

There were some poor roles—her first one in the movies, for instance. In *Only Yesterday*, she played a girl who shares an evening with a young soldier before he goes to war. She has his baby but, when he returns, he never recognizes her.

In spite of this unlikely premise and the soapsuds plot, Miss Sullavan made her heroine valiant and true, as all of her movie heroines were. Has anyone ever died so courageously on the screen as did her Patricia of *Three Comrades*? This was one of her rare great screen roles, her shopgirl of Ernst Lubitsch's *The Shop Around the Corner* being the only other in the thirties.

The rest of them were enhanced by the artistry of the actress, not because she was blessed by ideal parts. There was *The Good Fairy*, and actress after actress has failed in that role—the orphanage innocent on her own in a big, bad world. Miss Sullavan, suffice to say, was enchanting.

The Moon's Our Home was a gay trifle about a Hepburnish movie actress and a Richard Halliburton-style writer. The personalities and performances of Miss Sullavan and Henry Fonda made it much more than the kind of froth in which you normally saw a team like Ann Sothern and Gene Raymond.

Little Man, What Now? was episodic and choppy in its story of a young couple in post-WWI Berlin. But again, Miss Sullavan gave a performance of feeling.

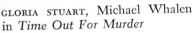

GLORIA STUART

She was capable of a performance. When Rouben Mamoulian took her in hand for *We Live Again*, and when King Vidor directed her in *The Wedding Night*, she showed much of what had been expected of her in the first place. But the damage had been done, the letdown had been too great. Now nobody paid any mind. Goldwyn dropped her.

A few years later, a minor studio, Grand National, brought her back in *Two Who Dared* and *Exile Express*. But these were not the films to re-establish a career which had never actually been established at all.

GLORIA STUART

Some publicist once called Gloria Stuart "orchidaceous." We're not sure just what that means, but if it refers to a fragile, flowerlike beauty, we'll go along with it. Because Miss Stuart certainly had that.

And every so often we could tell she had acting ability. Miss Stuart worked a great deal through the thirties, which was a boon. Few actresses were so ornamental. But "undemanding" is the word for most of the roles she played.

230

She was the one affecting character in a bleak domestic drama, *The Shining Hour*, as a wife driven to suicide by the infidelities of her husband. She was the chorus girl torn between her love of luxury and her feeling for a naive young soldier in a considerably laundered remake of the Nancy Carroll drama, *The Shopworn Angel*. She was a Southern plantation girl in a tiresome screen version of Stark Young's *So Red the Rose*. She was an actress whose career interfered with her marriage in *Next Time We Love*. Each of these pictures owed whatever distinction it had to the performance of Margaret Sullavan.

Finally, at the end of the thirties—so close to the end that it is usually listed as a 1940 picture—came *The Shop Around the Corner*. Many others shared the credit for that. It was Lubitsch's most charming movie and every role was perfectly cast and played. And the lyrical loveliness of Margaret Sullavan's performance was the principal delight in a film that was full of them.

MARGARET SULLAVAN, with Beulah Bondi, others, in *The Good Fairy*

MARGARET SULLAVAN in *So Red the Rose*

MARGARET SULLAVAN, Robert Taylor in *Three Comrades*

GLORIA SWANSON

Gloria Swanson was one star of the silent screen who made a successful transition to talkies. Her first picture in the new medium, *The Trespasser*, incongruously presented her as a naive girl, cast aside by the rich man she loves and then becoming an innocent victim of scandal. There was also some mother-love stuff with Gloria battling for her baby. They rather piled it on, but Miss Swanson's performance was hailed.

Yet she wasn't the Swanson we had come to expect—she of volatile temperament, of blazing jade eyes and those teeth, certainly Hollywood's most conspicuous teeth up to and including Burt Lancaster's. And her later talkies were simply weaklings—flimsy farces in which the firecracker Swanson personality was allowed to sputter out.

MARGARET SULLAVAN, Henry Fonda
in *The Moon's Our Home*

After the last of these, a British drawing room comedy-drama, *Perfect Understanding*, Miss Swanson gave it all up. She made one thirties stab at a return in *Music in the Air*, a film version of a Broadway operetta. But although she had the Kern score to sing (Miss Swanson's unexpectedly good singing voice had been a plus in her early talkies) and her role of a tempestuous prima donna was reminiscent of the old Swanson, the story line was foolish; they had eliminated the show's best songs, and there was no audience interest in movie operettas by this time anyway. So the comeback fizzled.

There would be *Sunset Boulevard* in her future—the high peak of her long career. But that was over fifteen years away, and in the thirties, all we knew was that another of the legends had gone out in something less than a blaze of glory.

GLADYS SWARTHOUT

On the heels of Grace Moore and Lily Pons came Paramount's contender for the operatic sweepstakes, the belle of the Metropolitan Opera, Gladys Swarthout. Miss Swarthout, needless to say, had the voice and the appearance. What she didn't have were the scripts.

The others both eventually failed on screen, but had some enjoyable films. However, Miss Swarthout had to contend with one horror after another. She went from an operetta version of the hoary *Rose of the Rancho* to a trio of extremely silly and dull comedies—*Give Us This Night, Champagne Waltz* and *Romance in the Dark*. There was that voice, of course, but it was lifted in a losing cause. She wound up her movie stay in a program melodrama, *Ambush*, in which she didn't sing a note.

GLORIA SWANSON, John Boles in *Music in the Air*

GLADYS SWARTHOUT in *Rose of the Rancho*

GLORIA SWANSON, Laurence Olivier in *Perfect Understanding*

JO ANN SAYERS

KATHRYN SERGAVA

JANET SHAW

GLORIA SHEA

ETHEL SHUTTA

NOTES ON OTHER "S" LADIES

Jo Ann Sayers had only a few look-ins in movies before going to Broadway and becoming *My Sister Eileen* and then leaving it all for a social marriage . . . *Mme. Ernestine Schumann-Heink* played Nino Martini's singing teacher in *Here's to Romance,* which gave her a chance to sing Brahms' "Lullaby" . . . *Margaretta Scott,* a British character actress, was seen here in a few pictures, most notably *Things to Come* . . . *Margaret Seddon* was one of the "pixilated" sisters of *Mr. Deeds Goes to Town* . . . Blonde *Miriam Seegar* played opposite Richard Dix and had a few lesser roles . . . *Blossom Seeley* sang some ragtime in *Broadway Through a Keyhole,* unaware that she'd be on the screen again one day, as impersonated by Betty Hutton . . . *Dorothy Ann Seese,* a precocious tot, was the youngest of *Five Little Peppers* . . . *Ruth Selwyn,* Buster Keaton's girl in *Speakeasily,* had a few other minor roles . . . *Kathryn Sergava* got more attention in fan magazines as a Garbo look-alike than for any screen work . . . *Athene Seyler* was a familiar figure among character actresses in British films . . .

Marla Shelton played a movie actress in *Stand In* but had few chances to live up to the role in other films . . . *Marion Shilling* was the leading lady in pictures like *Lord Byron of Broadway* and *Donovan's Kid* . . . *Ethel Shutta,* stage and radio star, had her one movie as Eddie Cantor's nurse in *Whoopee* . . . *Maria Sieber,* who played Marlene Dietrich as a child in *Scarlet Empress,* was Marlene's real life daughter

PAULINE STARKE

EVE SOUTHERN in *Fighting Caravans*

CAROL STONE

whom you would eventually know as Maria Riva . . . *Ginny Simms* moved over with Kay Kyser's band for *That's Right, You're Wrong* . . . *Diane Sinclair* was the lead in *Washington Masquerade* and a couple of other pictures . . .

Martha Sleeper always seemed to deserve more than she got—outside of a fair role in *The Scoundrel*, she got nothing much . . . *Queenie Smith*, from the stage, showed up in *Mississippi* and *Show Boat* . . . *Eve Southern* had bits in *Morocco* and *Lilies of the Field* . . . *Grace Stafford* played most impressively in *Confessions of a Nazi Spy* and *Indianapolis Speedway* . . . *Sally Starr* was a co-ed inspiration for the rivalry of those two new boys, Robert Montgomery and Elliott Nugent, in *So This Is College* . . . *Myrtle Stedman*, who had done them in silents, played only a few society matrons in talkies . . . *Leni Stengel* had supporting roles in pictures that ranged from Wheeler and Woolsey comedies to *The Animal Kingdom* . . . Brunette *Ruthelma Stevens* came along in the casts of a dozen or so movies (*The Mind Reader, Circus Queen Murder*, etc.) . . . *Margot Stevenson* made *Smashing the Money Ring* and *Invisible Stripes* at the end of the thirties with a few more to go in the early forties . . . *Sophie Stewart* was Celia in Bergner's *As You Like It* and also appeared in *Things to Come, The Man Who Could Work Miracles, Nurse Edith Cavell* . . . *Dorothy Stickney* had too little movie fortune in films like *Wayward, The Little Minister* and *I Met My*

SALLY STARR

235

GINNY SIMS, with Kay Kyser, in *That's Right, You're Wrong*

DOROTHY STICKNEY in *Working Girls*

ROSA STRADNER, with James Stewart, *The Last Gangster*

BLANCHE SWEET

Love Again . . . Fred Stone's daughters—*Carol, Dorothy, Paula Stone*—each had a movie or two, but nothing of consequence . . . *Rose Stradner*, esteemed in Europe, had to make do with a dull role in *The Last Gangster* for her American debut . . . *Mme. Sul-Te-Wan* was Tituba, the slave accused of witchcraft, in *Maid of Salem* . . . *Maxine Sullivan* swung her "Loch Lomond" in *St. Louis Blues* . . . *Eve Sully* had a hilarious moment or two in *Kid Millions* . . . *Nan Sunderland*, better treated on Broadway than in films, had a small part in *Sweepings* . . . *Blanche Sweet* was down from her silent celebrity to minor talkie roles . . . *Nora Swinburne*, a fine British actress, had mostly supporting roles in this era.

And a tip of the hat to *Virginia Sale, Ynez Seabury, Evelyn Selbie, Clarissa Selwynne, Effie Shannon, Sandra Shaw, Gloria Shea, Helen Shipman, Gertrude Short, Joan Standing, Kay Strozzi, Marina Schubert, Zelda Sears, Billie Seward, Elaine Shepard, Louise Stanley, June Storey, Jane Seymour, Janet Shaw, Katherine Sheldon, Dorothy Short, Gertrude Sutton, Kay Sutton, Betty Sinclair, Gay Seabrook, Flora Sheffield, Loretta Sayers, Edna Sedgwick, Jean Sharon, Eleanor Stewart, Peggy Stewart, Winifred Shotter, Ivy Stuart, Enid Stamp-Taylor.*

NORMA TALMADGE, with Gilbert Roland, in *New York Nights*

T

NORMA TALMADGE

Nobody, but nobody, was more intense in silent screen breast-heaving drama than Norma Talmadge. But her prestige didn't carry over into talkies. Unkindly they laughed, those few who saw them at all, at her dramatic efforts in *Du Barry, Woman of Passion* (the passion was all in the title) and *New York Nights*.

Even before her first talkie, she played the title character in *Woman Disputed*. It had a theme song, "Woman Disputed, I Love You"—and how the press ridiculed *that*, and indirectly, the star. It was almost as crushing a blow as that which hit John Gilbert when he shrilled "I love you, I love you" into the passive ear of Catherine Dale Owen.

Miss Talmadge got out of the rat race. After she had retired, she attended a public event where she was approached by autograph seekers. "Get away, dears," she said sweetly, "I don't need you any more."

LILYAN TASHMAN

Lilyan Tashman, being a tall and what they then called slinky blonde, was always getting stuck in those movies where she had to play some kind of chintzy vamp. But nobody ever took such roles very seriously, especially Miss Tashman herself. Her tongue was always planted so firmly in her cheek that it was fun to hoot at the overdrawn villainesses she played in things like *Murder by the Clock, The Road to Reno* and *Scarlet Dawn*.

She was much more at ease when she was playing something like the gay call girl in *Girls About Town* or dripping verbal acid in pictures like *Gold Diggers of Broadway* and *No, No Nanette*. Miss Tashman was usually heralded as one of Hollywood's "best-dressed women" and she made a point of living up to that title on the screen.

ESTELLE TAYLOR

Estelle Taylor, a Latin-looking brunette, seemed much too much the hot-eyed Hollywood temptress to be convincing as Mrs. Maurrant, the restless tenement mother, whose shabby affair leads to double murder in *Street Scene*. But King Vidor made all the things that seemed wrong about her casting work for her, and it became her one completely satisfying performance.

She was acceptable as Dixie Lee, a prostitute of the pioneer West in *Cimarron*. But she slitted her eyes and made like Theda Bara as Mme. Muskat, the carousel owner, in *Liliom* and as a lady with an unholy letch for Ronald Colman in *The Unholy Garden*.

VERREE TEASDALE

Verree Teasdale—wasn't she chic! With marcelled blonde hair, wearing the latest in Paris gowns, she gave her roles a sheen. In her best ones, *Desirable* and *First Lady*, she also showed an aptitude for murmuring the most malicious remarks without cracking that surface polish.

Actually, only these two pictures were at all worthy of her gifts. In *First Lady*, a too-talky version of a mildly successful Broadway play, she played a political wife fighting it out to become the Number One lady on the Washington social scene. Since her rival was Kay Francis, there would appear to be no contest. Miss Francis, being the bigger star, won out; but Miss Teasdale more than had her innings.

In *Desirable* she was a scintillating Broadway star who fears for her image and her lover when her unpublicized adolescent daughter turns up. Again, Miss Teasdale made much of this most un-maternal mama.

There were also pictures like *The Milky Way* with Harold Lloyd, in which she exhibited an unsuspected talent for slapstick . . . *A Midsummer Night's Dream*, in which she was a queenly Hippolyta . . . *Skyscraper Souls*, in which she played stronger drama than usual. But there were also too many time wasters like *The Firebird, A Modern Hero* and a couple of ZaSu Pitts-Slim Summerville epics. So Verree Teasdale never came close to reaching the movie position she rated.

LILYAN TASHMAN, Kay Francis in *Girls About Town*

VERREE TEASDALE (right) with Kay Francis in *Dr. Monica*

SHIRLEY TEMPLE

Shirley Temple was *Curly Top, Bright Eyes* and *Dimples*—and only slightly less obviously, *Rebecca of Sunnybrook Farm, Poor Little Rich Girl* and *Wee Willie Winkie*. But, strangely, not *Pollyanna*, which would have been ideal. Certainly nobody was a more incorrigible optimist. You could starve Shirley in a garret . . . let her be mistreated by stern spinsters, salty millionaires and Jane Withers—she would come smiling through because she knew everything always turns out right in the end.

Shirley was a phenomenon. It had never happened before, or since, that a tiny moppet had so completely taken over. The teenagers are always with us of course, and such kiddies as Jackie Coogan, Jackie Cooper, Baby Peggy, Freddie Bartholomew, and later Margaret O'Brien, Roddy McDowall and others had their pre-teen triumphs. But Shirley Temple was on top for good half-dozen of her child years, her appeal not to evaporate until well into adolescence.

She was just a cute tyke at first, with more curls and dimples than most, but still only for the childish bits. It was in such a subordinate role (in *Stand Up and Cheer*) that, attired in a polkadot doll's dress, she made her little curtsey and did her little time step as James Dunn sang "Baby Take a Bow."

Soon she was involved with a bunch of the quaintest Runyon underworld denizens, reforming them all as she lisped her prayers in *Little Miss Marker*, and turning such slickers as crooks Gary Cooper and Carole Lombard to righteousness in *Now and Forever*. Few hearts were stony enough to resist.

And then her pictures became "Shirley Temple Pictures"—all made from the same formula. She prattled her ditties: "Animal Crackers in My Soup," "On the Good Ship Lollipop," "When I'm With You." She tapped her dances—up and down stairs, with and without Bill Robinson. She sunnily settled marital upsets, worked out problems for countless adults simply by having heart-to-heart talks with the likes of Abraham Lincoln, Queen Victoria and various native chieftains, and melted the glacial hearts of such gorgons as Claude Gillingwater, Helen Westley, C. Aubrey Smith and Edna May Oliver. In her pantaloons or kilts or pinafores, she was winsome and winning—at least, at first. Later on, sterner souls might find her quite thoroughly resistible.

But nobody ever accused her of being untalented and she was remarkably free from self-consciousness. The parade of pictures went on—*The Little Colonel, The Little Princess, The Littlest Rebel, Heidi, Captain January*—and, if frequently there was more sugar and treacle than some could digest, they were well in the minority. Because it was almost unpatriotic not to love Shirley Temple and, in a pretty bleak time, nobody was ever more incurably cheerful.

ESTELLE TAYLOR, Ronald Colman in *The Unholy Garden*

SHIRLEY TEMPLE, Bill Robinson in *The Little Colonel*

SHIRLEY TEMPLE, Adolphe Menjou in *Little Miss Marker*

GENEVIEVE TOBIN

Genevieve Tobin started on the screen as a rather sedate paramour in pictures like *Seed* and *A Lady Surrenders*, turned kittenish for Maurice Chevalier in *One Hour With You*, and alternated those roles for the rest of her film career. Somehow she seemed too shrewd to be completely believable as a flibbertigibbet, although her best performances in this vein—the Chevalier film and *Goodbye Again*, in which she was a flirtatious, foolish wife—were amusing.

Although it was a comparatively small role for her, Miss Tobin may have been best served by *The Petrified Forest*. Here, as a bored society matron succumbing to excitement in the person of Mr. Bogart, she anticipated the general idolatry for him in the future.

THELMA TODD

Tall and blonde, with baby-blue eyes and deep dimples, Thelma Todd might have been a Lombard if she had had the material. That she wound up as a custard-pie comic instead of a high-style comedienne is probably because her pictures were planned by Hal Roach instead of Selznick and Paramount.

SHIRLEY TEMPLE in *Baby Take a Bow*

239

SHIRLEY TEMPLE

There was a time when she tried to get rid of Thelma Todd as a name and an image. So she called herself Alison Loyd and played in a picture called *Corsair*, fooling nobody and winning no laurels either. Actually she was never very good when she was playing straight.

But as a comic foil, she had few equals. She cavorted through short comedies with ZaSu Pitts and Patsy Kelly and was chasing, or chased by, the Marx Brothers, Wheeler and Woolsey, Laurel and Hardy, Buster Keaton, Jimmy Durante, Jack Oakie and Joe E. Brown.

It all stopped suddenly one night in a Hollywood garage with Thelma Todd as the victim of one of Hollywood's most baffling mysteries.

CLAIRE TREVOR

Claire Trevor was "The Queen of the B's" on the 20th Century-Fox lot. She played opposite people like Michael Whalen or the waning James Dunn in those fast-paced action melodramas that rounded off a double bill. One look at Claire and you knew she was much too clever for the B's, but Fox kept her there. She had a chance at another studio and seized it, even though the role was little more than a bit.

But try to find anyone who saw *Dead End* who doesn't vividly remember those few minutes of hers. She was Francey, who had been the first girl of Baby Face Martin, the gangster, and who is one of the reasons he had come back to his old neighborhood. And eventually she shows up—beaten down and sick now, a worn-out veteran of the streets.

It was only a moment, but it proved what program-picture audiences knew all along—here was an actress of major talent. It would be pleasant to report that, as a result, all the good roles started coming to her. But it wasn't true. The roles remained routine except for one in *The Amazing Dr. Clitterhouse*.

Until *Stagecoach*. John Ford's classic Western cast her as the archetypal good-bad girl—the whore who, cast out of one town, finds hope for better things on the long, suspense-filled trip on which she is an unwelcome passenger. At last, Claire Trevor had come into her own with the chance to play meatier roles— the kind you always knew she should be playing in those days when she was racing around the Fox lot as a demon girl reporter.

SOPHIE TUCKER

Sophie Tucker, the strutting "Last of the Red Hot Mamas" of the night clubs, was one thing; but Sophie, as a miserable momma of the movies, was zilch. She did some of the standard Tucker things in her movie, *Honky Tonk*, but she also had to participate in a schmaltzy mother-love plot about an entertainer whose daughter is ashamed of her.

THELMA TODD (then known as Alison Loyd) with Chester Morris in *Corsair*

GENEVIEVE TOBIN

THELMA TODD, Patsy Kelly

CLAIRE TREVOR, Edward G. Robinson in *The Amazing Dr. Clitterhouse*

CLAIRE TREVOR, with Allen Jenkins, Humphrey Bogart, in *Dead End*

It was enough to send Sophie right back to the real honky tonks where she stayed except for a couple of excursions back to the screen some eight years later. These routine roles (in *Broadway Melody of 1938* and *Thoroughbreds Don't Cry*) were easier to take, although they'd hardly satisfy anybody who had seen the real thing.

LANA TURNER

You might think that Lana Turner burst on the screen full-blown, all platinum and shiny and a star. You knew the story about her being discovered at the soda fountain, and then there was that first movie, *They Won't Forget*, with Lana taking a bouncy long walk, and the resulting "sweater girl" movie publicity.

After that, it had to be Gable and Taylor and super-stardom, didn't it? Well, no—not quite. Actually she worked out her apprenticeship in tiny roles in forgotten pictures and the obligatory appearances in chapters of the Andy Hardy and Dr. Kildare series. And then there were two in which her name came first in the cast list—*Dancing Co-Ed* and a particularly good college drama, *These Glamour Girls*.

The super-stardom didn't come until the next decade, but already you knew that Lana was on her way. She made it. And that has never really changed, has it?

HELEN TWELVETREES

Did anybody ever endure such tribulations as Helen Twelvetrees? She had the face for it—wispy eyebrows pointing plaintively up, tiny mouth curved downward, eyes always ready to brim with tears.

She started in pallid imitation of Lillian Gish but soon she had turned to sin. But sin was no fun for Helen. Consider the titles of some of her films and you can practically construct a Helen Twelvetrees script—*Panama Flo, Love Starved, Her Man, My Woman, Bad Company, A Bedtime Story, Unmarried, Unashamed, Disgraced, A Woman of Experience, She Was a Lady*.

Jokes about her being Rin-Tin-Tin's favorite actress must have bored her more than anybody; but her name, and the jokes about it, are virtually all that is remembered about her now—not the insipid roles she played.

SOPHIE TUCKER, with Robert Taylor, in *Broadway Melody of 1938*

LANA TURNER at time of *They Won't Forget*

LANA TURNER in *Dancing Coed* with Artie Shaw and orchestra

HELEN TWELVETREES

243

MARION TALLEY, Michael Bartlett in *Follow Your Heart*

NORMA TERRIS in *Cameo Kirby*

SHEILA TERRY

DOROTHY TREE

OLIVE TELL

NOTES ON OTHER "T" LADIES

Playing minor roles or "doing specialties" in a number of pictures were blonde, lissome *Sheila Terry* and brunette, bouncy *Ruth Terry*. There was also an *Ethelind Terry*, who had the lead in an early talkie, *Lord Byron of Broadway*, but then graced the screen no more.

June Travis was a pleasant leading lady but, outside of *Ceiling Zero* in which the feminine lead was hardly more than a walkthrough, her pictures were not the kind you would see unless you stayed for the second feature on a double bill. *Martha Tibbetts* had a *Ceiling Zero* bit, too, but nothing else of note.

From England came upper-class *Heather Thatcher*, complete with monocle, to play Lady Something-or-Other in pictures like *But the Flesh is Weak*, *Fools For Scandal* and *Tovarich* . . . *Valerie Taylor*, of *Berkeley Square* . . . *Dame Sybil Thorndike*, whose only appearance on American screens in the thirties was in a small character role in *Nine Days a Queen* . . . *Ann Todd*, with her heyday still to come but with a couple of thirties roles . . . and, representing the lower classes, at least in their movie roles, *Viva Tattersall*, of *Cynara*, and *Merle Tottenham*, of *Cavalcade* and *Night Must Fall* . . . dark-eyed *Linden Travers* . . .

There were those who had made their name somewhere else but whose thirties talkie appearances did not enhance them—*Marion Talley*, who wisely went right back to the Metropolitan Opera after a dreadful movie try in *Follow Your Heart* . . . *Lupita Tovar*, a South of the Border star, but confined to one or two small roles in nondescript American pictures . . .

RAQUEL TORRES, with Don Alvarado, in *Red Wagon*

JUNE TRAVIS, with James Cagney, in *Ceiling Zero*

LUPITA TOVAR

RUTH TAYLOR (right) with Alice White in *Gentlemen Prefer Blondes*

MARY TREEN

ANN TODD (left), Margaretta Scott in *Things To Come*

Norma Terris, original Magnolia of Broadway's *Show Boat*, with far less luck in her two movie musicals . . . *Rosemary Theby*, of early silents, back with other old-timers for a version of *Ten Nights in a Barroom* . . . *Helen Troy*, funny telephone girl of radio and vaudeville, in *Born to Dance* and *Broadway Melody of 1938* bits . . . *Kay Thompson* zinging through a specialty in *Manhattan Merry Go Round* . . . *Maidel Turner* repeating her *Another Language* stage role . . . *Olive Tell*, of the theatre and silents, playing some socialites, rather emotional ones, and *Vivian Tobin*, also of the stage, playing others of a giddier variety . . . *Ruth Taylor*, movies' Lorelei Lee of *Gentlemen Prefer Blondes*, with only a couple of third-rate talkies . . . *Dorothy Tree*, from the theatre, to a few meaty, if brief, supporting screen roles . . . *Raquel Torres*, lovely in *White Shadows*, but given only a few routine talkie appearances . . . *Ann Todd*, not to be confused with the British star, the dark-eyed child of *Intermezzo* and other movies . . . *Zeffie Tilbury*, who would be unforgettable as Grandma Joad, but mostly limited to tiny bits in this decade . . . *Nini Theilade*, fairy ballerina of *Midsummer Night's Dream* . . . *Mary Treen*, veteran of countless movies—a face you'd recognize but seldom in more than bits . . . *Carol Tevis*, one of Aline MacMahon's star diction pupils in *Once in a Lifetime* . . . *Mabel Todd*, a "comedienne" in some Warners musicals . . . and *Margaret Tallichet*, *Rosella Towne*, *Laura Treadwell*, *Helen Trenholme*, *Maude Truax*, *Lydia Yeamans Titus*, *Linda Terry*, *Avonne Taylor*, *Julia Thayer*, *Mary Taylor* . . .

HEATHER THATCHER, with Alice Brady, Gregory Gaye, Ivan Lebedeff, in *Mama Steps Out*

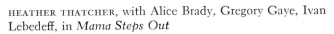

LENORE ULRIC, Robert Frazer in *Frozen Justice*

U~V

LENORE ULRIC

Lenore Ulric may have been one of David Belasco's biggest Broadway stars, but what passed for acting on the stage seemed ridiculously overdrawn on screen—at least in her first two talking pictures, made in the earlier days of that medium. The pictures themselves were no help—*Frozen Justice* and *South Sea Rose*, both old fashioned melodramas. Miss Ulric played a "child of nature" in each—a half-caste Eskimo in the first, a South Sea belle in the other. But she laid on the sultriness with a trowel.

A half-dozen years later, she tried Hollywood again. It was a secondary role in *Camille* as Garbo's friend, Olympe, but she was much more acceptably cast and had George Cukor as her director. This time, even within the limitations of the minor role, she managed to make something of an impact.

LUPE VELEZ

Lupe Velez was *Mexican Spitfire* and *Hot Pepper*. What Lupe was not was the dreary Russian peasant of *Resurrection*.

The thing about Lupe is that everybody knew all about her from the gossip columns and the fan maga-

zines and she seemed to be as fiery and gaily raucous in her private life as she was on the screen. One would never think of trouble, let alone tragedy, touching madcap Lupe. Perhaps that is why it seemed so particularly shocking when it actually happened.

So the sorrowful Katusha Maslova of Tolstoy's *Resurrection* didn't suit her at all, although she was effective in similarly muted performances as mournful Indian maidens in *The Squaw Man* and *Laughing Boy*. But usually she was a firecracker foil for Jimmy Durante, Laurel and Hardy, Leon Errol and a peppery partner in romance for anyone from Gary Cooper to Lawrence Tibbett—not to forget that old Quirt-Flagg team of Edmund Lowe and Victor McLaglen.

EVELYN VENABLE

In *Alice Adams*, Evelyn Venable played in poised contrast to the romantic dreamer of Katharine Hepburn. That may have been what happened to Miss Venable's career.

An unconventionally (by Hollywood standards) attractive actress, she impressed as sensible and matter-of-fact but possessed of very little of the stuff of dreams. Even in such an ideal role for a young actress as that of the mortal bewitched by Death (in *Death Takes a Holiday*) she seemed competent but somewhat earthbound.

Her other screen romances (principally opposite Kent Taylor) in films like *Cradle Song, Mrs. Wiggs of the Cabbage Patch, The Little Colonel* and a couple of Will Rogers films were antiseptic. You could (and we did) admire Evelyn Venable but you couldn't (at least, we didn't) ever warm to her.

HELEN VINSON

Helen Vinson had a kind of stylish primness about her—rather severely arranged dark blonde hair, a small, upturned mouth. But behind that pussycat smile were claws. Miss Vinson, at her best, was decidedly feline. But a very upper-class cat indeed.

In *Private Worlds* for instance, she was thoroughly shocking—an acquitted murderess who fooled around so with the husband of Joan Bennett that she drove poor Joan completely off her rocker. Miss Bennett managed to hold on to her sanity in *Vogues of 1938*, but it wasn't because Miss Vinson was not being as unpleasant as possible. And she was quite as aggravating to the nicer girls in most of her other pictures—*Age of Indiscretion, Broadway Bill, Transatlantic Tunnel, The Life of Virgie Winters* being only a sampling.

You could count her good ladies on one hand and you wouldn't find any of them very interesting. That would include the one with whom Paul Muni became temporarily involved in *I Am a Fugitive*.

The one exception was *The Wedding Night*. Miss Vinson was so charming as Gary Cooper's wife that it was hard to believe Gary's lusting after such a peasant lump as the one portrayed by Anne Sten. Certainly Miss Vinson could not have been more sympathetic. But maybe Gary had seen her other pictures, and remembered the claws behind the pussycat smile.

LUPE VELEZ, Lee Tracy in *The Half Naked Truth*

LUPE VELEZ

HELEN VINSON (right) with Ralph Bellamy, Anna Sten, Gary Cooper in *The Wedding Night*

EVELYN VENABLE, Kent Taylor in *Mrs. Wiggs of the Cabbage Patch*

HELEN VINSON

FLORENCE VIDOR, with Gary Cooper in *Doomsday*

VIRGINIA VALLI

NOTES ON OTHER "U, V" LADIES

Two who had been happier in silents tried talkies. But *Chinatown Nights* was enough for *Florence Vidor*. And *Virginia Valli* called it quits after three third rate quickies.

There was *Hilda Vaughn*, the Cockney crony of Beryl Mercer in *Three Live Ghosts* and the blackmailing maid of *Dinner at Eight* . . . *Alberta Vaughn*, popular in silent short comedies but with only bits in talkies . . . *Dorothy Vaughn*, who specialized in housekeeper and landlady-type bits . . .

There was a beauty named *June Vlasek*, who is covered in more detail under the name she later used, June Lang . . . *Virginia Verrill*, notable in films only because she introduced "That Old Feeling" in the film *Vogues* and dubbed other non-singers, like Harlow, in songs . . . *Myrtle Vail* of "Myrt and Marge" radio fame (they did one not very successful movie) . . . and a nod to *Minerva Urecal, Judith Vosselli, Edith Van Cleave, Blanca Vischer, Veola Von, Virginia Vale, Helen Valkis, Mildred Van Dorn, Joan Valerie,* and *Margaret Vyner.*

ALBERTA VAUGHN

248

NELLA WALKER (left) in *Three Smart Girls Grown Up* with Helen Parrish, Deanna Durbin, Nan Grey, Kathleen Howard

NELLA WALKER

Take a movie socialite mother in the thirties and chances are that she was played by Nella Walker. Miss Walker was also very right for the boss's wife, or a catty member of the country club set.

Actually, we found her quite charming, with her carefully coiffed grey hair and a nice twinkle in her eye that belied her occasional snobbishness. Except for Deanna Durbin's put-upon mama in *Three Smart Girls*, it's hard to remember any specific roles. But you saw her all the time during the period, even if it was in just a bit.

FREDI WASHINGTON

Imitation of Life was the first film to deal with attempts of a light-skinned Negro to pass as white. Fredi Washington played the part. (A white girl, Susan Kohner, took it over in the remake, which rather killed the point in spite of Miss Kohner's capabilities.) Miss Washington was effective in her portrayal although some of her moments with her grand old Mammy veered perilously close to the maudlin, as written and directed. She was also cast in *The Emperor Jones* and *One Mile From Heaven*, in which she played characters who were not "passing."

FREDI WASHINGTON, with Louise Beavers, in *Imitation of Life*

LUCILE WATSON (center) with James Stewart, Carole Lombard in *Made For Each Other*

VIRGINIA WEIDLER

MARJORIE WEAVER

LUCILE WATSON

That grandest of all grand dames, Lucile Watson, would have better movie roles in the era to come. In the thirties, her parts were fairly standard—usually someone to offer a bit of mature and considered advice to the ladies involved in such films as *The Women, What Every Woman Knows, Made for Each Other, Garden of Allah*. But she was such a brisk old lady, it was always a pleasure to see her.

MARJORIE WEAVER

Marjorie Weaver, with dancing dark eyes and bright grin, was rescued from Jones Family bits for good secondary roles in *Second Honeymoon* and *Three Blind Mice*, in which she proved to be a vivacious comedienne. She was more subdued, but quite pleasing as Mary Todd in John Ford's *Young Mr. Lincoln*. Then 20th Century-Fox gave her leads—but what leads, opposite actors who ranged from a has-been Warner Baxter to Stuart Erwin, the Ritz Brothers and the Cisco Kid. No wonder her career didn't live up to its early promise.

VIRGINIA WEIDLER

Of all the precocious mites of movies, Virginia Weidler was one of the least objectionable. As a matter of fact, given the right role, the pigtailed pixie could be a downright delight.

She was all of that as an offspring of *Mrs. Wiggs of the Cabbage Patch*, who was always threatening to hold her breath until she turned blue. And she was very much in her element as the mischievous maidens of *Laddie, Freckles, Scandal Street* and *Mother Carey's Chickens*, and especially so as John Barrymore's adoring daughter in *The Great Man Votes*. Most of these pictures weren't very popular and most of her others gave her limited opportunities. So she never even approached the popularity of someone like Jane Withers, who had her pictures—such as they were—tailored for her.

MAE WEST

"When I'm good, I'm very good—but when I'm bad, I'm better." "It's not the men in my life—but the life in my men—that counts." "Is that a gun in your pocket or are you just glad to see me?"

Who else? Mae West! There had been nothing like her before, and there has been nothing close to her since. Singlehandedly—maybe with just the tiniest help from such as Harlow and Cagney—she was responsible for the formation of the movies' moral code and the Catholic Legion of Decency.

Hers was the face that launched a thousand female impersonators. The queens adore her. She was out-

MAE WEST (right) with Alison Skipworth, George Raft, in *Night After
Night*

MAE WEST

MAE WEST, with Cary Grant, in *She Done Him Wrong*

The only way for the initial momentum to continue was for Mae to become ever more scandalous. But the censors wouldn't permit that. She still leered, swaggered across the screen, muttered innuendoes from the side of her mouth, sang in her adenoidal contralto. But her material grew more and more listless. And her pictures—*Goin' to Town, Klondike Annie, Go West, Young Man, Every Day's a Holiday*—grew more and more stale. And then, well before the finish of the thirties, it was all over for Mae in the movies.

There would be one successful comeback—fortified by the added presence of Mr. W. C. Fields—and comeback disasters, too. But those would be in other times.

HELEN WESTLEY

The owlish and imposing Helen Westley came from the theatre to exert her undeniable authority on a number of good movie roles. She was successively the matriarch of *The House of Rothschild*, the bitter spinster softened by *Anne of Green Gables* and the doughty Parthy Ann Hawks of *Show Boat*, and other such roles.

But then she went under contract to 20th Century-Fox and that meant she was tossed into everything that called for a gruff or supercilious oldster, whether or not the part was any good at all. Usually it wasn't. She had her moments like *Café Metropole* and *Wife, Husband and Friend* but more often she had to stooge for Shirley Temple, Jane Withers or even Joan Davis.

NYDIA WESTMAN

Nydia Westman, a dumpy little woman with a pudding of a face, specialized in maids and old maids, often frightened. While she had few chances to shine on her own (pictures like *Three Live Ghosts, Craig's Wife, A Feather in Her Hat, The Cat and the Canary* did give her moments), she was always well cast in support.

ARLEEN WHELAN

Arleen Whelan was one of the more fetching redheads of the thirties and early forties. But redheads are supposed to have fire. Miss Whelan hardly glimmered.

Perhaps it was her roles. In *Kidnapped*, she was dragged in to provide a feminine interest that hadn't occurred to Stevenson. In Ford's *Young Mr. Lincoln*, she was just a country girl looking worried in the courtroom as her young husband went on trial for his life. And she had leading roles in such pictures as *Thanks for Everything, Gateway* and *Sabotage*—but never mind the pictures. So how could a redhead flame?

rageous and ridiculous and marvelous as nobody else ever was.

Remember her very first picture, *Night After Night?* Mae undulates into George Raft's speakeasy, surrounded as always by a sufficient number of tall, dark and handsome types. "Goodness," says the hat-check girl, "what beautiful diamonds!" The Great One hardly paused. "Goodness had nothin' to do with it, dearie—goodness had nothin' to do with it."

Then there was *She Done Him Wrong*, which was as close to the forbidden *Diamond Lil* as La West could make it. Mae got mixed up in all kinds of melodramatic adventures in that one—yet she still had time to sway suggestively on a staircase—Mae always swayed—and murmur to Cary Grant, "C'mup and see me sometime—anytime."

She was involved again with Cary in *I'm No Angel*, in which the melodrama may have been even wilder and Miss West even less visibly affected by it. After a particularly nasty scene, she returned to her boudoir where her maid was waiting. Mae, never nonplussed, tossed it off: "Beulah, peel me a grape."

But then the censors got into the act. Another Mae movie was ready for release. *It Ain't No Sin* it was called. Sinful it was, decided the censors, and finally out came a laundered version known as *Belle of the Nineties*.

HELEN WESTLEY in *Anne of Green Gables*

NYDIA WESTMAN, Wallace Beery in *The Bad Man*

ARLEEN WHELAN, Freddie Bartholomew in *Kidnaped*

ALICE WHITE

Alice White was Warners' answer to Clara Bow in the last days of the silents. She was a jazzy brunette (later blonde) but her pictures were flimsy carbons and, even before Clara began her quick fall from favor, Alice was just about through.

After talkies came, she had a *Sweet Mamma* here, a *Naughty Flirt* there and even a *Show Girl in Hollywood*. But the days when White cheesecake dominated movie magazines were over. She wound up playing a few dizzy blondes (which is really what she had been doing all along), but these proceeded downward in the supporting cast list until, by 1937 and 1938, hers was the name at the bottom.

ELEANORE WHITNEY

Eleanore Whitney was a slim brunette who danced well—usually with Johnny Downs—in some of Paramount's minor musicals (*Turn Off the Moon, College Holiday, Thrill of a Lifetime, Three Cheers for Love,* etc.). Miss Whitney was in the storyline, too, such as it was, and, such as it was, it usually teamed her romantically with—you guessed it, Johnny Downs.

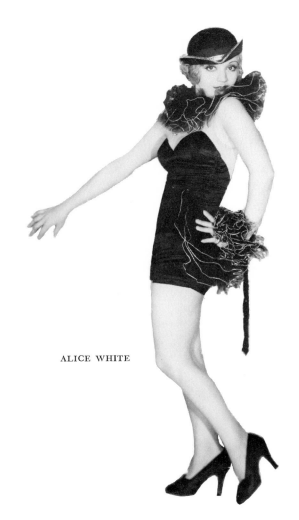

ALICE WHITE

ELEANOR WHITNEY, with Johnny Downs, in *Thrill of a Lifetime*

DAME MAY WHITTY, with Robert Montgomery, in *Night Must Fall*

DAME MAY WHITTY (center) with Basil Radford, Naunton Wayne, Margaret Lockwood, Michael Redgrave in *The Lady Vanishes*

DOROTHEA WIECK in *Cradle Song*

DAME MAY WHITTY

Our most memorable moment in Robert Montgomery's tour de force, *Night Must Fall*, belonged only incidentally to Mr. Montgomery. For it was Dame May Whitty, introduced to America in the film, who gave perhaps the most graphic study of hysteria ever put on the screen.

It is twilight. The complaining, overbearing invalid, played by Dame May, has been left alone. Gradually her mood shifts from annoyance, to exasperation, and then—as nobody comes and the shadows and sounds begin to assume alarming proportions—she becomes frantic. In a frenzy of fear, she cries desperately for her beloved Danny, the Irish handyman, new to her household but already dear to her heart. And then, finally, Danny is there and he comforts her as she sobs and babbles her terror. And, of course, we know that Danny is that psychopathic killer who has been roaming the neighborhood.

This would be the highlight of Dame May Whitty's career—she would go on playing in pictures like *I Met My Love Again* but never again would she have a part as demanding as this.

There was still one particularly notable role in the thirties—the title character in Hitchcock's classic, *The Lady Vanishes*. Here she was the bluff, hearty governess—or was she—and although most of the excitements of the movie occurred after she had disappeared, you were never unaware of her for a minute.

DOROTHEA WIECK

Dorothea Wieck, the compassionate schoolmistress of *Maedchen in Uniform*, was scarcely up to anticipations in her two American movies of the thirties. She played the distracted movie star–mother in *Miss Fane's Baby Is Stolen* and the nun of *Cradle Song*.

But there was very little glamour and surprising lack of emotion in the first, almost no radiance in the second. "Competent" may be the strongest adjective for her performances; perhaps the unfamiliarity of playing in a different language affected her, but she lacked the incandescence of her German screen personality. Dorothea Wieck in America was a disappointment.

DOROTHY WILSON

Dorothy Wilson was a quietly lovely girl—no flash at all and none needed—whose best performances were as troubled post-adolescents. She was believably in love in *The Age of Consent* . . . another schoolgirl, despondently realizing her pregnancy, in *Eight Girls in a Boat* . . . a shy, withdrawn daughter in *His Greatest Gamble* . . . a nursing student with problems in *The White Parade*.

She also played quite effectively opposite Harold Lloyd in *The Milky Way*, with Will Rogers in *In Old*

Kentucky and with Rosalind Russell in *Craig's Wife.* She faded from the screen—too soon, we thought. Perhaps it was her very lack of starlet artifice that caused her to be overlooked.

LOIS WILSON

Lois Wilson had a movie career that began before the twenties and continued well into talkies. Her first few of the latter—pictures like *Lovin' the Ladies, The Gamblers, The Furies, Wedding Rings*—gave her leads, but in films that were forgotten a month after their release.

With her plain, pretty face with its plaintive dark eyes, she found herself more successfully cast as mistreated wives (*Seed, There's Always Tomorrow*) and mothers of tots who ranged from Shirley Temple, Jackie Cooper and Dickie Moore to George Breakstone, the tormented youngster of Borzage's story of children at war, *No Greater Glory.*

MARIE WILSON

Marie Wilson, a bemused blonde, blinked her brown saucer eyes and chattered inanities as a minor nitwit in a number of thirties Warners movies (*Stars over Broadway, Colleen, Satan Met a Lady, Invisible Menace,* etc.). She had her chance to become a major nitwit when Marion Davies turned down the lead in *Boy Meets Girl* because, it is said, William Randolph Hearst objected to her playing an unmarried mother. Marie played the role and she wasn't unmarried either —the censors saw to that. The censors saw to a lot of the more mirthful moments from the play so you never saw them on the screen. And Marie went back to vacuous supporting parts—that is until the late forties and fifties, when *My Friend Irma* would come along.

TOBY WING

Toby Wing is about the only girl of whom we can think who achieved the status of a star name without being seen in anything more than extra parts and bits. Oh, she had a lead role here and there, but in pictures you never heard of (*Silks and Saddles, Sing While You're Able*).

The Toby Wing "name" was earned completely in the fan magazines, where she was always posing, curved and fluffy-haired, for cheesecake. In movies, you were lucky if you caught a glimpse of her among the Busby Berkeley beauties or the *Search for Beauty* and *Murder at the Vanities* girls.

DOROTHY WILSON

LOIS WILSON, with Frankie Darro (plaid shirt), George Breakstone (in arms), others, in *No Greater Glory*

MARIE WILSON, with James Gagney, Pat O'Brien, in *Boy Meets Girl*

TOBY WING

JANE WITHERS, John McGuire in *This is the Life*

JANE WITHERS

ANNA MAY WONG

JANE WITHERS

Jane Withers started as the female equivalent of Jackie Searle, that mean kid, and as long as she was persecuting Shirley Temple and demanding a machine gun for Christmas, she was a joy. With black button eyes . . . black straight Dutch bob . . . black disposition, she provided considerable contrast to Little Miss Sunshine.

But she got too popular too quickly—not as popular as Shirley, of course, but enough that they had to find "vehicles" for her. And since star vehicles don't go to brats, she became almost a low-grade Shirley in a series of B-minus movies. Her first few starring movies—*Ginger*, Tarkington's *Gentle Julia*, *Paddy O'Day*—were entertaining and Jane remained something of a rascal, although they never let her go much beyond making mischief.

But her movie stories became more and more hackneyed and her characters variations of the perennial Miss Fixit. Too, she grew up quickly—being quite a big girl before her parts grew up to her. Almost any Jane Withers picture would be worth seeing for moments she would contribute but, by the later ones, the moments were farther and farther apart.

CORA WITHERSPOON

Cora Witherspoon was blessed with a face that might have been drawn by one of those cartoonists who specialize in dealing with the "war between men and women." And she had a personality to match. Someone like Thurber might have known what to do with her, but Hollywood used her only in roles (in pictures like *Ladies of the Jury*, *Piccadilly Jim*, *On the Avenue*, *Professor Beware*) in which she played bumptious annoying specimens of the nouveau riche.

ANNA MAY WONG

Oriental ladies of the movies made so little splash that, when you think of an example, there's only one, Anna May Wong. Unfortunately there were far too few roles for her lacquered China-doll looks. And when such Occidentals as Helen Hayes, Luise Rainer, Sylvia Sidney, Loretta Young, Myrna Loy and Tilly Losch grabbed off some of the best of those, it left slim pickings for Miss Wong, the real thing.

So she played a series of inscrutable adventuresses—a vengeful daughter of Fu Manchu, for example—in program melodramas like *Daughter of the Dragon*, *Daughter of Shanghai*, *Limehouse Blues* and *Dangerous to Know* . . . traveled to England, where she had appeared in the silent days, for inept versions of *Java Head* and *Chu Chin Chow*, and really had only one talking picture role of any consequence—a courageous courtesan in *Shanghai Express*.

Even so, she remains the best-known Oriental actress of them all.

FAY WRAY, Robert Armstrong, Bruce Cabot in *King Kong*

CORA WITHERSPOON

FAY WRAY

FAY WRAY

Fay Wray once confessed to us that she was heartily sick of her reputation as a screamer and particularly fed up with herself as a shrieking blonde in the paw of that indescribable ape, known as Kong. We can sympathize with her feelings.

After all, Fay Wray was lovely and competent in dozens of pictures through the thirties, as well as in the silents opposite actors who ranged from Gary Cooper to Erich von Stroheim to Emil Jannings. But in talkies her pictures were a mixed bag and few of them gave her much more opportunity than to be present and pretty while the action was handled by Richard Arlen, Richard Dix, Jack Holt, George Bancroft or Wallace Beery.

There were exceptions, most of them in secondary roles. These would include Miriam Hopkins' secretary who posed as *The Richest Girl in the World*, the *One Sunday Afternoon* girl of Gary Cooper's dreams who turned out to be such a nightmare, and—our particular favorite—the gluttonous virgin, desired by both Fredric March and Frank Morgan in *The Affairs of Cellini*.

That leaves the horror heroines and—sorry, Fay—they're the ones for which you are particularly remembered. There were only five of them, all released within one year, but they kept Miss Wray's vocal cords working overtime. Scream she did, through the sinister experiments of *Dr. X*; the horrifying doings involved with *The Mystery of the Wax Museum*; the "Dracula"-type terrors of *The Vampire Bat*; the escape from a madman who hunts humans in *The Most Dangerous Game*.

And then there was *King Kong*, certainly the most magnificent monster ever conceived. Fay turned out to be his nemesis—"It was beauty killed the beast," said the philosophical movie producer—and like it or not, Kong was her greatest leading man—far and away more commanding than Beery, Bancroft and Jack Holt all put together.

257

JANE WYATT

Jane Wyatt was just the girl for Ronald Colman to find in Shangri-La—a lady of poise and breeding, and lovely to look upon, as well.

The girl in *Lost Horizon* was a role that many actresses wanted. Miss Wyatt, with only a few minor movies (*We're Only Human, Luckiest Girl in the World*, the first version of *Great Expectations, One More River*) and some short-run stage shows in her background, won it.

Strangely enough, it didn't establish her immediately—it was some three years before she got another movie lead and many more before there was a good one.

JANE WYMAN

Button-nosed, big-eyed, long-legged was Jane Wyman, just a starlet in the thirties. She would show for a minute or two in pictures like *Slim* and *The Singing Marine*, and when she did get a lead, it would be opposite somebody like Kenny Baker in something like *Mr. Dodd Takes the Air* or Joe E. Brown in *Wide Open Faces*. But then she played one of those amiable girls in *Brother Rat* and you could tell that you should expect more in those forties pictures to come. She delivered, too.

DIANA WYNYARD

Diana Wynyard, a lady of great dignity, was ideally cast as the prototype of all of those chin-up members of the gentry—most notably in *Cavalcade*. In Noël Coward's paean to the British Empire in the first three decades of the twentieth century, she played Jane Marryot, through whose eyes the "cavalcade" of the title is witnessed. Although her role in a much less distinguished film, *Men Must Fight*, was like a continuation of sequences from her Jane Marryot characterization, Miss Wynyard remained impressive.

But she seemed quite out of her depth in the rather racy comedy of *Reunion in Vienna*, substituting a ladylike pique for the beguiling wit with which Lynn Fontanne had played the role on the stage and proving no match at all for the colorful antics of John Barrymore. Other American Wynyard movies were pallid problem plays—*Let's Try Again, Where Sinners Meet, One More River*. Such failures sent her back to England, but her career was far from over. She would continue for years on the stage and screen there to do the kind of roles she played best.

JANE WYATT

258

DIANA WYNYARD, Clive Brook in *Let's Try Again*

JANE WYMAN, with Wayne Morris, in *The Kid From Kokomo*

DIANA WYNYARD, Dick Henderson, Douglas Scott in *Cavalcade*

259

WINIFRED WESTOVER (right),
Dorothy Janis in *Lummox*

ESTELLE WINWOOD in *Quality Street*

FRANCES WILLIAMS in
Broadway Through a Keyhole

ETHEL WATERS in *On With the Show*

NOTES ON OTHER "W" LADIES

Janet Waldo, a Paramount starlet . . . *Ethel Wales*, and *Charlotte Walker*, well-known silent character actresses who had a few bits in talkies . . . *Polly Walker*, who came from the theatre to play the lead in the first movie version of *Hit the Deck* . . . *Terry Walker*, who had minor leads in minor pictures like *23½ Hours Leave* . . . *Beryl Wallace*, transported from *Earl Carroll's Vanities* to the movie murder version . . . *Polly Walters*, just a bit-part blonde in films although she later scored on Broadway in *She Loves Me Not* . . . *Penelope Dudley-Ward*, of British films . . . *Helen Ware*, an efficient character actress in such early talkies as *The Virginian*, *One Night at Susies*, *Slightly Scarlet*, *Abraham Lincoln* . . . *Irene Ware*, who had a lead in her first picture (*Chandu the Magician*) but then went down into bits . . . *Linda Ware*, who sang with Crosby in *The Star Maker* . . . *Ruth Warren*, a busy small part character actress . . . the great *Ethel Waters*, who sang "Am I Blue?" in *On With the Show*, but whose dramatic movie debut would come in the Forties . . . *Linda Watkins*, from Broadway for leads in *Sob Sister* and *Good Sport*, but then relegated to the minors . . .

Barbara Weeks, brunette ingenue of *Palmy Days* . . . *Phyllis Welch*, opposite Harold Lloyd in *Professor Beware* . . . *Nancy Welford*, who had a lead in *Gold Diggers of Broadway* . . . *Jacqueline Wells*, who played in things like *Tarzan the Fearless*, *The Black Cat*, *The Bohemian Girl* (then, in the forties, would change her name to Julie Bishop and start a new

PATRICA "HONEYCHILE"
WILDER

MAJORIE WHITE

POLLY WALKER and boys in *Hit the Deck*

career) . . . *Doris Weston,* the Dick Powell leading lady whose name is forgotten even by the buffs (she was in *Singing Marine*) . . . *Winifred Westover,* who played *Lummox,* the most depressing drudge ever presented on screen . . .

Marjorie White, who performed energetically in films like *Sunny Side Up, Happy Days* and *Just Imagine* . . . *Patricia Wilder,* who had some movie bits but was better known to radio as Bob Hope's Honeychile . . . *Hope Williams,* for whom Philip Barry wrote some of his most popular plays but who had only a small part in *The Scoundrel* to represent her in films . . . *Kathlyn Williams,* who progressed up from serials in silents, but who had only a few talkie character roles . . . *Pat Wing,* Toby's brunette sister . . . *Linda Winters,* a bit player who would change her name in the forties and find a moment of movie immortality as Dorothy Comingore in *Citizen Kane* . . . *Jane Winton,* who had been doing moderately well in silents but was passed over quickly in talkies . . . *Estelle Winwood,* a welcome eccentric in *Quality Street* but with no more movies for a couple of decades . . . *Googie Withers,* who showed up briefly in such British films as *The Lady Vanishes,* but who would have better things to come . . . *Claire Windsor,* a name in the silents, but with little more than a look-in in talkies . . .

Dorothea Wolbert, a glum character actress (*Dangerous Paradise, Hallelujah, I'm a Bum*) . . . *Helen Wood* and *Judith Wood,* who had minor leads (*Champagne Charlie* for Helen, *Road to Reno* for

PEGGY WOOD, Colin Clive in *The Right To Live*

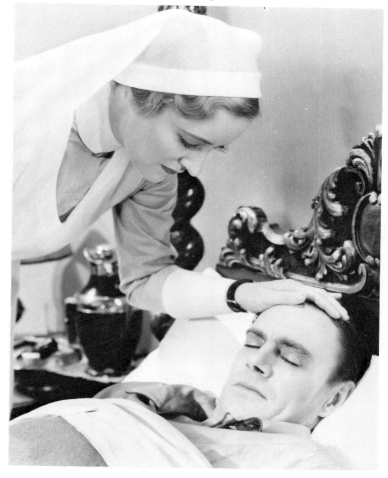

261

DORIS WESTON, Dick Powell in *The Singing Marine*

MARIS WRIXON

JUNE WALKER, with Robert Montgomery, in *War Nurse*

NANCY WELFORD (center), with Nick Lucas, Ann Pennington, Albert Gran, Winnie Lightner, Conway Tearle, Lilyan Tashman, others, in *Gold Diggers of Broadway*

Judith and one or two others for each) . . . Peggy Wood, noted in the theatre and later as TV's Mama, but unexciting on screen (in *Jalna, Wonder of Woman, Handy Andy,* etc.) . . . Joan Woodbury, who was in pictures like *Crashing Hollywood* and *Super Sleuth* . . . Sarita Wooten, the young Cathy in *Wuthering Heights* . . .

Charlene Wyatt, the child in *Valiant is the Word for Carrie* . . . Margaret Wycherly, with only the mediocre 1934 *Midnight* in this period . . . June Walker, a fine Broadway actress, suffering through the slush of her one starring movie, *War Nurse* . . .

And *Luana Walters, Eleanor Wesselhoeft, Lois Wilde, Thelma White, Barbara Worth, Josephine Whittell, Laska Winter, Isabel Withers, Constance Worth, Maris Wrixon, Charlotte Wynters, Lucille Ward, Lottie Williams, Renee Whitney, Frances Williams, Katherine Claire Ward, Claire Whitney, Ruth Weston, Marie Wells, Helen Wright, Adele Watson, Mildred Washington, Alice Ward, Dorothy Ward, Ada Williams, Gloria Williams,* and *Leah Winslow* . . .

LORETTA YOUNG, Richard Greene in *Four Men and a Prayer*

X ~ Y ~ Z

LORETTA YOUNG

It wasn't until a dozen years into her career that Loretta Young actually became a star. But what a leading lady she was for all that time! Take Colman or Cagney, Power or Gable, or even David Manners, and Loretta was just the girl to make them look their best—while looking ravishing herself.

Once in a while, she would be given a role that demanded more of her than being dewy-eyed and glistening-lipped and she was always equal to those assignments, too. You couldn't really think of her as a flaxen-tressed Hungarian orphan, could you? But she was—in the picturesque *Zoo in Budapest*. Add the drab prison girl in a maternity ward in *Life Begins*; a dedicated student nurse in *The White Parade*; and particularly, her part in *A Man's Castle*, the most pathetic waif since Janet Gaynor in *Seventh Heaven*. Miss Young's beauty was incidental in those roles, and would even have been distracting if her performances had not made the girls simple and real.

More often, she was very high style—the better to show off that model's figure and face. She had a fetching romantic comedy style, too, and the combination was felicitious in such enjoyable affairs as *Love Is News*, *Three Blind Mice* and *Wife, Husband and Friend*.

There were the "big" movies in which her function was primarily pictorial—*The Crusades, Clive of India, The House of Rothschild, Suez*. There were the program duds, forgotten except that she was in them.

But out of sixty-odd films in which Loretta Young appeared before the end of the thirties, there are others in which her contributions should be given at least a passing nod—*The Man From Blankleys*, that hilarious John Barrymore comedy; *The Devil to Pay* and *Bulldog Drummond Strikes Back*, both opposite Ronald Coleman; *Second Honeymoon* and *Café Metropole* with Tyrone Power; Cagney's *Taxi* and still more. *Wife, Doctor and Nurse, Kentucky, Grand Slam*. It would be nice to see any of them again—especially for the pleasure of gazing once more upon the face of Loretta Young.

BLANCHE YURKA

Somehow Blanche Yurka, long-time and sometimes distinguished star of the theatre, had never been given a movie role until 1935. And although it was her only film of the thirties (there would be others in the forties and fifties), her debut role was her most impressive.

She was Madame DeFarge in *A Tale of Two Cities*. Her sombre, hollowed eyes and deep-doom voice befitted the fanatic, fierce revolutionary, who knitted grimly as the guillotine claimed ever more aristocrats. She also had a no-holds-barred fight scene with Edna May Oliver, of all persons. Miss Oliver emerged victorious—but didn't she always?

LORETTA YOUNG, Leslie Fenton in *The Hatchet Man*

VERA ZORINA

The first ballerina to attract more than minimal attention in American movies was Vera Zorina (or simply Zorina, as she was first billed on the screen). In the thirties, she had only two roles (there were a few more in the following decade).

Dancing was the thing with Zorina and she did it beautifully in well-staged ballets in *The Goldwyn Follies* and in the vivid "Slaughter on Tenth Avenue" in *On Your Toes*, the only part of the movie that could approach the stage original. She had non-dancing sequences in both films and she handled them adequately enough. But when Zorina was acting, you did have a tendency to grow restless waiting for the next ballet.

BLANCHE YURKA (right) with Lucille La Verne, others, in *A Tale of Two Cities*

LORETTA YOUNG in *Zoo in Budapest*

BLANCHE YURKA, Edna May Oliver in *A Tale of Two Cities*

VERA ZORINA, Richard Greene in *I Was An Adventuress*

LORETTA YOUNG, with Joel McCrea, in *Three Blind Mice*

POLLY ANN YOUNG, George O'Brien in *The Border Patrolman*

GLORIA YOUNGBLOOD in *Adventures of Marco Polo*

CLARA KIMBALL YOUNG as she appeared in *Camille* (actor unknown)

OTHER "X, Y, Z" LADIES

After you have covered Loretta Young, Blanche Yurka and Vera Zorina, there is little left to say about the other "X, Y, Z" ladies. Loretta's sisters *Polly Ann* and *Georgianna Young* didn't approach the celebrity of their sibling—or even that of their other sister, Sally Blane. Polly Ann had a few roles in quickies, Georgianna was confined to *Alexander Graham Bell*, in which she joined the other three.

Another Young—*Clara Kimball Young*—was a great name of the early silent era. How sad to see her reduced to playing walk-ons in Westerns. There were also *Elizabeth Young*, no relation to any of the others, who had minor roles in *There's Always Tomorrow*, *Big Executive* and *Queen Christina*. And a sexy brunette, *Gloria Youngblood*, better known to Manhattan café society than for her short scene in *Trade Winds*. And to the other "Y" ladies, add *Lillian Yarbo*, who played a succession of dusky maids, most notably in *Destry Rides Again* and *You Can't Take It With You*.

And, with Zorina, they wind up the list of those ladies of the thirties.

THE YOUNG SISTERS—Polly Ann Young, Georgianna Young, Loretta Young and, in back, Sally Blane

FACES THEN

PART **2**

JACK HAMILTON'S
BIOGRAPHICAL NOTES

Mary Beth Hughes, Marsha Hunt, Jane Bryan, Lana Turner, Ann Rutherford, and Anita Louise in *These Glamour Girls*

INTRODUCTION

When I first arrived alone in New York in the late 1930s, I didn't know anybody—or even *like* anybody I saw—except Kay Francis, Claire Dodd, Greta Garbo, Margaret Sullavan, Beulah Bondi, Isabel Jewell, Jean Harlow, Patsy Kelly, May Robson, Glenda Farrell, and my other special friends who pulled me through the depression years in a small Pennsylvania town.

Walking along Broadway and down 42nd Street, quite homesick, I began to feel almost at home again when I saw their familiar, alluring faces on theater lobby posters inviting me to come in for a visit (for 55¢). I knew I could count on these courageous, unflappable women, whose faces, voices, and persuasive powers I admired so much, to give me courage to face this new city, and take my mind off my first terrible job and my antiseptic-smelling furnished room on West 74th Street.

Those were my purposely blind days when I wanted to believe they were goddesses from above, and I rather still do. Jean Harlow was up there flouncing, Patsy Kelly sassing, Bette Davis breathing defiance upon the mean and the selfish, and May Robson briskly taking over to make everything come out all right. They were so strong, they didn't need anybody's help. Why would they? I never gave any thought to studio moguls, producers, directors, etc., all those powerful people who "moulded" and even tyrannized my friends. Actually, as we all still know, only God could have created Claire Dodd.

I knew from *Photoplay* about movie stars' making big salaries—trillions more than my $100 a month—and living in big mansions, and driving Duesenbergs and V-16 Packards. I thought, that's just what they deserve, they bring so much happiness to the world. Now everybody knows that most of them didn't really earn all that much nor live in mansions, and a lot of them drove Model A Fords, and that the studios got their money's worth out of them, with those "suspensions" and all. The girls had to work so long and hard that many of them got divorces because of no home life, and went on binges in New York, after a six-day train ride away from Big Daddy's watchful studio. Kay Francis and Margaret Lindsay, finishing one movie in the morning, started another one they knew nothing about that same afternoon. Joan Blondell worked in three pictures at once. "It didn't make any difference," she said. "I always played the same character. They just changed the wardrobe." The studios ground out movies almost as fast as TV does today. It's now startling to realize that Kay Francis, Genevieve Tobin, and Claire Dodd had only 65 minutes to strut their stuff in *The Goose and the Gander*, and Bette Davis 72 minutes in *Dangerous*, and Garbo only 95 in *Anna Karenina*. Every studio shipped their mass-produced wares out fast, to wind up around the U.S.A. ultimately on double-feature bills, with bank nights and dishes thrown in.

All this turmoil and labor turned out luckily for all of us. That's why we can include in our book over 1,000 actresses, of breathtaking range and variety, a mass of staggering talent never surpassed in any other decade—some of them still with us, others who blossomed and were gone in a day. Immortally young, their faces and voices teasing our senses, they are even more secure and fixed in our mind's eye than all the Cleopatras of history and the Jane Eyres of literature.

For biographical data, I am indebted to a lifetime collection of movie reference books, magazines, and biographies, first-hand encounters, the Lincoln Center Library of Performing Arts, the American Academy of Dramatic Arts and Sciences Library, the Channel 13 WNET Library (once *Look's*), such detectives as Richard Lamparski in his "Whatever Became of . . . ?" series, the career articles in *Films in Review*, and to all our movie-lore friends in Hollywood and New York.

Unfortunately, it has been impossible to trace the whereabouts and current activities of all the surviving players of the 1930s as of mid-1974.

JACK HAMILTON

Julie Haydon, Mary Duncan, Irene Dunne, Myrna Loy, Kay Johnson, Marjorie Gateson; (foreground) Harriet Hagman, Peg Entwhistle; in *Thirteen Women*

KATHERINE ALEXANDER

Born in Arkansas, September 22, 1901, and married to Broadway producer William Brady, Jr. (who died in a fire in 1935), she was the sister-in-law of actress Alice Brady, and mother of actress Barbara Brady. In the 1920s and 1930s, she was a stage actress with the Theatre Guild. In 1949, she appeared in her last listed movie, *John Loves Mary*, and also on the London stage, as Linda in *Death of a Salesman*, with Paul Muni.

ELIZABETH ALLAN

Daughter of a Quaker doctor, she was born in Skegsness, Lincolnshire, April 9, 1908, and made her stage debut at nineteen with a walk-on at the Old Vic. She worked in Hollywood films until 1938, and then returned to England to resume her screen, stage, and later, television career, where she asserted herself as a breezier and stronger personality. She married publicist Wilfred J. O'Bryen.

GRACIE ALLEN

She was born in San Francisco, July 26, 1899, the daughter of a song-and-dance man, Edward Allen. At thirteen,

she was a "single" in the San Francisco area, and she later joined her three older sisters in an act, specializing in Irish brogue and colleen parts. She met George Burns, a vaudeville comedian, in 1923, and three years later they were married. The famous Burns and Allen radio show began on February 15, 1932, on NBC. They switched in 1950 to CBS, where, in addition to doing their radio show, they began a long career in television. Their act, in which Burns served as the perfect feeder, asking Gracie questions with increasing incredulity, stayed fresh and funny. Gracie retired in 1958.

In her last years, Gracie suffered several mild heart attacks but remained active in Hollywood society until the end. She died at Cedars of Lebanon Hospital, August 28, 1964.

JUDITH ALLEN

Born Marie Elliott in New York, January 28, 1913, she was educated there and in Providence, R. I. After a modeling career, she appeared on the Broadway stage in *The Trial of Mary Dugan*, *Skidding*, and *Interference*. In 1931, she married the world's heavyweight champion wrestler, Gus Sonnenberg ("Gus the

Goat"), at the Little Church Around the Corner, and divorced him at the time of her first movie. In 1935, she married Jack Doyle, a heavyweight boxer from Queensland, Ireland, who was also a part-time singer and actor. Miss Allen divorced Doyle in 1937, and then began a brief career as a night-club singer. In 1941, she married book publisher Rudolph Field (of the House of Field), then an Army private, and divorced him in 1944, saying: "Alas, I married brains."

ASTRID ALLWYN

She was born in South Manchester, Conn., on November 27. In her stage debut, she was one of the two nursemaids in Elmer Rice's *Street Scene* (1929). She made her first movie in 1931, and her career ended in the early 1940s. She first married actor Robert Kent and 'ter Charles Fee, of Beverly Hills.

ADRIENNE AMES

As Adrienne Ruth McClure, she was born August 3, 1907, in Forth Worth, Texas. She early married a Texas oil man, Derward Truax, and then a New York broker, Stephen Ames (1929—div. 1933), and became active in New York society. She had some still photographs made which showed off her dark beauty so strikingly that a Paramount official gave her a contract without a screen test. Her last film was *Zero Hour* in 1939. Two years before, she had divorced her third husband, actor Bruce Cabot. A witty radio commentator on the Hollywood-Broadway scene over station WHN for six years, she died May 31, 1947, after a long illness; but she had kept on working until two weeks before her death.

LONA ANDRE

She was born in Nashville, March 12, 1915, and named Laura Anderson. In 1933, she started to get a marriage license for a wedding to James Dunn, but changed her mind. In 1935, she was the wife of actor Edward Norris for four days.

HEATHER ANGEL

She was born in Oxford, England, February 9, 1909, daughter of Prof. Andrea Angel. She had a brief span on the stage in the plays of Shakespeare and Wilde before entering films in England, 1930. She was married and divorced from actors Ralph Forbes and Henry Wilcoxon. Her third, director Robert B. Sinclair, was stabbed to death by a prowler in their Montecito, Calif., home in 1970. She is the mother of two children.

ANNABELLA

Born on France's national holiday, Bastille Day, 1909, in a suburb of Paris, as Suzanne Georgette Charpentier, she was one of four children of a well-to-do French publisher. With her father's encouragement, she played a small role in Abel Gance's epic *Napoleon* in 1926, drawing her screen name from a childhood love for Poe's *Annabelle Lee*. She was first married to actor Jean Murat and is the mother of a daughter (Mrs. Oskar Werner). Annabella divorced her second husband, Tyrone Power, in 1948, and retired in 1950. She lives in Paris and on a farm in the French Pyrenees.

EVE ARDEN

Born in Mill Valley, Calif., April 30, 1912, she got the idea for her stage name from cosmetics jars on her backstage dressing table, combining the labels of "Evening in Paris" and "Elizabeth Arden," when she found she wasn't getting anywhere as Eunice Quedens. She played Broadway in two Ziegfeld Follies editions, 1936 and 1938. In 1941, she returned triumphantly in the musical *Let's Face It*, with Danny Kaye. Her stage, screen, radio and TV (as *Our Miss Brooks*) careers continued successfully thereafter. Her first husband was Ned

Bergen (1939-1947), by whom she had daughters Liza and Constance. She is now married to actor Brooks West, with two sons, Duncan and Douglas.

JEAN ARTHUR

She began her life as Gladys Georgianna Greene in New York, October 17, 1905, daughter of Herbert Sidney Greene, a professional photographer. After modeling for Howard Chandler Christy and other illustrators, she got a small part in her first movie in 1923, *Cameo Kirby*, with John Gilbert, followed by ingenue roles in Westerns.

Miss Arthur's first husband was photographer Julian Anker in 1928. The marriage was annulled. She married Frank Ross, a young singer, later to become a film producer, in 1932, and divorced him after seventeen years. Though mostly living a recluse-like life at her retreat in Carmel, Calif., she has made occasional forays out into the world on the stage, in television, and as a teacher of acting in colleges.

MARY ASTOR

In the 1930s, her career survived two off-screen scandals. In 1934, her tenacious parents sued her for non-support, because they had no money to continue improvements on the $75,000 house she had given them. A year later, her second husband, Dr. Franklyn Thorpe, divorced her, and was given custody of their daughter Marylyn (born June 15, 1932). Miss Astor sued to gain legal custody of her child. To prove that his wife was "a person of continuous gross, immoral conduct," Dr. Thorpe produced what he said was her diary, a detailed record of her alleged affairs with Hollywood celebrities, particularly the then-married George S. Kaufman. All this made good newspaper copy for months. But Judge Goodwin Knight (later Governor of California) attached small importance to the diary, ordered it burned, and gave custody of Marylyn to Miss Astor for nine months each year.

Born Lucile Langhanke, Quincy, Ill., May 3, 1906, Mary Astor began her screen career in September 1920. She was first married to director Kenneth Hawks in 1928; he was killed in an airplane crash three years later. After Dr. Thorpe, she married Manuel del Campo in 1937 (div. 1942), by whom she had a son Antonio, and Thomas Wheelock (1945-1953). She has written two accounts of her life, *My Story* and *My Life in Film*, as well as several novels.

OLGA BACLANOVA

Born in Moscow, August 19, 1899, she grew up on her parents' estate outside of Smolensk. At sixteen, she joined the Moscow Art Theatre, and made her New

York stage debut as Lysistrata with Russian players in 1925, and her first Hollywood movie, *The Dove*, with Norma Talmadge, in 1927. Her most famous silent film role was as Lou, in Josef von Sternberg's *Docks of New York* in 1928. After her Broadway appearance in *Murder at the Vanities* in 1933, she continued on the stage until 1942.

She became an American citizen in 1931, having married her second husband, Nicholas Soussanin, a Russian whom she met in Hollywood, in 1929. They were divorced in 1939, and she then married publisher Richard Davis of New York.

FAY BAINTER

Miss Bainter began as a child actress in her native Los Angeles (where she was born December 7, 1892), playing a little girl in *The Jewess*, with Nance O'Neil, 1898, and became a regular member of the Morosco Stock Co. Her first big success was as Ming Toy in *East Is West*. From then on, she was a Broadway star. Perhaps her most stunning stage role was as the desperate Fran Dodsworth in love with a young man in *Dodsworth*, with Walter Huston, 1934.

She married Lt. Commander Reginald Venable of the Navy in June 1922, and they had one son, Reginald, Jr. She died April 17, 1968.

LUCILLE BALL

The indestructible Lucy was born in Butte, Montana, August 6, 1911, but grew up in Jamestown, N. Y. While trying to get chorus jobs in New York, she found her first employment in a Broadway drug store. She became a fashion model for Hattie Carnegie and a "Chesterfield girl" before going to Hollywood in 1934 to be in the chorus of Sam Goldwyn's *Roman Scandals*, with Eddie Cantor. She Married Desi Arnaz in 1940, began her triumphant TV career with him, had two children, and finally divorced him in 1960. In 1961, she married night club comedian Gary Morton.

TALLULAH BANKHEAD

She never allowed anyone to forget that she was a Democrat from a famous Alabama political family (born January 31, 1902)—her father had been Speaker of the House of Representatives, and her grandfather and an uncle had been U. S. Senators, all Democrats from Alabama. She was born in Huntsville, and made her New York stage debut at sixteen. She became the scandalous darling of the London theatre between 1923 and 1930. After her first disastrous movie experiences, Tallulah became a triumphant stage star in New York, with her most famous success as Regina Giddens in *The Little Foxes* in 1939. She was briefly married to actor

TALLULAH BANKHEAD

John Emery. When she died of pneumonia, complicated by emphysema, December 12, 1968, she was 66 years old.

VILMA BANKY

She was born in Nagyrodog, near Budapest, January 9, 1898. Her screen career started in Hungarian films in 1921, and she also made films in Austria before being brought to the United States under contract to Sam Goldwyn to make her Hollywood debut in Rudolph Valentino's *The Eagle*.

Miss Banky married actor Rod La Rocque in 1927. The couple lived together, during their 42-year marriage, in an unostentatious home, without a swimming pool, in the Foothill Road area of Beverly Hills. Her husband died October 15, 1969.

LYNN BARI

The tall, affable Lynn Bari was born Marjorie Bitzer in Roanoke, Va., December 18, 1913. Her father was a clergyman, Rev. Robert H. Bitzer, who moved his family to Melrose, Mass., when his daughter was seven, and later to California, where he became the head of the Institute of Religious Sciences. Miss Bari began as a chorus girl in Joan Crawford's *Dancing Lady* at MGM in 1933, and was given a Fox contract a year later. Her first husband was agent Walter Kane (1939–div. 1943). Thereupon she married Sid Luft, then a test pilot for Douglas Aircraft, and had a son, John Sidney Luft, September 18, 1948. She divorced Luft in 1950. From 1958 to 1972 she was married to Dr. Nathan Rickles, a Beverly Hills psychiatrist.

BINNIE BARNES

Daughter of a London bobby, and christened Gertrude Maude Barnes (March 25, 1905), she is reputed to have been both a milkmaid and a nurse before going on the stage as a Tiller Girl in 1924. Then she was called "Texas Binnie Barnes" in a rope-spinning act in variety, and got her first good stage role as Fanny Bridges, the cabaret singer, in Noël Coward's *Cavalcade*, 1931. Once married to art dealer Samuel Joseph (1931–1936), she is now the wife of Columbia film producer Mike Frankovich and lives in Beverly Hills.

WENDY BARRIE

She is the daughter of a King's Counsel, F. C. Jenkins, and born in Hong Kong, April 18, 1912. She made her London stage debut in *Wonder Bar*, 1930, and her first British film two years later. After her movie career ended in 1942, she went to New York, and eventually wound up as one of TV's first talk show ladies.

ETHEL BARRYMORE

Miss Barrymore had been on the stage since she was fifteen, making her debut at the Empire as Julia in *The Rivals*, with her uncle John Drew. In 1909, she married socialite Russell Griswold Colt, and was the mother of two sons and a daughter. After a number of partings and reconciliations, she divorced him in 1923, when she was forty-four, and never remarried. Her last famous stage role was the schoolteacher Miss Moffat in *The Corn Is Green*, which she played three years. After 1946, she settled permanently in Hollywood, playing roles in twenty films. Born in Philadelphia, August 15, 1879, she died in Beverly Hills, June 18, 1959.

LOUISE BEAVERS

Miss Beavers was born in Cincinnati, March 8, 1902, studied at Pasadena High School in California, and entered movies as early as 1923 in *Gold Diggers*, with Hope Hampton. Between acting jobs, she worked as a personal maid to actress Leatrice Joy, then living in Beverly Hills. Her career hit full stride when sound came in, and, beginning with Mary Pickford's *Coquette*, 1929, she continued in movies through the 1950s. She played the title role in the *Beulah* TV series until her death of a heart attack October 26, 1962. She was married to Le Roy Moore.

JANET BEECHER

Born October 21, 1884, daughter of Herr Meysenburg, once German vice-consul in Chicago, and sister of actress Olive Wyndham. After studying at the Art Students League in New York, she turned to the stage, first as a walk-on in *The Two Orphans* at the New Amsterdam, New York, at twenty. She had a long Broadway career as leading lady and character actress, and when her movie career ended in 1943, she returned to Broadway as Catherine Apley in *The Late George Apley*, 1944. Miss Beecher was married twice, to Harry R. Guggenheimer and Dr. Richard H. Hoffman. She died August 6, 1955.

MADGE BELLAMY

Her father was William Bladsoe Philpott, dean of literature at the University of Texas, and she was born in Hillsboro, Texas, June 30, 1900. At five, she made her stage debut, and returned to acting ten years later as Pollyanna in a touring company. Her first movie was *The Riddle Woman* in 1920, with Geraldine Farrar. As a star in the 1920s, her films included *Lorna Doone*, *The Iron Horse*, *Ankles Preferred* and *Soft Living*. At her home in Ontario, Calif., she is writing her memoirs, *I was Madge Bellamy*.

CONSTANCE BENNETT

The eldest of three beautiful Bennett sisters was born in New York, October 22, 1904, and educated there and in Paris. In 1922 she made her movie debut in two Elaine Hammerstein features, *Reckless Youth* and *Evidence*. She married Philip Plant, heir to steamship and railroad fortunes, in 1925. She had previously been married, at sixteen, to Chester Moorehead, the son of a Chicago dentist, but this had been annulled. With Plant, she became one of "the darlings of the continental society set," and had a son, Peter Bennett Plant. This marriage ended in divorce in 1928, and Miss Bennett returned to movies. In 1931, she married, Henri Marquis de la Falaise de la Coudray and divorced him for desertion in 1940. A year later, she married actor Gilbert Roland. They had two daughters, Lorinda and Christina Consuelo ("Gyl"), and were divorced in 1944. Her fifth, final, and happiest marriage was to U. S. Army Col. John Couter in 1946. She died of a cerebral hemorrhage at Walson Army Hospital, Fort Dix, N. J., with her husband at her bedside, July 24, 1965.

JOAN BENNETT

She was born in Palisades, N. J., February 27, 1910, but says, "with all of Constance's juggling of dates through the years, I started out as the youngest, then became her twin, and wound up as the oldest sister."

She began her career with her father in an anti-Hollywood play, *Jarnegan*, in 1928. Prior to that in movies, she had played extras, and a small role in *Power* with William Boyd, before her real start as Ronald Colman's leading lady in *Bulldog Drummond*, 1929. From her long career, she selects only six films that satisfied her: three from the 1930s, *Little Women*, *Private Worlds* and *Trade Winds*, and three from the 1940s, *Man*

Hunt, The Woman in the Window and *Scarlet Street*. In marriage, she calls herself a "three-time loser." At sixteen, she married John Marion Fox, of Seattle, a young man on the fringe of the theatre and movies, and the father of her first daughter, Adrienne Fox Anderson. In March 1932, she married screenwriter Gene Markey, had a second daughter, Melinda (Mrs. Joseph Bena) and divorced him in 1937. In 1940, she married producer Walter Wanger, and had more daughters, Stephanie (Mrs. Frederick Guest) and Shelley. On December 13, 1951, Wanger shot Miss Bennett's agent, and his friend Jennings Lang, in the groin, telling the police "I've just shot the sonofabitch who tried to break up my home." He entered a plea of "not guilty by reasons of temporary insanity," and spent three months and nine days at the Wayside Honor Farm, Castaic, Calif. The Wangers were divorced in 1965, and he died in 1968. In 1953, Miss Bennett returned to the theatre, and made successful national tours with Donald Cook in *Janus* and *The Pleasure of His Company*. For four years, she appeared in the daytime TV serial, *Dark Shadows*, 1966–1970.

LEILA BENNETT

She was born in Newark. Her maid-in-blackface role in *The First Year* was a lucky one for her; she first played it on Broadway in 1920, repeated it in the London production of 1926, as well as in the 1932 movie version. She got her start with Harry Blaney's stock company in Brooklyn, and spent 53 weeks as a silent courtroom spectator in the long-run Broadway hit, *Lightnin'*. Her last film was *Fury* in 1936. She married Frank Keough.

INGRID BERGMAN

Born August 29, 1915, she is the daughter of Justus Bergman, who owned a camera shop, and his German-born wife, Friedel Adler, who died when Ingrid was two. Her father died when she was twelve, and she went to live with her father's brother and his five children. She was a scholarship student at the Royal Dramatic Theatre School, and made her film debut in 1934. She married dentist Petter Aron Lindstrom two years before coming to America. She has since been married to Roberto Rossellini (1950-1958) and Lars Schmidt, a Swedish theatrical producer. She is the mother of three daughters and a son.

ELISABETH BERGNER

Her birthdate is usually given as August 22, 1900, in Vienna, daughter to Emil and Anna Rosa Wagner Bergner. She studied for the stage at the Vienna Conservatory, from 1915 to 1919, and made her first success as Ophelia, with the German actor Alexander Moissi as Hamlet. With her Hungarian-born husband, director-producer Paul Czinner, she starred in German films in 1924. In 1943, she returned to Broadway in *The Two Mrs. Carrolls*. Her last appearance on the American stage was in the tryout of *First Love*, 1961, during which she and director Alfred Lunt had disagreements; she didn't go to Broadway with the play.

EDNA BEST

She was born in Hove, Sussex, March 3, 1900, and made her London stage debut at seventeen as Ela Delahay in *Charley's Aunt*. At the age of twenty, she was playing Peter Pan and getting married (to Seymour Beard), by whom she had twin sons. During the 1920s she was a favorite London star, with her biggest hits in *Fallen Angels*, with Tallulah Bankhead, and *The Constant Nymph*. After her divorce in 1928 she married actor Herbert Marshall. They had one child, actress Sarah Marshall, and divorced in 1934. In 1940 she married Nat Wolff. Her stage career, in London and New York, continued through the 1950s.

MARIE BLAKE

Offscreen, as the next elder sister of Jeanette MacDonald, she was born in Philadelphia, daughter to Daniel MacDonald, architect. In 1920, she was a chorus girl in New York, when her sister Jeanette made her stage debut. She also played in vaudeville and stock before making her first movie in 1937. She continued in the *Dr. Kildare* series through the 1940s. When appearing in the TV series *The Addams Family*, she changed her name again, this time to Blossom Rock.

CLARA BLANDICK

Born on an American ship in the harbor of Hong Kong, June 4, 1880, she grew up in Boston and made her stage debut there with E. H. Sothern in *Richard Lovelace*. She went to New York at the age of twenty-three for ingenue roles and was described as "a dainty, petite, graceful heroine." She made her talkie debut in 1929 in *Wise Girls*.

SALLY BLANE

She was born Elizabeth Jane Young in Salida, Colorado, July 11, 1910. All the Young children worked as movie extras after their mother, divorced, moved to Hollywood in 1915, and Sally alone worked as a sea nymph in *Sirens of the Sea*, with Jack Mulhall, in 1917. Her adult career started as the chum of Dorothy Gulliver in *The Collegians* series at Universal. She married actor-director Norman Foster in 1937, and has a son and a daughter.

JOAN BLONDELL

If ever an actress had a name that caught the flip, sexy essence of her personality it was Joan Blondell—yet Warner Bros. wanted to call her Inez Holmes! She was one of the three children of vaudevillians Eddie Blondell and Kathryn Cain, born August 30, 1909, in New York. From the age of three she was in her parents' act (Ed Blondell and Company), traveling around the world, appearing in Australia and Europe. At seventeen, she won a $2,000-prize beauty contest in Dallas, and, at twenty, finally made it to Broadway in George Kelly's *Maggie the Magnificent*, with James Cagney also in the cast. Blondell and Cagney were so good together that they were cast in *Penny Arcade* the following year. By 1971, Miss Blondell had appeared in over eighty movies, twenty-two stages plays, and at least fifty TV roles. She now lives alone in Santa Monica, Calif., after having been married and divorced three times: cameraman George Barnes (1932–1935), who provided Joan with "my first real home," then actor Dick Powell, "my broker and security man" (1936–1945), and finally Mike Todd, "my passion" (1947–1950).

ELEANOR BOARDMAN

Miss Boardman was the second aristocratic looking actress (the other was Florence Vidor) to become the wife of director King Vidor. She had started in silent films in 1922, and had a career of close to ten years at MGM, as leading lady to Conrad Nagel, John Gilbert, Lew Cody, Charles Ray, William Haines and others. She was born in Philadelphia, August 19, 1898, became the first "Eastman Kodak Girl," appeared on Broadway with Edna Hibbard, Louise Dresser, and Frank Morgan in *Rockabye Baby*, 1918, and in Arthur Hopkins' production of *A Very Good Man*. After her divorce from Vidor (whom she married in 1926), she married another director, Harry D'Abbadie D'Arrast, who died in 1968. She lives in Santa Barbara.

MARY BOLAND

Daughter of an actor, W. A. Boland, she was born in Philadelphia, January 28, 1880, when her father was on tour. The Boland home town was Detroit, where Mary attended Sacred Heart Convent. At twenty-one she made her debut and played in stock until her first New York play, as the heroine of *Strongheart*, with Robert Edeson, 1905. For several seasons, she was John Drew's leading lady at the Empire Theatre. During that time she was also the star of some early movies, made in New York, with Eugene O'Brien and Robert McKim. It was not until 1919 that she displayed her dazzling talents as a stately scatterbrain, as Mrs. Wheeler in Booth Tarkington's *Clarence*, with Alfred Lunt. From that time on, she was a favorite comedienne in New York, particularly in George Kelly's *The Torch Bearers*, 1922, and *Cradle Snatchers*, with Humphrey Bogart, 1925. In 1931, she returned to movies. Her last was in 1950, *Guilty Bystander*, with Zachary Scott, and her last play, *Lullaby*, in 1954, as an awesome, possessive mother in *The Silver Cord* vein, but with laughs. Her last years were described as "serene," divided between Hollywood and her suite at the Essex House, New York, where she died in her sleep on June 23, 1965. Miss Boland never married.

LILIAN BOND

She made her debut in *Dick Whittington*, a pantomime, 1924, in London (where she was born January 18, 1910)

JOAN BLONDELL

and came to the United States two years later. On Broadway, she appeared as Rosamanda in Earl Carroll's *Fioretta*, with Fanny Brice and Leon Errol, and *Stepping Out*, with Jobyna Howland and Lionel Atwill, both in 1929, *Stepping Out* became one of her first films in 1931, with Reginald Denny. She continued in movies into the 1950s. For a time, her name was linked romantically with Howard Hughes. She married Harry Shulman, and broker Sydney A. Smith (1935–1944). She now lives with a third husband in Northridge, Calif.

BEULAH BONDI

She was born in Chicago May 3, 1892, as Beulah Bondy, daughter of a real estate man. After she received her master's degree in oratory at Valparaiso University, she directed school and club dramatics there and did not make her debut on the professional stage until 1919, in Indianapolis with the Stuart Walker stock company, playing as her first role that of a very old lady. From the beginning, she

played only character roles, and her debut on Broadway in 1925 saw her as Maggie, the seventy-year-old servant in *One in the Family*, followed by *Saturday's Children*, *Cock Robin*, *Distant Drums*, and the adder-tongued Emma Jones of *Street Scene* that brought her to the movies. Miss Bondi never married ("I had to make a choice between marriage and a career"). She believes it is because her mother taught her to be "a lover of life and a student of human nature" that she has been able to act so convincingly.

OLIVE BORDEN

Born of Irish parents in Richmond, July 14, 1906, she was educated in Baltimore convents. Olive got started in Hal Roach comedies, but her career got its push when Tom Mix used her as leading lady in *My Old Pal* and *The Yankee Senor*. She married broker Theodore Spector and John Moeller, both divorced.

Falling on hard times, both Olive and her mother disappeared in the late 1930s. It turned out that Mrs. Borden had gone to the Skid Row section of Los Angeles to ask for help. Olive followed her there, scrubbed floors at the Sunshine Mission, and helped stage pageants. Although briefly a member of the WACS in 1943, she returned to Skid Row for periods of time. She was found seriously ill in a cheap Main Street hotel, and died at the age of 41, October 1, 1947. Among her possessions was a glossy 3" x 5" photograph of her, signed in white ink, "Sincerely, Olive Borden."

VEDA ANN BORG

Of Swedish-Scottish parents, she was born in Boston, January 11, 1915, went to schools there, and became an artist's model. In 1936, hailed· as "the most thrilling redhead since Clara Bow" (although she had reddish-blonde hair), she made her movie debut in *Three Cheers for Love*. She first married Paul Herrick. In 1946, while acting in *Mother Wore Tights*, she married Andrew Mc-Laglen, later a director, and son of actor Victor McLaglen. They had a son Victor, and were divorced in 1957. She died August 16, 1973, in Hollywood.

THE BOSWELL SISTERS

The Boswell Sisters were natives of New Orleans, growing up in a household that lived in the world of music. As children, the three sisters learned to play the cello, violin and piano, but their talents led to harmonizing as a trio. By 1935, their "Boswell Sound" achieved for them international fame on radio, in night clubs, the theatre, and European tours, as well as in movies. But it was in that year Vet married and left the trio,

BEULAH BONDI

274

followed a year later by Martha, who married George L. Lloyd, a retired major in the Royal Air Force and founder of Decca Records. (Martha died in 1958.) Only Connee (who is married to Harry Leedy, the sisters' manager) has remained in show business.

CLARA BOW

Clara Gordon Bow was born in Brooklyn, July 29, 1904, the only child of Robert and Sarah Bow, and grew up in an atmosphere of poverty and unhappiness. She daydreamed of becoming a movie star, entered her picture in the "Fame and Fortune" contest sponsored by movie magazines *Motion Picture, Shadowland,* and *Motion Picture Classic.* Her father hoped that she would win, but her mother warned, "She is going to a life of sin." Clara won the contest.

Her first role was in 1922, in *Beyond the Rainbow,* when at $50 a week, she played "a mischievous sub-deb." The movie that made her world famous was Elinor Glyn's *It,* 1927, and for three years she was Paramount's biggest star. In keeping with her zestful screen personality, she led an undisciplined private life. By 1931, she quieted down to marry cowboy star Rex Bell, and become the mother of two sons. In 1954, her husband was elected Lieutenant Governor of Nevada. But the couple had long since separated, and Clara lived alone in Culver City, under the care of a nurse and companion, treated by a neuro-psychiatrist after several nervous breakdowns. At Christmas, she sent cards inscribed "Remember me? Clara Bow." She died September 27, 1965.

DORRIS BOWDEN

She grew up in Memphis (though born in Coldwater, Miss., December 27, 1915) and was a graduate of Louisiana State University. In 1940, she became the third wife of film scenarist Nunnally Johnson (who, mentioning his two divorces, said "I always insist on custody of the mother-in-law"), and became the mother of two daughters and a son. Her last screen appearance was in *The Moon Is Down,* 1943.

GRACE BRADLEY

Grace was born in Brooklyn and began as a chorus girl in *The Third Little Show* and *Strike Me Pink.* She became the fifth wife of William Boyd (Hopalong Cassidy), and after 1950 lived with him in retirement in Palm Springs, a devoted and happy wife, until his death in 1972.

OLYMPE BRADNA

She was named for the Olympia The-ater in Paris—the equivalent to the Palace in New York in vaudeville fame—where she was said to have been born between the matinee and evening shows, on August 12, 1920. Her parents, Joseph and Jeanne Bradna, were presenting a dog act there. She became an acrobatic dancer at the Folies-Bergere, and later at the French Casino in New York, "where she stopped the show nightly." A Paramount contract followed in 1936. In 1941, she married Douglas Wood Wilhoit, a Santa Barbara socialite, and retired.

ALICE BRADY

Born November 2, 1892, she was the only child of the famous New York producer William A. Brady and his French-born wife, Rose Marie Rene, a dancer who retired from show business at her marriage. Her mother died when Alice was four, and her father married actress Grace George. She studied for the grand opera stage (she had a lyric soprano voice). Her first big roles in the theatre were in operettas, *The Mikado, H. M. S. Pinafore,* and *The Balkan Princess.* In 1912, she appeared in *Little Women,* playing Meg. In 1915, she opened on Broadway in Owen Davis' play *Sinners,* and until 1923 worked simultaneously on the Broadway stage and starring in silent films made in New York studios. She married one of her leading men, James Crane, in 1919, who became an alcoholic. They were divorced, and she never remarried. On Broadway she continued to play "lush ladies—women good enough, but also faintly bad" in a series of short-run plays. She was the first Nina Leeds in Eugene O'Neill's *Strange Interlude,* but a few weeks before it was scheduled to open, she collapsed and was replaced by Lynn Fontanne. She then undertook another O'Neill play—Lavinia in *Mourning Becomes Electra,* with Nazimova, in 1931, which established her reputation as a dramatic acress of emotional power. After 1933, she bought a house in Beverly Hills and settled down to making movies. She died of cancer, October 28, 1939, at LeRoy Sanitarium, New York.

EVELYN BRENT

Born in Tampa, Florida, October 20, 1899, as Mary Elizabeth Riggs, she grew up in Syracuse and Brooklyn. While a schoolgril, she and her classmates visited the film studios at Fort Lee, N. J., and "Betty" Riggs got her start as an extra in an Olga Petrova picture, 1914. From then on, until 1920, when she went to England, she played small parts in many movies, including *Raffles,* with John Barrymore, in 1917. She played leading roles in several English films. In 1922, she went to Spain to film *The Spanish Jade,* with David Powell and Marc MacDermott, released in the United States by Paramount. Her performance interested American producers in her once more, and she went to Hollywood for her real career. She was married to Bernie Fineman, songwriter Harry Edwards, and actor Harry Fox, with whom she appeared in vaudeville. In the 1950s, she worked as an actors' representative with the Thelma White Agency in Hollywood. After her third husband died in 1959, she lived with a longtime friend, Dorothy Herzog, in Westwood Village, California.

MARY BRIAN

As Louise Byrdie Dantzler, she was born in Corsicana, Texas, February 17, 1908, and attended public schools in Dallas. In 1924, she and her mother, Louise Dantzler, went to California to try to get the young sixteen-year-old girl in the movies. All attempts failed until she won second prize in a beauty contest, with a letter of introduction to a film executive as the consolation prize. This brought her to the attention of Paramount Pictures officials, and she was cast as the child Wendy in *Peter Pan,* with Betty Bronson. The good parts stopped coming to her around 1937. In 1940, she toured in a musical, *Three After Three,* with Simone Simon and Mitzi Green, and during World War II entertained American troops. In 1953, she played the mother in TV's *Meet Corliss Archer.* She married magazine illustrator Jon Whitcomb in May 1941 (divorced three months later), and later more happily, film editor George Tomasini, in 1947.

FANNY BRICE

She began life October 29, 1891, as Frances Borach on Forsyth Street, near Delancey, on the Lower East Side, daughter of Charles Borach, an Alsatian said to "own several saloons," and his wife, Rose Stern, Hungarian-born. She grew up in Brooklyn. In 1909, she married Frank White, a Springfield, Mass., barbershop owner (marriage annulled), and, in 1918, when she was twenty-seven, she married the gambler Nicky Arnstein—the marriage that gave drama to the stage-and-screen *Funny Girl.* Her last husband was impresario Billy Rose (1929-1938). Fanny, who then spelled her name Fannie, made her debut on an amateur night at Keeney's Theatre, singing "When You Know You're Not Forgotten by the Girl You Can't Forget," winning a five-dollar first prize. From 1910, until her last appearance in 1936, she was a Broadway favorite. She spent her last years in Beverly Hills, and died at the Cedars of Lebanon Hospital, of a cerebral hemorrhage, May 29, 1951.

HELEN BRODERICK

Born August 11, 1891, in New York, she was the daughter of an actor, William Broderick, wife of an actor, Lester Crawford, and mother of actor Broderick Crawford. She was in the first *Ziegfeld Follies* as a chorus girl in 1907, and later teamed with her husband in vaudeville for several years. On Broadway she played in such musicals as *Nifties of 1923*, *Puzzles of 1925*, and *Fifty Million Frenchmen*. She repeated her *Frenchmen* role in the movie of 1931, but didn't act on the screen again until *Top Hat*, 1935. Her last role was in Deanna Durbin's *Because of Him*, 1946. After a long retirement, she died at Beverly Hills Doctors Hospital, September 25, 1959.

SHEILA BROMLEY

To make her career even more confusing, she was also once known as Sheila Fulton, and was born in San Francisco, October 31, 1911. She studied at Berkeley, and entered movies after she was chosen "Miss California." Although her career ended around 1942, she came back in a small role, Mrs. Grandin, in *Hotel*, for Warners, 1967.

BETTY BRONSON

Born in Trenton, N. J., November 17, 1906, she was named Elizabeth Ada Bronson. At three, she was living in California with her parents, went to Catholic schools, and studied dancing under Michael Fokine. At sixteen, she started in movies in *Anna Ascends*, with Alice Brady, in a bit role. After *Peter Pan*, she became a special star at Paramount in little princess roles that were not in tune with the mood of the 1920s, and her popularity was short-lived. By 1927 the studio said good-bye to her in a Western, *Open Range*, with Lane Chandler.

She married Ludwig Lauerhaus, an executive in a pharmaceutical firm in Asheville, N. C., and later retired with him to live in Altadena, Calif. In 1962, she played a small part as a judge's wife in *Who's Got the Action?*, with Dean Martin, and also appeared on TV shows *Dr. Kildare* and *My Three Sons*. After a brief illness, she died October 19, 1971.

LOUISE BROOKS

The daughter of a lawyer, she was born in Cherryville, Kansas, November 14, 1906. Her mother, a musician, enrolled her at the Denishawn Dance Studios, to study with Ruth St. Denis and Ted Shawn in New York, and she toured with their company for two years. In 1924, she got a chorus job in George White's *Scandals*, with Winnie Lightner and Tom Patricola. Then she went to London to appear in a dance act at the Café de Paris, but returned to Broadway to appear in *Louie the 14th*, with Leon Errol in 1925, and was signed for movies by Paramount. She made her debut in a small part in *The Street of Forgotten Men*, with Percy Marmont and Mary Brain, 1925. Miss Brooks' only marriage was to director Eddie Sutherland, whom she divorced in 1928.

PHYLLIS BROOKS

Her father was an industrial engineer, her mother a dramatic coach, and she was born in Boise, Idaho, July 18, 1914, as Phyllis Steiller. She became a model to earn her tuition in a Chicago art school, after having gone to schools in St. Paul, Milwaukee, and Grand Rapids. On Broadway, in 1936, she played the part of Jean Maitland (Ginger Rogers' role on the screen) in *Stage Door*, with Margaret Sullavan, and also acted on Broadway, as a debutante in *Panama Hattie* with Ethel Merman, 1940. In the 1940s, she appeared in such films as Josef von Sternberg's *The Shanghai Gesture*, 1941, *Lady in the Dark*, 1944, and *The Unseen*, with Joel McCrea, 1945. That year, she married Torbert MacDonald, Jr., a Harvard football star, and retired.

IRENE BROWNE

Born in London, June 29, 1893, she went to schools in Germany and Switzerland. At seventeen she made her London stage debut as a dancer in *Robert Macaire*, with H. B. Irving, Sir Henry's son, and became a member of his company. Her long West End career included appearances in *The Nine O'Clock Revue*, as Lucille in *No, No, Nanette* (1925), and Noël Coward's *Cavalcade* and *Conversation Piece*. She died of cancer in London July 24, 1965.

VIRGINIA BRUCE

She was born as Helen Virginia Briggs in Minneapolis, September 29, 1910, daughter of an insurance broker. She grew up in Fargo, N. Dak., and Los Angeles, and made her screen debut in 1929. After her divorce from John Gilbert, her second husband was J. Walter Ruben, director-producer, whom she married in 1937. He died in 1942. In 1946, she married Ali Ipar, of Turkey, who had just been inducted into the U. S. Army. She returned to movies briefly as Kim Novak's mother in *Strangers When We Meet* in 1960, and since then has lived in Pacific Palisades.

JANE BRYAN

And, having proved she could do it, Hollywood-born and educated Jane (who

JANE BRYAN

had been born Jane O'Brien, June 11, 1918) turned her back on movies, married a Hollywood business man, Justin Dart, president of Rexall Drug., Inc., December 31, 1939, and resisted all attempts to lure her back to the screen, retiring at the age of twenty-one. She is the mother of two sons and a daughter, and lives in Beverly Hills.

DOROTHY BURGESS

A niece of Fay Bainter, and daughter of actress Grace Burgess, she was born in Los Angeles, March 4, 1907, and studied at Mrs. Dow's School of Acting in New York. She started her career as a specialty dancer in a *Music Box Revue*, then appeared with Helen Hayes in two plays, *Dancing Mothers* and *Quarantine*, both in 1924. In 1927, she played the lead role in a musical, *Bye Bye Bonnie*, with William Frawley, Georgie Hale, and Ruby Keeler in the cast. In 1932, Miss Burgess suffered a nervous breakdown as a result of an automobile collision in San Francisco. After the first part of her movie career ended in 1934, she played in *Lulu Belle* and *The Squall* on the Los Angeles stage, and succeeded Edith Barrett on Broadway in *Piper Paid*, with Spring Byington, 1935. Among her last movies *I Want a Divorce*, 1940, and *Lady for a Night*, 1942, both with Joan Blondell. In 1961, she was reported to be ill with "an undiagnosed ailment" at the Riverside General Hospital, and died in August, aged fifty-four.

BILLIE BURKE

She was born Ethelbert Burke in Washington, August 7, 1885, daughter of Billy Burke, a clown with the Barnum & Bailey Circus. She had her first success in the theater in London in 1903, in a musical, *The School Girl*. Her New York debut was at the Empire as John Drew's leading lady in *My Wife*. In 1914, she became the second wife of Florenz Ziegfeld, and kept that marriage intact until his death in 1932. Between 1916-1919, she starred in many silent films, produced in New York. On Broadway she was a favorite star in drawing room comedies, but the great successes of her career took place after 1932, and up to 1960, in Hollywood movies. Her only child, Patricia, married William Stephenson, and presented her with four grandchildren and four great-grandchildren. She died in Hollywood, May 15, 1970.

KATHLEEN BURKE

She had been a radio actress and fashion model in Chicago from the age of thirteen, and a leading lady in a stock company there at fifteen. She was born September 5, 1913, in Hammond, Ind., and, at twenty, married a Chicago photographer, Jack Reardon. They were divorced on their first wedding anniversary. Miss Burke lasted at Paramount three years, from 1933 to 1935, and during that troubled time of studio re-organization, she said, "I lost count of all the dinners welcoming new presidents I had to go to." She left Hollywood in 1938, and for a time acted in *Light of The World*, a series of Biblical dramas at NBC, around 1940. She became the wife of dancer José Fernandez, son of the former Spanish minister to Mexico.

MAE BUSCH

Stanley Laurel, who directed her in several Laurel & Hardy romps, esteemed her as the most versatile actress he ever worked with, asserting "she could do anything." She was born in Melbourne, Australia, June 18, 1895. Her father was a conductor of a symphony orchestra and her mother a grand opera singer. Mae went to Elizabeth Convent, Madison, N. J., before her stage debut in *Over the River*, with Eddie Foy. She began her screen career as a Mack Sennett bathing beauty. She worked in movies until 1941, and died in Hollywood on April 19, 1946.

SPRING BYINGTON

Born October 17, 1893, she was the daughter of Edwin Lee Byington, an instructor in English at Colorado College, and Dr. Helene Byington, one of the first women doctors in the West. She began her career with the stock company at Elitch's Gardens, Denver, and spent many years in stock, touring the United States and South America. She married a company manager, Roy Carey Chandler, and became the mother of two daughters, Phyllis Helene (Mrs. William Baxley) and Lois Irene (Mrs. Larry Dunn). When her marriage ended in divorce, Miss Byington returned to the stage—this time on Broadway, in 1924, playing Miss Hey in *Beggar on Horseback*. Thereafter, she was on Broadway each season until 1934. Miss Byington's screen and TV career (particularly as star of the popular series *December Bride*) continued in the 1960s. She died in Hollywood September 7, 1971.

MARION BYRON

Her real name was Miriam Bilenkin, born in Dayton, Ohio, March 16, 1910. She was a showgirl in Los Angeles when discovered for the movies, where her first important job was as Buster Keaton's leading lady in *Steamboat Bill, Jr.*, 1928.

MRS. PATRICK CAMPBELL

Daughter of an English father and an Italian mother, she was born February 9, 1865, as Stella Tanner in London. At nineteen, she married Capt. Patrick Campbell, and bore him a son and daughter before he was killed in the Boer War. She married again briefly in 1914, George Cornwallis-West, brother of the Countess of Westminster and the Princess of Pless. After becoming a London star in *The Second Mrs. Tanqueray* in 1893, she was also the star of London theatrical lore because of her temperament, wit, beauty, and her friendship with Bernard Shaw, who wrote *Pygmalion* for her. She died in Pau, France, April 9, 1940, preferring to live there rather than return to England because she couldn't get her Pekinese "Moonbeam" through quarantine.

KITTY CARLISLE

Daughter of a doctor who died when she was ten, she was born in New Orleans, September 3, 1914, and, with her mother, spent most of her girlhood in Europe. After making her society debut in Rome, she went to London to study at the Academy of Dramatic Arts, and to Paris under Charles Dullin. At eighteen, she made her first appearance as *Rio Rita* in a "tabloid" version, at the Capitol Theatre in New York. After making four movies, she returned to the stage in *White Horse Inn*, 1936, and *Three Waltzes*, 1937. She became the wife of playwright Moss Hart in 1945 (he died in 1961) and is the mother of two children, Chris and Cathy. Undoubtedly she is best known as a perennial panelist on TV's *To Tell the Truth*.

MARY CARLISLE

When she was four years old, her father died, and she and her mother left Boston (where Mary was born February 3, 1912) to live in Hollywood. She made her debut in the silent *Collegians* series, and her last film in 1942. She married her long-time friend, James Blakeley, later an executive with 20th Century-Fox, and became the mother of a son. Since 1951 she has been manager of the Elizabeth Arden Salon on Wilshire Boulevard, Beverly Hills.

SUE CAROL

Her real name is Evelyn Lederer, and she was born in Chicago, October 30, 1907. She studied at Kemper Hall in Wisconsin. One of her husbands was Nick Stuart, who was her leading man in *Why Leave Home?*, *Girls Gone Wild*, *Chasing Through Europe*, all 1929, and later in *Secret Sinners*, 1933. When her screen career fizzled, Miss Carol became an agent, with one particularly notable client —a boy she brought out of the extra ranks. The agent married the client, and Sue Carol became Mrs. Alan Ladd in 1942.

MADELEINE CARROLL

An intelligent, humorous, ash-blonde beauty, with a rich, warm voice, and whom audiences sensed had a smouldering sexual inner fire, she was born February 26, 1906, in West Bromwich, England, daughter of an Irish father and a French mother. She was graduated B. A. from Birmingham University, and for a while was a teacher in girls' seminary at Brighton. At twenty-one, in 1927, she made her stage debut, and her movie debut a year later. During World War II, she spent almost all of her time devoted to war work, and became entertainment director for the United Seamen's Service in 1942.

She has been married and divorced four times: to Capt. Philip Astley, actor Sterling Hayden, producer-director Henri Lavorel, and Andrew Heiskell, publisher of *Life*. Her only appearance on Broadway was in the hit *Goodbye, My Fancy*, in 1948, and in 1949 she made her last film *The Fan*, a remake of *Lady Windermere's Fan*.

NANCY CARROLL

She was born November 19, 1904, as Ann Veronica La Hiff, on New York's Tenth Avenue, one of the many children of Thomas and Anne La Hiff, both born in Ireland. By the time she was sixteen, she had left parochial school and was working in an office. With her sister Terry, she sang and danced at a neighborhood theatre's amateur night, and used the last name of Buddy Carroll, the master of ceremonies. Nancy Carroll made her Broadway debut in the chorus of *The Passing Show of 1923*, then appeared in *Topics of 1923* and *The Passing Show of 1924*, when she met and married her first husband, playwright Jack Kirkland. She became the mother of her only child,

NANCY CARROLL

Patricia Kirkland (Mrs. Don Bevan), on July 18, 1925. Kirkland's work took him to the West Coast, and Nancy went along. She made her debut as the girl friend of heroine Virginia Valli in *Ladies Must Dress* in 1927. She worked in movies until 1938, and thereafter appeared occasionally on the stage. After her divorce from Kirkland in 1931, she married Bolton Mallory, editor of the old humor weekly *Life*, and divorced him in 1934. Her third husband, in 1955, was C. H. J. Gröen, a Dutch sports-car manufacturer. She was appearing opposite Bert Lahr in a summer production of *Never Too Late* in Nyack when she was found dead August 6, 1965, in her New York apartment.

HELEN CHANDLER

Miss Chandler began as a child actress in the role of Marjorie Jones in *Penrod* on Broadway, 1918. She was born in Charleston, S. C., February 1, 1906. Through the 1920s and 1930s she was a popular Broadway actress. She was married and divorced twice: writer Cyril Hume and actor Bramwell Fletcher. She died April 30, 1965.

ILKA CHASE

Daughter of *Vogue* editor Edna Woolman Chase, she was born in New York, April 8, 1903. In 1925, she made her stage debut in *Shall We Join the Ladies?*, with Leslie Howard. Her best stage role

was Sylvia Fowler (played by Rosalind Russell in the movie) in Clare Boothe Luce's *The Women*, 1936. She also appeared in her own dramatization of her novel, *In Bed We Cry*, in 1944. Miss Chase has written an autobiography, *Past Imperfect*, 1942, *Always in Vogue*, with her mother, 1954, and several novels. She married actor Louis Calhern in 1926, William B. Murray in 1935, and Dr. Norton Sager Brown in 1946.

RUTH CHATTERTON

Miss Chatterton was born in New York, December 24, 1893, the daughter of Walter Chatterton, an architect, and his wife, Lillian Reed. She was educated at Miss Hagen's School in Pelham Manor. Her stage career began in stock in Washington and Milwaukee, and by 1911 she was on Broadway. In 1914, she became a star in Henry Miller's production of *Daddy Long-Legs*, and remained a star from that time on. She began her film career in 1928, after Emil Jannings saw her on the stage in Los Angeles and asked for her as his leading woman in *Sins of the Fathers*.

She first married English actor Ralph Forbes, her leading man in films and theatre; they divorced in 1932. That year, she married film actor George Brent (divorced 1934) and later, in a happy marriage, actor Barry Thomson, who died in 1960. Her last Broadway play was a revival of *Idiot's Delight*, 1951. Miss Chat-

terton was a licensed pilot who flew her own plane across the country, as well as the author of four novels. She died November 24, 1961, after a brief illness.

VIRGINIA CHERRILL

Miss Cherrill was born in Carthage, Ill., April 12, 1908, and attended Kemper Hall, Wisconsin, along with Sue Carol. Her last movie was a curiosity, directed by the silent film director Lois Weber in Hawaii, *White Heat*, 1934, in which she played "an American girl of the San Francisco sugar aristocracy," who withered away emotionally and physically under the pressure of the tropics. She has been married five times: to Irving Adler, William Rhinelander Stewart, Cary Grant (his first wife), the ninth Earl of Jersey (1937–1946), and Florian Martini, one-time RAF pilot, later a missile engineer in Santa Barbara.

MADY CHRISTIANS

Viennese born (January 19, 1900), daughter of actors Rudolphe and Bertha Klein Christians, she studied for the stage under Max Reinhardt. With the Berlin company of UFA during the silent film years, she acted in *The Waltz Dream* and *Queen Louise*, and as Conrad Veidt's leading lady in the talkie *The Black Hussar*, 1932.

After her disappointing Hollywood career she returned to the stage, playing Hesione Hushabye in Orson Welles' production of *Heartbreak House*, Gertrude to Maurice Evans' *Hamlet*, Sara Muller in Lillian Hellman's *Watch on the Rhine*, and her most famous American role, Mama in *I Remember Mama*, 1944. She was married to and divorced from Sven von Mueller. At her death October 28, 1951, Elmer Rice wrote in the *New York Times* that she had been hounded to death in the McCarthy era.

MARGUERITE CHURCHILL

Born in Kansas City, December 25, 1909, she attended the Professional Children's School and Theatre Guild Drama School in New York. On her thirteenth birthday she made her Broadway bow in *Why Not?* with Gene Raymond. In 1932, she returned to Broadway to play Paula Jordan in the hit play *Dinner at Eight*. She married Western star George O'Brien in July 1933, and divorced him in 1948. They have two children, a daughter Orin and a son Darcy.

BERNICE CLAIRE

Unlike Jeanette MacDonald, Miss Claire had no Broadway experience, but did appear in West Coast productions of *Babes in Toyland*, *The Desert Song*, and

CLAUDETTE COLBERT

MAE CLARKE

Mlle. Modiste. She was born in Oakland, Calif., March 22, 1907. She made her last film in England in 1935, in American director William Beaudine's *Two Hearts in Harmony.* From 1937 until 1945, she sang in civic light operetta productions throughout the United States, and once played in a road company production of *Golden Boy*, with Eric Linden.

INA CLAIRE

Her real name was Fagan, and she was born in Washington, D. C., October 15, 1892. Her father was killed in an auto accident four months before her birth. She studied at Holy Cross Academy, and went on the stage at seventeen in vaudeville. In her long Broadway career she worked for David Belasco and Florenz Ziegfeld, and from the 1920s well through the 1950s she was the chic star of plays by Maugham, Behrman, Lonsdale, George Kelly, T. S. Eliot. She married three times: newsman James Whittaker (1919–1925), film star John Gilbert (1929–1931), and San Francisco lawyer William R. Wallace, Jr.

MAE CLARKE

The daughter of a motion picture theatre organist, she was born August 16, 1907, in Philadelphia, and made her debut as a dancer in New York cabarets in 1924. She played Georgie in the drama *The Noose*, with Barbara Stanwyck in 1926, and was with Ed Wynn and Elizabeth Hines in the musical comedy *Manhattan Mary*. She made her movie debut in 1929 in *Nix on Dames*, with Robert Ames. She has been married to Lew Brice, Stephen Bancroft, and Herbert Langdon.

JUNE CLYDE

Miss Clyde had better parts on the stage, from the time she appeared in vaudeville, in 1917, as the Baby Tetrazzini. She was born in Saint Joseph, Mo., December 2, 1909, and grew up in San Francisco. In 1925, she was in the cast of *Topsy and Eva* with the Duncan Sisters, and during the 1930s she had leads in London musicals *Lucky Break*, with Leslie Henson, and *The Flying Trapeze*, with Jack Buchanan. On Broadway, she was with Ed Wynn in *Hooray for What!* in 1937. She also has had a career in British films. She married director Thornton Freeland.

CLAUDETTE COLBERT

Her real name is Lily Chauchoin, daughter to a banker, George Chauchoin, and his wife, Jeanne Loew. She was born in Paris, September 13, 1905. In 1910, her parents went to New York, where she studied at Washington Irving High School and the Art Students League. She made her stage debut in Anne Morrison's play, *The Wild Westcotts*, with Elliott Nugent, 1923, with three lines. Two years later, she was a star in *A Kiss in the Taxi*, which ran for a year. From 1925 through 1929, she was one of the leading young stars of Broadway. In 1955, she returned to Broadway, briefly replacing Margaret Sullavan in *Janus*, and then on to her own plays, *The Marriage-Go-Round*, with Charles Boyer, *Julia, Jake and Uncle Joe*, and *The Irregular Verb to Love.*

In 1928, she married actor Norman Foster (divorced 1935). That same year she married Dr. Joel Pressman, who died in 1968. Miss Colbert lives at Belle Rive, her house on Barbados.

CONSTANCE COLLIER

Miss Collier was born January 22, 1875, in Windsor, England, as Laura Constance Hardie, daughter of actors. In her long distinguished career in London and New York, she appeared in Shakespeare with Sir Beerbohm Tree, with the Barrymores in *Peter Ibbetson*, as Gertrude to John Barrymore's *Hamlet*, as the Duchess de Surennes in Maugham's hit comedy *Our Betters*, and as Charlotte Vance (the Marie Dressler screen role) in *Dinner at Eight*.

She married English actor Julian L'Estrange in 1912, but they separated before he died in 1918. She was more fortunate in her friendships with the theatrical elite: Noël Coward, Eva Le Gallienne, Ivor Novello, Katharine Cornell, and her most devoted and valued friend in later years, Katharine Hepburn. Just a week before her death (April 25, 1955), she had given a lecture on the plays of Shakespeare.

CORA SUE COLLINS

Cora Sue was born in Clarksburg, Va., April 19, 1927, and, according to her early publicity, "She got her first job in movies due to her ability to cry easily." The fan magazines said that Greta Garbo personally chose Cora Sue to represent herself as a child in *Queen Christina*. Cora Sue also played a small role in another Garbo film, *Anna Karenina*, 1935. Her movie career ended as one of Rosalind Russell's large brood of children in *Roughly Speaking*, 1945. She now lives in Mexico, where her parties are "social events."

JUNE COLLYER

Born August 19, 1907, her real name was Dorothea Heermance. Her mother, Carrie Collyer, was an actress before her marriage, and her grandfather, Dan Collyer, was an actor for fifty-four years. Her brother was Bud Collyer, master of ceremonies on television. Miss Collyer was discovered for the screen by director Allan Dwan, who cast her as a society girl in the silent film *East Side, West Side*, with George O'Brien, 1927.

She married the character comedian Stuart Erwin, whom she met when both were at Paramount filming *Dude Ranch* in 1931. In the early 1950s, she teamed with him in *The Trouble with Father* television show. Erwin died December 21, 1967, at their Beverly Hills home, and she less than three months later, March 16, 1968.

BETTY COMPSON

Miss Compson was the daughter of a mining engineer, and was born March 18, 1897, in Beaver City, Utah. She got her start in show business as a violinist in a Salt Lake City vaudeville house at $15 a week, and touring as the "Vagabond Violinist" (accompanied by her mother) in the West. At eighteen, she started in movies in one-reel comedies produced by Al Christie. Along with Lon Chaney, she became a star when *The Miracle Man* was released in 1919, and from then until 1925 she was one of the Paramount stars. Between 1923 and 1926, she made occasional films in England. Back in America, she continued to work steadily. She married three times: to director James Cruze, divorced 1929, producer Irving Weinberg, and then to a one-time boxer, Silvious Jack Gall, who started an ashtray manufacturing business, which she managed after his death in 1962. Always frugal, she is a wealthy woman, living in Glendale, Calif.

JOYCE COMPTON

This bubbling blonde was born in Lexington, Ky., January 27, 1908, and was educated mainly in Tulsa, Okla. A beauty contest winner, she entered movies in 1925, and next year was selected as a Wampas Baby star, along with Joan Crawford, Janet Gaynor, and Mary Astor. She had few roles after 1950. Except for a three-month marriage in 1956, she lived with her parents. She now lives with another family in Sherman Oaks, Calif., and works as a part-time nurse.

PEGGY CONKLIN

She was born November 2, 1910, in Dobbs Ferry, N. Y., and made her debut on the stage as a dancer in *The Little Show*, 1929, with Constance Cummings also in the chorus. Upon returning to Broadway in 1937, she starred in the comedy *Yes, My Darling Daughter*, with Lucile Watson; appeared with the Group Theatre in *Casey Jones*; in the title role of *Miss Swan Expects*; and as Mrs. North in *Mr. and Mrs. North*, 1941. Among her last appearances was as Flo Owens in William Inge's *Picnic*, 1953. She married James D. Thompson, living for many years at 142 East 71st Street, New York.

DOLORES COSTELLO

She was born in Brooklyn, September 17, 1904, one of the two daughters of the early matinee idol Maurice Costello. At five, she made her debut in movies, playing a little boy. Later, she became a New York model, and was signed for movies when she was a chorus girl in Chicago on tour with George White's *Scandals* with her sister Helene. John Barrymore saw her wandering around the Warners lot in 1926, and she became his leading lady in the silent version of *Moby Dick*, retitled *The Sea Beast*. He called her "the most preposterously lovely creature in the world, a charming child, slender and shy and golden-haired," and married her in 1928. She held the longevity record as a John Barrymore wife—seven years, and two children, Dolores Ethel Mae and actor John, Jr. In 1939, she married a Beverly Hills physician, John Vruwink, and once again came back into the newspapers at their acrimonious divorce in 1960. Miss Costello lives on a ranch at Del Mar, Calif.

HELENE COSTELLO

Helene Costello—however undistinguished her career—was one of the silent screen's most hauntingly beautiful girls, as vivid in dark, dramatic looks as Joan Crawford. Her life was dogged by ill health and bad luck. She was born in New York, June 21, 1905, and went to school at Ladycliffe-on-the-Hudson. In 1925, she had a small part in *Bobbed Hair* (along with Dolores), and next year she was, briefly, a star in *The Love Toy*, with Lowell Sherman (who became her

second husband) and Myrna Loy in the cast. From then on, she played roles in support of other stars. She was married and divorced four times: John Reagan, Lowell Sherman (1930–1932), sportsman Arturo de Barrio, artist George Lee Le-Blanc. Occasionally, when not too ill (tuberculosis) to work, she found jobs as an extra and as a reader for 20th Century-Fox. In 1942, she filed bankruptcy proceedings, and engaged in a long court battle with her fourth husband over their daughter's custody. Destitute, she died January 27, 1957, at Patton State Hospital, in California, where she had been committed for narcotics addiction.

INEZ COURTNEY

She grew up in New York, and left school to become a milliner. After five years in vaudeville, she appeared in Rudolf Friml's *The Wild Rose*, 1926; as Babe O'Day in *Good News*, 1927; and the Rodgers-Hart *Spring Is Here*, with Glenn Hunter and Charles Ruggles, 1929. In 1931, she returned briefly to Broadway for the musical *America's Sweetheart*, with Harriette Lake (Ann Sothern), and again in 1933 in *Hold Your Horses*, with Joe Cook, Ona Munson, and Stanley Smith. First married to broker Howard S. Paschal (1931–1933), she next married a titled Italian wine merchant, Luigi Filiesi, and now lives in Rome.

JOAN CRAWFORD

She was named Lucille Fay LeSueur, born in San Antonio, Texas, on March 23, 1908. Her parents were soon divorced. Her mother married Henry Cassin (divorced 1915), and for a time her daughter was known as Billie Cassin. She went to St. Agnes Convent, Kansas City, and for four years to a private school called Rockingham. For a few months, in 1921, she attended Stephens College, Columbia, Mo. After that she worked in a department store, won an amateur dance contest, and became a dancer in night clubs in Chicago and Detroit. On Broadway, in 1924, she was a dancer in *Innocent Eyes*, with the eternally youthful French star Mistinguett, and was one of forty-five dancers in *The Passing Show of 1924* at the Winter Garden, appearing as a Beaded Bag in a "living curtain," and as Labor Day in a Holiday sketch. Harry Rapf of MGM saw her, gave her a screen test, and a contract at $75 a week. Joan Crawford made her movie debut as a chorus girl in *Pretty Ladies* in 1925 at MGM, and stayed with that studio until 1943. She has never really ever stopped working, as either a star or as a business executive. Her most romantic marriage was her first, to Douglas Fairbanks, Jr. (1929–1933). She then mar-

ried actor Franchot Tone (1935–1939), actor Philip Terry (1942–1946), and Pepsi-Cola executive Alfred N Steele, who died in 1959.

LAURA HOPE CREWS

She was one of four children born to a carpenter, John Thomas Crews, and his wife, Angelina Lockwood, who until Laura's birth (December 12, 1879), was a member of the California Stock Company in San Francisco. At the age of four, she made her debut in *Bootle's Baby* there, and "retired" at seven to go to school. She returned to the stage at nineteen as an ingenue with the Alcazar Stock Company. At twenty-two she first played New York and for a time was leading lady to stars such as Robert Edeson and Henry Miller. During the 1920s, she hit her stride as a character star in *Ariadne*, Judith Bliss in Noël Coward's *Hay Fever*, and, of course, Mrs. Phelps in *The Silver Cord*. She entered films in 1929, and made her last—*The Man Who Came to Dinner*—in 1941. The next year, she succeeded Josephine Hull briefly in *Arsenic and Old Lace*, with Erich von Stroheim as her eccentric brother. Miss Crews died at Le Roy Sanitarium, New York, November 13, 1942. She never married.

HENRIETTA CROSMAN

A grand-niece of songwriter Stephen Collins Foster, Miss Crosman was born September 2, 1861, in Wheeling, W. Va., where her father, an Army major, was stationed. She made her debut in 1883 at the Pittsburgh Opera House in *The White Slave*. Eventually she became a star under the managements of Augustin Daly, Charles Frohman, and David Belasco, with her forte in light, piquant comedy. Her own favorite roles were Rosalind in *As You Like It* and *Sweet Kitty Bellairs*. Her marriage to Maurice Campbell, a newspaperman who became her manager, was a happy one. In 1914, she was one of the earliest of the big stage stars to try out the movies, appearing in *The Unwelcome Mrs. Hatch*, with Harold Lockwood, for Famous Players. She died at her Pelham Manor home, October 31, 1944.

CONSTANCE CUMMINGS

An American from Seattle, she has never assumed a British accent, though she has acted more in London than Broadway or Hollywood. She was born May 15, 1910, as Constance Halverstadt, and educated at St. Nicholas School there. On Broadway in 1928, she was a chorine in the Gershwins' *Treasure Girl* and the 1929 *Little Show*. In 1933, she married British playwright Benn W. Levy, and next year made her London

JOAN CRAWFORD

stage debut in *Sour Grapes*. She returned to Broadway in 1937 as the star of two plays, *Young Madame Conti* and *Madame Bovary*. Next year, she played the wife, Katherine, in the stage *Goodbye, Mr. Chips*, with Leslie Banks, in London. From then on, her career was chiefly in England, on both stage and screen. In 1945, she played the suspicious wife Ruth in the famous screen version of Noël Coward's *Blithe Spirit*, with Rex Harrison and Kay Hammond. Recently she appeared in a stage revival of Coward's *Fallen Angels* with Joan Greenwood, and, in 1972, added new dimension to her reputation as Mary Tyrone in O'Neill's *Long Day's Journey into Night*, with Laurence Olivier, receiving the most respectful notices of her unique career.

CECIL CUNNINGHAM

The tall (5' 8"), Amazonian Miss Cunningham was born August 2, 1888, in Saint Louis, daughter of Patrick Cunningham, whom she described as a professional baseball player and man-about-town. In Saint Louis, she went to Humboldt School and Central High School, sang in a church choir, and was a switchboard operator at the National Bank of Commerce. Going to New York at eighteen, she became a photographer's model and a chorus girl in *Mlle. Modiste*, with Fritzi Scheff. In a subsequent career as a singer, she appeared in *Iolanthe* in New York, 1913, and in *Parsifal* in Paris. By 1915, convinced by her husband, writer Jean Havez (1915–1917) that she was essentially a comedienne, she tried vaudeville, becoming a headliner at the Palace in New York. She remained on the stage until 1929, when she went to Hollywood to manage Ciro's night club for Barney Gallant for one season, and to start her film career of seventeen years (until 1946). She died in Los Angeles, April 17, 1959.

ESTHER DALE

Miss Dale was born in Beaufort, S. C., November 10, 1885. After attending Leland and Gray Seminary, Townsend, Vt., she studied music in Berlin. Under the management of her husband, agent-producer Arthur Beckhard, she had a successful career as a *lieder* singer, and later as an actress in summer theatres. She began her Broadway career in the title role of his production *Carrie Nation* in 1933, supported by James Stewart, Mildred Natwick, and Joshua Logan. Her movie career began with the Charles MacArthur-Ben Hecht *Crime Without Passion* in 1934, and ended in 1957, with *The Oklahoman*. Her husband died in March 1961, and she died four months later, July 23, 1961, after surgery, in Queen of Angels Hospital, Hollywood.

LILI DAMITA

She was born at Bordeaux, France, July 19, 1901, the daughter of a civil servant, and was trained for the stage at the Paris Opera. At eighteen, she was a leading member of the Folies-Bergere and a year later succeeded Mistinguett as the star of the Casino de Paris. In 1921, she made her cinema debut in *L'empereur des pauvres*, and thereafter made films in France, Germany, Austria, and England, before coming to the United States to make her first Hollywood film, *The Rescue*, in 1929.

After a much publicized affair with Errol Flynn, Miss Damita married him in June 1935. She is singled out for special loathing in Flynn's autobiography, *My Wicked, Wicked Ways*. Their son Sean was born May 31, 1941. A year later, Miss Damita divorced Flynn, with an alimony settlement of over $1,000,000. In 1962, she married Allen R. Loomis.

BEBE DANIELS

In the silents, Bebe Daniels—of Scottish-Spanish ancestry—had enough fire and versatility to play anything from princesses to poor girls, exotics to dancing flappers, and in everything from costume dramas to Westerns. Popular and outgoing, she sped through the 1920s as one of Paramount's top stars. She had been in show business from childhood. Born in Dallas, January 14, 1901, the daughter of show people, she played the infant Duke of York in Shakespeare's *Richard III*, at the age of four, and appeared in a variety of child roles in Los Angeles stock companies. When she was fourteen, she played her first "adult" role —with the Hal Roach company in movies—and for four years was featured with Harold Lloyd in "Lonesome Luke" films, making over 200 of them. Cecil DeMille gave her her first role in a feature film, as a Babylonian slave in a flashback sequence of *Male and Female* in 1919, and she worked at Paramount from then until 1928. In November 1943, Bebe was the star of *Panama Hattie* at the Piccadilly in London, becoming probably London's favorite star of the wartime years. She played "Hattie" for a year in the West End, then toured in the provinces, and re-opened the show again in London in 1945. Along with her other activities, she compiled *The Complete Book of Salads* in 1942, and with her son ran an antique shop on Kensington High Street. At 62, she suffered a stroke, the first of many, and she died March 16, 1971, of a cerebral hemorrhage at her home in London.

LINDA DARNELL

The third of five children of a postal clerk, she was born October 16, 1921, in Dallas, and christened Monetta Eloyse.

Her stagestruck mother prodded her lovely daughter into becoming a model at eleven (giving her age as sixteen) and getting some acting experience with the Catholic Players of St. Matthews, and the Dallas' New Theatre Group. Encouraged by a talent scout from 20th Century-Fox, her mother took her daughter to Hollywood, and the young girl, now named Linda Darnell, made her bow in *Hotel for Women* in 1939. She was placed under contract with 20th Century-Fox and remained with them until 1952. In 1943, she married a cameraman, Peverell Marley, many years her senior, as his third wife; they were divorced in 1952. Her second husband was Philip Liebmann, of the New York brewery family, 1954–1955. An airline pilot, Merle Roberton, was her third husband, from 1957 to 1963. She was visiting her onetime secretary, Mrs. Jane Curtis and her daughter, in Glenview, a suburb of Chicago, when she suffered burns that covered 80 per cent of her body, and died April 10, 1965.

DANIELLE DARRIEUX

For forty years, from the age of fourteen, this dainty, still youthful looking star has had a career almost record-breaking for its consistent, top-level excellence. Daughter of an eye specialist and his wife, an Algerian singer, she was born in Bordeaux, May 1, 1917, and was educated to be a musician, playing the piano and the cello, intending to enter the Paris Conservatory. Instead, she was sidetracked by reading an advertisement for a young girl to play the leading role in *Le Bal*, based on a popular novel by Irene Nemirowski, which young Danielle had read. This was in 1931, and her career began; she reached top-ranking status overnight. But she had to wait until 1936 to play her first serious dramatic role, the Baroness Marie Vetsera in *Mayerling*, with Charles Boyer, a film that made them both international stars

She first married director Henri Decoin in 1935, divorced 1941. Her second husband was Porfirio Rubirosa, whom, it was said, she "rescued from a German prison," and married him in 1942. She divorced Rubirosa, who was in the diplomatic service at the Dominican Republic's embassy in Paris, in 1947, and the following year married George Mitsinkides, a Greek-born writer and producer of several of her films. They live in a house thirty miles from Paris, and own a private island off the Brittany coast.

JANE DARWELL

Her father was president of the Lousiville Southern Railroad when she was born, as Patti Woodward, in Palmyra, Mo., October 15, 1879. Young stage-

MARION DAVIES

struck Patti studied instrumental music, voice and dramatics, and hoped to appear either in opera or the circus. Her father disapproved of any career, but while on a visit to Chicago, his daughter got her first job, a part in a stock company production, and she worked for the rest of her life. When she was thirty-five she made her first movie, *Rose of the Rancho*, with Bessie Barriscale, and another, *The Only Son*, with Thomas W. Ross, but she didn't continue until she returned to the screen for good in *Tom Sawyer* in 1930. Thereafter, the robust personality of Miss Darwell took over, and her real career began. She was last seen as the "bird woman" in Walt Disney's *Mary Poppins* in 1964. On August 14, 1967, she died at the Motion Picture Country Home, after having suffered a stroke.

MARION DAVIES

Even at her death in 1961, the Hearst newspapers kept a veil over her intimate, lifetime relationship with their chief, the powerful tycoon-publisher.

Marion Cecelia Douras was born in Brooklyn, January 3, 1897, youngest of the five children of a minor politician who later became a city magistrate, Bernard J. Douras. She went to Public School 93 in Brooklyn and the Convent of the Sacred Heart, Hastings, N. Y. Her first stage job was in the chorus of *The Sunshine Girl* in 1913. She was a model for magazine covers and illustrations by Harrison Fisher and Howard Chandler Christy, became a *Follies* girl in 1916, and had featured parts in other musicals, *Betty* and *Oh, Boy!*

Mr. Hearst fell in love with the teenage girl when she was in the *Follies of 1916*, and decided to make her a film star.

Miss Davies began her movie career as a star in *Runaway Romany*, which she also wrote, in 1917. At first, she made her movies at a studio purchased for her at Second Avenue and 127th Street, in New York; later Hearst transferred his operations to Culver City, founding Cosmopolitan Pictures, for release by MGM, at Culver City. It was estimated that Mr. Hearst lost $7,000,000 (which now seems a conservative figure) in his futile attempt to make her the nation's top star.

Mr. Hearst, who was thirty-four years her senior, died at her Beverly Hills home in 1951, aged eighty-eight, confident that the bulk of his publishing empire would go to her. This did not happen. Two months after his death, she "eloped" to Las Vegas with Capt. Horace G. Brown, Jr., a retired Military Sea Transport Captain, a former Hollywood stunt man, and once the husband of Mrs. Lawrence Tibbett. She twice filed suit for divorce, but withdrew both times, and was still married to him at her death from cancer (after a three-year illness) at Cedars of Lebanon Hospital, September 22, 1961.

BETTE DAVIS

Ruth Elizabeth Davis was born in the mill city of Lowell, Mass., April 5, 1908. Her father, Harlow Davis, was a lawyer, and she was named for her mother, Ruth Favor. After the Davises divorced (when Bette was eight), Mrs. Davis earned a precarious living as a photographer, moving from town to town with her two daughters. For a time, Bette attended Newton, Mass., High School (where she met her first husband) and Cushing Academy, Ashburnham, Mass., and first became involved in theatricals there. Between 1926 and 1928, she attended John Murray Anderson's dramatic school, and for a time she was a member of the stock company of George Cukor in Rochester (Cukor gave her only two roles), and later was with the Provincetown Playhouse in New York. Her Broadway debut was as the ingenue in *Broken Dishes*, with Donald Meek, for 200 performances. She made her film debut in 1931 in *Bad Sister*. Studio head Carl Laemmle, Jr., said: "I can't imagine anyone giving *her* a tumble." Universal put her in two more movies, and began lending her to other studios for equally poor roles. Miss Davis said, in retrospect, "I learned about my trade with those two years of horrible films." George Arliss was the first to recognize her dynamism, and cast her in a leading role, that of a young girl infatuated with a famed violinist, in *The Man Who Played God*, 1932.

She married her schoolmate, band leader Harmon "Ham" Nelson in 1932 and divorced him in 1938; next she married Arthur Farnsworth in 1940. He was an assistant manager of a resort hotel, and later an aircraft executive. He died in August 1943, while walking on a Hollywood street. William Grant Sherry, painter and amateur boxer, was her third husband from 1945 to 1949, and the father of her daughter, Barbara Davis Sherry, born May 1, 1947, now Mrs. Jeremy Hyman, of Weston, Conn. In 1950, she married her leading man in *All About Eve*, Gary Merrill, adopted two children, Margo and Michael, and divorced him ten years later. Miss Davis lives in Westport, Conn., still appears occasionally in movies and television.

JOAN DAVIS

This mistress of the loose-jointed, skittery skid and pratfall unashamedly carried on the tradition of hoary slapstick in vaudeville, movies (from 1934 to 1951), and television. Born in St. Paul, June 29, 1907, the daughter of a train dispatcher, she was named Madonna Josephine Davis. In 1931, she met and married Serenus (Si) Wills, and joined his vaudeville act, now called Wills and Davis. When they began to realize the great days of vaudeville were over, they settled in Hollywood in 1934 with their baby daughter, Beverly. Miss Davis made her debut as a hillbilly in *Way Up Thar*, a comedy short. While making movies, she made her radio debut as Rudy Vallee's guest on his show, 1941. When he joined the Coast Guard in 1943, she took over, and in 1945 she signed a radio contract with the United Drug Co. for $1,000,000 a year for four years. In the 1950s, she formed her own production company, making movies and the TV series *I Married Joan*. After her divorce in 1944, Miss Davis never re-married, and lived in Bel-Air and Palm Springs, where she died of a heart attack, May 23, 1961.

LARAINE DAY

Her great-grandfather, Charles C. Rich, was one of the apostles of the Mormon church who came across the plains to settle in Utah. She was born a twin, as La Raine Johnson (with her brother La Mar) in Roosevelt, Utah, October 13, 1917, one of the seven children of Clarence Johnson, a grain dealer and a government interpreter for the Utes tribe. She attended Long Beach, Cal. Junior High School and became a member of the Little Theatre Guild there, where she was seen by a scout. Her career reached its peak in the 1940s, but she has acted sporadically from 1954 to 1960. Miss Day has been married to singer Ray Hendricks (1942–1947), baseball's Leo Durocher (1947–1960), and now to Michael Grilikhas, a TV producer.

FRANCES DEE

Miss Dee was born in Los Angeles, November 26, 1907, daughter to a civil

BETTE DAVIS

engineer. When she was seven, her family moved to Chicago, where she went to Hyde Park High School and the University of Chicago for two years. During a college vacation before her junior year, she got a small part in *Follow Thru* with Buddy Rogers and Nancy Carroll, in 1930. Maurice Chevalier noticed her on the lot and asked that she be tested for the leading lady role in his *Playboy of Paris*, and she got the part. Her long career, which extended up to 1953, followed. In 1933, she married actor Joel McCrea. They have three sons: David, who manages his father's ranch in Shandon, Calif., actor Jody, and Peter. They live on a ranch in Camarillo, Calif.

OLIVIA DE HAVILLAND

She was born in Tokyo, July 1, 1916, to a patent attorney, Walter de Havilland. At her parents' divorce, she and her sister, Joan Fontaine, lived with their mother in California, where Olivia was a scholarship pupil at Mills College. She was given her first screen role by the German producer-director Max Reinhardt, who was attracted by her "esthetic face." She played in twenty-six Warner films between 1935 and 1943. In 1946, she married novelist Marcus Goodrich, eighteen years older, and divorced him in 1953. Two years later she married Pierre Paul Galante, editor of *Paris-Match*.

CLAUDIA DELL

Born Claudia Dell Smith in San Antonio, January 10, 1910, she went to schools there and in Mexico City. By 1927, she was on Broadway in the *Ziegfeld Follies of 1927* as a showgirl and understudy to Irene Delroy. It was said that she was "visiting her parents in Hollywood" when she made her screen debut. Miss Dell was last reported to be a receptionist in a beauty salon. In 1934, she married Edwin Silton, a theatrical agent.

DOROTHY DELL

Born in Hattiesburg, Miss., daughter of Elbert and Lillian Goff, January 30, 1915, she won her first beauty contest at the age of thirteen months as "the most beautiful baby in Hattiesburg." From the age of ten she lived in New Orleans, and went to Sophie B. Wright High School for Girls. At fifteen she won the titles of "Miss America" and "Miss Universe," and went on a Fanchon and Marco vaudeville tour for six months. Arriving in New York she immediately got a job in the *Ziegfeld Follies of 1931*, and was given a solo number, "Was I Drunk?," to sing in her deep, throaty voice.

All three of her Paramount films were released in 1934, the year of her death

in an auto crash, June 8, 1934. With her escort, Dr. Carl Wagner (also killed), she had left an all-night party at an inn at Altadena, and was headed for Pasadena in the early morning hours when the car, driven by Wagner, plunged off the highway, mowed down a telephone pole, caromed off a palm tree, and rammed into a boulder. Miss Dell, pinned in the wreckage, was killed instantly; Wagner died hours later.

DOLORES DEL RIO

The eternal Dolores Del Rio was born August 3, 1904, in Durango, Mexico, daughter to a banker, J. L. Asunsolo. She as educated at the Convent of St. Joseph in Mexico City, and went to Spain to study voice and dancing. In 1921, she married an attorney, Jaime Martinez Del Rio, of Mexico City. When an American director, Edwin Carewe, saw her dancing at a party, he suggested that she should act in the movies. Encouraged by her husband, who thought it would be a lark, she went to Hollywood in 1925 for her film debut in Carewe's *Joanna*, which starred Dorothy Mackaill. From the beginning, she took her career seriously. She made her first hit as Charmaine in *What Price Glory?* with Victor McLaglen and Edmund Lowe, in 1926, and went on to become the star of such silent films as *Loves of Carmen, Revenge, The Trail of '98* and *Evangeline*.

When her career in Hollywood seemed finished in 1942, she returned to Mexico to star in films there. One of them, *Maria Candelaria*, was awarded the best-film prize at the 1946 International Exposition in Cannes. In 1947 she played a leading role in John Ford's *The Fugitive*, filmed in Mexico, and returned to Hollywood for several films, including Ford's *Cheyenne Autumn*.

Her first husband died in Berlin after an operation in 1928. She married MGM set designer Cedric Gibbons in 1930, and divorced him eleven years later. She is now the wife of Lewis Riley, producer, whom she married in 1959.

KATHERINE DeMILLE

Said to be the only child of Edward Gabriel Lester, and his wife, Cecile Colani, and born in Vancouver, B. C., June 29, 1911, her father was killed in World War I. At the death of her mother, she was placed in a Los Angeles orphanage, and at nine was adopted by producer-director Cecil DeMille and his wife, Constance, as one of their four children. In 1934, she made her movie debut in *Viva Villa!* and appeared in only two of her father's films: *The Crusades*, 1935, and *Unconquered*, 1947, when her career ended. On October 2, 1937, she married actor Anthony Quinn and had four chil-

dren: Christina, Kathleen, Duncan and Valentina. The Quinns are divorced.

GLORIA DICKSON

Born as Thais Dickerson in Pocatello, Idaho, August 13, 1917, she was the second daughter of a banker, Fred Dickerson, and his wife, Emma Starrett. Her father died when she was twelve, and Mrs. Dickerson took her two daughters to live in Long Beach, Calif. She was graduated from Polytechnic High School in 1932, joined the Wayside Colony Players in Long Beach, and toured briefly with the Hart Players, a tent show. She was given the role of Diane in *Seventh Heaven*, which she played for four weeks at the old Mason Theatre in Los Angeles, and then in *Smilin' Thru* and *The Devil Passes*. Max Arnow, a Warner Brothers scout, saw her and signed her to a Warner contract in November 1936, changing her name to Gloria Dickson. Along with another girl from Idaho, Lana Turner, she made her debut in Mervyn LeRoy's *They Won't Forget* in 1937. By early 1940, she was out of Warners. While there, she married and divorced makeup man Perc Westmore (1938-1940), then married director Ralph Murphy (1941-1944) and ex-Marine and onetime middleweight boxer William Fitzgerald (1944). She died mysteriously in a fire in the Hollywood Hills home she had rented from Mrs. Sidney Toler a year before, on April 10, 1945. Apparently trapped on the upper level of the house, she had made her way to the bathroom, where her body was found.

MARLENE DIETRICH

Details of her early life have always been hard to come by. But after World War II, the Russians found her birth certificate in East Berlin, and ungallantly disclosed that she was born December 27, 1901 as Maria Magdalene Dietrich, and her father was Erich Otto Dietrich, a lieutenant, not in the cavalry as had been said, but in the Royal Prussian Police. Long ago, Dietrich herself said: "Just say I'm seventy-five, and let it go at that." She grew up wanting to be a concert violinist, practicing six hours a day, but muscle damage put an end to such a career. Her first verifiable film is *Die Tragodie der Liebe*, with Emil Jannings, in 1923. Before that, she had studied in Max Reinhardt's drama school in 1921 and met Rudolf Sieber, then a young assistant director, whom she married in 1924. Her biggest stage success in the 1920s was in Reinhardt's production of the American play *Broadway*, and in that same year, 1927, she made her first record, "Peter." In German movies she had a small part in *Joyless Street*, in which Garbo made her first notable suc-

MARLENE DIETRICH

cess, 1925; played Michelin in *Manon Lescaut*, with Lya de Putti, 1926; and appeared in *Cafe Electric, Princess Olala, I Kiss Your Hand, Madame, Three Loves* and *Ship of Lost Men*. Then came Lola in *The Blue Angel* and, before its Berlin premiere, she was on her way to America with a Paramount contract. In 1938 she became an American citizen.

JEAN DIXON

She was born in Waterbury, Conn., July 14, 1896, went to St. Margaret's School in New York and also studied in Paris, where she made her stage debut with Sarah Bernhardt. On Broadway, she first appeared in small roles in two plays with Helen Hayes, *Golden Days* and *To the Ladies*, in 1921-1922. After spending three years in stock companies, she returned to New York in 1926, made her first big hit as Lucille in *June Moon*, the George S. Kaufman-Ring Lardner comedy, 1929, and continued her success as the tart "voice coach" May Daniels in *Once in a Lifetime*, by Kaufman and Moss Hart, a year later. Her screen career began in *The Lady Lies*, 1929, filmed at Paramount's Astoria studio, but she didn't make another film until 1933, with *Kiss Before the Mirror*. Her last was in *Holiday*, 1938. She married Edward Ely.

CLAIRE DODD

Miss Dodd was born in New York, December 29, 1908, and studied under tutors. At twenty she was a show-girl in Ziegfeld's *Whoopee!* with Eddie Cantor, and later was in Ziegfeld's *Smiles*, with Marilyn Miller. She got her movie start in a small bit in *Our Blushing Brides* in 1931, and made her last film in 1942, in *The Mad Doctor of Market Street*. She has been married to Jack M. Strauss, then to H. Brand Cooper. She died in Beverly Hills, November 23, 1973.

RUTH DONNELLY

Daughter of a newspaperman, she was born in Trenton, N. J., May 17, 1896, and started her career as a chorus girl in a touring company of *The Quaker Girl* in 1913. A year later she was on Broadway in *A Scrap of Paper*, playing a telephone operator. Her movie career dates from 1927, with a small part in *Rubber Tires*, with Bessie Love and Harrison Ford. Miss Donnelly was happily married from 1932, until his death in 1958, to Basil de Guichard, an aircraft company executive. Her last movie was in 1957, *The Way to the Gold*. She now lives in New York.

MARY DORAN

She grew up in New York, where she was born September 3, 1907, and attended Teachers College, Columbia University.

She cut classes there to take tap dancing lessons at Ned Wayburn's Dancing School, and got her first stage job in Ziegfeld's production of *Betsy*, with Belle Baker, in 1926, and later in his *Rio Rita*. In California, she played the ingenue in the Los Angeles stage production of *Saturday's Children* with Douglas Fairbanks, Jr. Miss Doran first appeared in silent films, beginning with *Half a Bride*, with Esther Ralston, 1927, and later got an MGM contract. Her screen career ended in 1936. She married Joseph McGillicuddy Sherman.

FIFI D'ORSAY

Her real name is Yvonne Lussier, one of twelve children of a post office worker in Montreal, where she was born April 16, 1904. She stresses she has never set foot in Paris, though a professional "French bombshell" throughout her career. Following her schooling at the Academy of the Sacred Heart, she became a typist, and then decided to go to New York in 1923 to look for a job on the stage. Through Gus Edwards, she became a chorus girl in the *Greenwich Village Follies*, and was seen by Gallagher and Shean, who worked in a part for her in their act. Thereafter, she worked steadily in vaudeville, until Will Rogers asked for her to be in his *They Had to See Paris* in 1929. The Fox studios signed her to a long-term contract, and took her movie name, D'Orsay, from a perfume bottle. From 1935 on, she worked only occasionally in movies, vaudeville, TV, and night clubs, and had two unhappy marriages. After finding religion from a little book, *My Daily Bread*, by a Jesuit, Anthony Paone, Miss D'Orsay went on the women's club lecture circuit, using as her theme, "I'm Glad I'm Not Young Any More." In 1971, aged 67, she made her Broadway debut in *Follies*.

CATHARINE DOUCET

She was born June 20, 1875, the daughter of Joshua E. Green and his wife, Clarinda Provost. It wasn't until 1906 that her stage career began as Marian Thorne in *Brown of Harvard*, with Henry Woodruff and Laura Hope Crews, in New York, at the Princess Theatre. Before that she had been a school teacher, and married to actor Paul Doucet. Her career on Broadway was spotty until she made a hit in J. P. McEvoy's *The Potters*, as Ma Potter, with Donald Meek as Pa, in 1923. Her last movie, *Family Honeymoon*, was in 1949. She died June 24, 1958.

BILLIE DOVE

During her silent screen career, she was called simply "the American Beauty" and

starred in a movie of that name in 1927 just to prove it. She was born May 14, 1900, in New York, as Lillian Bohny, and went to George Washington High School and a business school before going on the stage as a show-girl in Ziegfeld's *Midnight Revue* and his *Follies* and *Sally*. In 1921, she got a small part in *Get-Rich-Quick Wallingford*, with Norman Kerry, and a lead in *At the Stage Door*, with Huntley Gordon, before going to Hollywood to begin her career there in *Polly of the Follies*, with Constance Talmadge. During the 1920s she became a star at First National. She was the wife of director Irvin Willat from 1923 to 1929. She has been married to multimillionaire Robert Kenaston since 1933, with homes in the Pacific Palisades and Palm Springs. In 1962, Miss Dove returned briefly to movies to play a nurse in *Diamond Head*, with Charlton Heston.

FRANCES DRAKE

She was born in New York, October 22, 1908, daughter of Edwin Morgan Dean, of Newcastle, Northumberland, England, and Toronto; was educated at Havergal College, Toronto, and in a finishing school at Arundel, England. Under her real name, Frances Dean, she danced in London night clubs with Gordon Wallace, played a cockney maid in a play, *Little Earthquake*, 1933, and acted in two British films, *Two Hearts in Waltz Time*, with Carl Brisson, and *The Jewel*, with Jack Hawkins and Hugh Williams. This opened the way to Hollywood, where she made her debut in *Bolero*, 1934. Paramount changed her name from Frances Dean to Frances Drake, to avoid conflict with another Paramount player, Frances Dee. She married the Hon. Cecil John Arthur Howard, son of the nineteenth Earl of Suffolk, February 12, 1939, and a year later made her last film, *I Take This Woman*. The Howards live in Beverly Hills.

LOUISE DRESSER

Born Louise Kerlin, the daughter of a railroad man, in Evansville, Indiana, October 5, 1878. When she was sixteen, she ran away from home to join a singing troupe that got her to her wished-for destination, Chicago. There, when auditioning for a roof-garden show, she aroused the interest of song-writer Paul Dresser ("On the Banks of the Wabash"), who had been befriended by her father when he was a "candy-butcher" on the Wabash Railroad. Dresser introduced Louise Kerlin around Chicago as "my kid sister, Louise Dresser," giving her a new name and a career boost—and eventually, a song to introduce, "My Gal Sal." In 1906, she got to Broadway in the musical *About Town*, with her new husband, Jack

MARIE DRESSLER

Norworth (who later married Nora Bayes). Oddly, her Broadway career was mainly filled with vaudeville, musicals, and farce. It was the movies that discovered her dramatic strength. At the age of forty-four she made her bow in *Enter Madame*, with Clara Kimball Young. Her most famous roles in silent films were as the Empress Catherine the Great in *The Eagle*, with Rudolph Valentino, and the title role in *The Goose Woman*. After *Maid of Salem* in 1937, Miss Dresser's career came to an end. She claimed that this was due to a false report that she was deaf. Her second husband was "Handsome Jack" Gardner, who originated *The Chocolate Soldier* role in America, and later a Hollywood casting director. He died in 1950, after a 42-year marriage. In her last years, she lived alone in an apartment in Glendale, and died in the Motion Picture Country Hospital, April 24, 1965.

MARIE DRESSLER

Even when young, Marie Dressler, of light brown hair and green eyes, was always a large woman—weighing over 150 pounds and 5′ 8″ tall—"too homely for a prima donna, too hefty for a soubrette", she said. The bulk of her body never deterred her—it was the bulk of her personality that gave her star quality all her life.

Miss Dressler was born Leila Marie Koerber, in Cobourg, Ont., November 9, 1868, younger of two daughters of Alexander Rudolph Koerber, an Austrian piano teacher and his Irish-Canadian wife. The small bungalow in which she was born is still a popular tourist Mecca. When she was about fourteen, she left home with her sister Bonita to go on the stage, taking her stage name from an aunt who lived in Germany. By 1892, she was on Broadway in a comic opera, *The Robber of the Rhine*, written by Maurice Barrymore. Her most durable stage success came in 1910, as the boarding-house drudge Tillie Blobbs, in *Tillie's Nightmare*, in which she sang "Heaven Will Protect the Working Girl." Tillie inspired her famous early movie, *Tillie's Punctured Romance*, 1914, produced by Mack Sennett, in which the towering Miss Dressler all but eclipsed even Charlie Chaplin and Mabel Normand. Although she made a few more Tillie movies around this time, Marie Dressler was too strong a personality, like Chaplin, to fit into the ensemble style of the Sennett company.

The 1920s were bad financially for her: only two Broadway shows. In 1927, she was living in a room usually occupied by hotel servants at the Ritz, New York. In 1932, when she had come into the money once more, she bought the Georgian mansion of King Gillette in Beverly Hills, and gave extravagant parties for all her friends.

Her marital life was rather mysterious. She was married to a George E. Huppert, probably from 1894 to 1896, but never explained who he was in any of her reminiscences. It was rumored she had a child who died either in childbirth or infancy. Then she listed, in *Who's Who in the Theatre*, J. H. Dalton as her husband. Dalton was her manager from 1907. It later developed that they couldn't marry because his wife refused to divorce him. Miss Dressler said, "He and his wife had never been able to get along, and there was every reason why she should divorce him. She laughed at us, and refused. Since that time, Mr. Dalton has always been my manager." He died in 1921.

At her own death July 28, 1934, she left an estate of $300,000, including a bequest of $50,000 to her Black maid of twenty-five years.

ELLEN DREW

Ellen Drew was born November 23, 1915, in Kansas City, daughter of a barber, who later moved to Chicago with his wife and daughter. She got as far as the third year in the Parker High School, when she quit to go to work at Marshall Field's department store, then went back to Kansas City, where she ran an elevator in the Aladdin Hotel at $14 a week, rejoined her family in Englewood, Ill., where she got a job in the Grant store. When the manager of the store entered her in a beauty contest sponsored by the Kiwanis Club, she won the thing, and, moviestruck, decided to go along with a young couple to California in their rattletrap flivver. In Hollywood, she got a job at Brown's Confectionary on Hollywood Boulevard at $11.50 a week, where she met her future husband, film make-up man Fred Wallace, and an agent, William Demarest, who got her a studio test and a $50-a-week contract to play extras and bits. After her divorce from her first husband, she married writer Sy Bartlett (1941-1949) and then William Walker, of Detroit, an advertising executive and oilman, in 1951.

MARGARET DUMONT

Miss Dumont didn't think it was fair to be called a "stooge". She said, "I'm a straight lady, the best straight woman in Hollywood."

She was the daughter of William Lawrence and Lillian Harvey Baker, and was born in Brooklyn, October 20, 1889. At eighteen, she was on Broadway in a play with George M. Cohan, and then toured Europe as an ingenue singer in revues in London, Paris, Vienna, and Berlin. She retired from the stage for several years, but returned to Broadway in 1922. By 1925 she became a fixture with the Marx Brothers in their first Broadway show, *The Cocoanuts*, and made her bow in the movie version in 1929. She appeared in seven of their films. By no means was her movie career confined to the Marxes; she also appeared with W. C. Fields, Laurel and Hardy and Jack Benny, among others. She worked until the last, and died at her home March 6, 1965.

STEFFI DUNA

She was born in Budapest, daughter of a vintner. She first appeared as a child in the ballet of the Budapest Opera, and at fifteen was a dancer in Salzburg and subsequently throughout Europe. In Berlin, she played opposite Francis Lederer in *Wonder Bar*, in London in Noël Coward's *Words and Music* with John Mills, 1932, and in New York, 1933, as Polly Peachum in *The Threepenny Opera*, with Burgess Meredith. From there, she went to Hollywood to make her first American movie, *Man of Two Worlds*, 1934, with Francis Lederer also in his Hollywood debut. She married actor Dennis O'Keefe in 1940 and retired. Her husband died in 1968.

DIXIE DUNBAR

Christina Elizabeth Dunbar was born January 19, 1919, in Montgomery, Ala., and educated in public schools there. As a teenager she was a chorus girl at the Paradise Restaurant on Broadway, and in August 1934, played at the Winter Garden in *Life Begins at 8:40*, with Bert Lahr. That same year, she made her movie debut in *George White's Scandals*, with Rudy Vallee and Alice Faye. In 1938 she wound up her movie career. She is married to millionaire Jack L. King, of Miami Beach, and is always called "Chris" for Christina, never "Dixie."

MARY DUNCAN

The daughter of William and Ada Douglas Duncan, she was born in Luttrellville, Va., August 13, 1903, was educated at Wirtland Seminary in Virginia and Cornell University, and studied acting one year with Yvette Guilbert. She made her Broadway bow in *Face Value* in 1921. Her most successful stage appearance was as Mother Goddam's daughter Poppy in *The Shanghai Gesture*. Her first movie was the silent *Very Confidential*, with Madge Bellamy, 1927. She was once married to Lewis Wood Jr.

THE DUNCAN SISTERS

Rosetta was born November 23, 1897, and Vivian, June 17, 1899, in Los Angeles, daughters to a violinist turned salesman. In 1911, they began their careers in the cast of Gus Edwards' *Kiddies' Revue*, and in 1917 made their first important Broadway appearance in *Doing Our Bit*, with Ed Wynn and Frank Tinney, at the Winter Garden. Thereafter, they played in vaudeville, night clubs, and musicals in New York and London. Together they wrote part of the music for their smash hit, *Topsy and Eva*, in which they first appeared in 1923. They were still appearing together in clubs, when Rosetta was killed in an automobile accident, December 4, 1959.

Vivian divorced Nils Asther in 1932. They had a daughter, Evlyn. Vivian was also married briefly to cowboy actor Rex Lease. In 1947, she married architect Frank Herman and lives in Atherton, Calif., when not touring the club circuit as a single.

JOSEPHINE DUNN

Mary Josephine Dunn was born May 1, 1906, in New York, and was educated at Holy Cross Convent there. At fifteen, she was a member of the chorus of her first Broadway show, *Good Morning, Dearie*, with Louise Groody and Oscar Shaw. In 1926, she was among the young people chosen by Paramount Studios for their acting school, and made her movie bow, along with other debutantes, in the school's production, *Fascinating Youth*. Her movie career ended in 1933, when she was playing small parts. Thereafter, until the early 1940s, she played mostly in summer stock. Miss Dunn married William P. Cameron, a Philadelphia engineer, in 1925, who claimed she deserted him two days after marriage. She then married Clyde Greathouse, an Oklahoma oil man (div. 1931), Philadelphia attorney Eugene J. Lewis (1933-1935), and Carroll Case, son of Frank Case, the owner of the Algonquin Hotel, New York, in 1935.

IRENE DUNNE

Miss Dunne was born December 20, 1901 in Louisville, Ky., where her father, Joseph John Dunne, built and operated river boats. Her mother was a pianist who saw to it that their daughter received thorough musical training. She made her debut in a road company of *Irene* in 1920. She had her first starring role in *Luckee Girl*, 1928, for the Shuberts, with Irving Fisher and Harry Puck, and, in Chicago, played Magnolia in *Show Boat*.

In twenty-two years of movies, she made forty-two films, with her last, *It Grows on Trees*, in 1952

In 1928, she married dentist Dr. Francis J. Griffin, who died in 1965. They had one daughter.

MINNIE DUPREE

Miss Dupree devoted fifty-six years to the theatre, from her childhood debut in 1887 until her last Broadway appearance in Jed Harris's production of *Dark Eyes*, 1943. She was born January 19, 1875, in San Francisco. For years, she was a popular leading lady to such stars as Richard Mansfield, William Gillette, Nat Goodwin, and David Warfield. In *The Road to Yesterday*, 1906, she became a star herself, praised for the delicacy and lightness of her comedy style. Miss Dupree had appeared briefly as a night club attendant in a crudely made early talkie *Night Club*, with Fanny Brice, 1929, before *The Young in Heart*, 1938. She also had a small part in *Anne of Windy Poplars* in 1940. She died May 23, 1945.

DEANNA DURBIN

Deanna Durbin felt comfortable only as a singer, never as an actress, and was terrified of the camera. In 1948, after eleven years, she left the movies and Hollywood without a tinge of regret, for a life of total retirement in a remote village of France. She was christened Edna May Durbin, the younger of two daughters

IRENE DUNNE

of English-born James Durbin and Ada Read Durbin, and was born December 4, 1921, in Winnipeg. From the age of six months, she lived in Los Angeles, where her father, an industrial blacksmith, set up his own wrought-iron business. She attended Manchester Grammar School and Bret Harte Junior High School in South Los Angeles. She could sing with unusual clarity almost from babyhood, and became locally famous in school productions. An actor's agent who had heard her sing recommended her to MGM in 1935 when that studio needed a child to play the diva Mme. Schumann-Heink as a child, in a proposed biography of the opera star. This was never made, but MGM put her in a short subject with Judy Garland, then dropped her contract. Universal Pictures wanted Judy, but were told they would have to take "the other one."

At twenty, she married Vaughn Paul, and divorced him in 1943. In 1945, she married producer Felix Jackson, by whom she had a daughter, Jessica, in 1946, and divorced him in 1948. Her third husband is director Charles David, with a son, Peter.

ANN DVORAK

Her real name is Ann McKim, born in New York, August 2, 1912, one of the two children of Sam McKim, then a director at the Biograph Studios, and his actress wife, Anna Lehr. Ann went to St. Catherine's Convent in New York, and the Page School for Girls in Los Angeles. In 1920, her parents divorced, and Ann stayed with her mother. When Ann went into the movies she decided on the name Dvorak, taken from her mother's family tree in Bohemia. She was an assistant dance director at MGM for the early musicals, and was a chorine in *Hollywood Revue of 1929*. Her first break came from Howard Hughes, who gave the dark-haired girl the lead opposite Spencer Tracy in *Sky Devils* and as Paul Muni's sister in *Scarface*. Warners bought her contract from Hughes; and then began her up-and-down career marked by her rebellious walk-outs, suspensions, lawsuits, and slow-boats to Europe that won her the displeasure of Jack Warner. Miss Dvorak said it wasn't the money that was involved, but the parts they stuck her with. In 1940, she and her husband of eight years, Leslie Fenton, returned to his native England, where he served as a naval liaison officer and she drove an ambulance in England and Scotland. She also made three films there, notably *Squadron Leader X*, with Eric Portman, in 1943. Two years later, she was back in Hollywood, as leading lady to John Wayne in *Flame of Barbary Coast*. Her movie career ended in 1951. On Broadway, she

starred in Sartre's *The Respectful Prostitute*, which ran for 314 perforances in 1948. After her divorce from Fenton in 1944, she married dancer Igor de Navrotsky in 1947—divorced 1951. She is now married to architect Nicholas Wade, with residences in Malibu Beach and Honolulu.

JEANNE EAGELS

Jeanne Eagels was born in Kansas City, June 26, 1890, and went to St. Paul's parochial school and Morris Public School. She quit school at fourteen to work in a department store, and, at fifteen, was touring with Dubinsky Brothers' Tent Show. She married the man who played the villains, Morris Dubinsky, and bore him a son, whom she entrusted to friends. Her son never knew who his mother was. She first attracted notice in a musical, *Jumping Jupiter*, with Richard Carle and Ina Claire, in New York, 1911. By 1918, she applied to the autocratic David Belasco for a star part in *Daddies*, and got it. But she had to wait four more years for the big hit of her career, the role of Sadie Thompson in *Rain*, 1922, which she played for two years, and then returned to it for a tour, 1925-1926, a total run of 1500 performances.

She had appeared in movies as early as 1916, as the star of *The World and the Woman* and *Under False Colors*, among others. In 1927, she made another silent, *Man, Woman and Sin*, with John Gilbert. Her second husband, whom she divorced, was the Yale football star, Ted Coy; she was the second of his three wives. Her extremely nervous condition, frail physique, and drug and drinking habits required that she be treated medically for nine years before her death. She died broke, October 3, 1929, from a dose of chloral hydrate.

MAUDE EBURNE

She was born 1875 in Bronte-on-the-Lake, a Toronto suburb, of Scotch-Irish parents, and went to Toronto schools and Havergal College. In later life, she said she got on the stage "by stealth" against the wishes of her parents. She made her first hit as Coddles, a Cockney maid-of-all-work in *A Pair of Sixes*, with Ann Murdock and Hale Hamilton, in 1914. She was a popular stage character actress until 1930, when she transferred her style to the movies. Miss Eburne was married to E. J. Hall. She died October 15, 1960.

HELEN JEROME EDDY

She was born in New York, February 25, 1897, and grew up in Los Angeles, where she made her movie debut in 1915 with Dustin Farnum in *The Gentleman from Indiana*. She was the star of King Vidor's first film, *Turn in the Road*, 1918, was George Beban's leading lady in all his

movies, and was the star of a typical Eddy drama of "home life pathos" in *An Old Sweetheart of Mine*, with Elliott Dexter, in 1923. Her last appearance was in *Strike Up the Band*, 1940.

SALLY EILERS

Born in New York, December 11, 1908, daughter to Peter and Paula Eilers, she was educated in Hollywood at Fairfax High School, and studied dancing with Ernest Belcher. She began her movie career in Pathé shorts and played bits in *Cradle Snatchers*, *Slightly Used*, and a party girl in King Vidor's *The Crowd*. After she played the heroine in two Westerns with Hoot Gibson in 1930, she married the cowboy star at his ranch June 27, 1930. After her divorce from Gibson in 1933, she married producer Harry Joe Brown; she later became the wife of Hollingsworth Morse. Miss Eilers retired in 1943, but returned briefly in *Stage to Tucson* in 1950.

FLORENCE ELDRIDGE

Born Florence McKechnie in Brooklyn, September 5, 1901, she became a chorus girl at seventeen in *Rock-a-Bye Baby*, after leaving Girls' High School. She rushed to the top fast, as Annabelle West in *The Cat and the Canary*, Daisy Fay in *The Great Gatsby*, the Stepdaughter in *Six Characters in Search of an Author*. In 1927, when touring for the Theatre Guild, she met and married actor Fredric March, and her career became largely intertwined with his through the years, on both stage and screen.

MARY ELLIS

Miss Ellis was born in New York, June 15, 1899, studied art for three years, then singing, and made her debut at the Metropolitan Opera in 1918. She married four times: to L. A. Bernheimer, producer Edwin Knopf, actor Basil Sydney and Muir Stewart Roberts, who left her a widow. Since the 1930s, except for her brief Hollywood movie career, she has worked principally in England.

PATRICIA ELLIS

As Patricia Gene O'Brien, she was born in Birmingham, Mich., May 20, 1916, and had three years' stage experience before she became, as she said, "Queen of B Pictures" at Warner Brothers", beginning in 1932. After her marriage in 1941 to George T. O'Maley, later president of Protection Securities Systems, Kansas City, she retired. She died of cancer, March 27, 1970.

MADGE EVANS

Madge Evans was one of the earliest

and most ethereal of child actresses, starting at five in 1914, appearing with adult stars Marguerite Clark, Pauline Frederick, Ethel Clayton, and Alice Brady. She was also the child model who sat on a Fairy Soap bar, and asked, "Have you a little fairy in your home?" She was born in New York, July 1, 1909, and worked on the stage and in movies until her retirement, as wife of playwright Sidney Kingsley, in the middle 1940s. On Broadway, she appeared with John and Lionel Barrymore in *Peter Ibbetson*, in Noël Coward's *The Marquise*, with Billie Burke, 1927, George Kelly's *Philip Goes Forth*, 1931, Philip Barry's *Here Come the Clowns*, 1938, and her last, her husband's *The Patriots*, 1943.

FRANCES FARMER

She lived her stormy, tragic life as an uncompromising rebel. Born September 19, 1913, in Seattle, daughter of a lawyer, she first stirred up things by winning a national essay prize from *Scholastic* magazine, for a paper called "God Died," and became "the freak of West Seattle High." At the University of Washington (graduating 1935), she won another essay prize, this time from a radical magazine, *The Voice of Action*, with a trip to the Soviet Union as first prize. On her way back home, she met producer Shepard Traube in New York, who introduced her to Paramount executives for a screen test. Her debut was in *Too Many Parents*, 1936. She never adjusted comfortably to Hollywood values, and cherished her brief career with the Group Theatre in New York as the high point of her professional life. Just before this, she met her first husband, actor Leif Erickson, whom she married in 1936, and who followed her to New York.

After making *Son of Fury* in 1942, she began a tortured period of drunkenness,

arrests, and horrifying internments in mental hospitals. Having precariously regained her mental health, she became hostess of a popular TV program in Indianapolis, was an actress in residence at the University Theatre at Purdue. She married twice again, Seattle engineer Alfred Lobley and Indiana business man Lee Mikesell, and divorced both. Her last years were spent on a farm northwest of Indianapolis. She told the story of her shattered life in a posthumously published autobiography, *Will There Really Be a Morning?*, 1972. She stipulated that all proceeds from her book go into a special fund set up "to decorate and brighten state asylums throughout the land." She died of cancer, August 1, 1970.

GLENDA FARRELL

She was born in Enid, Okla., June 30, 1904, made her debut at seven as Little Eva, and thereafter spent most of her life in the theatre and movies. Her movie career went straight through the 1930s. Thereafter she alternated between stage and screen. During the stage run of *Forty Carats* in New York, 1969, she became ill, and died at her home on Park Avenue, May 1, 1971. As the wife of Dr. Henry Ross (former colonel in the U. S. Army), she is the only actress buried in the cemetery of the U. S. Military Academy at West Point.

ALICE FAYE

Alice Jeanne Leppert, later to become Alice Faye, was born in a Hell's Kitchen tenement, on New York's West Side, May 5, 1912, and attended P. S. 84. While a dancer in George White's *Scandals* she was noticed by its star, Rudy Vallee, who signed her as his lead singer on his radio show and band tours. In 1934, she and Vallee appeared together in a screen version of the *Scandals*, and her

movie career continued until 1946. She married band leader Phil Harris on May 12, 1941, and is the mother of two daughters, Alice and Phyllis. In 1962, she returned to movies once more as the mother of Pat Boone and Pamela Tiffin in *State Fair*, and to Broadway in 1973 in *Good News*.

LOUISE FAZENDA

Born June 17, 1895, in Lafayette, Indiana, she went to high school in Los Angeles, made her debut in 1912, in a one-reel Universal comedy, and really got going in Mack Sennett's slapstick comedies. She married film director Noel M. Smith, and after her divorce, producer Hal B. Wallis in 1927. They had one son, Brent, a psychologist. She ended her 27-year career in 1939. An astute business woman, she personally managed her many properties, and she was generous in both time and money to many charities. She died of a cerebral hemorrhage at her home in Holmby Hills, Hollywood, April 17, 1962.

EDITH FELLOWS

Her parents separated shortly after her birth in Boston, May 20, 1923. Edith Marilyn Fellows was brought up in Charlotte, N.C., by her grandmother, Elizabeth Lamb Fellows, a onetime singer, who took in sewing to support them. From the age of three little Edith was singing, dancing, and doing imitations at every church entertainment, club benefit, and amateur show in town. Her enraptured grandmother took the talented tot to Hollywood. Edith played bits and extras in picture after picture, getting her first good part in Ruth Chatterton's *Madame X*, in 1929. On the Los Angeles stage, she acted in revivals of *The Drunkard* and *Ten Nights in a Barroom*, and had a vaudeville night club act with Tommy Dix. By 1945, she got to Broadway as a comedienne in a musical, *Marinka*, with Harry Stockwell and Joan Roberts. She was once married to CMA head agent Freddie Fields.

BETTY FIELD

Born in Boston, February 8, 1918, she grew up in Kew Gardens, a section of New York City, and studied at the American Academy of Dramatic Arts. Her first acting job was as a maid in *The First Mrs. Fraser*, in a summer theatre in 1933, and she became one of George Abbott's favorite ingenues in his light comedy productions of the late 1930s. Her later screen roles were few but memorable; in *King's Row*, *Tomorrow the World*, *The Southerner*, *Picnic*, *Bus Stop*, *Peyton Place*. Her first husband was playwright Elmer Rice (1942–1956), by

ALICE FAYE

GERALDINE FITZGERALD

whom she had three children, and who wrote three plays for her: *Two on an Island*, *A New Life* and *Dream Girl*. After her divorce, she married Edwin J. Lucas, and after him, painter Raymond Olivere. She died September 13, 1973.

VIRGINIA FIELD

Born in London, November 4, 1917, as Margaret Cynthia Field, she was the daughter of a King's Counselor, St. John Field, and went to schools in Paris and Vienna. With the help of her aunt, Auriol Lee, actress-director, she got her start in the theatre. She appeared on the London stage with Leslie Howard in *This Side Idolatry*, 1933, and also in British films. Her first husband was actor Paul Douglas, by whom she had a daughter, Margaret; her second, composer Howard Grode, whom she also divorced. Miss Field continued in movies until 1962.

GRACIE FIELDS

The British claimed that their Gracie was the highest paid film actress in the world. She was born in Rochdale, Lancashire, January 9, 1898, and made her debut at eight singing between shows in a cinema. For her first husband, Archie Pitt, she starred in *Mr. Tower of London*, which ran between 1918 and 1925 for 4000 performances, and followed with *By Request* for another three years. After her American movie career ended in 1945, she retired, living in Capri. Her second husband, actor-producer Monty Banks, who had once acted in Mack Sennett comedies, died in 1950.

GERALDINE FITZGERALD

Daughter of an attorney, and niece of an Abbey Theatre actress, Shelah Richards, she was born in Dublin, November 24, 1914. At first she studied art, but was persuaded by her aunt to try acting. She appeared in British films from 1934 to 1937. Orson Welles brought her to the United States for her stage debut here in his Mercury Theatre production of *Heartbreak House* in 1938. This led her straight to Hollywood, and from then on she divided her career fairly evenly between stage and screen. Miss Fitzgerald first married an Irish horse breeder, Edward Lindsay-Hogg, whom she divorced in 1943. She married her second husband, Stuart Sheftel, grandson of the founder of Macy's, and dollar-a-year financier, in 1946. She has a son, Michael Lindsay-Hogg, and a daughter, Susan Sheftel.

SUSAN FLEMING

Born in New York February 19, 1909, she danced in the *Scandals* and *Follies* and made her movie debut in 1931. She married Harpo Marx in 1936, and they adopted four children. Her career ended in 1937, playing bits in *Gold Diggers of 1937* and *God's Country and the Woman*.

JOAN FONTAINE

A year younger than her sister, Joan de Beauvoir de Havilland was born in Tokyo, October 22, 1917. She and her sister Olivia grew up near San Francisco, after their mother divorced their father and re-married a man named George Fontaine. She made her debut with a little theater group in San Jose, and her movie debut at eighteen, playing a thirty-five-year-old woman who lost Robert Montgomery to Joan Crawford in *No More Ladies*. She married three times: actor Brian Aherne (1939–1944), producer William Dozier (1946–1951), and producer Collier Young, 1952.

LYNN FONTANNE

She had made two brief appearances in silent films: *Second Youth*, with Alfred Lunt, 1924, and *The Man Who Found Himself*, with Thomas Meighan and Virginia Valli in 1925. But her entire life was devoted to the theatre from 1905, when she toured with Ellen Terry in *Alice Sit-by-the-Fire*. She made her New York debut in 1910. She first appeared with Alfred Lunt on the stage in the Theatre Guild's production of *The Guardsman* in 1924. They had married May 26, 1922. After years of speculation, it now appears that Miss Fontanne's birthdate is December 6, 1887.

SIDNEY FOX

The very tiny Miss Fox (less than five feet tall, under 100 pounds), whose father's name was Jacob Liefer, was born in New York, December 10, 1910. After studying law at Columbia University, she worked for a time as a legal secretary, but changed her mind about a career and briefly attended Louise Gifford's acting school. She made her debut with the Civic Theatre in Johnstown, Pa., and her Broadway debut as the ingenue lead in *It never Rains*, 1929. Between 1931 and 1935, she made thirteen films, including one in France for G. W. Pabst, opposite the great Russian basso, Feodor Chaliapin, in *Don Quixote*, 1934. She returned to the stage in April 1937, to replace Margo in *The Masque of Kings* and, that July, Katherine Locke in *Having Wonderful Time*. In December 1932, she married playwright-novelist-producer Charles Beahan. She was found dead in her Hollywood home, November 14, 1942, aged thirty-one, from an overdose of sleeping tablets.

KAY FRANCIS

She was the daughter of a businessman, Joseph Gibbs, and an actress, Katherine Clinton, and was born in Oklahoma City on January 13, 1903. Her first jobs were selling real estate, in public relations, and arranging parties for the rich. She made her stage debut as the Player Queen in *Hamlet* with Basil Sydney in 1925, and played her first important part opposite Walter Huston in Ring Lardner's *Elmer the Great* in 1928, which led to films. Her four marriages, to Dwight Francis, William Gaston, John Meehan, and actor Kenneth MacKenna, ended in divorce. She ended her career in summer stock. She lived, practically a recluse, in New York on East 64th Street and in a house near Falmouth, Cape Cod. She died of cancer August 26, 1968, and willed most of her estate of $1,000,000 to the Seeing Eye, Inc.

NOEL FRANCIS

She was born in Temple, Texas, and grew up in Dallas. She attended Southern Methodist University and Columbia. After her stage career (in the *Follies*) she made her debut in 1930 in *Fox Movietone Follies*. Her screen career ended in 1938, opposite Buck Jones in the horse opera *Sudden Bill Dorn*.

PAULINE FREDERICK

Ironically, this regal stage actress, of a long, distinguished career, had more success in silent films than in talkies. Between 1915 and 1937, she made sixty-five movies. Her roles in silents varied from smoldering melodramas (*Madame X*) to sophisticated comedy (Lubitsch's *Three Women*).

She was born Pauline Libbey in Boston on August 12, 1883, the only child of Richard O. Libbey (later spelled Libby), yardmaster for the Old Colony Railroad. She made her debut as a chorus girl in 1902, changed her name to Pauline Fred-

GRETA GARBO

erick in 1908, and played her last role, Empress Elizabeth of Austria in the Theatre Guild's New York production of Maxwell Anderson's *The Masque of Kings*, 1937. She was married five times: New York architect Frank Mills Andrews (1909–1913), actor-playwright Willard Mack (1917–1920), Seattle physician Dr. Charles Rutherford (1922, divorced), hotel man Hugh C. Leighton (1930, annulled) and Col. Joseph A. Marmon, 1934. She died of an asthmatic attack September 19, 1938, in her big Sunset Boulevard house in Hollywood.

FRANCES FULLER

A niece of U. S. Senator James F. Byrnes, she was born October 4, 1907, in Charleston, South Carolina. She studied acting at the American Academy of Dramatic Arts in New York, where she later was a teacher for many years. She is the wife of producer Worthington Miner. On Broadway, she played opposite Leslie Howard in *The Animal Kingdom*, 1932, and had the role of Kaye Hamilton (the actress suicide played by Andrea Leeds in the movie) in *Stage Door*, 1936. She lives in New York.

BETTY FURNESS

She was born in New York, January 3, 1916, daughter of a Union Carbon and Carbide Corporation official. At sixteen, she became a model for John Robert Powers agency, and got a Hollywood contract with RKO a year later in 1933. Her movie career ended in 1937. She has been married four times: to orchestra leader Johnny Green (1937, div.); radio producer Hugh (Bud) Ernst, who died in 1950; drama teacher Denton Snyder, and TV producer Leslie Midgeley. In March 1967, President Lyndon Johnson named her as his special assistant for consumer affairs.

FRANCISKA GAAL

Miss Gaal was born in Budapest, February 1, 1904, the thirteenth and youngest child of an aristocratic Budapest family. She started her career as a cabaret and ballad singer, and married Francis Dajkovich, also a singer. On the stage, she appeared in Molnar plays, and began her Hungarian movie career in 1933. She also made films in Berlin, Vienna, and Monte Carlo, before going to Hollywood in 1938, at the age of thirty-four. Cecil DeMille made her obligations even weightier by describing her to the press as "a combination of Helen Hayes, the early Mary Pickford, Elisabeth Bergner, and Clara Bow." In 1940, she departed hurriedly for Budapest to visit her sick mother, was stranded in Budapest for the duration of the war, and by 1946 had lost

most of her family, "several houses, a castle, 200 horses, and all her land." In 1951, she returned to Broadway, succeeding Eva Gabor in *The Happy Time*.

KETTI GALLIAN

Born in Nice, December 25, 1913, she worked in her mother's dressmaking shop, and began her career as a chorus girl in 1928 before going into French films. On the London stage in 1933, she appeared in a murder mystery, *The Ace*, with Raymond Massey. She returned to France and acted in six movies between 1937 and 1955. She was the wife of director Pierre Billon and died in December 1972.

GRETA GARBO

In 1963, I asked Mary Pickford, certainly the most influential star in movie history, who in her opinion, male or female, of whatever country, she considered to be the most significant artist the movies have given us. She paused a moment, and said, "Unquestionably, Greta Garbo."

Greta Lovisa Gustafsson was born September 18, 1905, the youngest of three children, in a four-room, cold-water flat in the Soder, the poorest district of Stockholm. Her father, Karl, made his living as an unskilled laborer. He had come from a farm in southern Sweden, and married a plump young woman, Anna Karlsson, also from the country, a round-faced woman with heavy arms and a thick neck. In 1919, Greta dropped out of school when her father became seriously ill, to nurse him while the family worked. In 1920, at his death, she became a soap-latherer in barbershops, and later a shopgirl on the fourth floor millinery department of the PUB department store. While working there, she appeared in two advertising films, and in 1922 played in a slight Sennett-like comedy, *Peter the Tramp*. This led to her being accepted as a scholarship pupil at the Royal Dramatic Theatre's training school, and her ultimate introduction to the director Mauritz Stiller, who took her life and career into his own hands. Before coming to America in 1925, she made two feature films, *Gösta Berling's Saga*, with Lars Hanson, in Stockholm, and *Joyless Street*, directed by G. W. Pabst, in Berlin. From 1926 to 1941, she worked exclusively as a star for MGM. Upon the disastrous failure of her last, *Two-Faced Woman*, Garbo, always easily discouraged, decided to leave films, at first only temporarily, but as time went on, she departed permanently, leaving behind a priceless legacy to the world.

JUDY GARLAND

She was the third daughter of Frank A. and Ethel Milne Gumm, who, as

JUDY GARLAND

"Jack and Virginia Lee, Sweet Southern Singers," toured as a vaudeville act. She was born in Grand Rapids on June 10, 1922, christened Frances Gumm. Her mother then changed the family act to "the Gumm Sisters." From the start, her entire life took on aspects of a potential script for a gay and sad musical comedy, of a lost era in American stage and screen life, of dizzying success snatched from sordid beginnings; but a script alive with more tragic and subtly sinister implications than most. Only the magnitude of Judy Garland's acting talents and gift of gaiety and song to the world saved her life from being just another show-business cliché of laugh, clown, laugh. She made movies from 1936 to 1950, and then, at irregular intervals, up to 1963. She was found dead in her London flat, June 22, 1969, aged forty-seven, after having tried suicide many times over many years, survived by her fifth husband and three children.

GREER GARSON

She was born in the County Down, North Ireland, September 29, 1906, only child of George Garson, a native of the Orkney Islands, and his wife, Nora Greer, descended from the Rob MacGregor clan of Scotland. The name "Greer" is a corruption of the clan label, "the name that was no name." Her father, engaged in the import business, died when Greer was four months old, and her mother, when Greer was in her teens, moved to London. There, the young woman became a scholarship pupil at London University, graduated B. A. with honors, and then did postgraduate work at the University of Grenoble in France. Her first job was with the Lever Brothers combine in London, where she became head of the market research and information department, and one of the best-paid young career women in London. But this was keeping her from her first love, the theatre, and she quit her job to make her professional

JANET GAYNOR

debut with the Birmingham Repertory Company in 1932, as Shirley Kaplan in Elmer Rice's *Street Scene*. Her first London hit was as Fanny Field in *The Golden Arrow*, with and directed by Laurence Olivier, 1935. From then on, she was a popular young star on the London stage. Louis B. Mayer saw her as Geraldine in Keith Winter's *Old Music*, and signed her to an MGM contract at $300 a week. She was with MGM fifteen years, and eventually in her career there earned more than $150,000 a year.

Miss Garson was first married to Edward A. Snelson, whom she divorced, and then to actor Richard Ney, who had played her son Vin in *Mrs. Miniver*, in 1942; they divorced in 1947. She then married Elijah E. ("Buddy") Fogelson, a Dallas oil executive, rancher, geologist, and sportsman, in 1949. They have houses in Dallas, and Bel Air, as well as a cattle ranch, Forked Lightning Ranch, in New Mexico.

MARJORIE GATESON

The granddaughter of Rev. John D. Kennedy, rector of St. Mark's Episcopal Church, Brooklyn, she was born January 17, 1891, and attended Brooklyn University. She made her stage debut in *The Little Café*, with Hazel Dawn, at the New Amsterdam, 1913. She had a varied stage career: in Shakespeare, vaudeville, in a musical with the Astaires. Her first movie was *Beloved Bachelor* in 1931, and she worked steadily through 1944. She returned to the stage in 1947 as Dame Lucy in a revival of *Sweethearts*, with Bobby Clark. Her last movie was *The Caddy*, with Jerry Lewis, 1953.

JANET GAYNOR

She was born October 6, 1906, in Philadelphia, and christened Laura Gainor. She grew up in Chicago and San Francisco, graduating from the Polytechnical High School there in 1923. Moving to Hollywood, she was put on a $50-a-week salary at Universal to play both extras and leads in two-reel comedies. Her first big break was in *The Johnstown Flood* at Fox in 1926. She left the screen in 1938, returning only once to play in *Bernardine*, 1957. She married Gilbert Adrian, the movies' top costume designer, in 1939. (She had been previously married to a San Francisco lawyer, Lydell Peck, from 1929 to 1934.) The Adrians had a son, Robin, born July 6, 1940, now national sales manager at CBS-TV, Hollywood. Several years after Adrian's death in 1957, Miss Gaynor married again, stage and screen producer Paul Gregory, fourteen years her junior. They live in the Palm Springs desert.

GLADYS GEORGE

She said her father was Sir Arthur Evans Clare, an actor, and her mother was Alice Hazen, a Boston girl. Gladys was born September 13, 1904, in Patton, Maine, while her parents were on tour. She went to school whenever the company paused long enough to permit it. She began her career as Little Tommy in *Back Among the Old Folks* at the age of three, at the Poli Theatre, Waterbury, Conn. At eight, she was star of her own vaudeville act, "Little Gladys George and Co." and later toured with a medicine show. She made her New York debut as the beggar's daughter in Maeterlinck's *The Betrothal*, with Isadora Duncan, at the Shubert in 1918, then spent a decade as star of stock companies throughout the country. Her biggest stage success was as the touring movie star, in *Personal Appearance*, 1934, a role played by Mae West on the screen.

In movies, she appeared as early as 1919 in *Red Hot Dollars*, with Charles Ray. Her real screen career began in 1934 and continued until her death. She was married four times: actor Ben Erway (1922–1929), manufacturer Edward H. Fowler (1933–1935), actor Leonard Penn (1935–1944), and bellhop Kenneth Bradley (1946–1950). She died of cancer of the throat in Hollywood, December 8, 1954, in Cedars of Lebanon Hospital, after having been found unconscious in her one-bedroom apartment. She had no survivors and $500 in the bank.

WYNNE GIBSON

Wynne was born Winifred Gibson in New York, July 3, 1905, and attended Wadleigh School for Girls. She began as a chorus girl in Lew Fields' *Snapshots of 1921*, and earned a listing in *Who's Who in the Theatre* in spite of the fact that most of her stage career was spent in touring companies, her only really big Broadway play being *Jarnegan*, with Richard Bennett in 1928. She also played in vaudeville. Her screen career began in 1929, and ended in 1943. For a long time after retiring from acting, she was an actors' agent in New York with Beverly Roberts. They live in West Babylon, Long Island.

LILLIAN GISH

This actress of spiritual fragility had a steely durability that other D. W. Griffith stars couldn't match. She was born October 14, 1893, in Springfield, Ohio, the elder of the two Gish girls. With her sister Dorothy, she started working on the stage as a child, in touring companies and in New York. In 1912, their friend Gladys Smith, who had become Mary Pickford, introduced them to the director, Mr. Griffith, at the Biograph Studio at 11 East 14th Street, and the Gishes started to work for him at $5 a day each, as extras. Thus began one of the most fabled screen liaisons in history (*Birth of a Nation, Intolerance, Broken Blossoms, Way Down East, Orphans of the Storm*). From 1926–1928, she was one of the stars at MGM, and, briefly in 1930, at United Artists. After the 1930s, she appeared only occasionally in movies, notably in *Duel in the Sun*, 1947, Charles Laughton's *Night of the Hunter*, 1957, and *The Comedians*, with Elizabeth Taylor and Richard Burton, 1967.

Miss Gish's stage career became a distinguished one. In 1930, she returned to Broadway as Helena in *Uncle Vanya*. In the years that followed, she played in, among many others, Sean O'Casey's *Within the Gates*, as the Young Whore; as Ophelia in *Hamlet*, with John Gielgud,

1936; Maxwell Anderson's *The Star Wagon*; Katerina in *Crime and Punishment*; *All the Way Home*; and *I Never Sang for My Father*, 1968. The next year, her autobiography, *The Movies, Mr. Griffith, and Me*, appeared, which occasioned a country-wide lecture tour.

PAULETTE GODDARD

She was born in Whitestone, Long Island, June 3, 1911, and when very young lived with her mother when her parents separated. She went to school at Mt. St. Dominic's in New Jersey, and the Ursuline Academy in Pittsburgh. Her mother re-married (to a Mr. Levy) and the family moved to Great Neck, where she met Florenz Ziegfeld, a guest of her uncle, Charles Goddard, president of the American Druggists' Syndicate. Ziegfeld offered her a small part in his musical *Rio Rita*, 1927. After her first marriage to Edward James, president of Southern States Lumber Co., ended in divorce, Paulette went to Hollywood, where she appeared in Hal Roach comedies and as a chorus girl in Eddie Cantor's *Kid from Spain*. She clipped together footage from these films to show Charlie Chaplin, searching for a newcomer to play opposite him in *Modern Times*. She got both the job and him. They succeeded in concealing their 1936 marriage for some time. They divorced in 1942. Two years later she married actor Burgess Meredith. They were divorced in 1950. Her fourth, and happiest marriage was to novelist Erich Maria Remarque, whom she married in 1958. They lived at Porto Ronco, on the Swiss shore of Lake Maggiore. He died in 1970.

MINNA GOMBELL

The daughter of a physician, she was born in Baltimore, May 28, 1893, and made her stage debut in 1912. On Broadway, she played in the farces of the period up to 1930. She continued her specialty of brassy, faded blondes in movies from 1930 to 1951. Miss Gombell was married to Howard C. Rumsey and Joseph Sefton, Jr., and lived at Laguna Beach. She died April 14, 1973.

MARY GORDON

Biographical data is scant on Mrs. Gordon. She was probably born in Scotland, in 1882, née Mary Gilmour, and under that name toured with Sir Harry Lauder at the turn of the century. She entered American films around 1925. Her best-known part was as Mrs. Hudson, housekeeper for Sherlock Holmes, both in movies and on radio. She retired in 1950, and died August 23, 1963, aged eighty-one, survived by a daughter.

BETTY GRABLE

Daughter of a wealthy stock broker, Conn Grable, she was born in Saint Louis December 18, 1913. After attending a school there, she went on vacation to Southern California in 1929, and she and her mother decided to stay. Betty became a student at Hollywood Professional School, and studied dancing with Albertina Rasch and Ernest Belcher. In 1930, she made her movie debut in a specialty number in *Let's Go Places*, and became a member of the old Fox chorus line of early musicals. As a star in the 1940s, she was a bouncy tootsie, with every measurement right to become the favorite "pin up girl" of World War II. She even made a movie of that title in 1944 to prove it. She married Jackie Coogan in 1937, divorced 1940, and Harry James in 1943, and divorced him after a long marriage. She had two daughters, Victoria and Jessica. She died of lung cancer, July 3, 1973.

MARGOT GRAHAME

Although born in Canterbury, Kent, February 20, 1911, she grew up in South Africa, where she was a student at Ladies' College, Durban, and where she made her stage debut in 1926 with a visiting touring company headed by Dennis Neilson-Terry. She returned to London with his company in 1927. In English films from 1929, she made her American debut in 1935 in *The Informer*. Her husbands have included actor Francis Lister, Alan MacMartin, and literary agent-film producer Augustus Dudley Peters.

BONITA GRANVILLE

Though she played naughty little girls in her screen career, Bonita Granville (born Chicago, February 2, 1923, daughter to Bunny Granville of the Ziegfeld shows) became a pillar of the Beverly Hills community as an adult. She married Texas oilman Jack Wrather, and eventually (after becoming the mother of four children) became a director of the Wrather Corp., which has business interests in all parts of the U. S., including the Disneyland Hotel in Anaheim, the Muzak Corp., and TV series *Lassie*, *The Lone Ranger* and *Sgt. Preston*.

MITZI GREEN

The daughter of Joe Keno and Rosie Green, a vaudeville act, who named her Mitzi for the star Mitzi Hajos, she was born in the Bronx, October 22, 1920. She joined her parents' act in Pittsburgh three years later, and was eventually given

LILLIAN GISH

WYNNE GIBSON

top billing in the act. The first child actress to be signed to a multi-picture contract at Paramount, she made eleven films for them between 1930 and 1932. In 1937, she returned to the stage in a hit musical, Rodgers and Hart's *Babes in Arms*, and introduced "The Lady Is a Tramp." After her marriage to film director Joseph Pevney, and becoming the mother of four children, her appearances were few. She died May 24, 1969, of cancer, in Huntington Beach, Calif.

CHARLOTTE GREENWOOD

This eccentric comedienne, once billed as "The Only Woman in the World Who Can Kick a Giraffe in the Face," was born in Philadelphia, June 25, 1893, and made her debut as a chorus girl in *The White Cat*, at the New Amsterdam in New York in 1905. Her biggest stage success was as Letty Robins, in a series of shows that began in 1916 with *So Long Letty* and went on to *Linger Longer, Letty* and *Let 'Er Go, Letty*, 1922. She made her first film, *Jane*, in 1918, but didn't return until 1928, in *Baby Mine*. Her most notable appearances after the 1930s were in Cole Porter's stage musical *Out of This World*, in 1950, and as Aunt Eller in the screen version of *Oklahoma!* in 1955. She is married to musical comedy composer Martin Broones.

NAN GREY

She was born in Houston, Tex., July 25, 1918, as Eschol Miller. On a holiday visit to Hollywood in 1934 with her mother, she met an actor's agent, one of her mother's friends, who got her a role in *The Firebird*, with Ricardo Cortez and Verree Teasdale. Her movie career ended in 1941. Her first husband was jockey Jackie Westrope. She then married singer Frankie Laine.

VIRGINIA GREY

Daughter of a film comedy director, Ray Grey (who died 1925) and his wife Florence, a film cutter at Universal, she was born in Hollywood, March 22, 1917. She studied dancing at the Meglin studios and was one of the original "Meglin Kiddies," and attended North Hollywood High School. In 1927, she was Little Eva in *Uncle Tom's Cabin*, second version of the Harriet Beecher Stowe classic, a silent film still shown around the United States. Miss Grey continues to make occasional appearances, usually in small roles in Ross Hunter movies (*Madame X*, 1966; *Airport*, 1969). In movie-magazine annals, she was long known as a great friend of Clark Gable.

CORINNE GRIFFITH

She was born in Mineral Wells, Texas, circa 1896, and began her screen career with Vitagraph in 1915. She was a star there many years until joining First National Pictures as a star in 1924. Miss Griffith, who invested wisely in Beverly Hills real estate, became one of the richest women in Hollywood. She is also the author of several books, including an autobiographical one, *Father's Delicate Condition*.

SIGRID GURIE

She was born in Brooklyn (May 18, 1911) and lived in the Flatbush section there until she was taken, age three, to Norway by her parents. She attended schools in Oslo and Brussels. She went to Hollywood in 1934, was "discovered" by Sam Goldwyn, and was launched as "the siren of the fjords" when she made her debut opposite Gary Cooper in 1938. It wasn't discovered she was Brooklyn-born until she filed suit for divorce, with another surprise for Goldwyn: a hitherto unsuspected husband, Thomas Stewart of California. Reeling, but recovering to make the best of it, Sam Goldwyn exclaimed: "The greatest hoax in movie history!" She married again in 1939, to Dr. Laurence Spangard, a Hollywood physician, and made her last movie in 1948. She died August 14, 1969, in Mexico City.

LOUISE CLOSSER HALE

Louise Closser Hale was born October 13, 1872, in Chicago, and went to school in Indianapolis and at the American Academy of Dramatic Arts in New York. In 1899 she married Walter Hale, after having been on the stage since 1894. Her long stage career had as highlights *Ruggles of Red Gap*, *Miss Lulu Bett* and *Peer Gynt*. She made her movie debut in *Hole in the Wall* in 1929, shot at Paramount's Astoria studios. She died of heat prostration while shopping in Hollywood, July 27, 1933.

MARGARET HAMILTON

She was a kindergarten teacher in her native Cleveland (where she was born September 12, 1902) and later joined the Cleveland Playhouse. From 1933, she was set in the movies as a favorite character type. Once married to landscape architect Paul Meserve, she has a son, Hamilton Meserve, an officer with the First National City Bank in New York. She lives near Gramercy Park.

ANN HARDING

The daughter of Col. George G. Gatley, she was born at Fort Sam Houston, Texas, August 7, 1901, christened Dorothy Walton Gatley, and educated at Bryn Mawr. When she decided to go on the stage, her father wrote her: "You have chosen the inevitable Road to Hell. What do you think my feelings must be to have my daughter's painted face on exhibition for harlots and perverts to jape at? Do not use my name on the stage." She used, instead, the name of the then current President of the United States, and made her debut at the Provincetown Playhouse in New York, 1921, as Madeline Morton in *Inheritors*. The starring part of her American screen career lasted from 1929 to 1936. Thereafter, she played character roles in a number of movies. Miss Harding has been married to actor Harry Bannister (1926–1932), with a daughter, Jane, and conductor Werner Janssen, from 1937 to 1962. She lives in Westport, Conn.

JEAN HARLOW

In retrospect, probably the most lovable and tragic star of the 1930s, Jean Harlow was the only child of Dr. and Mrs. Montclair Carpenter (her mother's maiden name was Jean Harlow), and she was born Harlean Carpenter in Kansas City, March 3, 1911. From the age of ten, she lived with her family in California, and attended the Hollywood School for Girls for three years. Later, she went to the Bigelow School in Kansas City, and the Ferry Hall Seminary, Lake Forest, Illinois. At sixteen, she ran away and married Charles F. McGraw II, a young Chicago bond broker. They divorced in 1930. She began her career in Richard Dix's *Moran of the Marines*, at Paramount in 1928, played in two-reelers at the Christie and Hal Roach studios, and with Clara Bow in *The Saturday Night Kid*. Then came *Hell's Angels*, and the real start of her career. Her second marriage was to producer Paul Bern, who either committed suicide or was murdered three months after their marriage in 1932. She married Harold G. Rossen, cameraman, in 1933, divorced 1935. At the time of her death from uremic poisoning, June 7, 1937, she was the fiancée of star William Powell, whose picture of grave-side grief is memorable to this day.

LILIAN HARVEY

Born in Edmonton, England, on January 19, 1906, as Helene Lilian Muriel Pape. She and her family (her father was an accountant) moved to Berlin one month before World War I broke out. Lilian was sent to Switzerland to live with an aunt, but returned to Berlin to attend high school and ballet classes. She made her debut in German films in 1925, and by 1940 had made some 50 movies. She spoke 13 languages and made movies in four. She was married three times, most notably to German actor Willy

JEAN HARLOW

Fritsch, her co-star in *Congress Dances*. During World War II, she lived in the United States, working as a nurse in a Los Angeles hospital and appearing on the stage, touring Pacific Coast theaters with Reginald Denny and Mona Barrie in *Blithe Spirit*. She spent her last years at Juan-les-Pins, Antibes, where she died July 27, 1968.

JULIE HAYDON

Born as Donella Donaldson in Oak Park, Ill., June 10, 1910, she went to school in Hollywood, where, in 1931, she made her stage debut with Mrs. Fiske in *The Lower Depths*. After she had been off the screen since 1937, she made her last film, *Citizen Saint*, in 1948. Two

years before his death at seventy-six, the perennial bachelor, drama critic George Jean Nathan, married Miss Haydon in 1955.

HELEN HAYES

Miss Hayes made her stage debut when a child of five in her native Washington, D. C., where she was born October 10, 1900, and has devoted her entire life to acting. She managed to include during her movie years two of her biggest stage successes: *Mary of Scotland* in 1933, and *Victoria Regina*, which she played, on Broadway, tour, and revival, from 1935 to 1939. Miss Hayes became the second wife of playwright Charles MacArthur in 1928 (he died in 1956) and was the mother of Mary MacArthur, who died

of polio at nineteen, in 1949, and of her adopted son, actor James MacArthur.

SUSAN HAYWARD

She grew up in a life of poverty in the Flatbush section of Brooklyn, where she was born in a tenement on June 30, 1918, and named Edythe Marrener, the youngest of three children of Walter Marrener, a Coney Island barker and later a subway guard, and his Swedish-born wife, Ellen. During her childhood years, she delivered newspapers, and studied stenography and dress designing in high school to try to make more money. Her first job was as a model, and a picture of her on the cover of *The Saturday Evening Post* when she was twenty attracted the attention of George Cukor, who suggested that David

O. Selznick bring her to Hollywood to try for the Scarlett O'Hara role in *Gone With the Wind*. She stayed on in Hollywood and became the tawny redhead Susan Hayward, a star able to play a winner or a loser with equally intense conviction. She married actor Jess Barker in 1944, and became the mother of twin sons, Timothy and Gregory, born February 19, 1945. After a quarrelsome marriage and a divorce, she married Floyd Eaton Chalkley, a lawyer and former FBI agent, in 1957. He died in 1966.

RITA HAYWORTH

Born as Margarita Carmen Cansino, of a family of dancers, October 17, 1918. At thirteen, she says, her "summer camp" was dancing at Tijuana. She was seventeen when she made her film debut in *Dante's Inferno*.

She has married five times: to business man Edward Judson (1937-1943); Orson Welles (1944-1947), by whom she has a daughter, Rebecca, married to a sculptor; Aly Khan (1949-1953), with another daughter, Princess Yasmin; singer Dick Haymes (1953-1955); and producer James Hill (1958-1961). She lives alone in her house in Beverly Hills, and maintains she never got "a dime" from any of her husbands. But newspaper reports said that her lawyer negotiated a $1,000,000 divorce settlement from Aly Khan. Miss Hayworth still appears occasionally in movies.

SONJA HENIE

She seemed a grown-up Shirley Temple. But even then, she was a woman with a taste for luxury and business that made her one of the world's richest women. Sonja was the daughter of an Oslo, Norway, fur mechant, and was born April 8, 1910. Her father gave her skates when she was six and also encouraged her to study ballet. At eight, she won her first figure skating championship. In 1927, she won the first of ten consecutive skating titles at Oslo, and won three Olympic titles (1928, 1932, 1936). Darryl F. Zanuck signed her to a 20th Century-Fox contract in 1936, and in the next dozen years her movies are said to have grossed $25 million. Her last film was in 1948, *The Countess of Monte Cristo*.

She became an American citizen in 1941, and married Daniel Topping (divorced 1946) and Winthrop Gardiner, Jr. (divorced 1956). In 1956, she married her childhood sweetheart, Neils Onstad, who had become a Norwegian ship owner. The Instads gave Norway an art museum, and 250 of their paintings, in August, 1968. In the last nine months of her life she was ill with leukemia, and died on an ambulance plane flying from Paris to Oslo, October 12, 1969.

CHARLOTTE HENRY

Charlotte Henry as both the winner and the victim of a nation-wide search launched by Paramount Pictures in the early 1930s to bolster a shaky regime. Charlotte was born March 3, 1914, in Brooklyn, and appeared on the stage from the age of five. On Broadway, she played in *Courage*, with Janet Beecher, and made her movie debut in the screen version, 1930. In 1933, Paramount announced its wish to cast an unknown as Alice in *Alice in Wonderland*, and received between 6,500 and 7,000 applications from all over the world. Charlotte was acting in a stage production of *Growing Pains* at the Pasadena Playhouse, but took time off to ask for a test. She was the 57th girl to try out for the role and, some time later, she was called back for a second test. Then, sending out charming publicity photos of Charlotte dressed as little Alice, Paramount announced her as the winner. In spite of the high-pressure publicity and the all-star cast, the picture was a flop. After 1936, she returned to the stage, playing in stock; returned to Hollywood in 1941, and got a job in *Bowery Blitzkrieg*, with the East Side Kids. She is now said to be living in San Diego.

KATHARINE HEPBURN

She was the second of the six children of Dr. Thomas Norval Hepburn, a urologist, and Katharine Houghton Hepburn, a suffragette and advocate of birth control, and was born in Hartford, Conn. November 8, 1907. After graduating from Bryn Mawr, she made her stage debut in 1928 in Baltimore in *The Czarina* in Edwin H. Knopf's stock company, and in New York as one of the hostesses in *Night Hostess*. Her first big part was as the ingenue Judy Bottle in *Art and Mrs. Bottle*, with Jane Cowl, in 1931. Possibly her most glamorous stage success was as Tracy Lord in *The Philadelphia Story* in 1939, which rejuvenated her film career in 1940.

Miss Hepburn married Ludlow Ogden Smith, a Philadelphia socialite, December 12, 1928, and was separated from him for four years before their divorce in 1934. Her most famous romance, a carefully kept and respected open secret for many years, was with her co-star Spencer Tracy. They made nine films together (the last, *Guess Who's Coming to Dinner?* the year of his death, 1967). To this day, Miss Hepburn remains a superstar.

IRENE HERVEY

Daughter of an artist-photographer, she was born Irene Herwick July 11, 1910, in Los Angeles, and was graduated from Venice High School. She entered movies through the MGM School of Acting,

where some of the other pupils have been Robert Taylor, Judy Garland and Deanna Durbin. She worked steadily in movies until 1943, with appearances in some ten more after 1948 through 1971. First married at seventeen, she gave birth to a daughter, Gail, and ended her marriage after four years. Her next husband was Allan Jones in 1936. Their son Jack was born in 1941 and they divorced twenty-one years later.

WENDY HILLER

She was born at Bramhall, Cheshire, England, August 15, 1912, and was educated at Winceby House School in Bexhall. As a student with the Manchester Repertory Theatre, she made her debut there as the Maid in *The Ware Case* at the age of eighteen. She became an instant star in London as Sally Hardcastle in Ronald Gow's *Love on the Dole* in 1935, and repeated her success in New York a year later. A year after that, she married Mr. Gow. She continues to divide her time between stage and screen.

HARRIET HILLIARD

She was born into a theatrical family in Des Moines, July 18, 1911, the daughter of Roy E. Hilliard, a stage director, and Hazel McNutt Hilliard, an actress. She attended the St. Agnes Academy in Kansas City. She started early in the theatre, at the age of six weeks, and toured with her parents in vaudeville. Her first break was as a featured singer with the band of Ozzie Nelson, at the New Yorker Hotel, Glen Island Casino, and the Ambassador in Los Angeles. She married Ozzie on October 8, 1935, and became the mother of sons David Ozzie (October 24, 1936) and Eric (Ricky) Hilliard (May 8, 1940). She and her family went on to wider fame on the *Adventures of Ozzie and Harriet* radio show, beginning in 1944, and later on the *Ozzie and Harriet* TV show.

ROSE HOBART

The daughter of musicians, she was born in New York, May 1, 1906, and originally intended to follow a musical career. But after playing Betsy in *Cappy Ricks* with a Chautauqua stock company in 1920, she was hooked by the theatre and spent most of the 1920s and 1930s on Broadway. Her outstanding stage roles were Grazia in *Death Takes a Holiday*, with Philip Merivale, 1929, and Cynthia in *I Loved You Wednesday*, with Humphrey Bogart, 1932. She married William M. Grosvenor, Jr., in 1931, and lives in Sherman Oaks, Calif.

VALERIE HOBSON

Daughter of Commander R. G. Hob-

KATHARINE HEPBURN

MIRIAM HOPKINS

son, Royal Navy, she was born in Larne, Ireland, April 14, 1917, and studied at St. Augustine's Priory, London, and the Royal Academy of Dramatic Art. She made her British film debut in 1933, and her first Hollywood movie in 1935. After the 1930s, her career highlights were as Estella in *Great Expectations*, 1946, *Blanche Fury*, 1947; in *Kind Hearts and Coronets*, 1949, and *The Rocking Horse Winner*, 1949, all British-produced. On the stage, Miss Hobson appeared in the Gertrude Lawrence role in the musical *The King and I*, with Herbert Lom, at the Drury Lane, 1953. First married to British producer Anthony Havelock-Allan (1939-1952), she retired when she married Baron John Dennis Profumo in 1954. He was the British War Secretary when his career was shattered by a spectacular political scandal in 1963. His wife remained with him throughout his troubles.

FAY HOLDEN

Under the name of Gaby Fay, she had spent over thirty years on the stage, beginning her career in childhood, before her Hollywood screen debut in 1936. She was the daughter of Dr. Harry Hammerton, was born in Birmingham, England, September 26, 1895, and was married to David Clyde, brother of the comedian Andy Clyde. She died June 23, 1973.

MIRIAM HOPKINS

"Our finest Southern actress" (as Tennessee Williams has called her) was born in Bainbridge, Ga., October 18, 1902, and educated in the North at Goddard Seminary in Vermont. At nineteen, she went on the stage as a chorus girl in Irving Berlin's *Music Box Revue*. During the

1920s and 1930s, she appeared in such Broadway shows as *Little Jessie James*, *An American Tragedy* and *Excess Baggage*. While appearing as one of the Amazon maidens in *Lysistrata* in 1930, she commuted to Paramount's Astoria studio for her debut in *Fast and Loose*.

She married four times: Brandon Peters, playwright Austin Parker, director Anatole Litvak, and Raymond B. Brock. She died in New York, October 9, 1972.

HEDDA HOPPER

Miss Hopper was born May 2, 1885, in Hollidaysburg, Pa., as Elda Furry, the daughter of a "struggling meat dealer." She never graduated from grammar school, and left home early to go on the stage, making her debut in the chorus of a New York opera company. As the fifth wife of comedian De Wolf Hopper (a man older than her father), she became the mother of actor William Hopper (born January 26, 1915—died March 6, 1970). In 1916, when her husband was in California making pictures for the old Triangle Film Co., she made her debut as William Farnum's leading lady in *The Battle of Hearts*, and by 1918 was appearing in movies regularly. The Hoppers were divorced in 1920. Miss Hopper's spotty acting career went through 1942, with occasional guest appearances thereafter, notably *Sunset Boulevard*, 1950. Active to the end, she died of double pneumonia, in Hollywood, February 1, 1966.

LOUISE HOVICK

Her full name was Rose Louise Hovick, and she was born January 9, 1914, in Seattle. Her father, a *Seattle Times* re-

porter, and her mother, Rose Thompson, divorced shortly after the birth of their second child, June (Havoc). Then began the saga of "Gypsy"; the children's act in vaudeville, tours on the Keith-Orpheum circuit, the days in burlesque. Billy Minsky introduced Miss Lee (then using the name Rose Louise) to burlesque in New York at the Republic Theatre, 42nd Street, on April 1, 1931. An arrest got her picture on the front pages of the tabloids, and Florenz Ziegfeld offered her a bit in *Hotcha!* From then on she was in the big time: the *Follies, Scandals,* and *Streets of Paris* at the World's Fair in 1939-1940. She became fashionable with writers and intellectuals, and wrote books of her own (*The G-String Murders* and *Mother Finds a Body*, besides her memoirs). In her last years, she lived alone in a seventeen-room mansion in Beverly Hills, while being the hostess of a syndicated talk show, *Gypsy*, that she commuted to San Francisco to do.

She was married three times. Her first husband was Arnold R. Mizzy, a manufacturer, in 1937. After divorce, she married actor-producer Alexander Kirkland, in 1942, and had a son, Erik, born December 11, 1944 (later revealed to be the son of producer Otto Preminger). Her third husband was artist Julio de Diego, 1948-1955. She died of cancer at U.C.L.A. Medical Center, April 26, 1970.

JOBYNA HOWLAND

This tall, Amazonian actress was born March 31, 1880, in Indianapolis, and began her career as a Gibson girl. At nineteen she began her long stage career, playing in a succession of farces and musicals. As early as 1918, she acted in two Norma Talmadge silents, but her real movie career began in 1930, and ended in 1933. She was once married to novelist Arthur Stringer. She died June 7, 1936.

ROCHELLE HUDSON

Born in Oklahoma City, March 6, 1914, she began taking dancing lessons when she was three, and went to school there until her family moved to Los Angeles in 1928, where she continued to study dancing under Ernest Belcher. She made her movie debut in 1930. During World War II, she married Harold Thompson, a naval reservist, and worked with him in Naval Intelligence in Mexico and Central America. Her first marriage ended in divorce in 1947, as did her second marriage, to writer Dick Irving Hyland, in 1950. After the war, she made only occasional movie appearances, notably as Natalie Wood's mother in *Rebel Without a Cause*, 1955. On TV, she had a 39-week run in *That's My Boy*, with Eddie Mayehoff, in 1954-1955. In

1969, she moved to Palm Desert, Calif., where she opened a real estate brokerage office, and divorced her third husband, hotel executive Robert Mindell, in 1971, after a marriage of eight years. Miss Hudson was found dead in her home at the Palm Desert Country Club, January 18, 1972, by her real estate partner, Walter Price.

JOSEPHINE HULL

She might have looked dear and dumpy, but she was filled with surprises. She had a feminine balkiness and a fey, almost evil mischief about her that enabled her to stand up to the world of men and win her points. Born Josephine Sherwood in Newton, Mass., January 3, 1884, she made her stage debut under that name after having graduated from Radcliffe College. When she married Henry Hull's elder brother, the matinee idol Shelley Hull, in 1910, she changed her stage name. After her husband's death at the age of thirty-five of flu in 1919, she retired from the stage for three years. She never re-married. She died of a paralytic stroke at St. Barnabas Hospital, the Bronx, March 12, 1957.

BENITA HUME

Born in London, October 14, 1906, she trained for the stage at the Royal Academy of Dramatic Art, made her professional debut in 1924, and her silent screen debut in 1926.

Miss Hume was first married to Eric Siepman. On September 30, 1938, she became the wife of Ronald Colman. This was a happy marriage, and in 1951 the couple began a successful TV series, The Halls of Ivy, which ran for five seasons. They lived in Beverly Hills and in Santa Barbara, where they were part owners of a resort called San Ysidro. After Mr. Colman died in 1958, Miss Hume returned to Europe, and married actor George Sanders in Spain on February 10, 1959. She died in Egerton, England, November 1, 1967, with her husband and her daughter, Juliet Colman, at her bedside.

MARSHA HUNT

The daughter of Earl R. Hunt, a civic leader and insurance company executive, and Minabel Hunt, onetime opera and concert singer, she was born in Chicago, October 17, 1917. She grew up in New York, attending the Horace Mann School for Girls and the Theodora Irvine School of the Theatre. After being a model for John Roberts Powers agency in New York, she visited friends in Hollywood, who spread the word that "New York's most famous model" had arrived, but wasn't interested in movies. The next

day, she had three contract offers, and made her screen bow as the heroine in The Virginia Judge in 1935. She appeared regularly in movies to 1949, and in The Happy Time, Bombers B-52 (1957), and Blue Denim (1959). She first married Jerry Hopper, a cousin of Glenda Farrell and an assistant chief cutter at Paramount (1938), and then in 1946 Robert Presnell, Jr., a TV and movie writer. She is a member of the U. N. Association, Community Relations, U. S. Committee for Refugees, and the Freedom-from-Hunger Campaign.

RUTH HUSSEY

Born in Providence, R. I., October 30, 1913, the daughter of George and Julia Corbett Hussey, she was graduated Bachelor of Philosophy, Pembroke College. She worked as an advertising copy writer, and also was a member of the Providence Players, 1933-1935, and of a summer stock company in Michigan, 1934-1935. Her first breaks came in national tours of The Old Maid and Dead End, in which she played the society girl Kay, in 1937. She was seen by MGM scouts when Dead End played Los Angeles, and made her movie bow in Gladys George's Madame X. She worked steadily until 1953, and occasionally afterwards. In August 1942, she married TV producer C. Robert Longenecker, and is the mother of two sons and a daughter. Occasionally she appears on TV.

JOSEPHINE HUTCHINSON

The daughter of a stage actress, Leona Roberts, she was born in Seattle, October 12, 1904. As a child, she appeared in a Mary Pickford film, A Little Princess, 1917. She won a scholarship at Maurice Browne's Dramatic School, made her stage debut with the Ram's Head Players in Washington, and stayed with them three years. The important part of her career started in 1926, when she joined Eva Le Gallienne's Civic Repertory Theatre, on 14th Street, New York. She remained with Miss Le Gallienne for seven years, playing Maria in Twelfth Night, Wendy in Peter Pan, Nina in The Sea Gull, and Alice in Wonderland. She was first married to Robert Bell, a Washington newspaperman and grandson of Alexander Graham Bell. They had a bitter divorce in 1930. In 1935, she married her agent, James Townsend, and in 1972, actor Staats Cotsworth, with whom she had acted at the Civic Repertory Theatre forty years before.

LEILA HYAMS

The daughter of vaudeville stars Leila McIntyre and John Hyams, she was born May 1, 1905, in New York, spent five

years in vaudeville, and later with William Collier, Sr. At twenty, she started to play small parts in movies (she was a chum to Clara Bow in Dancing Mothers), and later elevated to leading lady in the silent movies of Johnnie Hines, Edmund Lowe, Monte Blue, George Walsh, and George· O'Brien.

FRIEDA INESCORT

Scottish-born (in Edinburgh, June 28, 1901), she was the daughter of John and Elaine Inescort Wightman. During World War I she became Lady Astor's secretary, later publicity director for G. P. Putnam's Sons in New York. She married writer Ben Ray Redman in 1926. She made her stage debut in 1922 at the Booth, in New York, in The Truth About Blayds, and spent the 1920s on the New York stage, her best part probably being Sorel Bliss in Noël Coward's Hay Fever, in 1925. Her stage career continued until her film debut in 1935, in The Dark Angel. Her last film was in The Eddy Duchin Story in 1956.

SYBIL JASON

The child of Jack and Mary Jacobs, she was born November 23, 1929, in South Africa. Sybil came to the attention of comedian Archie Pitt (then Gracie Fields' husband), who featured her in his British movie, Barnacle Bill, 1935. That same year, she made her Hollywood debut.

GLORIA JEAN

Gloria Jean Schoonover was born April 14, 1927 in Buffalo, and grew up in Scranton, Pa., as one of the four daughters of Forman Schoonover, a piano salesman. Gloria became a local celebrity, singing in school, church, and community entertainments, and finally made it to New York as a radio singer. Producer Joe Pasternak heard about her, and signed her to a Universal contract in 1939, to appear, as they said at the time, in "Deanna Durbin's outgrown scripts." She continued her education in the studio school, with Ann Blyth, Sabu, and Donald O'Connor as classmates. She could never seem to get her career going after 1950. She got a starring part as the gold-rush actress Lotta Crabtree in a half-hour Death Valley Days segment in 1956. In 1960, she was working in a Tahitian restaurant in the San Fernando Valley, and appeared occasionally on TV. She is now employed as receptionist by a Los Angeles cosmetics firm.

ISABEL JEWELL

The daughter of a doctor and medical researcher, she was born July 19, 1909, in Shoshoni, Wyo., and was educated at St. Mary's Academy in Minnesota, and

Hamilton College in Kentucky. Before making her Broadway debut in *Up Pops the Devil* in 1930, she had had several years of training in stock. In her first movie, *Blessed Event*, in 1932, she repeated the role she had created on Broadway. She acted in movies through 1949, with two brief returns thereafter. She died April 5, 1972, in Santa Monica.

ZITA JOHANN

Hungarian born (July 14, 1904), she came to New York at the age of seven, and made her Broadway debut for the Theatre Guild at twenty in *Man and the Masses*. Later she acted with the Lunts in *The Goat Song*, 1926; with Clark Gable in *Machinal*, 1928; and had a good role in Philip Barry's *Tomorrow and Tomorrow*, 1931, later played by Ruth Chatterton in movies. After her screen career ended, she was in Archibald MacLeish's *Panic*, on radio with Orson Welles, 1936. She married producer-director John Houseman; John McCormick, Colleen Moore's first husband (1935-1938); and economist and publisher Bernard E. Shedd.

KAY JOHNSON

Daughter of an architect, she was born November 29, 1904, in Mount Vernon, N. Y., and studied at Grew Seminary and the American Academy of Dramatic Art. In 1923, she made her Broadway debut in *Go West, Young Man*. She was acting in *The Silver Cord* in Los Angeles when seen by C. B. DeMille. After her last movie in 1943, she returned to Broadway in *State of the Union*, 1945, with Ralph Bellamy, Ruth Hussey, and Kay Francis. Miss Johnson was once the wife of director-actor John Cromwell.

RITA JOHNSON

She was born in Worcester, Mass., August 13, 1912, and studied the piano at the New England Conservatory of Music. She began her acting career with a Worcester stock company, moved on to summer theaters, and appeared on Broadway in two Theatre Guild productions, *Fulton of Oak Falls* and *If This Be Treason*. Her first movie was *London by Night* in 1937. In the 1940s, her best roles were in *Edison, the Man, They Won't Believe Me, My Friend Flicka, Here Comes Mr. Jordan* and *The Major and the Minor*. She married L. Stanley Kahn (1940-1943). Miss Johnson retired in 1951 when a hair dryer fell on her head, causing brain damage. She died on October 31, 1965.

MARCIA MAE JONES

A Hollywood child, she was born August 1, 1924, and made her debut as a baby of two in Dolores Costello's *Manne-*

quin. She struggled through the 1940s in such cheapies as *Secrets of a Co-Ed, Lady in the Death House* and *Street Corner*. At seventeen, she had married a Merchant Marine, Robert Chic (sic). After their marriage ended, she had two children to support. In 1952, she was discovered as a switchboard operator in lawyer Greg Bautzer's Beverly Hills office. From 1956 to 1963 she was married to TV writer Bill Davenport, and still appears occasionally on television.

DOROTHY JORDAN

Born in Clarksville, Tenn., August 9, 1908, she studied at Southwestern University, and the American Academy of Dramatic Arts, before becoming a chorus girl in some choice 1920s musicals: *Garrick Gaieties* and *Twinkle Twinkle, Funny Face*, with the Astaires, and *Treasure Girl*, with Gertrude Lawrence and Clifton Webb. She retired upon her marriage to film producer Merian C. Cooper, but came back briefly in the fifties for small roles in John Ford's *The Sun Shines Bright* and *The Searchers*.

MIRIAM JORDAN

Born March 3, 1908, in London, she went to Skinner's School for Young Ladies. While employed as a typist, she entered, and won, a beauty contest. This publicity gave her an introduction to the theater in London. In New York, she was said to have received $100 a week walking down a flight of stairs "clad in a beautiful evening gown" in the musical *Three Cheers*, with Will Rogers, in 1928. She also appeared with Philip Merivale in *Cynara*, 1931. Her Hollywood screen career lasted barely two years, 1932-1934. In 1938, she again showed up on Broadway in *Michael Drops In*, with Arlene Francis and Onslow Stevens—the play ran eight performances. She was married to Joseph Davis in 1926. They separated in 1929 and divorced in 1933.

LEATRICE JOY

Born as Leatrice Joy Zeidler, November 7, 1896, in New Orleans, she was raised there and studied at the Sacred Heart Academy. She is the daughter of Dr. Edward Joseph Zeidler. She is said to have made her screen debut with the Nola Film Co., Wilkes-Barre, Pa., and to have appeared with a stock company in San Diego for eight months. One of her first Hollywood films was as an extra, one of the crowd, in Mary Pickford's *The Pride of the Clan*, 1917. In the 1920s, she became a Paramount star, in DeMille's *The Ten Commandments* and *Manslaughter*, and in light comedies *Changing Husbands, The Dressmaker from Paris* and *Bachelor Daddy*. Miss Joy was in the

chic, tailored woman tradition of Irene Rich, and her movies were mainly addressed to women.

She was the wife of the star John Gilbert from 1922 to 1924 and had a daughter, Leatrice, who, as Leatrice Gilbert Fountain, is a novelist (*Love to the Irish*, 1967). In 1931, she married William Spencer Hook. She lives in Riverside, Conn.

BRENDA JOYCE

Born as Graftina Leabo in Kansas City, February 25, 1916, she grew up in Los Angeles and was a student at University of Southern California. She was a model before entering films. She is married to Owen Ward.

ARLINE JUDGE

Arline was born in Bridgeport, Conn., February 21, 1912, and was convent-educated. She got her start in *The Second Little Show*, at the Royale, New York, in 1930, with Al Trahan and Jay C. Flippen, and later was a part of Jimmy Durante's old night club act. On the train to Hollywood, she met movie director Wesley Ruggles, who directed her first movie, *Are These Our Children?*, 1931. She married Ruggles the same year (divorced 1937). Until her second marriage, she worked steadily in movies.

A tabulation of her subsequent marriages: (2) "tin-plate heir" Dan Topping (1937), (3) Capt. James Addams of the Royal Air Force—father of actress Dawn Addams (1942), (4) advertising man Vincent Morgan Ryan (1945), (5) her onetime brother-in-law, Bob Topping (1947), (6) the "heir of an insurance tycoon," George Ross Jr. (1948), (7) Edward Heard, Beverly Hills businessman (1955). She divorced him in 1960 and never remarried. Miss Judge died in Hollywood on February 7, 1974.

HELEN KANE

She was the daughter of a German father, Louis Schroeder, and an Irish mother, Ellen Dixon, was born in the Bronx, August 4, 1903, and attended St. Anselm's Parochial School there. In 1920, Helen got her first professional job in an act with the Marx Brothers; she played with them on the Orpheum vaudeville circuit, and on the London music hall stages. She stayed with the Brothers for two seasons, then played other vaudeville dates and night clubs until her musical comedy debut in 1927 in *A Night in Spain*, which ran fifty performances. It was staged by her future mother-in-law, dancer Gertrude Hoffman, and a member of the cast was a future husband, Dan Healy.

In 1928, while featured at the Paramount Theatre, she created her own show-business legend when, in rehearsing "That's My Weakness Now," she tossed in a few squeaky "boop-boop-a-doops" to flavor the original lyrics, and so entranced her accompanist and stage-crew members that she put the trick that became her trademark into her act.

Later that same year, Helen became the leading lady in *Good Boy*, introducing "I Wanna Be Loved by You." The show, with Eddie Buzzell and Charles Butterworth, ran 253 performances. This led directly to her screen career at Paramount.

After her short Hollywood career, she continued in vaudeville, night clubs, and again starred in a Broadway musical that ran only thirty performances. She also unfortunately suffered a nervous breakdown, and made unlucky investments which eventually forced her into bankruptcy.

She married four times: Joe Kane, a businessman (1924-1928); Bill Girard, of Hollywood; actor Max Hoffman, Jr. (divorced 1933); and actor-singer Dan Healy (1939), long known as the "Night Mayor of New York" and one of the leading Masters of Ceremonies in 52d Street night clubs. Her marriage to Healy was a happy one. In her last years, she underwent surgery for breast cancer, and received 200 radiation treatments as an outpatient at Memorial Hospital in Queens. The night before she died (September 26, 1966) she stayed up with her husband to watch a TV showing of *Three Little Words*, in which Debbie Reynolds mouthed her recording of "I Wanna Be Loved by You."

RUBY KEELER

She was born in Halifax, Nova Scotia, August 25, 1909, and moved with her parents to an East Side, New York, tenement when she was three. She went to school at St. Catherine of Siena's on East 69th Street. This girl who, in movies, always seemed to be of the dewiest rosebud innocence, started to buck-and-wing dance in speakeasies (including Texas Guinan's) at the age of thirteen. In 1923, she got her first Broadway chorus job in *The Rise of Rosie O'Reilly*, and remained in chorus work for some years. By 1927, she had featured parts in musicals such as *Lucky*, with Mary Eaton, and *Sidewalks of New York*, with Smith and Dale, and in 1929 Ziegfeld made her a star in *Show Girl*. A year before, she had married, as his third wife, the great Broadway star Al Jolson, and stayed married to him for eleven years. In 1932, she made her movie debut in *42nd Street*, and the rest is tap-dance history. She retired from movies in 1941, after *Sweetheart of the Campus*, married John Lowe, a socially prominent broker, and became

RUBY KEELER

the mother of five children. Mr. Lowe died in 1968. She returned to Broadway in 1971 as a part of inspired casting, along with Patsy Kelly, in a revival of *No, No, Nanette*.

NANCY KELLY

She was born in Lowell, Mass., March 25, 1921, and, as a child of one, modeled for James Montgomery Flagg's commercial advertisements. In 1926 she began her career as a child actress in Gloria Swanson's *Untamed Lady*, and appeared thereafter in about fifty features. Her last child role was in Jean Hersholt's *The Girl on the Barge* in 1929. She appeared on *March of Time* regularly from 1932 to 1937, as well as other radio shows. Her first hit as an adult actress was as Gertrude Lawrence's daughter Blossom in Rachel Crothers' play *Susan and God* in 1938, and she returned to movies again that same year, staying in Hollywood until 1946. Married three times, she was divorced from Warren Caro in 1968. She has a daughter, Kelly Caro, born 1958.

PATSY KELLY

She was born January 12, 1910, in Brooklyn, and wanted to be a fireman. She began as a stooge for Frank Fay in vaudeville at the Palace, buck-danced with Ruby Keeler in night clubs, appeared in *Earl Carroll's Vanities*, with Jimmy Savo and Jack Benny, 1930, and in *Wonder Bar*, with Al Jolson, before going into the movies in 1933. After 1943, to the disappointment of millions, she appeared only occasionally in movies. She lives in Hollywood when not appearing on the Broadway stage.

PERT KELTON

The child of a vaudeville couple, Ed

and Susan Kelton, she was born October 14, 1907, on her grandmother's cattle ranch near Great Falls, Mont. She first appeared in the family act at the age of three, and went out as a "single" at twelve. On Broadway she appeared in the musicals *Sunny*, with Marilyn Miller, and *The Five O'Clock Girl*, with Mary Eaton, and made her film debut in 1930. She appeared in films until 1937, returning in 1962 to repeat her stage role as Marian the Librarian's mother in *The Music Man*. Her last Broadway appearance was in *Spoffard*, with Melvyn Douglas, 1967. She was married to Ralph Bell and had two sons. She died of a heart attack while swimming, October 30, 1968.

BARBARA KENT

Born as Barbara Clowtman, in Gadsby, Alberta, December 16, 1906, she was a student there until she moved to Holly-

PATSY KELLY

305

wood, where she was a pupil at Hollywood High School. After winning the title "Miss Hollywood," she entered movies in 1925.

She also played Gypsy in *Emma*, with Marie Dressler, in 1932, and Rose Maylie to Dickie Moore's *Oliver Twist* in 1933. Her last movie was in 1935. She married (December, 1932) Harry E. Eddington, head of an agency handling topflight stars such as Garbo, Dietrich, Ruth Chatterton, and Ann Harding.

DOROTHEA KENT

Her real name was Dorothea Schaffer, and she was born June 7, 1917, in Saint Joseph, Mo. Before her movie debut in 1934, she was a model. She made her last film in 1946.

DORIS KENYON

Her father was a clergyman-poet, James Benjamin Kenyon, of Syracuse, New York, where she was born September 5, 1897. At nineteen, she made her stage debut as Coralie Bliss in *Princess Pat*, with Eleanor Painter. A year later, she made her film debut in *The Pawn of Fate*, directed by Maurice Tourneur, and became a star in melodramas and serials. In the 1920s, she played Lady Mary to Rudolph Valentino's *Monsieur Beaucaire*, and was a leading lady to Thomas Meighan, Percy Marmont, Lewis Stone, and Milton Sills, whom she married in 1926. He died in 1930. She later married producer Arthur Hopkins, who died in 1950, and Albert D. Lasker. She was then married to a musician, Bronislaw Mlynarski, of Beverly Hills; he died in 1971. Her son, Kenyon Sills, a geologist, died the same year. Her last movie was in 1939.

EVALYN KNAPP

She was born in Kansas City, June 17, 1908, the sister of Orville Knapp, later an orchestra leader, and made her first stage appearance in her home town. On Broadway she first appeared in Channing Pollock's *Mr. Moneypenny*. In her movie debut, she played a nurse in a short comedy, *At the Dentist's*, 1929. Her last film was in 1941. She married Dr. George A. Snyder.

MARILYN KNOWLDEN

According to her studio biography, "she sings and dances, ballet and tap, and is golden-haired and blue eyed," and was born in Oakland, Calif., May 12, 1925. Her father was Robert E. Knowlden, who practiced law there, and in Hollywood from 1931 on, and was later killed in an automobile accident. Marilyn was his only child. Her last listed movie was in a small role in *Hidden Power*, 1939.

MILIZA KORJUS

The sumptuous Miliza Korjus was born in Warsaw, August 18, 1900, daughter of a Swedish diplomat and his Polish wife, and studied in several musical conservatories, mainly in Kiev, Moscow, Vienna, and Dresden. In both opera and concert, she sang in Kiev and Warsaw, 1925-1926, in Moscow, 1927, and later in Leningrad, Stockholm, and Vienna. As a favorite of the German conductor Wilhelm Furtwangler, she appeared for several seasons at the Berlin Opera. In 1932 she married Kuno Foelsch, by whom she had a daughter. Irving Thalberg discovered her for movies, and, for her single U. S. film, she learned English and took off forty-five pounds. After *The Great Waltz*, she pursued her singing career briefly in Los Angles and San Francisco, in Mexico, and at Carnegie Hall in New York, 1944. She married Dr. Walter E. Shector, of Beverly Hills, in 1952, and retired.

ALMA KRUGER

Born in Pittsburgh, September 13, 1871, she made her stage debut as a child, and her long career included membership in the Sothern and Marlowe company performing Shakespeare; the role of Laura Fenner and directing George Kelly's play, *Daisy Mayme*, in 1926; association with Eva Le Gallienne in the Civic Repertory Theatre, 1927–1931; and the role of Lady Catherine de Bourgh in *Pride and*

DOROTHY LAMOUR

Prejudice at the Music Box in 1935. Her movie career ended in 1947 in *Forever Amber*. She lived in Stamford, Conn., until 1955, when she went to a nursing home in Seattle, where she died April 5, 1960.

HEDY LAMARR

306

HEDY LAMARR

She was born in Vienna, November 9, 1913, daughter of Emil Kiesler, a banker, and studied at private schools there and in Switzerland. She was acting in movies as early as 1930. In 1933 she appeared in *Ecstasy*. Her American movie debut was in 1938.

She's had six marriages: international financier and "munitions king" Fritz Mandl; writer Gene Markey; actor John Loder (by whom she had two children, Denise and Anthony); Acapulco real-estate man Teddy Stauffer; Texas oil man Howard Lee; and a sixth that she does not name, referring to him as "the attorney." Her ghost-written "autobiography," *Ecstasy and Me*, a best-seller, she claims is filled with falsities and misrepresentations. She says she earned nothing from the book's world-wide sales. This is only one of the misfortunes and pieces of bad luck that have plagued her for many years.

DOROTHY LAMOUR

Her real name is Dorothy Leta Kaumeyer, and she was born in New Orleans, December 10, 1914. After a year at business college there, she managed a real estate office. In 1930 she got her first job, along with her friend Dorothy Dell, as a dancer in a Fanchon & Marco vaudeville act, and in 1931 won the title "Miss New Orleans." She then tried her luck in Chicago, but wound up as an elevator operator at Marshall Field's. Finally, she got a chance to try out as a singer at a Chicago hotel, and band leader Herbie Kaye, whom she eventually married, signed her with his orchestra at the Black Hawk Café, which led to a contract with NBC in New York and Los Angeles, and her screen career, beginning in 1936.

After her divorce from Kaye in 1936, she married William Ross Howard III, then an Air Force lieutenant, and became the mother of two sons, Ridgely and Tom. The Howards are neighbors of Bob Hope, with whom Dorothy still appears at benefits.

ELSA LANCHESTER

Her real name is Sullivan; she took her mother's maiden name as her stage name. Born in Lewisham, England, October 28, 1902, she started the Children's Theatre, Charlotte Street, in Soho, London, in 1918, and later the Cave of Harmony (a cabaret) in Gower Street, where she produced plays by Luigi Pirandello, A. E. Housman, and Anatole France. Her professional career began humbly as the Second Shop Girl in *Thirty Minutes in a Street* in 1922. In 1927, she appeared in Charles Laughton's first hit play, *Mr.*

Prohack. They married in 1929, and first appeared in New York together in 1931 in *Payment Deferred*. The couple spent a season with the Old Vic in 1933 before settling down in Hollywood. Laughton died in 1962. Miss Lanchester continues to act in films.

ELISSA LANDI

Born in Venice, Italy, December 6, 1904, she was the daughter of Richard Kuehnelt, Austrian cavalry officer and government official, and was christened Elizabeth Marie Christine Kuehnelt. After her mother's second marriage to an Italian nobleman, Count Carlo Zanardi-Landi, she took her stepfather's surname. Miss Landi was educated by private tutors in Canada and England. She made her London stage debut as Selina in *The Painted Swan*, by Princess Elizabeth Bibesco (sister to director Anthony Asquith), in 1924, and appeared regularly on the London stage until 1930, when she made her Broadway debut as Catherine in *A Farewell to Arms*, with Glenn Anders. In 1943, she made her final film, *Corregidor*, with Otto Kruger, then returned to Broadway and appeared regularly there and on tour until 1945. She also wrote four novels, and was popular on the lecture circuit. When she was twenty-four, she married a London attorney, John Cecil Lawrence, whom she divorced in 1936. In 1943, she married writer Curtis Thomas, of Newburyport, Mass. She died of cancer, October 21, 1948, after ten days in Kingston Hospital, Kingston, N. Y.

LOLA LANE

There were five Lane sisters (née Mullican) from the corn belt in Iowa, but only Lola, always slightly frayed looking; Rosemary, the very pretty one; and plump and sincere Priscilla, the real ingenue of the family, made it in the movies. The other two older sisters were Leota, who had a brief stage career, and Martha, who married an English instructor. Lola was born in Macy, Ind., May 21, 1909, and grew up in Indianola, Iowa, where her father, Dr. L. A. Mullican, was a dentist. Between the ages of twelve and fourteen, she was a pianist in the local movie theater. After high school, she worked her way through two years at Simpson College, the local conservatory of music. Her sister Leota was discovered in an Iowa theater by impresario Gus Edwards, who changed her name to Lane (eventually the entire family changed their name). When Leota went to New York, Lola went along as a chaperone, and both made their Broadway stage debuts in *Greenwich Village Follies*, and later toured in vaudeville. After Lola appeared with George Jessel on Broadway in

The War Song in 1928, she made her movie debut and stayed in films until 1946. She married five times: actor Lew Ayres, in 1931, director Alexander Hall, Henry Clay Dunham, director Roland West, and aircraft executive Robert Hanlon. She lives in Pacific Palisades, near her sister Rosemary.

PRISCILLA LANE

The youngest of the Lane girls, Priscilla was born June 12, 1917, in Indianola, Iowa. Her early life and career were closely linked with those of her sister Rosemary, with whom she appeared with Fred Waring's Pennsylvanians. At twenty, she made her movie bow in *Varsity Show*, with the Pennsylvanians and Dick Powell. After her 1940 divorce from Oren Haglund, whom she had married a year before, she married a building contractor of Andover, Mass., Joseph Howard, by whom she has two sons and two daughters.

ROSEMARY LANE

The fourth Lane daughter, she was born in Indianola, Iowa, April 4, 1914, and, with her younger sister Priscilla, she got her start as a singer with Fred Waring's Pennsylvanians, after finishing her education at Simpson College. She was ready for the movies when her film career started in 1937. In 1941, she appeared on Broadway in *Best Foot Forward*, with Nancy Walker and June Allyson. She made her last movie in 1945. She married Bud Westmore.

JUNE LANG

Her career extended from 1931 to 1944. She was born Winifred June Vlasek, in Minneapolis, May 5, 1915, daughter of a railway inspector, who later transported his family to Hollywood. From the age of five, she studied dancing, and was a graduate of Beverly Hills High School. She first married agent Victor Orsatti, May 29, 1937, and separated from him

THE LANE SISTERS, Priscilla, Rosemary, and Lola

GERTRUDE LAWRENCE

July 12. Next she married John Roselli, then Lt. William Morgan, of Chicago, in 1944.

FRANCES LANGFORD

She was born April 4, 1914, in Lakeland, Fla., and studied music from childhood under the encouragement of her mother, Annie Newbern, a concert pianist. She got her start with Rudy Vallee, who introduced her on his coast-to-coast radio show. In 1933, she appeared in *Here Goes the Bride* on Broadway, and was signed to a movie contract by Walter Wanger. Besides her movies, she was the star of radio's *Texaco Star Theatre* in 1939, and was with Bob Hope in his Pepsodent radio series. She also traveled with Hope on his trips to war zones during World War II. After her divorce from actor Jon Hall in 1955, she married Ralph Evinrude, of the Evinrude Outboard Motor Co., and lives in Florida.

LAURA LA PLANTE

It's her real name (her father was a French dancing teacher) and she was born in Saint Louis on November 1, 1904, going to school there and in San Diego. When she was fifteen, she landed a job in Christie Comedies because she looked like Jiggs' blond daughter in the George McManus cartoons, "Maggie and Jiggs." At Universal, she became a leading lady in Hoot Gibson Westerns and Reginald Denny farces, before she became their top star at $3,500 a week in such comedies as *Her Big Night*, *The Love Thrill*, *The Beautiful Cheat* and *Poker Faces*. One of her best performances was as the shimmering, shuddering Annabelle in the spooky classic, *The Cat and the Canary*, in 1927. She married director

William Seiter in 1926. After their divorce in 1932, she married producer Irving Asher in Paris, 1934. The couple lived in London for several years. She is the mother of two children by Asher, Tony and Jill. The Ashers now live in Palm Desert, near Palm Springs.

GERTRUDE LAWRENCE

Half-Danish, half-Irish, Gertrude Alexandra Dagmar Lawrence Klasen was born in London, July 4, 1898, daughter of troupers Arthur Klasen and Alice Louise Banks. At ten, she was a child dancer in the pantomime *Dick Whittington*, and toured the provinces as dancer and singer for many years. Her first big hit was in America, in *Charlot's Revue*, with Beatrice Lillie, at the Times Square Theatre, January 1924; it ran for a year and repeated in London in 1925. From then on she was an international stage star, in revues, musicals, and plays. Her first husband was Francis Gordon-Howley, by whom she had a daughter, Pamela, born May 28, 1918. Her second was socialite–theatrical producer-diplomat Richard Stoddard Aldrich, whom she married on her 42nd birthday in 1940. Her last movie was *The Glass Menagerie*, in which she played the Laurette Taylor role of Amanda in 1950, and her last stage appearance was in one of her greatest triumphs, *The King and I*. After her death in 1952, Aldrich wrote an intimate biography of her and their love story, *Gertrude Lawrence as "Mrs. A,"* one of the very best theater biographies.

EVELYN LAYE

Miss Laye was born in London July 10, 1900, and went on the stage at fifteen. During her long stage career, she starred chiefly in musicals and revues (most notably Noël Coward's *Bitter Sweet*, in both New York and London), and occasional light comedies. As of 1973, still appearing in the West End, she hasn't played an old-lady role yet. She was married to musical star Sonnie Hale (1926-1931), and to actor Frank Lawton (*David Copperfield*) from 1934 to his death in 1969.

DOROTHY LEE

Dorothy Lee began life as Marjorie Millsap in Los Angeles on May 23, 1911, and went to school there at Virgil Junior High. At eighteen she was in the movies, in *Syncopation* 1929. Ten years later, she made her last movie, *SOS Tidal Wave*. Once married to gossip columnist Jimmie Fidler, she now lives in Chicago.

GWEN LEE

Born in Hastings, Nebr., November 12, 1904, she shortened her name from

Gwendolyn LePinski. She went to school in Omaha, and was briefly on the stage, where she was discovered by film director Monta Bell. She made her debut in 1924, and her last film was *Corruption*, for a quickie company in 1933. She died August 20, 1961.

LILA LEE

She was born Augusta Appel in New York, July 25, 1901, and began her long career as a child named Cuddles Edwards in Gus Edwards' famous old "School Days" vaudeville act, with George Jessel, Walter Winchell, Eddie Cantor, Eddie Buzzell, and Gregory Kelly. At seventeen, she made her movie debut in *The Cruise of the Make-Believe*, with Harrison Ford at Paramount, and spent the major part of her silent-screen career with that company. She played leading ladies to Thomas Meighan, Wallace Reid, Harry Houdini, Jack Holt, William Boyd, and James Kirkwood (whom she married in 1923 as the third of his five wives). In the latter part of the 1920s she worked mainly for the "quickies" (Anchor, Quality, Chesterfield, Tiffany, etc.) until her career was given a new spurt by the talkies, when she began to appear again with the major companies. She has a son, novelist Jim Kirkwood (born August 22, 1925). After her divorce from actor Kirkwood, she married broker John E. Murphy, whom she divorced in 1949. She died of a stroke November 13, 1973.

ANDREA LEEDS

Of English-French-Italian descent, she was born Antoinette Lees in Butte, Mont., August 18, 1914, the daughter of a mining engineer. Before entering movies in 1935, she studied at the University of California and the Chicago Conservatory. Upon her marriage to millionaire Robert S. Howard, of Burlingame, Calif., she retired from the movies in 1940.

VIVIEN LEIGH

She was born Vivian (she wasn't Vivien until 1935) Mary Hartley in Darjeeling, India, November 5, 1913, daughter of Ernest Richard Hartley, a stockbroker in Calcutta, and his Irish wife, Gertrude Robinson. Her parents took her back to England when she was six to enroll her at the Convent of the Sacred Heart, outside London. Her schooling was continued in France, Italy, and Germany. From adolescence she was determined to be an actress. At nineteen, she married Herbert Leigh Holman, a barrister, and became the mother of her only child, Suzanne Holman, on October 12, 1933. A year later, she got her acting start as a schoolgirl in *Things Are Looking Up*, with Cicely Courtneidge, and in 1935 had her

VIVIEN LEIGH and Laurence Olivier

first stage success as one of the four leads in Ashley Dukes' comedy *The Mask of Virtue*. This won her a five-year film contract with Alexander Korda. After making two movies with Laurence Olivier, he encouraged her to work with the Old Vic in Shakespeare, and in 1937 she played Ophelia and Titania. When Olivier went to America to film *Wuthering Heights*, Miss Leigh impulsively followed him. Olivier asked his agent, Myron Selznick, if he would suggest to his brother, David O. Selznick, that Miss Leigh was exactly right for Scarlett O'Hara. On January 13, 1939, a month after production had started, it was publicly announced that the part every actress in Hollywood wanted was given to a little-known English actress. Miss Leigh and Olivier married in 1940, and divorced twenty years later. They played in *That Hamilton Woman* together, and also appeared on the stage in *Romeo and Juliet* on Broadway, in Old Vic productions in London and New York. They last appeared together at Stratford-on-Avon. In all, Miss Leigh made nineteen films, winning a second Oscar for her Blanche DuBois in *A Streetcar Named Desire* in 1951. Her last stage appearance was on Broadway in Chekhov's *Ivanov*, with Sir John Gielgud in 1966. Her later life was plagued by years of illness. She was found dead in her London apartment, in Eaton Square, on July 8, 1967.

WINNIE LIGHTNER

Christened Winifred Josephine Reeves, she was born in Greenport, L. I., September 17, 1899, and was raised by an aunt and uncle named Hanson in Buffalo, N. Y., where she went to school. When she won first prize singing in a contest at a local theater, she went to New York, and briefly was a member of Gus Edwards' road show production of *School Days*. George White saw her in vaudeville and liked her so much that he gave her a lead part in his *Scandals of 1923*, in which she stopped the show with George Gershwin's first hit, "I'll Build a Stairway to Paradise," backed by Paul Whiteman's Orchestra. She appeared in two additional *Scandals*, and in 1924 introduced another Gershwin evergreen, "Somebody Loves Me." From there, she was the lead in two Shubert productions of *Gay Paree*, and in *Delmar's Revels*, 1927, with Frank Fay, Bert Lahr and Patsy Kelly. Between 1929 and 1933, she was the star of ten musicals for Warners, and appeared in her last at MGM, *Dancing Lady*, with Joan Crawford and Clark Gable. Miss Lightner married four times: John Patrick; William Harold; George Holtrey, a broker; and Roy Del Ruth, who directed four of her pictures. He died in 1961, and she on March 6,

1971, at their home in Sherman Oaks, Calif., survived by two sons.

BEATRICE LILLIE

Beatrice Gladys Lillie was born May 29, 1898, in Toronto, daughter of John Lillie, onetime British Army officer in India and a Canadian government official, and Lucie-Ann Shaw, a concert singer. At fifteen, she left St. Agnes' College in Ontario to go on the stage with her mother and sister Muriel as the Lillie Trio. In 1914, she made her debut in London in the revue *Not Likely*, but she didn't have a big international hit until the magical *Charlot's Revue of 1924* in both New York and London. Thereafter, she became a theatrical commuter. In 1920, she married Sir Robert Peel, 5th Baronet, and became the mother of a son, who succeeded to his father's title in 1934. Sir Robert Peel, 6th Baronet, was killed in the bombing of the H.M.S. *Hermes* in Colombo Harbor, at the age of twenty-two, in 1942. Her autobiography, *Every Other Inch a Lady*, was published in 1972.

MARGARET LINDSAY

Born as Margaret Kies in Dubuque, Iowa, September 19, 1910, she studied at National Park Seminary in Washington and the American Academy of Dramatic Arts in New York. After a brief stage career, she made her first movie appearance in a small role in *Okay America*, with Lew Ayres and Maureen O'Sullivan, in 1932. Her career went fairly steadily through 1948, and thereafter she returned occasionally, most notably in *Please Don't Eat the Daisies* in 1960. Miss Lindsay lives in Los Angeles.

MARGARET LIVINGSTON

Of Scotch-Swedish descent, she was born in Salt Lake City, November 25, 1900, and educated there. At the age of sixteen, she went to Hollywood with her mother, with the firm intention of getting into the movies. By 1919, she was getting featured leads, and she worked steadily through the 1920s in "other woman" roles. She was Paul Whiteman's fourth wife. In 1933, she collaborated with Isobel Leighton on a book, *Whiteman's Burden*, dealing with her overweight husband's diet.

DORIS LLOYD

Born in Liverpool, on July 3, 1900, she went to school there and made her debut with the Liverpool Repertory Theatre Company in 1914, remaining with them for six years. After a short London stage career, she went to Hollywood to visit her sister and remained there for a movie career, beginning with *The Lady*,

with Norma Talmadge, in 1925. She made only one appearance on Broadway, as the selfish Mrs. Birling in J. B. Priestley's *An Inspector Calls*, with Thomas Mitchell, in 1947. She died at her sister's house, Santa Monica, May 21, 1968.

MARGARET LOCKWOOD

She was born Margaret Day in Karachi, India, September 15, 1916, and went to schools in London. At twelve she appeared as a fairy in *A Midsummer Night's Dream* at the Holborn Empire, and later in pantomime and as a walk-on in *Cavalcade* at Drury Lane. Then she studied at the Royal Academy of Dramatic Arts before returning to the stage in 1934, and making her film bow that same year in *Lorna Doone*. Miss Lockwood's last British film was made in 1955, but she still appears occasionally on the West End stage. She married and divorced Rupert W. Leon, and has a daughter, actress Julia Lockwood (born August 23, 1941), who made her debut as a child in her mother's *Hungry Hill*.

JACQUELINE LOGAN

Daughter of an architect, Charles A. Logan, and his wife Marion, onetime prima donna of the Boston Opera Co., she was born in Corsicana, Texas, November 30, 1901. Before going on the stage, she was a newspaper reporter. She made her debut in a revival of *Floradora* in New York in 1920, and in the same year was in the *Follies*. In 1921, she began her screen career. She has been married to Robert Gillespie and Larry Winston.

CAROLE LOMBARD

Among her fellow artists and studio workers, she was perhaps the most widely loved star that Hollywood has ever known. Of Scotch-English ancestry, she was born October 6, 1908, in Fort Wayne, Ind., and named Jane Alice Peters. After her divorce, her mother, Elizabeth Knight Peters, took her daughter, age eight, and two older brothers to live in Los Angeles. When she was twelve, she was playing baseball on the street with other kids when director Allan Dwan saw her and gave her a part as Monte Blue's daughter in *A Perfect Crime*. Jane Peters and her mother haunted the movie lots for more jobs, but to no avail. At Los Angeles High School, she won medals for sprinting and high-jumping, and later was a star pupil at the Marian Nolks Dramatic School. She then landed a job as the heroine in a Buck Jones Western, *Hearts and Spurs*, in 1925, at $75 a week, leading the way to a five-year contract with Fox. An automobile accident—when a car in front of her slid backwards down a hill and she was thrown against the

CAROLE LOMBARD

windshield—cut her face from the corner of her nose to her left cheekbone, and left a permanent scar that was always faintly noticeable in spite of make-up and expert lighting. Her Fox contract lapsed during her convalescence; she returned to movies in 1927 as a Mack Sennett bathing beauty, and at that time changed her name. She married two major stars: William Powell (in 1931, divorced 1933), with whom she appeared in *Man of the World* and *Ladies' Man*, and Clark Gable, whom she had first met while making *No Man of Her Own*, her only film with him, in 1932. The Gables married in Kingman, Ariz., May 29, 1939. After finishing her last film, *To Be or Not to Be*, shortly before Pearl Harbor, Miss Lombard set out on a bond tour, selling $2,000,000 worth. She perished when a TWA skyliner crashed head-on into Table Rock Mountain, thirty miles southwest of Las Vegas, on January 16, 1942.

PAULINE LORD

She was born on a fruit ranch near Hanford, Calif., on August 8, 1890, one of the three daughters of Edward Lord. She went to school in Hanford, studied for the stage under Jennie Morrow Long, and at thirteen, made her debut as the Maid in *Are You a Mason?* with the Belasco Stock Company in San Francisco. In 1912 she made her Broadway debut, and became a star when she created the title role in Eugene O'Neill's *Anna Christie* in 1921. Her last role was as Amanda in a tour of *The Glass Menagerie*. Her two films were made in 1934 and 1935. She died at midnight, October 10, 1950, in the Champion Memorial Hospital, Alamogordo, New Mex., from asthma and a heart ailment.

ANITA LOUISE

Born in New York, January 9, 1915, and named Anita Louise Fremault, she was an actress on stage and screen from childhood. Her career spanned more than seventy pictures, and ended in 1946. By that time, she had been married for six years to Buddy Adler, later head of 20th Century-Fox, who, when he died in 1960, willed her several million dollars. Two years later she married Henry Berger, an importer, and became increasingly active in the film colony's social scene and in philanthropic causes. She died of a massive stroke April 25, 1970, at her Holmby Hills home in West Los Angeles.

BESSIE LOVE

D. W. Griffith gave her the name Bessie Love when she made her debut in *Intolerance*, as the Bride of Cana, in 1916. Her real name is Juanita Horton,

and she was born in Midland, Tex., September 10, 1898, daughter of an ex-cowboy and bartender, who later took his family to Los Angeles, where he became a chiropractor. Miss Love worked in American films until 1931, becoming a dramatic actress of affecting poignancy. She married William B. Hawks (brother of director Howard Hawks), who was then a Pasadena stockbroker, in 1929. In 1932, her daughter, Patricia, was born, and she retired temporarily. On a European tour in 1935, she decided to live in London, and divorced her husband in 1936. She has continued to work on the stage, screen, and television there ever since. In 1972, she played Aunt Pittypat in the musical stage version of *Gone With the Wind* in London.

MYRNA LOY

Myrna Loy, née Myrna Williams, had carroty red hair and freckles; was tall and lanky, with long, skinny arms; and when she finally talked in movies, her voice carried a faint Montana twang. Yet she got away with playing sinuous Orientals and exotic vamps for years.

She was born on a ranch in Crow Creek Valley, Mont., August 2, 1905, of Welsh-Scottish descent. Her father, who died when Myrna was thirteen, was a rancher, who served in the Montana Legislature. After her husband's death, Myrna's mother took the family to California, where her daughter went to West-lake School for Girls and Venice High School. She has married and divorced four times: producer Arthur Hornblow, Jr. (1936-1942); rent-a-car tycoon John Hertz, Jr. (1942-1943); writer Gene Markey, once husband of Joan Bennett and Hedy Lamarr (1946-1950); government official Howland Sargeant (1951-1960). Miss Loy worked as a member of the UNESCO Commission for five years in Washington, and is active on the National Committee Against Discrimination in Housing. She lives in New York, and appears occasionally on both the stage and TV.

IDA LUPINO

Ida Lupino was born in London, February 4, 1916. Her parents were Stanley Lupino and Connie Emerald, both stage performers of generations-old acting families. Ida studied for the stage at the Royal Academy of Dramatic Arts, and became a film actress accidentally when she accompanied her mother, who was applying for the starring role of *Her First Affair*, 1933, directed by the American Allan Dwan, then working in England. Dwan preferred the daughter to the mother, and Ida made her debut in a leading role. She made her Hollywood debut in 1934.

She first married English actor Louis Hayward in 1937, and divorced him in

IDA LUPINO

1945. In 1949, she married Collier Young and a year later began directing and producing films with him (they divorced in 1950). Her third husband is actor Howard Duff (1951), with whom she appeared in a TV series, *Mr. Adams and Eve*. She continues as an actress and TV director and lives in the Brentwood section of Hollywood.

SHARON LYNN

It seems her name was really D'Auvergne Sharon Lindsay, born April 9, 1907, in Weatherford, Texas. On Broadway she appeared in C. B. Dillingham's musical *Sunny Side Up*, before making her movie debut in *Clancy's Kosher Wedding*. She made her last film in 1941. Married twice, to screen writer Barney Glazer and Beverly Hills business man John Sershen, she died of multiple sclerosis, in Hollywood Presbyterian Hospital, May 26, 1963.

JEANETTE MacDONALD

A realistic woman, she toyed with the idea of using "The Iron Butterfly" as the title of her autobiography (still unpublished): "It might help sell copies."

Of Scottish, Irish and English ancestry, she was born in Philadelphia, the third daughter of Daniel and Anne Wright MacDonald. All three daughters eventually went on the stage. In 1920, young Jeanette first appeared on the stage at the Capitol Theatre in New York, in the chorus of Ned Wayburn's *Demi-Tasse Revue*. It's not generally known that she spent the entire decade of the 1920s on Broadway because her stage career never reached the splendor of her movie stardom. She starred in *Sunny Days*, with Lynne Overman, 1928; *Angela*, with Roy Hoyer and Alison Skipworth; and *Boom Boom*, with Stanley Ridges and Archie Leach (Cary Grant), 1929. That same

MYRNA LOY

JEANETTE MAC DONALD

year she made her screen debut in Ernst Lubitsch's *The Love Parade*, opposite Maurice Chevalier. She made her last movie appearance in a Lassie film, *The Sun Comes Up*, in 1949, seven years after her great days with Nelson Eddy were over. On June 17, 1937, she married actor Gene Raymond. On January 14, 1965, she died at the Methodist Hospital, Houston, Texas, before open-heart surgery could be performed. Her husband was at her bedside.

HELEN MACK

Helen Mack (née McDougall) was born in Rock Island, Ill., November 13, 1913. Her parents took her to New York when she was a child, and enrolled her in the Professional Children's School. She played in silent films, made in and around New York, during 1923-1924: *Zaza*, with Gloria Swanson, *Little Red Schoolhouse*, with Elmo K. Lincoln, *Pied Piper Malone*, with Thomas Meighan and Lois Wilson, and *Grit*, with Glenn Hunter and Clara Bow. On Broadway, she appeared with Ernest Truex in *Pomeroy's Past*, 1926, and was discovered for adult roles when she was playing in the murder mystery hit, *Subway Express*. Her adult movie career began in 1931, and continued into the 1940s. Miss Mack first married Charles Irwin, Fox West Coast Theatre executive (1935), and had a son. In 1942, she married radio producer Tom McAvity, gave birth to another son. In 1944, Miss Mack was producer of a radio show, *A Date with Judy*, and in 1965, under the name of Helen McAvity, she was the co-author, with Eleanor Harris Howard, of *The Mating Dance*, with Van Johnson, which closed after one performance.

314

DOROTHY MACKAILL

Born March 4, 1903, in Hull, England, she began her career as a chorus girl in London and with Ziegfeld in New York, and made her American movie debut in Marshall Neilan's *Bits of Life*, 1921. Through the 1920s, she worked chiefly at First National (later Warner Bros.), best remembered as Jack Mulhall's co-star in such froth as *Subway Sadie*, *Smile, Brother, Smile*, *Ladies' Night in a Turkish Bath* and *Children of the Ritz*. Miss Mackaill married and divorced director Lothar Mendes (1926-1928), singer Neil Miller, and Harold Patterson. She has lived many years at the Royal Hawaiian Hotel in Honolulu.

ALINE MacMAHON

She was the only child of William Marcus MacMahon, onetime broker and later editor-in-chief of *Munsey's Magazine*, and his wife Jennie Simson, and was born May 3, 1899, in McKeesport, Pa. She grew up in Brooklyn and Manhattan and was a Barnard graduate in 1920. At the age of twenty-two, she made her debut as a thirty-nine-year-old spinster in *The Madras House* at the Neighborhood Playhouse in New York, and first became noticed for her wicked impersonations in *The Grand Street Follies*, and later in *Artists and Models*. Her first dramatic success was in a revival of O'Neill's *Beyond the Horizon* in 1926, a performance described by Noël Coward as "astonishing, moving and beautiful." She was discovered by Hollywood when she played the wise-cracking "voice-culture" teacher in *Once in a Lifetime* in its Los Angeles production in 1931. She continues to appear on the stage and occasionally in movies. Since 1928, she has been married to the

ALINE MAC MAHON

distinguished New York architect, Clarence S. Stein (New York's most famous synagogue, Temple Emanu-El).

MARJORIE MAIN

She was the daughter of a Church of Christ mininster, born near Acton, Ind., February 24, 1890. After three years at the Hamilton School of Dramatic Expression, Lexington, Ky., she went out on the Chautauqua circuit, giving readings from Shakespeare and Dickens. From there she went into stock companies and vaudeville, changing her name from Mary Tomlinson because her family didn't approve of a stage career. In 1921, she married Dr. Stanley Krebs, a psychologist and lecturer on salesmanship and personality development. He died in 1935, after fourteen years of a happy marriage.

On Broadway, Miss Main appeared in *Burlesque* with Barbara Stanwyck, played Mae West's mother in *The Wicked Age* and the gangster's mother in *Dead End*. At the end of her career in 1957, she had appeared in some eighty-two movies, and will always be remembered as Ma Kettle, a role she first created in *The Egg and I* in 1947. She lives alone in Cheviot Hills, near Los Angeles.

BOOTS MALLORY

Patricia Mallory was born October 22, 1913, in New Orleans. At twelve, she was a banjo player in a girls' band and at sixteen a dancer in vaudeville. On Broadway she was a chorus girl in *George White's Scandals* and appeared in Ziegfeld's musical *Hot-Cha!* with Bert Lahr, Buddy Rogers, and Lupe Velez, when she was discovered for the movies. She made her debut in 1932 in *Handle with Care*, with James Dunn, with whom she also appeared in *Hello, Sister* a year later. Her last movie was *Here's Flash Casey*, with Eric Linden, in 1937. She married three times: actor Charles Bennett; producer William Cagney (divorced 1946); then became the fourth wife of star Herbert Marshall in 1947. He was at her bedside when she died of a chronic throat ailment in St. John's Hospital, Santa Monica, December 1, 1958.

MARGO

In her screen career, Margo—of heart-shaped face, electric eyes, gentle voice—was largely consigned to play doleful girls of tragic fates. Unfortunately, she was never given a chance in a role that would display the rollicking humor and sophistication of her private personality. The daughter of a Spanish surgeon, Dr. Amedio Bolado, she was born in Mexico City, May 10, 1917, and named Maria Margarita Guadalupe Teresa Estella Castilla Bolado y O'Donnell. Margo grew up in the United States, and made her debut at eleven at the old Mexican Theatre at First and Main Streets, in Los Angeles. She became a specialty dancer in hotels, particularly the Waldorf-Astoria in New York, where her uncle, Xavier Cugat, was conducting his orchestra at the Starlight Roof. Her most famous role was as Mirianne, in *Winterset*, Margo was first married to actor Francis Lederer, and then, from 1945, to actor Eddie Albert. They live in Pacific Palisades.

SARI MARITZA

Named Patricia Detering Nathan, she was born in Tientsin, China, March 17, 1910, daughter of British Major Walter Nathan and his Viennese wife. After schooling in England, Switzerland, Germany, and Austria, she took her mother's name for the screen, making her debut in Vienna. She did films later in Budapest, Berlin, and London. In 1934, she departed films to marry Paramount official Sam Katz, and confessed (in 1948): "I quit the screen because I couldn't act."

The Katzes were divorced in 1938. During the war, she worked for a lens manufacturer, and is credited with devising a method of polishing plastic gunsights. She married an Air Force navigator, George Glatthar, and lived with him in Georgetown, Md.

JOAN MARSH

Her father, Charles Rosher, was Mary Pickford's cameraman, and his daughter Dorothy (born in Porterfield, Calif., July 10, 1913) played children in such Pickford films as *Daddy Long-Legs* and *Pollyanna* in 1919 and 1920. She first used the name Joan Marsh in *The King of Jazz* in 1930. She had roles in two Garbo films (*Inspiration*, 1931, and *Anna Karenina* in 1935). Her career extended to *Follow the Leader* for Monogram in 1944. She was once married to screenwriter Charles Belden, and she married for a second time in 1943. She owns a Los Angeles stationery business, Paper Unlimited.

MAE MARSH

Next to Lillian Gish the most famous of the D. W. Griffith actresses, Miss Marsh was born as Mary Warne Marsh on November 9, 1895, in Madrid, New Mexico. Growing up in Los Angeles and going to the Convent of the Immaculate Heart in Hollywood, she was introduced to movie-acting by her sister Marguerite, six years her senior, who had joined D. W. Griffith's Biograph company, then shooting in Los Angeles for its second winter. Griffith changed her name to Mae, to distinguish her from Mary Pickford, and she started out in extra and bit roles in 1912. After her Griffith years, she became

a Goldwyn star from 1917 to 1919, and during the 1920s made films in England and Germany. In 1923 she rejoined Griffith for one picture, *The White Rose*, with Ivor Novello and Carol Dempster. In 1918, she married Lee Arms, then a Goldwyn studio publicity man, later an attorney, and became the mother of two daughters and a son. From time to time, she played small parts, many of them for John Ford; the last, *Two Rode Together*, in 1961. She died at her home in Hermosa Beach, February 13, 1968.

MARIAN MARSH

She was born Violet Krauth in Trinidad, October 17, 1913, and grew up in Hollywood, where she went to Hollywood High School. After appearing on the local stage, she started in movies in small parts in 1930. Her career ended in 1941. She married stockbroker Albert Scott in the later 1930s, and next Cliff Henderson. She lives in Palm Desert, Calif.

ILONA MASSEY

Born Ilona Hajmassy in Budapest in 1910, she began her career as a singer with the Vienna Volksoper, and later the Vienna State Opera, in 1934 and 1936. Her first movies were made in Austria in 1935. She was discovered by Louis B. Mayer and brought to America by MGM for her debut in *Rosalie* in 1937, singing and speaking her lines phonetically. Her career ended in 1959 with *Jet Over the Atlantic*. Miss Massey married Nicholas Szavozd, of Hungary; actor Alan Curtis (1941-1942); New York jeweler Charles Walker (1952-1955); and Gen. Donald S. Dawson. The Dawsons live in Bethesda, Md.

JESSIE MATTHEWS

The only star appearing exclusively in British films to become famous in America, Miss Matthews was born in Soho, London, March 11, 1907, and made her stage bow at ten in *Bluebell in Fairyland*. By 1924, she was in the chorus of *Charlot's Revue* and was an understudy to Gertrude Lawrence; in the *Charlot Show of 1926*, she was the star. Thereafter she became a London favorite in light and airy musicals (*Evergreen*, *This Year of Grace*, *Wake Up and Dream*); she also came to New York with the latter in 1929, with Jack Buchanan.

She made her first two movies in 1923 and 1924, and her talkie debut in 1931 in *Out of the Blue*. She married and divorced three times: Henry Lytton, Jr.; her co-star Sonnie Hale; and Brian Lewis. She now lives in the Northwood section of London with her sister Rosie.

MAY McAVOY

She was born September 8, 1901, in New York, and was a student at St. Bartholomew's Convent and Wadleigh High School. At seventeen, she became an extra in New York film studios, soon played featured parts, and at twenty, went on to Hollywood, where she played leads at Paramount, Warners and MGM. Although she had appeared in relatively few MGM movies that company placed her under contract to play extras and bits, under its pension policy, from 1940 to the mid-1950s. Miss McAvoy married Maurice Cleary, vice president and treasurer of United Artists, and later with Lockheed Aircraft, in 1929, and has a son, Patrick. They live in a small house off Wilshire Boulevard, Beverly Hills.

HATTIE McDANIEL

Miss McDaniel was one of thirteen children of a Baptist minister of Wichita, Kansas, and was born June 10, 1895. She spent two years at East Denver High School, and won a medal in dramatic art from the White Women's Christian Temperance Union in Denver. Beginning as a singer with Prof. George Morrison's Colored Orchestra in Denver, she toured the West with this band, through the South for the Shrine and Elks circuit, and the Pantages circuit in 1924-1925. On the stage, she played in road companies of *Show Boat*. In 1931 she first appeared in movies, and her career went up to *Family Honeymoon* in 1949. In the meantime, she became the original *Beulah* on both radio and television. Miss McDaniel was married twice, to James Crawford and Larry Williams, both of whom she divorced. She died of cancer October 26, 1952.

NINA MAE McKINNEY

She was born in Harlem, daughter of John and Nina McKinney, non-professionals, and educated in public schools. She said she was fifteen years old when she played the lead in *Hallelujah!* and that her career had begun as a dancer and blues singer in Harlem. Miss McKinney also sang in night clubs and music halls in London, Paris, Budapest, Dublin, and Athens in the late 1940s and 1950s.

BUTTERFLY McQUEEN

Born Thelma McQueen in Tampa, Fla., January 8, 1911. Her father was a stevedore and her mother a domestic. She received her early education from Catholic nuns at St. Benedict's Convent in Augusta, Ga. In Harlem in 1935, with Venezuela Jones's Negro Youth Group, she danced in the "Butterfly" ballet of *A Midsummer Night's Dream* and acquired her stage name. On Broadway, she became a favorite of George Abbott, who gave her parts in his productions of *Brother Rat*, *Brown Sugar* and *What a Life!* between 1936 and 1938. In the 1940s, she played in six movies, including *Mildred Pierce*. Afterwards, between jobs on the stage, she has worked in New York in a factory, as a waitress and a dishwasher and a playground assistant. She made another personal hit in the Hollywood spoof, *Curley McDimple*, an off-Broadway production in 1968.

BERYL MERCER

She was born in Seville, Spain, of English parents, August 13, 1882, and was educated in England. At four, she made her stage debut as Little Willie in *East Lynne* and played regularly on the London stage until 1924, when she came to America for both stage and screen engagements. During the first World War, she went to France as an entertainer of British troops, and received the Queen Alexandra medal. She returned to America, this time for good, and played many character roles in Hollywood films. Miss Mercer was once the wife of actor Holmes Herbert. She worked until the end, and died July 28, 1939.

UNA MERKEL

One of the least egotistical of all actresses, she made every role count in her rich and varied career. She was born in Covington, Ky., December 10, 1903, only child of Arno and Bessie Phares Merkel. After schools in Covington and Philadelphia, she started her career as a cigarette girl in *Montmartre* on Broadway in 1922. During the 1930s, she made fifty-nine movies. In one year, 1933, she worked in three movies at the same time, and made thirteen in all.

Besides movies, she has appeared in television, and on Broadway in *Take Me Along*, with Jackie Gleason, in 1959. She was married to Ronald L. Burla, an aviation designer, in 1932; they were divorced in 1946. She now lives with her father in Los Angeles.

ETHEL MERMAN

Ethel Agnes Zimmerman is the only child of Edward Zimmerman, an accountant, and his wife Agnes Gardner, onetime school teacher, and was born in Astoria, L. I., January 16, 1908. After graduating from Bryant High School, she became secretary to the president of the B. K. Vacuum Booster Brake Co. Evenings and weekends, she sang in clubs and at weddings, and got her first chance in vaudeville in the act of Clayton, Jackson and Durante at the Palace when she was twenty-one. A year later, she became a Broadway star in the Gershwin musical *Girl Crazy*, the beginning of a long, unchallenged reign in Broadway musicals. In 1953, she starred in *Call Me Madam* and in 1954, *There's No Business Like Show Business*, in the movies. She's been married and divorced four times: actors' agent William B. Smith (1940-1941); ad man Robert Leavitt; airlines executive Robert F. Six (divorced 1961); and actor Ernest Borgnine (1964).

MAYO METHOT

She was the daughter of Jack Methot, a sea captain on the Orient run, and his wife, newspaperwoman Evelyn Wood, born in Portland, Ore., March 3, 1904. On the stage from childhood, she made her Broadway debut in *The Mad Honeymoon* in 1922. Her best Broadway role was in Kenyon Nicholson's *Torch Song* in 1930. She made her movie debut in 1931, ending with a small role in *Brother Rat and a Baby* in 1940. Humphrey Bogart was her third husband, and she his third wife; they married August 20, 1938 and divorced May 10, 1945, after exhausting themselves as the "Battling Bogarts." Miss Methot left Hollywood forever to go to Portland to live with her mother. She died at Holladay Park Hospital, Multhomak, Ore., June 9, 1951.

GERTRUDE MICHAEL

Born in Talladega, Ala., June 1, 1910, she went to high school there, and at seventeen appeared on a local radio station as a household adviser, singer, piano and violin soloist. Later she went to the University of Alabama and Converse College of Cincinnati, where she made her stage debut with Stuart Walker's stock company in 1929. After playing on Broadway in the Rachel Crothers comedy, *Caught Wet*, 1931, she made her movie bow as Richard Arlen's fiancée in *Wayward*. After 1944, Miss Michael appeared only occasionally, most notably in a small role in Joan Crawford's *Flamingo Road* in 1949, and her last, *Women's Prison*, 1955. She died unmarried at her home in Hollywood, January 1, 1965.

ANN MILLER

The nimble Miss Miller was born Lucille Ann Collier, Chireno, Texas, April 12, 1919, on her grandparents' ranch, daughter of J. A. Collier, a Houston lawyer. She took dancing lessons, and made her first public appearance at seven as a Pink Rosebud at a Police and Firemen's Ball. She and her mother went to Hollywood to try to get into show business. Ann enrolled in Fanchon and Marco's dancing school. As a tender teen-ager, she danced at the Sunset Club, a small place with gambling upstairs, at $25 a week, trying out her machine-gun taps for the first time. Then she played other joints, and vaudeville, before making *New Faces of 1937*, with Milton Berle. Her movie career was maintained steadily through 1956, with a Broadway interruption for *George White's Scandals*, with Willie and Eugene Howard, 1939. She didn't get back to Broadway until 1969, as the last and most athletic of the musical stage *Mames*, and later toured the country.

She made three short-lived marriages: Reese Milner (1946—div. 1947); William Moss (1958—div. 1961); Arthur Cameron (1961—annulled 1962).

MARILYN MILLER

At the age of four, she made her bow in vaudeville billed as "Miss Sugar Plum," and it was this sugar-plum ethereality that she retained throughout her life that made her Florenz Ziegfeld's most popular singing-and-dancing star. Her real name was Mary Ellen Reynolds, born in Evansville, Ind., September 1, 1898. She joined her parents, her stepfather Caro Miller and her mother Lyn Reynolds, in their act, "The Five Columbians," and toured all over the world. She made her Broadway debut in *The Passing Show of 1914*, and her last show was *As Thousands Cheer*, another of her many hits, in 1933. Her three movies were made between 1929 and 1931. Miss Miller first married Frank Carter, a singing juvenile who was killed in an automobile accident in 1920, a year after their marriage. Her second husband was film star Jack Pickford, from 1922 to 1927. In 1934, she married Chester O'Brien, a chorus boy in *As Thousands Cheer*. She died in Doctors Hospital, New York, of a sinus infection, April 7, 1936.

PATSY RUTH MILLER

Born in Saint Louis, June 22, 1905, she went to the Visitation Convent and St. Mary's Institute there. When she was in her early teens, her father, a newspaperman, moved the family to Los Angeles. At fifteen, she made her movie bow in a small role, and worked steadily throughout the 1920s. Her most famous role was as Esmeralda in Lon Chaney's *The Hunchback of Notre Dame* in 1923. Never a star, she served well as a pert leading lady to Monte Blue, Glenn Tryon, Kenneth Harlan, Sydney Chaplin, and George Jessel. After her screen career ended in 1931, she wrote radio scripts, short stories, a novel (*That Flanagan Girl*, 1939), and the book for a musical based on the life of Tschaikowsky, *Music in My Heart*, produced on Broadway in 1947, with Robert Carroll and Vivienne Segal. Her 1929 marriage to director Tay Garnett ended in divorce. She married a New York importer, E. S. Deans, in 1951. They live in Stamford, Conn.

COLLEEN MOORE

The light comedienne who set the pace for the movie flappers of the 1920s was born Kathleen Morrison in Port Huron, Mich., August 19, 1900, with, as well documented in the fan magazines, one brown and one blue eye. Her father was an irrigation engineer who moved his family to Tampa, Fla., where young Kathleen studied piano and went to the Convent of the Holy Name. Later she went North to study music at the Detroit Conservatory. Her uncle, Walter Howey, then managing editor of the *Chicago American*, arranged for his niece to be hired for extra work at the Essanay Studios in Chicago in 1916, and that same year she and her grandmother, Mrs. Mary Kelly, were inspired to go to Hollywood to try the youngster's luck there. She made her Hollywood debut in *Bad Boy*, with Robert Harron and Mildred Harris, in 1917, and began to get leading-lady parts with Tom Santschi, Charles Ray, Tom Mix, Sessue Hayakawa. In 1923, her flapper heroine of *Flaming Youth* made her a star—even though she had been in movies six years—and she was soon earning $12,500 a week, a record, as her career progressed in frothy fare. Only rarely did she have a chance to show her dramatic force—as the Dutch farmer's wife, in *So Big*, 1924, and the French war heroine of *Lilac Time*, with Gary Cooper, 1928. Her movie career ended in 1934.

Miss Moore first married John McCormick, First National Studios production head, in 1923, and divorced him in 1930. From 1932 to 1934, she was married to New York stock broker Alfred P. Scott. From 1937 until his death in 1966, she was the wife of a Chicago broker, Homer P. Hargrave.

GRACE MOORE

Christened Mary Willie Grace Moore, she was born in Slabtown (later Nough),

GRACE MOORE

Cocke Co., Tenn., December 5, 1901, one of the four children of Col. Richard L. Moore. She grew up in Knoxville and in Jellico, where her father became a partner of the Baird Dry Goods Co. As a choir singer, she dreamed of being a missionary, but changed her mind when she studied voice at the Ward-Belmont School in Nashville, and the Wilson-Greene School of Music in Washington. When a schoolgirl in 1919, she made her first concert appearance at the National Theatre in Washington on a program with Giovanni Martinelli, singing the aria "Ritorna vincitor" from *Aida*. Her first New York stage appearance was in *Hitchy Koo 1920*, with Raymond Hitchcock and Julia Sanderson. By 1923 she was the leading prima donna of Irving Berlin's *Music Box Revue*, followed by a second *Revue* in 1924. In that year she met the millionaire music patron Otto Kahn, who befriended her and urged her to study opera. Four years later, she made her operatic bow as Mimi in *La Boheme* at the Metropolitan, and was a member of the company until 1931. After her first two disastrous movies at MGM, she left Hollywood, vowing to get even. In 1934 (after a triumph in *The Dubarry* on Broadway in 1932), she did so, at Harry Cohn's Columbia studio. She married Valentin Parera, and was killed January 26, 1947, when a Royal Dutch Airlines DC-3 crashed and burned on the runway of Copenhagen's airport.

NATALIE MOORHEAD

Born Nathalia Messner in Pittsburgh, July 27, 1905, she went to Peabody High School there. While in New York on a visit, she got her first stage job as a bridesmaid in *Abie's Irish Rose*, during that play's long run, and then joined Charles Brian's Stock Company in Trenton, N. J., for two years. She went to Hollywood, and was placed under contract by Fox in 1929, making her debut in *Thru Different Eyes*. Her career ended in 1940.

LOIS MORAN

She was christened Lois Darlington Dowling, and was born in Pittsburgh, March 1, 1907, daughter of Roger and Gladys Evans Dowling. Later she became a stepdaughter to Dr. T. G. Moran. She studied at Linden Hall Seminary, Greensburgh, Pa., and the Lycee de Tours, France. She acted in two French films, *La Galerie des Monstres* and Marcel L'Herbier's *Feu Mathias Pascal*, with Ivan Mosjoukine and Michel Simon, 1925. Producer Sam Goldwyn, then touring Europe seeking a Juliet for a proposed Shakespearean film, discovered her. When he decided to make *Stella Dallas* instead, she got the role of Laurel. Her movie

HELEN MORGAN

career extended from 1925 to 1931. Before leaving the screen for good, she played the heroine, Emma Krull, in Robert E. Sherwood's *This Is New York*, on Broadway, for thirty-nine performances in 1930. After her personal success as Mary Turner in *Of Thee I Sing*, 1931, and its sequel, *Let 'Em Eat Cake*, 1933, it's surprising that impressionable Hollywood didn't beseech her to return to movies. On February 10, 1935, she married Col. Clarence M. Young, assistant Secretary of Commerce under Hoover and Roosevelt (1929-1933), later vice president of Pan American Airways, and has a son, Timothy. In 1951, she was senior artist-in-residence at Stanford University at its speech and drama department, played the lead in their production of *Biography*, and lectured on the dance. She also conducted a dance therapy course at the Veterans Hospital in Palo Alto, and later in the decade had the lead in a TV drama series.

POLLY MORAN

Born Pauline Therese Moran in Chicago, June 28, 1884, she went to public schools there and St. Patrick's Convent. She claimed to be "the most traveled vaudeville performer in the world," and as a "single" toured America, Europe, and Africa. She made her film debut for Mack Sennett circa 1913, and played in *Sheriff Nell* comedies. After that she returned to the stage, but in 1926, director Tod Browning persuaded her to come back to movies for good, and gave her parts in three Lon Chaney pictures, *Blackbird*, *The Road to Mandalay* and *London After Midnight*, all at MGM. She died January 25, 1952.

HELEN MORGAN

The illustrator James Montgomery Flagg

317

JEAN MUIR

described her as "the composite of all the ruined women in the world." She was the only child of a farmer and a school teacher, Frank and Lulu Riggins, and was born in Danville, Ill., August 2, 1900. When her mother divorced and married Thomas Morgan, Helen took her step-father's name. In Danville, she went to public schools and sang in a church choir. All this time she was studying singing and dancing, and after leaving high school she went to Chicago to go on the stage. Instead, she got a job packing crackers for the National Biscuit Co.; worked in a department store, and as a manicurist. Her first singing job was in a Chicago cabaret. She was noticed by a drama critic, Amy Leslie, who helped the young girl get her start on Broadway. Her first New York job was in the chorus of Ziegfeld's *Sally*, with Marilyn Miller, 1920, and her first singing job was at the Back-stage Club. It was in this little speakeasy, one night in 1922, that she got on top of the grand piano, because the place was so small and crowded that this was the only spot where she could be seen and heard. This gimmick became her trademark. In the musical *Show Boat* she turned a secondary role, the tragic mulatto Julie, into a star part forever associated with her name. She played Julie in revivals many years later on both stage and screen. Through Prohibition days, she was a singer in, and manager of, several speak-easies. She married Maurice Maschke, Jr., son of the Republican Party leader in Cleveland (1933-1935), and Lloyd Johnson, Los Angeles used car dealer, on July 27, 1941. She died shortly before midnight at the Henrotin Hospital, Chicago, October 8, 1941, of cirrhosis of the liver and chronic nephritis, brought on by the alcoholism that had plagued much of her life and career.

318

PATRICIA MORISON

Eileen Patricia Augusta Fraser Morison was born March 19, 1914, in New York, daughter of writer Norman Rainey Morison and his wife, Selena Carson, a theatrical agent. After graduation from Irving High School, she studied at the Art Students League, and for six months was a designer at Russeks Department Store. She then became a model and joined the Neighborhood Players. After a bit in *Victoria Regina* and appearing with Lenore Ulric in *The Road to Paradise* on the old "subway circuit," Miss Morison won her first attention as one of the two young girls in Marc Connelly's *The Two Bouquets*, 1938. She went directly to movies, working through 1948, when she returned to the stage for her biggest triumph in *Kiss Me Kate*, which she played two years and also in London. She took the Gertrude Lawrence role in *The King and I*, with Yul Brynner, on the road in 1954, and toured with the show two years. In 1960, she returned to movies briefly in *Song Without End*. She often works in West Coast musicals.

KAREN MORLEY

She was born Mabel Linton in Ottumwa, Iowa, December 12, 1905, and lived there until she was thirteen, when her family moved to Hollywood. There she went to Hollywood High School and the University of California, leaving school to join the Pasadena Community Players. She began in movies in 1931 at MGM, playing bits in *Never the Twain Shall Meet* and *Politics* before being promoted to leading-lady roles. She quit movies in 1940, she said, because "I was shuttling from studio to studio. There was one hand-wringing part after another." In 1941-1942, she appeared in three short-lived Broadway plays. In 1951, she was called upon to testify before the House Un-American Activities Committee, defended by her attorney, Vito Marcantonio. She ran for the office of Lieutenant-Governor on the ticket of the now defunct American Labor Party, in New York, 1954. Miss Morley was first married to director Charles Vidor (1934), with a son, Michael. She next married actor Lloyd Gough.

JEAN MUIR

Born Jean Muir Fullarton in New York, February 13, 1911, she studied at the Dwight School, Englewood, N. J. As Jean Fullarton she spent three years on the stage, with her first part as a maid in *The Truth Game*, with Ivor Novello, in 1930, on Broadway. She made a personal success as Nadja in *Saint Wench*, winning her a Warners contract. Using the name of Jean Muir for the first time, she started in movies in *The World Changes*, with

Paul Muni. In the late 1930s she returned to the stage for a time, and acted in London in J. B. Priestley's *People at Sea*, 1937. Her last movie was *The Constant Nymph* in 1943.

Miss Muir became the acting profession's cause célèbre when she was listed in *Red Channels*, a privately compiled political directory of who was unsuitable for employment because of "Communist sympathies," in 1950. She was playing Henry Aldrich's mother in *The Aldrich Family* on TV and was promptly dropped from the cast. This all but ruined her career and her private and emotional life, leading to a bout with alcoholism and her divorce from attorney Henry Jaffe, the father of their three children. By 1960 she was "cleared," and allowed to appear once more on television.

ONA MUNSON

She was born in Portland, Ore., June 16, 1906, and went to schools there. At sixteen she first appeared in vaudeville, and at twenty she succeeded Louise Groody as Nanette in *No, No, Nanette* at the Globe Theatre in New York. This made her a star, and later in 1926 she played the lead in *Twinkle, Twinkle*, a musical with Joe E. Brown; the title role in *Manhattan Mary*, with Ed Wynn, 1927; and in *Hold Everything*, with Victor Moore and Bert Lahr, 1928. After her brief movie career in the 1930s, she returned to the stage to play more dramatic roles, including that of Regina in Nazimova's famous revival of *Ghosts* in 1935. Her last movie was *The Red House*, with Edward G. Robinson in 1947, and her last play, a revival of *Kind Lady*, with Helen Gahagan, 1952. Miss Munson was married to actor-director Eddie Buzzell and to Stewart McDonald, before her third marriage to artist and designer Eugene

ONA MUNSON

Berman (they were married in 1949 at the home of Igor Stravinsky in Beverly Hills). Her husband found her dead, of sleeping pills, in their New York apartment on February 11 1955. She had left a note: "This is the only way I know to be free again . . . Please don't follow me."

MAE MURRAY

Miss Murray retained her glamour-star looks for so long that it was hard to believe she made her Broadway debut as long ago as 1906 in *About Town*, with Lew Fields and Edna Wallace Hopper. Of Belgian-Austrian parentage, she was born Marie Adrienne Koenig in Portsmouth, Va., May 7, 1889. After her debut, she appeared in three editions of the *Ziegfeld Follies*—1908, 1909 and 1915. But she was born to be a silent-screen movie star, and she was one from the beginning of her career in 1916 in *To Have and to Hold*. She was fortunate to become the wife of director Robert Z. Leonard, who guided her career as a star at Universal from 1917, and later in the early 1920s, at Paramount and Metro. She is best remembered for *The Merry Widow*, with John Gilbert, directed by Erich von Stroheim, who had epic rows with Miss Murray during production, in 1925. Miss Murray is said to have made a fortune estimated at around $3,000,000, and lost it all in an acrimonious life filled with court fights over salary agreements, damages, bankruptcy, and divorces. She was married to W. N. Schwenker, Jr., a son of a millionaire; Jay O'Brien, then known as the "Beau Brummel of Broadway"; director Robert Z. Leonard; and finally to Prince David Mdivani (1926-1933), and became the mother of a son, Koran. In February 1964, Miss Murray was found wandering, penniless, in the streets of Saint Louis. She died at the Motion Picture Country Home, March 23, 1965.

CARMEL MYERS

Daughter of Rabbi Isadore Myers, she was born in San Francisco, April 9, 1901, and grew up in Los Angeles, where she went to public schools. She started in movies in 1916, became a leading lady to Douglas Fairbanks and Harold Lockwood, and a star at Universal in such items as *A Society Sensation*, *The Gilded Dream* and *Little White Savage*, working through the 1920s with the elite: Rudolph Valentino, Rod La Rocque, John Barrymore, John Gilbert, Milton Sills. Her career officially ended in 1934, but she returned in 1942 for *Lady for a Night*. Miss Myers married I. Kornblum in 1921, attorney Ralph Blum in 1929 (he died in 1950), and A. W. Schwalberg, then president of Paramount Film Distributing Corp., in October 1951. She lives in New York.

ANNA NEAGLE

ANNA NEAGLE

An institution in her own land (she was made a Dame of the British Empire in 1969), Anna Neagle began her unique career as a chorus girl named Marjorie Robertson. She was born at Forest Gate, a London suburb, October 20, 1904, the only daughter of Herbert and Florence Neagle Robertson. After she spent three years in musical choruses in London and New York, and work as a model, Jack Buchanan gave her her first break as his leading lady in *Stand Up and Sing* in 1931, the year she also made her film debut in *Should a Doctor Tell?* Producer Herbert Wilcox put Miss Neagle under contract in 1932, and began to guide her career to the heights it achieved in British film history. They married in 1943. By 1964, Mr. Wilcox's producing organization went into bankruptcy, and Miss Neagle put her London apartment and its contents up for sale to help pay her husband's debts. A year later, their luck returned; Miss Neagle starred in a musical, *Charlie Girl*, which ran for six years in London and Australia and rescued them from bankruptcy.

POLA NEGRI

One of the more interesting of the smouldering, exotic stars of the silents, in both Berlin and Hollywood. Her life has been cluttered with emotional upheavals,

star glamour, titled husbands, unrequited love (Valentino), and political mystery (she made films in Nazi Germany). She was born December 31, 1894, in Yanowa, Poland, and grew up in Warsaw. She made her first movie in 1914 in Poland, and became a great German star under Ernst Lubitsch, working mainly with him from 1918 to 1922. Her American debut was in *Bella Donna* in 1923. Her tempestuous reign at Paramount as a rival to Gloria Swanson (who made most of her films in New York) came to an end in 1928. Her last film was in *The Moon-Spinners* for Walt Disney in 1964. She lives in San Antonio, Texas, as heiress to the fortune of oil millionairess Margo West.

GRETA NISSEN

Born Grethe Ruzt-Nissen in Oslo, Norway, January 30, 1906, she first appeared in ballet at the age of six, studied under Michel Fokine, and toured extensively in Europe. She made her American debut on Broadway in *Beggar on Horseback*, 1924, and later played in Ziegfeld's *No Foolin'* in 1926. Her Hollywood career began with Paramount in 1925, and she appeared with such stars as Adolphe Menjou, Clive Brook, Edward Everett Horton and Ricardo Cortez. Even after *Hell's Angels* proved a debacle for her, Miss Nissen appeared in some fifteen films in both Hollywood and England, the last in 1937. She married actor Weldon Heyburn (né Franks), onetime University of Alabama football star, in March 1932, and got the marriage annulled in April 1936.

MARION NIXON

Born October 20, 1904, in Superior, Wis., she went to school in Minneapolis and worked in a department store there. She started her career by dancing in a stage show prologue in a Minneapolis movie theater, then joined a vaudeville troupe as a chorus girl, touring West to Los Angeles. When the company became stranded, she got a job in a Mack Sennett comedy in 1922, and later became a leading lady in Westerns with Buck Jones and Tom Mix, and in comedies with John Gilbert, Reginald Denny, and Edward Everett Horton. Her movie career ended in 1936. She married Joe Benjamin (1925-1926); Edward Hillman, Jr. (1929); director William Seiter (1934—died 1964); and actor Ben Lyon (1972).

DORIS NOLAN

She was born July 14, 1916, in New York City, and grew up in New Rochelle. She made her stage debut in stock, and her most successful stage appearance was in the wartime comedy *The Doughgirls*, which ran for a year in 1942.

Laurence Olivier and MERLE OBERON

She is married to actor-writer Alexander Knox.

MERLE OBERON

She was born as Estelle Merle O'Brien Thompson, February 19, 1911, in Tasmania, daughter of an English railway official. At the age of seven she moved with her mother to India, where she was enducated in British schools in Bombay and Calcutta. As a teenager she went to London with an uncle, who allowed her to remain there (with a return ticket to Calcutta) to try the movies. Under the name of Queenie O'Brien, she worked as a dance hostess at London's Café de Paris, and for two years played bit roles in movies. She was first known as Merle O'Brien, later magically changed to Merle Oberon. She met producer-director Alexander Korda, then forming his own film company, who gave her a five-year contract and the leading-lady role in *Wedding Rehearsal*, 1932, opposite Roland Young. From 1939 to 1945, she was married to Korda, then to cinematographer Lucien Ballard (1945-1949).

Miss Oberon was most recently married to Italian-born Bruno Pagliai, living in Mexico, where his interests include steel, aluminum mining, publishing, and several estates.

ERIN O'BRIEN-MOORE

Born in Los Angeles, May 2, 1908, Miss O'Brien-Moore trained to be an artist, but went on the stage instead, making her debut in 1926. Perhaps her most famous stage role was Rose Maurrant in *Street Scene*, which she played in both London and New York, 1929-1930. Her 1930s screen career lasted only two years, 1935-1937, but she returned twice in the 1950s, in *Phantom of the Rue Morgue* and *Peyton Place*. She is married to Mark Baron.

UNA O'CONNOR

Her real name was Agnes Teresa Mc-Glade, born in Belfast, October 23, 1880. She studied for the stage at the Abbey Theatre in Dublin, and in 1911 made her debut there as Jessie in Shaw's *The Shewing-up of Blanco Posnet*, a play which took her to New York. She never acted in her native land again, and spent the rest of her career in both London and New York; and after 1932, when she made her Hollywood debut as Ellen Bridges in *Cavalcade*, in the movies. Her last stage and screen appearance was in Agatha Christie's *Witness for the Prosecution*. She died at the Mary Manning Walsh Home, New York, February 4, 1959, after a long illness.

MAUREEN O'HARA

Born Maureen Fitzsimmons in Milltown, a suburb of Dublin, August 17, 1920, she was one of six children of a wholesale hatter in Dublin. One of Maureen's sisters became the actress Sheila Sim. She studied acting with the Abbey Players, but said, "I never got the chance to do anything worthwhile at the Abbey." Charles Laughton is credited for discovering her, and she made her Hollywood film debut at nineteen, in a career that continued fairly steadily until 1966. She has been married three times: to George Brown; Will Price, by whom she had a daughter Bronwyn (born June 30, 1944); and Charles Blair, retired Air Force Brigadier General (1968).

EDNA MAY OLIVER

Although she always seemed virginal (with maternal feelings), Miss Oliver was once married to a D. W. Pratt. Her maiden name was Nutter, and she was born in Boston, November 9, 1883; after studying music, made her debut there at the age of twenty-eight. Five years later, she first appeared on Broadway in *The Master*. The stage didn't make as rich use of her as the screen, but she had good roles as Hannah in Owen Davis' *Icebound*; as one of the *Cradle Snatchers* (along with Mary Boland); and her immortal Parthy Ann Hawks in *Show Boat*, which she also played in movies. Miss Oliver also appeared in eight Paramount silents between 1924 and 1929. Her last film was *Lydia* in 1941. She died on her fifty-ninth birthday in Hollywood in 1942.

BARBARA O'NEIL

Stories about her stressed her aristocratic Irish heritage: she was a descendant of the Kings of Ireland; her father, David O'Neil, was a rich businessman who retired to travel and write poetry; her grandfather O'Neil founded the Artists Guild; she was a cousin of the playwright George O'Neil. She was born in Saint Louis, July 10, 1910. As a child, she traveled abroad with her parents, and learned to speak several languages. She was graduated from Sarah Lawrence College, and introduced to society in 1929.

Along with Henry Fonda, Margaret Sullavan, James Stewart, Joshua Logan and others, she was one of the founders of the University Players, and appeared with them in Falmouth, Mass., and Baltimore. She made her Broadway debut, speaking one line, in *Carrie Nation*, 1933, with Esther Dale, James Stewart, and Joshua Logan. Her appearance in *Ten Million Ghosts*, with Orson Welles, 1936, brought her to the attention of Hollywood, and she made her movie debut in 1937 in *Stella Dallas*. In 1958-1960, she was an artist-in-residence at the University of Denver. She married director Joshua Logan June 18, 1940; they were later divorced.

SALLY O'NEIL

One of 11 children of Judge Thomas Noonan, of Bayonne, N.J., she was born October 23, 1908, as Virginia Louise Concepta Noonan, nicknamed "Chotsie." She was educated at convents in Trenton and in Canada, and was briefly on the stage as a child. Her movie career began at the top, as Mary, one of the three gold-digging chorus girls, in *Sally, Irene and Mary*, with Constance Bennett and Joan Crawford, in 1925, and she was a star in her next, Marshall Neilan's *Mike*, with William Haines, in 1926. She was at MGM until 1928.

When her screen career ended in 1936, she appeared on Broadway, and at the Pasadena Playhouse in DeWitt Bodeen's *Bright Champagne*, based on the life of actress Lotta Crabtree, and also his adaptation of Edith Wharton's *The Bunner Sisters*, with Lenore Ulric. Mr. Bodeen says: "Sally had a surprisingly deep, resonant voice for such a small girl." In 1953, she married S. S. Battles, president of the Midwest Manufacturing Co., Galesburg, Ill. Her death on June 18, 1969, in Galesburg, was caused by a stomach ulcer.

VIVIENNE OSBORNE

Born in Des Moines, Iowa, December 10, 1896, she was an actress from the age of five. On Broadway, her best roles were Climene in *Scaramouche*, with Sidney Blackmer, 1923; the title role in *Aloma of the South Seas*, 1925; and Lady de Winter in Ziegfeld's musical version of *The Three Musketeers*, with Dennis King, 1928. As early as 1920, she made her movie debut in *Over the Hill to the Poorhouse*, the famous old tear-jerker with Mary Carr. After her retirement from films in 1946, she is said to have been a department store saleslady, and died June 10, 1961.

MAUREEN O'SULLIVAN

She was born in Roscommon, Ireland, of a prominent Irish military family, on May 17, 1911, and educated at convents in Dublin and London, and a finishing school in Paris. When she was nineteen, she was discovered by American director Frank Borzage when he was making *Song of My Heart*, with the Irish tenor John McCormack, in Dublin. The company had to go to Hollywood to complete the film, and Maureen's life in America began. On September 12, 1936, she married John Farrow, (Feb. 10, 1906-Jan. 27, 1963), a Catholic writer of ecclesiastical history as well as a Hollywood writer-director-producer. The first of their seven children was born three years later: Michael, then Patrick, Mia, John, Prudence, Stephanie, and Tisa. She still divides her career among movies, television, and the stage.

RAFAELA OTTIANO

The character actress who could make "even winding a clock seem sinister" was born in Venice, March 4, 1894, of Italian-French descent. She grew up in England and in Boston, and later said she acquired a "New England British accent." At eighteen, she started her career in vaudeville on the B. A. Rolfe circuit, toured in plays with Leo Dietrichstein and William Gillette. In 1917, she appeared in a movie, *The Call of Her People*, with Ethel Barrymore, filmed in Jacksonville, Fla. Miss Ottiano's most notable Broadway appearances were as Rita Christiana in Mae West's *Diamond Lil*, 1928, and as Suzette in *Grand Hotel*, 1930. She was the only member of the latter play's cast to appear in the movie of 1932, as Garbo's maid. Her last film was *Adventures of Martin Eden* in 1942, and she died that year on August 18, at her parents' home in East Boston.

MARIA OUSPENSKAYA

Certainly she was one of the great scene-stealers. Her five-minute appearance as the rigid matriach in *Dodsworth* in 1936 was enough to ensure her movie roles for the next 13 years.

Born July 29, 1876 in Tula, Russia, daughter of a lawyer who died when she was thirteen, she went to the Warsaw Conservatory to study singing, and later Adasheff's School of the Drama in Moscow. She began as an actress in the Russian provinces and later joined the Moscow Art Theatre, under Stanislavsky, becoming one of the most distinguished members of the troupe. When the company came to America in 1922 she remained behind, to appear on the Broadway stage. With Richard Boleslavsky, she founded the American Laboratory Theatre to teach the Stanislavsky method, and in 1929 founded the Maria Ouspenskaya School of Dramatic Art in New York and Hollywood. Her last Broadway appearance was in *Outrageous Fortune*, with Elsie Ferguson, in 1943; her last movie, *A Kiss in the Dark*, 1949. She died December 3 of that year from burns suffered while smoking in bed at her Hollywood apartment.

CATHERINE DALE OWEN

In 1925 she was acclaimed as one of the ten most beautiful women in the world. She was born in Louisville, Ky., July 28, 1900, and graduated from Brantwood Hall in Bronxville, N. Y., and the American Academy of Dramatic Arts. At twenty, she made her debut on Broadway in *Little Women*. She had appeared in a silent, *The Forbidden Woman*, with Jetta Goudal, 1927, before making her talkie debut in 1929. Her last movie was *Behind Office Doors*, in 1931. She was married to Milton Davis, Jr., a New York broker, from 1934 to 1937, then to advertising executive Homer P. Metzger. She died of a stroke at Lenox Hill Hospital, September 7, 1965.

ANITA PAGE

Of Spanish descent, she was born Anita Pomares in Murray Hill, Flushing, Long Island, August 4, 1910, daughter of an electrical engineer, Marino Pomares. She went to Washington Irving High School in New York, and started as an extra in movies at the Paramount studios in Astoria. The millionaire Harry K. Thaw, dabbling in show business, gave her a leading role in a Kenilworth production in 1928, but apparently the picture was never released. In any event, her contract was bought by MGM, and Miss Page began her Hollywood career in *Telling the World*, as William Haines' leading lady. She married songwriter Nacio Herb Brown in 1934, then Naval officer Herschel A. House in 1937, upon her retirement from the screen. She lives in Coronado, Calif.

GALE PAGE

Gale Page was born Sally Perkins Rutter in Spokane, Wash., July 23, 1913, the daughter of R. L. Rutter, an attorney, and niece of Sen. Miles Poindexter. Her career began in stock companies in Spokane, Seattle, and Tacoma. She sang with Ted Weems' band, and acted on radio in Chicago in *Today's Children* and *Fibber McGee*. In 1938, she made her movie bow in *Crime School*, and continued until 1941. In 1944, she was on NBC's *Star Playhouse* in New York. Miss Page came back briefly to movies in 1948 and 1949, and again in 1954. She married Fred Treitschler, a Chicago investment banker, and divorced him in 1940. Next, she married Count Aldo Solito de Soltis, a concert pianist and composer, in

1942, and is the mother of Juan Antonio, and twins Giovanni and Francesca.

CECILIA PARKER

She was born April 26, 1905. After a childhood spent in Canada and England, she and her family settled in Hollywood, where she went to Hollywood High School. She started in movies as an extra, became a leading lady in Westerns in 1932, and got her first break as Garbo's young sister in *The Painted Veil*, in 1934. She married actor Robert Baldwin in 1938, and became the mother of a daughter and two sons. The Baldwins live in Ventura, where Mr. Baldwin is a realtor.

JEAN PARKER

Born Mae Green in Deer Lodge, Mont., August 11, 1912, she grew up in California, and was graduated from a Pasadena high school. She made her movie debut in 1932, and her career kept going healthily through 1944. On Broadway, 1946, she appeared in two plays, the Jed Harris production of *Loco*, and as Bonnie (originated by Barbara Stanwyck) in a revival of *Burlesque*, with Bert Lahr. Later, she toured in *Born Yesterday*. After 1950, she again began to appear occasionally in movies. Miss Parker was married to George MacDonald (1936-1940); Douglas Dawson (1941); Curtis Grotter, her manager (1944-1949); and actor Robert Lowery (1951-1957).

HELEN PARRISH

She was born March 12, 1922, in Columbus, Ga., and spent her childhood in Los Angeles, where she went to Fairfax High School. Her brother, Robert Parrish, later became a director. She played the daughter of Babe Ruth in *Babe Comes Home*, in 1927, and was in *Our Gang* comedies for a time. Her movie career continued until 1942. In New York, 1945, she was hostess on *The Hour Glass* television show for two years, before returning to Hollywood to appear regularly on TV. Before her death, she was women's editor of *Panorama Parade*, an early morning show. Miss Parrish married film writer-actor Charles Lang in 1942, divorced 1954. Two years later, she married TV producer John Guedel, who was at her bedside when she died of cancer at Hollywood Presbyterian Hospital, February 22, 1959.

PAT PATERSON

She was born in Bradford, Yorkshire, on April 7, 1911, and appeared in British films before going to Hollywood in 1934. She married Charles Boyer the same year, and retired from the screen in 1939. Their only child, Michael, born December 10, 1943, shot himself in Hollywood in 1965.

GAIL PATRICK

As Margaret LaVelle Fitzpatrick, she was born in Birmingham, Ala., June 20, 1911. After being graduated B. A. from Howard College in 1932, she became assistant dean of women there, before her screen debut at Paramount in 1933. Her first husband was Robert Cobb, owner of the Brown Derby Restaurant (1936-1940); her second, Arnold White (1944-1946); and third, TV producer Thomas Cornwall Jackson (1947—divorced 1969). Miss Patrick's movie career ended in 1946, and she herself went into TV as a producer, most notably of the successful *Perry Mason* series with Raymond Burr.

ELIZABETH PATTERSON

Miss Patterson was born in Savannah, Tenn., November 22, 1875, daughter of Judge E. D. Patterson, and educated at Martin College, Pulaski, Tenn., and Columbia Institute in Columbia, Tenn. In defiance of her parents, she announced she was going on the stage, and with an inheritance from her grandfather, went to Chicago to attend a drama school. There she joined Ben Greet's touring Shakespearean players, traveling with them three seasons and playing twenty-three roles. Next came roles with the Washington Square Players in New York, and with Stuart Walker's stock companies in Cincinnati and Indianapolis, for several seasons. Booth Tarkington saw her in the latter city, and recommended her for his play *Intimate Strangers*, to be produced in New York; at the age of forty-six, she made her Broadway bow, with Billie Burke as its star. Thereafter, she appeared regularly in character roles on Broadway, in the movies, and on television. Miss Patterson was living in a Hollywood hotel when she became ill, and was taken to Good Samaritan Hospital, where she died January 31, 1966.

JOAN PEERS

She was born in Chicago, August 19, 1911, daughter of an actor, Frank Peers. She went to school in both Los Angeles and Chicago, and married businessman Christy Allen. As a child, she performed as a dancer with the Chicago Symphony Orchestra, toured with Guy Bates Post in *The Masquerader*, and was an extra in Mary Pickford's *Rosita*. Miss Peers' adult screen career lasted only from 1929 to 1931.

BARBARA PEPPER

Daughter of a manager of the Astor Hotel, New York, she was born May 31, 1912, and began her career in *George White's Scandals* and *Ziegfeld Follies of 1931*, when she was discovered by Eddie Cantor. The following year, she made her movie debut in Cantor's *Roman Scandals*, and in 1934 had a leading role in King Vidor's *Our Daily Bread*. After her husband, actor Craig Reynolds', death in an auto accident, 1949, she worked infrequently. Her last screen bit was as a street lady who danced on a table with Stanley Holloway in *My Fair Lady*, 1964. She died of a coronary in Panorama City, Calif., July 18, 1969.

DOROTHY PETERSON

This handsome Nordic woman, whose screen career lasted from 1930 through 1947, was born Bergetta Peterson, in Hector, Minn., and went to school in Chicago and at Columbia University, New York. When appearing on Broadway in a murder mystery, *Subway Express*, in 1929 (with Helen Mack, Barton MacLane, Edward Ellis also in the cast), she was given a screen test in Astoria, leading to her movie debut in *Mothers Cry*. In the 1950s, she appeared in television, and off-Broadway in the 1960s.

MARY PICKFORD

It is unfortunate that this great star did not find a script that would establish her in talking pictures. She had entered movies in 1909 as a trained stage actress, and in 1933, twenty-five years and over 200 films later, she retired. From the beginning she had helped to write film history.

She was born Gladys Smith on April 9, 1893, in Toronto, and made her stage debut in 1898 as Cissy Denver in *The Silver King*. She married three actors: Owen Moore (1911-1920), Douglas Fairbanks (1920-1935), and Charles "Buddy" Rogers (1937). After her retirement, Miss Pickford worked hard for many causes, but the closest to her was the well-being of actors, through the Motion Picture Relief Fund and the Motion Picture Country House.

NOVA PILBEAM

She was born in Wimbledon, England, November 15, 1919, daughter of Arthur Pilbeam, and went to school there and at Blackheath. She studied for the stage under Gertrude Burnett, and made her debut at the Savoy, London, as Marigold in *Toad of Toad Hall* in 1931. She made her movie debut in 1934. Between movies, she continued on the stage, playing Peter Pan twice (in 1935 and 1938), and with the Old Vic. She married twice: film director Penrose Tennyson, great-grandson to the poet, in 1939 (he was killed in action in 1941); and Alexander Whyte.

ZASU PITTS

She got her name ZaSu from combining the syllables of the names of two of her father's sisters: Eliza and Susan. She was born in Parsons, Kansas, January 3, 1898, and moved with her family to Santa Cruz, Calif., as a child, where she attended public schools. Her first screen role, in 1917, was with Mary Pickford in *The Little American*, and her last, as a telephone operator in *It's a Mad, Mad, Mad, Mad World* in 1963. She married Tom Gallery, a leading man (later head of NBC-sports) in 1921 and divorced him in 1926. In 1933, she married John E. Woodall, a Los Angeles businessman and former tennis champion. She died of cancer at Good Samaritan Hospital, Los Angeles, June 7, 1963, survived by her husband, a daughter, Mrs. Ann Gallery Reynolds, and an adopted son, Don Mike Gallery, the son of actress Barbara Lamarr.

LOUISE PLATT

She was twenty-three when she made her movie debut in *I Met My Love Again* in 1938. Miss Platt was born in Stamford, Conn., August 3, 1915, daughter of Lt. Commander Daniel Louis Platt, and went to schools in New York, Manila, and Hong Kong. She acted on Broadway in *A Room in Red and White*, *Spring Dance, Promise*, and, in 1941, alternated with her sister Jean in playing Belinda in *Johnny Belinda*, succceeding Helen Craig. Her last movie was *Street of Chance*, 1942. She married director Stanley Gould, and producer Jed Harris (divorced 1944). In 1948, she played Mary Boleyn in *Anne of a Thousand Days*, with Rex Harrison, and in 1949 acted in Jed Harris's production of *The Traitor*, with Lee Tracy.

LILY PONS

Probably the most chic of the opera stars, certainly one of the most durable (thirty years at the Metropolitan Opera House, 280 performances), Miss Pons was born at Cannes, April 12, 1898, daughter of French-Italian parents. Her father was a violinist, her mother a singer, and both Lily and her two sisters are pianists. Miss Pons studied voice under Alberti de Gerostiaga, and made her debut in *Lakme* at the Mulhouse Municipal Opera in France, 1928. By 1931, she was ready for the Metropolitan, and made her bow in the coloratura role of *Lucia di Lammermoor* in January 1931. Her sensational debut still echoes in operatic history; after her "mad scene," she took sixteen curtain calls.

Miss Pons was first married, 1923, to August Mesritz, who had encouraged her to pursue singing as a career, instead of

the piano. They divorced in 1933. In 1938, she married conductor Andre Kostelanetz, with whom she often appeared in concert. After their divorce twenty years later, she did not remarry. She has homes in Dallas and Palm Springs. A town in Maryland was named Lilypons in her honor.

She retired in 1962, but made a triumphant "surprise" appearance at Philharmonic Hall in New York on May 31, 1972.

ELEANOR POWELL

Miss Powell was born in Springfield, Mass., November 21, 1912, and studied dancing from childhood. At the age of thirteen, she made her debut in a Gus Edwards show at the Ritz Grill in Atlantic City. On Broadway she appeared in *Follow Thru*, 1929, *Fine and Dandy*, 1931, and *Hot Cha!* 1932, and in night clubs. In 1935, she danced in her first movie. In 1943, she married actor Glenn Ford, then in the Marine Corps, and became the mother of their child, Peter, now also an actor. Her son persuaded her to make a comeback in 1961 and, in a 55-minute act assisted by four male dancers, she made a sensation at the Latin Quarter in New York and the Sahara in Las Vegas. Then Miss Powell (divorced from Ford in 1959) returned to her church work, as a member of a religious group called the Symposium.

MARIE PREVOST

Marie Prevost had a puckish personality and a crooked, elfish smile that curled at one end, and was a good frothy light comedienne, as director Ernst Lubitsch, fresh from UFA in Berlin, discovered when he directed her in *The Marriage Circle* in 1924. Her real name was Marie Bickford Dunn, born in Sarnia, Ontario, November 8, 1898. She went to school at the Laurette Sisters' School in Denver, and St. Mary's Convent and Manual Arts High School in Los Angeles. Mack Sennett made her one of his bathing beauties in 1917, and she worked from that time on in pictures. In the 1920s, she was a star in films at Universal, Warners, and Pathé. She married twice: H. C. Gerke (1918-1923) and actor Kenneth Harlan (1923-1927). At the death of her mother in an automobile accident, Miss Prevost took to drinking, lost her figure, and found jobs scarce. On January 23, 1937, she was found dead in a cheap Hollywood rooming house, an empty whisky bottle on the dresser.

AILEEN PRINGLE

She was born July 23, 1895, in San Francisco, daughter of George W. Bisbee, was educated there, and in London and

Paris. While in London, she married Sir Charles Pringle, later Governor General of the Bahamas, with whom she quarreled when she decided to go on the stage in London. She made her debut in *The Bracelet* in 1915, and acted on Broadway in *The Green Goddess*, with George Arliss. In 1920, she made her first film, *Honor Bound*, with Frank Mayo, Dagmar Godowsky, and Rudolph Valentino, shot at Fort Lauderdale, Florida. Then she made her way to Hollywood, where through the 1920s, she worked chiefly at MGM. Elinor Glyn chose her for two of her "daring" stories, *Three Weeks*, with Conrad Nagel, 1924, and *His Hour*, with John Gilbert the same year. She made her last movie in 1939.

After her long separation and final divorce from her first husband, she married, briefly, novelist James M. Cain (*The Postman Always Rings Twice*). She lives in New York.

JUANITA QUIGLEY

A Hollywood-born child (June 24, 1931), she was the daughter of Wayne and Martha Quigley, and made her baby bow at two and a half in a short, *Gimme My Quarter Back*. In 1944, she made three final movies, most notably as Elizabeth Taylor's sister, Marvolia Brown, in *National Velvet*.

LUISE RAINER

Viennese-born (January 12, 1910) and educated, she made her stage debut in Dusseldorf, Germany, in 1928, and for a time was a member of Max Reinhardt's company in Berlin. When she first came to the United States, she studied English under Constance Collier before making her screen debut in 1935 in *Escapade*. After her days at MGM were over, she appeared in London at the Shaftesbury Theatre in *Behold the Bride* in 1939, and on Broadway in Barrie's *A Kiss for Cinderella*, with Ralph Forbes, at the Music Box, 1942. She made only one additional Hollywood film, an anti-Nazi melodrama, *Hostages*, in 1943, for Paramount. She was married to playwright Clifford Odets from 1937 to 1940, then, in 1945, to publisher Robert Knittel, and lives in London.

JESSIE RALPH

She was the thirteenth child of Capt. James C. Chambers, a seafaring man of Gloucester, Mass., and was born there November 5, 1864. At the age of sixteen, she made her stage debut in Boston, and was on the stage for over forty years. She cited as one of her most notable roles that of the Nurse to Jane Cowl's Juliet, on Broadway, 1923. Ten years later, she was brought to the movies to re-enact her stage role of Aunt Minnie in *Child of Manhattan*, with Nancy Carroll, and remained in Hollywood from that time on, as one of the movies' most popular character actresses. She married a Saint Louis actor, William Patton, who died many years before her own death. After an operation that required the amputation of one of her legs, she returned to her birthplace to live with a nephew, Carleton H. Parsons, and died three years later, May 30, 1944.

ESTHER RALSTON

She was born in Bar Harbor, Maine, September 17, 1902, and as "Baby Esther" traveled with her parents, Harry and May Ralston, in a family act that presented Shakespearean and other classic dramatics in vaudeville and Chautauqua for a decade. By 1916, the Ralstons settled in Southern California, where Esther almost immediately went into movies as a dancer, expert horseback rider, and blonde beauty. In 1920, she played the heroine in *Huckleberry Finn*, and Rose Maylie in *Oliver Twist*, with Jackie Coogan in 1922, but it wasn't until she was the saintly Mrs. Darling in *Peter Pan* in 1924 that her career was really launched. She stayed at Paramount until 1930, as a leading lady, and as a star. She made her last movie in 1941. She married and divorced three times: actor-agent George Webb (1925-1933); singer Will Morgan (1934-1938); newspaper man Ted Lloyd (1939-1954). Miss Ralston has played in radio soap opera, toured the summer theaters, worked at B. Altman's in Manhasset (1956-1961) and appeared on television. She became vice-president of the Kerr Talent Agency in New York.

MARJORIE RAMBEAU

The only child of a French-born businessman, Marcel Rambeau, and his wife, Dr. Lillian Kindleberger Rambeau, one of the first woman physicians in the West, she was born July 15, 1889, in San Francisco. After her parents separated, Marjorie went with her mother to Alaska during the Gold Rush of 1899 to set up a clinic for miners, traders, and Eskimos. On returning to California, Marjorie went to dancing school, and, in 1901 made her stage debut at the Alcazar Theatre. She spent many years in stock companies before her Broadway debut in 1913 in *Kick In*, with Willard Mack—a role that made her a Broadway star and got her her first husband, Mr. Mack. As a darkly attractive young woman, she appeared in *Cheating Cheaters*, *Daddy's Gone A-Hunting*, as Rosalind in *As You Like It*, among others, until 1926. She had appeared in movies as early as 1916 in *The Dazzling Miss Davison* before her

talking picture debut in 1930 in *Her Man*. In 1940, she was nominated for an Oscar for *Primrose Path*, and again in 1953 for *Torch Song*. After her marriage to Willard Mack ended in divorce, she married and divorced actor Hugh Dillman. She was left a widow by her third husband, Francis A. Gudger, a former vice president at the Goldwyn Studios. After her retirement in 1957, she lived in Palm Springs and died at her home there, July 7, 1970.

MARTHA RAYE

Martha Raye, as a true professional, literally knocked herself out all her life giving audience-satisfying performances in movies, on the stage, on TV, and entertaining troops in Vietnam. Her real name was Maggie Teresa O'Reed, born in a Butte, Mont., charity ward, August 22, 1916, while her parents, the vaudeville team of Reed & Hooper, were on tour. She traveled with her family on their endless migrations around the country, making her debut at three, clad in home-made overalls, singing "I Wish I Could Shimmy Like My Sister Kate." At thirteen, she was a specialty singer with Paul Ash's orchestra in New York and Chicago, and played on Broadway in *Earl Carroll's Sketch Book*, and Lew Brown's *Calling All Stars*, with Gertrude Niesen and Jack Whiting, in 1934. Her movie career went steadily through 1941, then came war work. Perhaps the triumph of her movie career was as Charlie Chaplin's indestructible wife in *Monsieur Verdoux*, in 1947. Her last movie appearance was with Doris Day in *Jumbo* in 1962. She has been married and divorced six times: make-up man Bud Westmore (three months in 1937); composer David Rose (1938); hotel manager Neal Lang (1941); dancer Nick Condos (1944-1953), with whom she ran the Five O'Clock Club in Miami and father to her only child, Melodye; dancer Edward Begley (1954); and a Westport, Conn., policeman, Robert O'Shea, who sued *her* for $100,000 at their divorce in 1959. Miss Raye made the first of her several trips to Vietnam in 1963.

DOROTHY REVIER

Born in San Francisco as Doris Velegra, April 18, 1904, she was the daughter of a musician and the niece of an opera singer. After leaving Oakland High School, she danced as a soloist at Tait's Café in San Francisco. Her screen debut was in 1922. Specializing in blonde vamps, she played in such movies as *The Siren*, *The Tigress*, and *Beware of Blondes*, as well as Milady de Winter in Douglas Fairbanks' *The Iron Mask* in 1929. She ended her career in *The Cowboy and the Kid*, with Buck Jones, in 1936.

FLORENCE RICE

Throughout her career, she must have wearied of everybody feeling obliged to identify her as "the daughter of the popular sports writer Grantland Rice" whenever her name was mentioned, because she had a respectable career all her own. She was born in Cleveland, February 14, 1907, and was graduated from the Dwight High School, Englewood, N. J. Miss Rice said: "I had absolutely no training whatever for the stage. Ring Lardner gave me a bit part in *June Moon* because he knew my father." (This was in the revival of that comedy in 1931.) She also appeared on Broadway in *Once in a Lifetime*, and in a good role in *She Loves Me Not* for a long run in 1933-1934, that brought her to the attention of Hollywood. Her movie debut was in *The Best Man Wins*, 1935. In February 1945, she briefly replaced Betty Field as Sally Middleton in *The Voice of the Turtle* during its long Broadway run. When she was nineteen, she married a New York broker, Sydney A. Smith, and divorced him in 1931. Her next husband was Robert Wilcox, screen actor, in 1939, and then Frederick Butler, a La Jolla, Calif., business man, in 1946. She died of lung cancer in Honolulu on February 23, 1974.

IRENE RICH

Born Irene Luther in Buffalo, October 13, 1891, she was educated at St. Margaret's School for Girls there. While still young, she and her family moved to the West Coast. She married Elvo Deffenbaugh in 1909, by whom she had a daughter, Frances Luther Rich, born January 9, 1910, a sculptor. Her second husband was Charles H. Rich (1912), by whom she had a second daughter, Jane Luther Rich, born December 13, 1916, later an actress. Before she started her screen career as an extra in Mary Pickford's *Stella Maris* in 1918, she sold real estate, but thereafter worked steadily in movies until 1932. In 1933, she started her national radio show, *Dear John*, sponsored by Welch's Grape Juice, and appeared for over a decade. Miss Rich also acted on Broadway in a revival of *Seven Keys to Baldpate*, with George M. Cohan, 1935, and, more triumphantly, as the President of the United States, Lucille Thompson Wellington, in *As the Girls Go*, with Bobby Clark, at the Winter Garden, 1948. With her final husband, George Henry Clifford, a wealthy New York businessman, whom she married in 1950, she lives at the Hope Ranch in Santa Barbara, Calif.

ELIZABETH RISDON

She chalked up one of the longest career listings on record on stage and

MAY ROBSON

screen both in England and the United States. She was born in London, April 26, 1887, and made her stage debut in 1910. In the early silent films of England, she was a star from 1913 to 1917, and she married her American film director, George Loane Tucker (chiefly remembered for his silent, *The Miracle Man*, with Lon Chaney and Betty Compson), who died in 1921. After 1917, Miss Risdon lived and worked entirely in America, and became a Theatre Guild actress. She made her Hollywood debut in 1935, and worked regularly thereafter until 1952. Her second husband was Brandon Evans, whom she married in 1926. She died in Santa Monica, December 20, 1958.

LYDA ROBERTI

A sort of platinum blonde Lupe Velez (but more good-humored in her uninhibited pursuit of men), Lyda Roberti, one of two daughters of a famous Continental circus clown, was born in Warsaw, Poland, May 20, 1906. She spent her early years touring Europe and Asia in circuses as a trapeze artist. Once, when stranded, she worked as a waitress in a Shanghai café. Her first appearance in the United States was in vaudeville in Brooklyn; and with her sister Manya, she toured the country. She made her bow as a musical comedy comedienne as Fanny in *You Said It*, with Lou Holtz, on Broadway in 1931. She started to make movies in 1932 in *Dancers in the Dark*. First married to R. A. Golden, she married Bud Ernst in 1935. According to her friend and co-star, Patsy Kelly, she died instantly of a heart attack while bending over to tie a shoelace, March 12, 1938, in Hollywood.

BEVERLY ROBERTS

Born in New York, May 19, 1914, she went to Girls' High School, and Lockwood Academy in London. She made her debut on an acting scholarship, with Eva Le Gallienne's Civic Repertory Co., and after her film career was over, appeared with Miss Le Gallienne for a year in the hit *Uncle Harry*, in 1942. Her screen career lasted from 1936 through 1939. She is now executive head of Theatre Authority in New York, a union clearing house protecting actors who appear in benefits across the country from getting bilked.

FLORA ROBSON

Now a Dame of the British Empire, she was born March 28, 1902, in South Shields, Durham, and studied at the Royal Academy of Dramatic Arts. At nineteen, she made her debut as Queen Margaret in *Will Shakespeare*. During her long stage career, she appeared happily on Broadway in *Ladies in Retirement*, 1940, *The Damask Cheek*, 1942, *Macbeth*, 1948, and *Black Chiffon*, 1950. She is still working in films and plays.

MAY ROBSON

The marvelously raspy Miss Robson, whose horse-sense withered all cant and hypocrisy, was born in Melbourne, Australia, one of the four children of a British Navy captain, on April 19, 1858. Her name was Mary Jeanette Robison. She was educated at the Sacred Heart Convent, Highgate, London, and in Brussels and Paris. At sixteen, she ran away from home to marry Charles Livingston Gore, aged eighteen, and the young couple settled in Fort Worth, Texas, to try ranching. After many struggling years of failure, they went to New York, where her husband died, leaving her three small children. She tried to make a living by teaching art and in embroidering. (Two of her children, a boy and a girl, died of diphtheria and scarlet fever.) On an impulse, when passing a theatrical agency, she went in to apply for a job, and began her career in 1884, at twenty-six, as an ingenue, Tilly, in *The Hoop of Gold*. Her long stage career followed—and she acted in a Los Angeles production of *Kind Lady* over fifty years later. In her youth, she acted in Shakespeare, was a member of Charles Frohman's famous Empire Theatre Company (1893-1896), but she didn't hit her stride as a character star until her triumph in *The Rejuvenation of Aunt Mary* in 1907, a role she played off and on for three years, and in a 1927 silent film. As early as 1915, she appeared in movies, in *How Molly Made Good*. Between 1926 and 1927, she made five silents. Miss Robson's last movie was

Joan of Paris, 1942. Her second husband was Dr. A. H. Brown. She died October 20, 1942.

GINGER ROGERS

She was born Virginia Katherine McMath in Independence, Mo., July 16, 1911. During her childhood, her parents, Eddins and Lela Owens McMath, became estranged, and her father twice "kidnaped" Virginia away from her mother. He died when Virginia was eleven. In the years that followed, mother and daughter traveled to Kansas City, Washington, Fort Worth, and Galveston (where Mrs. Rogers had married and divorced insurance-man John Logan Rogers). Mrs. Rogers worked variously as newspaper writer, publicist, theatre critic, and playwright. Her daughter appeared in one of her plays, *The Death of St. Dennis*, while a student at Fort Worth's Central High School. In 1925, Ginger won a Charleston contest and toured a theatre-circuit in Texas and Oklahoma, with two runners-up, as "Ginger and Her Redheads." For the next three years, she toured in vaudeville in the Midwest and South, with her mother as manager. At last she got to New York as a featured singer with Paul Ash and his orchestra in 1929. Success came fast, with George Gershwin's *Girl*

GINGER ROGERS and Fred Astaire

325

Crazy in 1930. That same year, she made her first movie. In 1928, at seventeen, she married a childhood sweetheart, Jack Pepper, a marriage that lasted ten months. Next came actor Lew Ayres in 1934, separated 1936, divorced 1940. She then married actor Jack Briggs in 1943, divorced 1949; and then French actor Jacques Bergerac (1953-1957). Her present estranged husband is actor William Marshall (1961). Since the fall of 1971, Miss Rogers has been fashion consultant to the J. C. Penney chain.

SHIRLEY ROSS

Her real name is Bernice Gaunt; she was born in Omaha, January 7, 1914, and studied at U.C.L.A. In 1934-1935, she was the featured singer with Gus Arnheim's band at the Beverly Wilshire and at the St. Francis Hotel. She made her debut in a small role in Jean Harlow's *Bombshell* in 1933; her last film was *A Song for Miss Julie* in 1945. She married agent Ken Dolan in 1938, who died in 1951. She is the mother of two sons. Her present husband is Edward Blum.

LILLIAN ROTH

In her autobiography, *I'll Cry Tomorrow*, she recited a painful chronicle of her life as a tormented alcoholic. She was born Lillian Rutstein in Boston, December 13, 1910, one of two daughters of stagestruck parents, who put Lillian and her sister Ann in movies playing bits at the old studios in Fort Lee, N. J., in 1916, and later as singers and dancers in vaudeville. Ann escaped show business for a happy marriage; but Lillian acted on Broadway in plays and musicals, including *Artists and Models*, Texas Guinan's *Padlocks of 1927*, Earl Carroll's *Vanities*, until resuming her movie career in 1929 in *Illusion*. Her first marriage was to William C. Scott, a twenty-two-year-old flying student and son of a Pittsburgh lumber magnate, in April 1931. They were divorced the following year. Her second husband was Judge Benjamin Shalleck, a Mayor Jimmy Walker appointee. They were married in 1933 and divorced in 1939. In September 1940, she married Eugene Wiener, who had once broken her jaw in three places, and had the marriage annulled in July 1941. By 1947, she became a member of Alcoholics Anonymous and met T. Burt McGuire, Jr., of the Social Register (and the Funk & Wagnalls publishing fortune), whom she married. They had a stormy divorce in 1963. Her other husbands, in no particular chronological order, have been David Lyons; Willie Richards, an Air Force cadet; Edward Goldman; and Mark Harris.

326

ROSALIND RUSSELL

She was born in Waterbury, Conn., June 4, 1907, one of seven children of James E. Russell, a trial lawyer, and his wife Clara McKnight; and was educated at Marymount College, Tarrytown, N. Y., and the American Academy of Dramatic Arts. She got her start in a stock company at Saranac Lake, N. Y., and in the fall of 1929 played a season with E. E. Clive's stock company at the Copley Theatre, Boston. In 1930, she made her Broadway debut in the last *Garrick Gaieties*. Her stage career went on unexcitingly between stock companies and flop plays, before she went to Hollywood for a screen test by Universal. While waiting for them to make up their mind, she made a test for MGM and was given a contract as a waiting-in-the-wings replacement for Myrna Loy, who was then being difficult with Louis B. Mayer about her salary. Miss Russell made her debut in 1934 in a Loy film, *Evelyn Prentice*. In 1941, she married producer Frederick Brisson, son of the dimpled Danish matinee idol, Carl Brisson, and is the mother of one son, Lance, born May 7, 1943, now a journalist.

ANN RUTHERFORD

Born in Toronto, November 2, 1917, she is the daughter of John Rutherford (known on the stage as John Guilberti), onetime tenor with the Metropolitan Opera Co., and his wife, a cousin of the actor Richard Mansfield. Ann first appeared with her parents in stock at five, and later played roles "from babies to old women" in Los Angeles radio shows. Her first movie was in 1935. She will always be remembered as Andy Hardy's jealous Polly Benedict, but another highlight of her career was as giddy Lydia Bennet, who disgraced her hysterical mother and unmarried sisters by running off with a caddish army officer in *Pride and Prejudice*. She was first married to David May of the department store family from 1942 to 1953, is now married to producer William Dozier, and lives in Beverly Hills.

DOROTHY SEBASTIAN

Born in Birmingham, Ala., April 26, 1903, of a family of clergymen and missionaries, she studied at the University of Alabama, before going to New York to become a model and a chorus girl in George White's *Scandals*, in 1924. When the show went to Los Angeles, she stayed there and made her movie debut in 1925 in *Sackcloth and Scarlet*, with Alice Terry. She was married to William ("Hopalong Cassidy") Boyd—from 1930 to 1936, and later to aircraft technician Herman Shapiro. She died after a long illness at the Motion Picture Country House, April 9, 1957.

VIVIENNE SEGAL

Daughter of Dr. Bernard Segal, she was born April 19, 1897, in Philadelphia, and from girlhood studied voice and appeared

ROSALIND RUSSELL and Robert Montgomery

in amateur theatricals with the Philadelphia Operatic Society. She made her Broadway debut in *The Blue Paradise*, produced by the Shuberts in 1915, and stayed in this show until 1917. During her long career as a Broadway prima donna, she appeared in such hits as *Ziegfeld Follies of 1924*; *The Desert Song*; as Constance in Ziegfeld's *The Three Musketeers*; and *The Chocolate Soldier*. After her movie career, she continued to have a prosperous one on Broadway, particularly as Countess Peggy Palaffi in *I Married an Angel*, 1938; the predatory Vera Simpson in *Pal Joey*, 1940 (and its revival); and Queen Morgan le Fay in a revival of *A Connecticut Yankee*, 1943. She was the third of the four wives of actor Robert Ames from 1923 to 1926, and later married, and was separated from, TV executive Hubbell Robinson, Jr. She lives in Hollywood.

PEGGY SHANNON

Born in Pine Bluff, Ark., January 10, 1907, she went to Sacred Heart Convent there. Her parents divorced when she was 15, and Peggy supported her mother, her younger sister, and herself from then on. After studying dancing with Ned Wayburn in New York, she began as a chorus girl in *Ziegfeld Follies of 1923*, with Fanny Brice, at the New Amsterdam, and again in 1924, with Will Rogers, Ann Pennington, and Imogene Wilson (Mary Nolan), followed by two editions of Earl Carroll's *Vanities*. She made her acting debut in *What Ann Brought Home* in 1927, with Mayo Methot as Ann. She continued on Broadway until 1931, when she first went into movies. Her last movie was in 1940, *House Across the Bay*. Miss Shannon was first married to actor Allan Davis. After her divorce, she married motion picture cameraman Albert G. Roberts in October 1940. Six months later, May 11, 1941, after returning from a fishing trip, he found his wife dead, sitting at a table, with an empty glass and a burned out cigaret near her hand. Death was attributed to a liver ailment caused by alcoholism.

WINI SHAW

Wini Shaw, of Hawaiian descent, was born in San Francisco as Winifred Lei Momi (translated as "wreath of pearls"), February 25, 1910. She was the youngest of thirteen children in a show-business family. As a child of eleven, she started traveling with the family act on nationwide vaudeville circuits. Later, as a "single," she sang with Phil Baker in the Little Club, New York; then appeared in Broadway musicals *Rain or Shine*, *Simple Simon* and *Ziegfeld Follies of 1931*; and later returned to night clubs. In 1934 she made her first movie, *Three on a Honeymoon*, at Fox, and Warners signed her to be a sort of studio contract singer, beginning with *Sweet Adeline*, with Irene Dunne. Married at fifteen to Leo Cummins, and widowed at twenty-five, she is the mother of three children. She subsequently married Frederick Vosberg, and, since 1956, New York theatre treasurer Bill O'Malley, with whom she lives in Sunnyside, Long Island.

NORMA SHEARER

The imperial Miss Shearer was born August 10, 1900, in Montreal, one of the three children of Andrew Shearer, a Scot, and his English wife, Edith Fisher. She grew up in Westmount, a suburb, where she attended high school for two years. During the depression of 1920, Mrs. Shearer and her two daughters and son went to New York to look for work, and rented a $7.50-a-week room at 57th Street and 8th Avenue. Norma found a job selling sheet music, and played the piano in a small 8th Avenue movie theater. She also earned $5 a day sitting for artists James Montgomery Flagg and Charles Dana Gibson, and became the "Miss Lotta Miles" of the Springfield Tire ads. She worked as an extra in D. W. Griffith's *Way Down East*; in *The Restless Sex*, with Marion Davies; and in *The Flapper*, with Olive Thomas. She began to get bigger roles, and one of them, as a clergyman's daughter in *The Stealers*, in 1922, attracted the attention of Irving Thalberg, then working for Carl Laemmle at Universal. When signed as chief of production for Louis B. Mayer, Thalberg gave Norma a five-year contract at $110 a week. She arrived in California early in 1923, with her mother and sister, and began her long Hollywood career that ended with her retirement in 1942. She did not make her first MGM film until 1924, but remained with the company from that time on. When she married Thalberg in 1927, she was already a star. When her husband died in 1936, he left her $8,000,000 and an iron-clad contract. After Miss Shearer retired, she married ski instructor Martin Arrouge, some twenty years her junior. Since then, they have lived in Hollywood and Squaw Valley.

ANN SHERIDAN

She was a unique product of Hollywood—a surprised beauty contest winner who hadn't planned to be an actress, and yet, when pushed around, fought her way to the top as an original and individual screen personality. She was a forthright, hearty redhead, with few pretensions and no dishonesty, and a fighter to the end. As Clara Lou Sheridan, she was born in Denton, Texas, February 21, 1915, youngest of four girls and a boy to a mechanic, G. W. Sheridan, and his wife Lula Warren. While she was attending North Texas State Teachers' College, her sister Kitty submitted a photograph of her to a "Search for Beauty" contest being run by Paramount Pictures. Clara Lou, then seventeen, was one of the six winners, was willy-nilly given a Paramount contract, and dropped after eighteen months. Rather than admit defeat, she stayed on in Hollywood and, in 1934, moved over to Warner Bros. at $75 a week. Through the rest of the 1930s, she went through the Warners mill, and didn't get her first really good role—that of Randy Monaghan in *Kings Row*—until she went on suspension in her first major act of rebellion. From then on, she was treated as a star, and her career sailed through the 1950s. Her first two marriages, to actors Edward Norris (1936-1943) and George Brent (1942-1943), ended in divorce. She then had a long romance with public-relations man Steve Hannagan, whom she couldn't marry for religious reasons (he died in 1953). At the time of her own death, from cancer, January 21, 1967, she was the star of a TV series, *Pistols 'n' Petticoats*, and had recently married actor Scott McKay.

ANNE SHIRLEY

As Dawn O'Day (her real name was even more theatrical: Dawn Evelyeen Paris), she appeared in many silent films, including Pola Negri's *The Spanish Dancer* in 1923. She changed her name in 1923 to Anne Shirley. She was born in New York, April 17, 1918, and went to Lawlor Professional School. Her husbands include actor John Payne, by whom she had a daughter, Julie; writer-producer Adrian Scott; and writer Charles Lederer. Her last film was *Murder, My Sweet*, with Dick Powell, produced in 1944.

ANN SHOEMAKER

Born of a seafaring family in Brooklyn, January 10, 1891, she was the daughter of Capt. Charles Shoemaker, Chief of the U. S. Revenue Cutter Service (later the Coast Guard) and sister to Rear Admiral W. R. Shoemaker. She grew up in Washington and on her father's farm in Woodstock, Va. The first member of her family to go on the stage, she made her debut with the Keith Stock Co. in Philadelphia, and her Broadway debut in a small role in David Belasco's production, *Nobody's Widow*, with Blanche Bates in 1910. Thereafter, she appeared in stock, vaudeville, and in many Broadway plays, including Eugene O'Neill's *The Great God Brown*, *The Noose*, and more recently, *The Bad Seed* and as Sara Delano Roosevelt in *Sunrise at Campobello* (a role she also played on the screen). In 1931, she went to Hollywood with her husband, the British actor Henry Stephenson, and appeared regularly in movies.

SYLVIA SIDNEY

She was born Sophia Kosow, the only child of Victor Kosow and his wife Rebecca Saperstein, Russian immigrants, in New York, August 8, 1910, and, while still a child, she was adopted by her mother's second husband, Dr. Sigmund Sidney, a dental surgeon. In 1925 she joined the Theatre Guild School, and made her Broadway debut in the starring role of the school's graduation play, *Prunella*. This led to ingenue roles in Broadway plays and stock engagements in Denver and Rochester. Her first screen role was as a witness in a courtroom trial, in *Thru Different Eyes*, but, dissatisfied, she returned to Broadway to play Dot in *Bad Girl* in 1930. Her hit in that role got her a Paramount starring contract. In 1937, she returned to Broadway for the Theatre Guild's *To Quito and Back*, and for the Group Theatre's *The Gentle People*, 1939. In the 1940s and 1950s, Miss Sidney made eight more films. She continues to appear on the stage and on television. Her three husbands, all divorced, were publisher Bennett Cerf for a few months in 1935, actor Luther Adler (1939-1947), by whom she had a son Jody, and agent Carlton Alsop (1947-1950). She has written a book on her hobby, needlepoint, and lives in Washington, Conn., where she breeds prize dogs—many champions. In 1974, she received an Academy Award nomination as best supporting actress for *Summer Wishes, Winter Dreams*.

SYLVIA SIDNEY

328

SIMONE SIMON

She was born in Marseilles, April 23, 1910, and with her mother and stepfather, the manager of a graphite mine in Madagascar, she moved there at the age of three. She attended schools there, as well as in Berlin, Budapest, and Turin, before moving to Paris in 1930. On the stage, she appeared mainly in musicals, and started her movie career in 1931 in *Le Chanteur inconnu*, and her Hollywood career in 1936. After her hit in *La Bête Humaine*, Hollywood offered her another chance in *All That Money Can Buy*, screen version of *The Devil and Daniel Webster*, in which she played Belle, the Devil's handmaiden. But her famous 1940s films are the horror classics *Cat People* and *Curse of the Cat People*. She continued to make movies in France. She never married.

PENNY SINGLETON

Mariana Dorothy McNulty was born in Philadelphia, September 15, 1908, niece of onetime Postmaster General James A. Farley. After going to the Alex McClue School and Columbia University, she got a job as a singer and acrobat on Broadway in the musical *Good News* in 1928, and later was featured in *Follow Thru*, 1929, *Walk a Little Faster*, 1932, and *Hey Nonny, Nonny*. In 1930, she made her first two movies, *Good News* and *Love in the Rough*, but wasn't much heard from filmically until she played the part of a nightclub dancer, in *After the Thin Man*. She continued as Dorothy McNulty until, after marrying a dentist, Dr. Lawrence Singleton, in 1937, she decided to change her name to Penny Singleton. The original feature film *Blondie* was made in 1938 on a low budget by Columbia Pictures. Her last, *Blondie's Hero*, was made in 1950. She divorced Dr. Singleton in 1939, and in 1941 married Robert Sparks, who produced the *Blondie* movies for a time. She is active in the American Guild of Variety Artists, representing dancers and singers. She returned to Broadway briefly in the summer of 1971, briefly replacing Ruby Keeler in *No, No, Nanette*.

ALISON SKIPWORTH

Alison Skipworth, a minor Marie Dressler in her screen career (but who, unlike Miss Dressler, was once a great beauty), was born in London, July 25, 1863, daughter of Dr. Richard Ebenezer Groom, and early married an artist, Frank Markam Skipworth. With her duchesslike beauty and her masses of auburn locks, she was his favorite model. She didn't make her stage debut until she was thirty-one (in *A Gaiety Girl* at Daly's Theatre, London, 1894), because "I was

poor and had to go on the stage." A year later, she appeared on Broadway in *An Artist's Model*. She went back to England for two brief stage jobs, and then returned to New York in November 1897 to join Dan Frohman's company at the Lyceum. She never acted again in England. During her long stage career (her last play was *Lady of the Valley*, 1942, on Broadway), she played in Shakespeare, *The Prisoner of Zenda*, *The Torch Bearers*, *The Grand Duchess and the Waiter* and many others. Between 1925 and 1930, she claimed she appeared in twenty-one consecutive failures, so she was glad to accept film offers in 1930. Her last movie was *Wide Open Faces* in 1938. She died July 5, 1952.

KATE SMITH

The songbird of the South, Kathryn Elizabeth Smith, was born in Washington, D. C., May 1, 1909, and began as a choir singer as a child of four. In September 1926, she made her Broadway debut billed as Tiny Little in Eddie Dowling's musical, *Honeymoon Lane*, followed by *Hit the Deck*, with Charles Winninger and Louise Groody, 1927, and *Flying High*, as Bert Lahr's stooge, in 1930. But the stage was not to be her kingdom: by the time she was twenty-three, her longtime manager, business partner, confidant, and impresario, Ted Collins, had transformed her into an $18,000-a-week radio star. By 1969, she had starred in 15,672 radio broadcasts, 1280 hours of live network TV, and recorded 2,260 songs, more than any other living performer. She introduced "God Bless America" on Armistice Day in 1938. During World War II, she single-handedly raised $600 million worth of savings bonds. She no longer has her own radio or TV shows, but appears as a guest on variety shows.

GALE SONDERGAARD

A native of Litchfield, Minn., born February 15, 1899, she graduated from the Minneapolis School of Dramatic Art, and the University of Minnesota, where her father was a professor. On the stage, she first toured as Jessica in *The Merchant of Venice* with John Kellard, and then joined Jessie Bonstelle's famous stock company in Detroit tackling any part assigned her —"hags and ingenues, mothers and daughters, wantons and nuns." The The-

atre Guild signed her to a five-year contract, and she played leading roles in *Red Rust*, *American Dream*, *Doctor Monica*, and followed Judith Anderson as Nina in *Strange Interlude*. She was first married to Neill O'Malley (1922-1930). She had met and married director Herbert Biberman in New York, in 1930, and, when he went to Hollywood, she went with him, not expecting to go into movies. In 1948, Miss Sondergaard was blacklisted following the House Un-American Activities Committee's investigation of the movie industry. Her husband, one of "the Hollywood Ten" who refused to give testimony, was sent to prison. The long hiatus in her career followed. During 1967-1968, she was a member of the Minnesota Theatre Company of the Tyrone Guthrie Theatre, where she played the Lynn Fontanne role in *The Visit*, among other major roles. Her alma mater, the University of Minnesota, gave her its "outstanding achievement award" in 1968 for her acting work.

ANN SOTHERN

Her paternal grandfather, Simon Lake, invented the submarine, her maternal grandfather was a Danish violinist, and she was born as Harriette Lake, January 22, 1909, in Valley City, N. D., daughter of Walter Lake and his wife Annette Yde, onetime concert soprano. As a child, she often went on tour with her mother, and at eleven she was already an accomplished pianist. At Central High School, Minneapolis, she won first prize three consecutive years for her original compositions. In 1931, she made her Broadway debut as Geraldine in a musical, *America's Sweetheart*, and succeeded Lois Moran in *Of Thee I Sing* in June, 1933. When she made her first movie that year, *Let's Fall in Love*, she changed her name to Ann Sothern. She had a lively career up to 1953. She returned briefly to movies in 1964 and 1965 in *The Best Man*, *Lady in a Cage* and *Sylvia*. Miss Sothern also had an active TV career with *Private Secretary* and *The Ann Sothern Show*, as well as running a Swiss Chalet in Sun Valley, the A bar S Music Publishing Co., and the A bar S Cattle Co. in Idaho, where she owns a breeding herd. She married and divorced twice: actor-musician Roger Pryor (1936-1942) and actor Robert Sterling (1943-1946), father of her only child, Tisha Sterling.

Richard Carlson with ANN SHERIDAN

BARBARA STANWYCK

BARBARA STANWYCK

This brassy-with-class star was born Ruby Stevens in Brooklyn, July 16, 1907, youngest of the five children of Byron Stevens, a laborer, and his wife, Catherine McGee, who died when Ruby was two years old (her father died shortly thereafter). Ruby was brought up by her showgirl sister Mildred, and at fifteen got a job as a night-club dancer and a bit in *Ziegfeld Follies of 1922*. This led to jobs in the choruses of *Keeping Kool, A Night in Spain*, another *Follies*, before making her bow as a dramatic actress playing Dot, a cabaret girl, in Willard Mack's *The Noose* in 1926. It was Mack who thought up the name Barbara Stanwyck. She married Broadway star Frank Fay in 1928, and traveled to Hollywood with him in 1929 after having made *The Locked Door* in New York. Since then, she has made over eighty movies. She divorced Fay in 1935 and was given custody of their adopted son, Dion. In 1939, she married Robert Taylor; they were divorced in 1952.

FRANCES STARR

She was born in Oneonta, N. Y., June 6, 1886, went to schools in Albany, and made her stage debut there in 1901. She was a longtime star for impresario David Belasco, from 1906 until 1922, a record in stage annals. Her most famous plays were *The Rose of the Rancho*, 1906, and *The Easiest Way*, 1909-1911. Her movies were made between 1931 and 1932. Highpoints of her later stage career were her soft and lovely portrayal of the dying Mrs. Brown in *Claudia*, with Dorothy McGuire, 1941, and in Dorothy Parker's mordant comedy, *Ladies of the Corridor*, with Edna Best, June Walker, Betty Field, and Walter Matthau, in 1953. She married twice: painter Haskell Coffin (divorced) and banker Ronald G. Donaldson. She died June 11, 1973.

ANNA STEN

Born in Kiev, Russia, December 3, 1908, she was the daughter of a Russian ballet master (who died in 1922) and a Swedish mother. Encouraged by Stanislavsky, she entered the Moscow Film Academy, and started to make films under her real name, Anjuchka Stenska, in the Crimea and Moscow (*Girl with the Hatbox*, 1927, *The Yellow Ticket*, 1928). Her role as Grushenka in *The Brothers Karamazov*, filmed in Germany, caught producer Sam Goldwyn's attention, and he brought her to America in 1932. Two years later, after she had been tutored in English, and the big guns of her publicity campaign had been fired (and later backfired), her *Nana* was released. In 1960, she appeared briefly as Jenny in the long-run *Threepenny Opera* in New York. First married to Fedor Ozep, director of *The Brothers Karamazov*, she married that film's producer, Eugene Frenke, in 1932. She and her husband live in Beverly Hills, and as a painter she has had successful one-woman shows in Los Angeles and New York.

GLORIA STUART

The glossy Miss Stuart, who always looked like a rich girl, was born in Santa Monica, July 14, 1910, and went to schools there and the University of California. Before her movie debut in 1932, as Allan Dinehart's daughter in *Street of Women*, with Kay Francis, she had played on the West Coast stage in *The Sea Gull* and *The Second Man*. She was first married to Blair Gordon Newell, and then, in 1934, she married screenwriter Arthur Sheekman (*Monkey Business, Duck Soup, Roman Scandals*). After her retirement in 1946, she took up painting, and had a one-woman show in New York in 1961. She lives in California.

MARGARET SULLAVAN

She was born May 16, 1909, in Norfolk, Va., daughter of a broker, Cornelius H. Sullavan, and his wife, Garland Council. Stagestruck from the age of six, she had trouble with her parents who resisted her theatrical ambitions while she attended three private schools and Sullins College in Bristol, Va. They finally permitted her to go to Boston, where she studied dancing and then enrolled in the E. E. Clive Dramatic School. In 1928, she joined the University Players Guild, a theatre at Falmouth, Mass., where she first met Henry Fonda. That winter she returned to Norfolk to make her social debut, then returned to Falmouth for another season, and rejoined the University Players in Baltimore, where they had a season of stock. There she and Fonda were married; they divorced within a year. She made her debut on Broadway in the lead role, that of Teddy, in Elmer Harris's *A Modern Virgin*. The play was called a "dank mess" by one critic, but Miss Sullavan was hailed as a find. Her next four Broadway plays were also flops, but she finally got a part worthy of her when she succeeded Marguerite Churchill as Paula Jordan in *Dinner at Eight*, and won a movie contract with Universal. In 1935, she married William Wyler, who was directing her in *The Good Fairy*. Two years later they were divorced. In 1936, she returned to Broadway as Terry Randall in the hit play *Stage Door*. During its run, she married her agent, Leland Hayward, by whom she had two daughters and a son. When they divorced in 1947, she married Kenneth A. Wagg, a director of a British malted milk firm, the father of four children of his own, and this marriage was successful from the beginning. Her biggest stage success was as Sally Middleton in John van Druten's light comedy, *The Voice of the Turtle*, in 1943, in which she played for two seasons. For a star of her importance and popularity, Miss Sullavan's record is sparse: sixteen movies and, in the last sixteen years of her life, only five plays. During the New Haven tryout of *Sweet Love Remember'd*, she was found unconscious by her husband in her room at the Taft Hotel, and was dead on arrival at Grace-New Haven Community Hospital, January 1, 1960. Her death resulted from an overdose of barbiturates. Miss Sullavan had long been fighting deafness and had been constantly in terror of missing her cues.

GLORIA SWANSON

Her father, Joseph Theodore Swanson, was of Swedish-Italian descent; her mother, Adelaide Klanowski, of Polish-French-German extraction. This accounts for the impression that their only child, Gloria Josephine May Swanson, gave of having a faintly foreign air that enhanced her glamour. She was born in Chicago, March 27, 1897. Her father was a civilian employee of the U. S. Army, who later enlisted, and young Gloria spent her childhood in Army posts in Florida and Puerto Rico, with only one year in high school. After her parents separated, Gloria and her mother moved back to Chicago, where the youngster began her movie career playing bits in Essanay's one- and two-reel comedies in 1914. Two years later, she married an Essanay comedian, Wallace Beery, separated from him a month later, though they didn't divorce for three years. Her

MARGARET SULLAVAN

GLORIA SWANSON

Hollywood-based career began with Mack Sennett in 1916, not as a bathing beauty, but as a featured comedienne and leading lady with Bobby Vernon. But Cecil B. DeMille, who liked Gloria's dignity in the midst of the Sennett mayhem, gave her career its real start in *Don't Change Your Husband* in 1919, and Swanson became his slinkiest star, in golden bed-and-bathtub dramas with high-society backgrounds.

Her career as the biggest star on the Paramount lot lasted until 1927, when she joined United Artists. After the 1930s, she appeared in only three films; her last, *Three for Bedroom C*, in 1952. But she worked on radio, television, and the stage, with a spectacular run in *Butterflies Are Free*, both on the road and on Broadway, 1971-1972.

After her first marriage, she had four more husbands, all divorced: Herbert Somborn, owner of the Brown Derby in Hollywood (1919-1920), by whom she had a daughter; Marquis Henri de la Falaise de la Coudraye (1925-1931); Irish sportsman Michael Farmer (1931-1934), with another daughter; and broker William N. Davey, for 44 days. She was also a close friend to Joseph P. Kennedy, who produced five of her United Artists films, 1927-1930. She also has one adopted son, Joseph, who she frankly denies was sired by Mr. Kennedy.

GLADYS SWARTHOUT

She was born December 25, 1904, in Deepwater, Mo., and studied music at the Bush Conservatory of Music in Chicago,

for three years. At twenty, she was hired by the Chicago Civic Opera Co., making her debut as an off-stage shepherd in *Tosca*. She made her debut at the Metropolitan Opera Co. in *La Gioconda* and, until 1945, she was one of its most glamorous stars and leading mezzo-soprano singers. Her most famous role was *Carmen*. Her Paramount movies were made between 1935 and 1939. She continued in concert after her operatic career ended, until a heart valve condition required an operation in 1956. Her first husband, Harry Richmond Kern, died in 1931, after six years of marriage. Her second husband was Frank Chapman, a singer and also her manager, who died in 1966. They lived in New York, and had a villa, La Ragnaia, near Florence, Italy, where Miss Swarthout died July 7, 1969.

NORMA TALMADGE

"The lady of the great indoors," as one critic quipped—and a great silent-film star—was born in Jersey City, May 26, 1897, the eldest of the three daughters of a salesman, Frederick T. Talmadge, and his Spanish-born wife, Margaret L. Jose, who, as Peg Talmadge, was a favorite wit in Hollywood. Her younger sisters, Constance (born April 19, 1899) and Natalie (April 29, 1900), were also actresses, with Constance being on as high a level as a comedienne as Norma was in melodrama (she couldn't be called a tragedienne). Norma grew up on Fenimore Avenue in Brooklyn, and by 1910 was working in the Vitagraph Studios in Brooklyn as an extra, then in bits, then as a leading lady. By 1915, she had made 250 movies for Vitagraph, and in 1916 she married Joseph Schenck, who produced Norma Talmadge films. In 1920, she began her career as a star at First National Studios and made her most famous films there in the 1920s, including *Smilin' Through*, 1922, and *Secrets*, 1924. Eugene O'Brien was her most durable leading man, appearing with her in ten films. She made no movies after 1930. After a long romance with Gilbert Roland, leading man in four of her pictures, she divorced Mr. Schenck in 1934, having been separated from him for seven years. She then married George Jessel instead of Roland, but divorced him in 1939. In 1946, she married Dr. Carvel James, a Las Vegas physician, and died from crippling arthritis at their home there December 24, 1957.

LILYAN TASHMAN

She has become a dim, legendary figure in movie history, a tough, worldly actress who died young. Her rather undistinguished, but very active, career didn't prevent her from being a style-setter and

a café social leader. She was born in Brooklyn, October 23, 1899, as plain Lillian, the seventh and last child of Maurice Tashman, a children's clothing manufacturer. Beginning as an artist's model at fifteen, she was soon flashing about in four Ziegfeld shows—two *Follies* (1916, 1917), *The Century Girl* and *Miss 1917*. Her gay swagger and sophistication made her at once a name as a smart clothes-horse and a comedienne, with a deep, throaty, insinuating voice, good at imitations. From musicals, she went into farce comedy: the long-run *Gold Diggers*, with Ina Claire, *A Bachelor's Night* and *Lady Bug*. In 1921, she made a movie in the East, with Richard Barthelmess and Marjorie Daw, called *Experience*. She wound up her Broadway career in the part of Hazel in *The Garden of Weeds* in 1924, and repeated her role in a Paramount picture that same year, with Betty Compson and Warner Baxter. From then until her death, she worked steadily, usually playing second-lead sophisticates, in support of such stars as Gloria Swanson, Norma Talmadge, Corinne Griffith, Billie Dove, Marie Prevost, and on into the talkies, when she had her greatest success in Paramount Pictures.

Miss Tashman first married Al Lee, a vaudeville player, who appeared on bills with Eddie Cantor. In 1919, she met Edmund Lowe, when he was Lenore Ulric's leading man on Broadway in *The Son-Daughter*. They married September 1, 1925, the second marriage for both. Miss Tashman died March 21, 1934, following an emergency operation for an advanced tumorous condition. At her services at Universal Funeral Chapel, Rev. Dr. Samuel H. Goltenson, rabbi of Temple Emanu-El, officiated. The streets around its address, 597 Lexington Avenue, were blocked off to accommodate 3000. That same day, a cheapie back-stage story called *Wine, Women and Song*, with Lew Cody (who died two months later), her last movie, opened on Broadway.

ESTELLE TAYLOR

She was born in Wilmington, Del., May 20, 1899, and at fourteen married a banker, Kenneth Malcolm Peacock. They separated in 1918, when she went to New York to study acting at Sargent's Dramatic School, and become an artist's model for Howard Pyle and Boardman Robinson. In a Broadway musical, *Come On, Charlie*, she became known as "the girl in the red beads," and was picked out of the chorus line for her first job in movies. This was in 1920. Thereafter, through the decade, she played Miriam, the sister of Moses, in the first *Ten Commandments*; Mary Queen of Scots in Mary Pickford's *Dorothy Vernon of Haddon Hall*; Lucrezia Borgia in John Barrymore's *Don Juan*, among others. After she was Jack Dempsey's leading lady in *Manhattan Madness*, in 1925, she became the boxing champion's wife, and appeared with him on the Broadway stage in *The Big Fight*, 1928, produced by David Belasco. Their marriage ended in divorce in 1931. In 1943, she married Paul Small, agent-producer, and divorced him in 1946. She had made her last movie, *The Southerner*, the year before. She died of cancer at her Hollywood home, April 15, 1958.

VERREE TEASDALE

The daughter of Clement and Mattie Wharton Teasdale, she was born in Spokane, Wash., March 15, 1906. Her old Warner Bros. studio biography says that two of her cousins were the poet Sara Teasdale and the novelist Edith Wharton. Ambitious to go on the stage, she studied at the New York School of Expression, and made her Broadway debut in Philip Barry's *The Youngest*, with Henry Hull and Genevieve Tobin, 1924. She worked steadily on Broadway until 1931, with high-lights a two-year run in *The Constant Wife*, with Ethel Barrymore, and the role of one of the predatory girls, Jean, in *The Greeks Had a Word for It*, with Dorothy Hall and Muriel Kirkland, 1931. In 1929, she had made her first movie, *Syncopation*, but her film career didn't get going until 1932, and ended with *Come Live With Me*, 1941. When she was twenty-one, she married musical comedy singer William J. O'Neal and divorced him in 1933. She became the third wife of Adolphe Menjou on August 24, 1934, and is the mother of a son, Peter Adolphe Menjou.

SHIRLEY TEMPLE

The tot who won a special Academy Award in 1935 for cheering up a Depression-weary nation was born in Santa Monica, April 23, 1928, to banker George Temple and his wife Gertrude. Shirley was their third child and only daughter. When she was four, she was picked out at dancing school by Charles Lamont, a director and talent scout at Educational Studios, for parts in comedy features called Baby Burlesks, takeoffs on adult movies. She starred as "The Incomparable More Legs Sweetrick," a satire on Marlene Dietrich, and played Lulu Parsnips, poking fun at Louella O. Parsons. Then Shirley acted in feature-length films, including *Red-Haired Alibi*, with Merna Kennedy, *To the Last Man*, with Randolph Scott, and *Out All Night*, with ZaSu Pitts, who said, "She's marvelous—she's going to be really great." In 1934,

she was chosen out of nearly 200 applicants for the tiny-tot role in *Stand Up and Cheer*, and that same year made six more movies.

Shirley became the number one box-office attraction in America in 1936, 1937, and 1938, and by 1940 had earned close to $3 million. Did the hard work spoil her childhood, as in so many other cases? "She didn't act or make pictures," said director David Butler. "She played wonderful games. She got into fairyland, she believed it all herself, and that's why you believed it." She was also backed by parents of commonsense, who loved her and didn't exploit her.

In 1945, at seventeen, she married actor John Agar, but parted from him acrimoniously after a year, and the birth of a daughter, Linda Susan. She then married, more happily, Charles Alden Black, a wealthy marine-development specialist, and is the mother of a son and daughter, Charles, Jr., and Lori. Mrs. Black became a conservative Republican, and was defeated in a Congressional primary in 1967 by Paul N. McCloskey, Jr. In 1969, President Nixon appointed her to the five-member U. S. delegation to the session of the United Nations. She is now Deputy Chairman to the U. N. Conference on the Human Environment and a co-founder of the International Foundation for Multiple Sclerosis.

Bill Robinson and SHIRLEY TEMPLE

GENEVIEVE TOBIN

The roguish Miss Tobin was born in New York, November 29, 1901, and went to schools there and in Paris. As a child she appeared on New York and Chicago stages, and made her adult debut as Genevieve in *Oh Look!* on Broadway in 1918. Two years later she made a hit as Patricia O'Day in *Little Old New York*, then as Polly in *Polly Preferred*. At the end of the decade, she was playing in *Murray Hill*, with Leslie Howard, as Mary Dugan in the London production of *The Trial of Mary Dugan*, and as Loo-loo Carroll in the musical *Fifty Million Frenchmen*, with William Gaxton and Helen Broderick, when she was signed for the movies. She spent the bulk of her screen career at Warner Bros., and married a Warner director, William Keighley in 1938. He died in 1972. She lives in Paris.

THELMA TODD

Thelma Todd was perfect for what she was: a blithe and breezy blonde, who liked to sign her letters "your hot Toddy," and the ideal, busty foil for knockabout comics, both male and female. She grew up in Lawrence, Mass., where she was born July 29, 1905, and went to State Normal School, working part-time as a fashion model. For a time she taught school. But when she won a beauty contest as Miss Massachusetts, she abruptly ended her teaching career, and signed with Paramount to attend its acting school in New York. With "junior stars and debutantes," she made her debut in the school's production, *Fascinating Youth*, in 1926. In 1932, she eloped with her agent, Pat di Cicco (later a husband of Gloria Vanderbilt) and divorced him two years later. With her good friend, producer-director Roland West, she operated Thelma Todd's Sidewalk Café, in Santa Monica. She was found dead of carbon monoxide poisoning in her car, parked in the garage behind this restaurant, on December 16, 1935, aged thirty. It has never been determined whether her death was murder, suicide, or an accident.

CLAIRE TREVOR

Claire Trevor was born March 8, 1909, the only child of Noel B. Wemlinger, a successful Fifth Avenue merchant tailor of French descent, and his wife Edith Morrison, from Belfast. Claire went to high school in Mamaroneck, and for a time studied art at Columbia before enrolling in the American Academy of Dramatic Arts. At twenty, she started her stage career with Robert Henderson's Repertory Players in Ann Arbor, Mich. Her Broadway debut was the lead opposite Ernest Truex and Edward Arnold in a hit comedy, *Whistling in the Dark*, in 1932. She next appeared in a flop, *The Party's Over*, with Ross Alexander and Peggy Conklin, in 1933, and listened to the New York office of Fox Pictures when they offered her a film contract. She arrived in Hollywood in May 1933, and immediately went to work in her debut, as leading lady in a Western, *Life in the Raw*, with George O'Brien. Never a star, but a favorite with the public and the critics, she worked steadily thereafter, and in 1948 won an Oscar for her performance in *Key Largo*. She was married to CBS producer Clark Andrews (1938-1942) and Navy Lt. Cylos William Dunsmoore (1943-1947), and is mother to a son, Charles. She is now married to producer and real-estate businessman Milton H. Bren, and they live at Lido Isle, Newport, Calif.

SOPHIE TUCKER

She was born Sophie Abuza, January 13, 1884, daughter of Russian-Jewish parents who had fled their homeland. The first eight years of her life were spent in Boston, and then her family moved to Hartford, where they opened a 25-cent-dinner restaurant. Sophie and her two brothers and a sister worked there, and she discovered she could pick up dimes singing for the customers. In 1906, she went to New York to start her long career in clubs, vaudeville, the *Follies*, and musicals. Her biggest successes, though, were in nightclubs, from the Catskills to Miami Beach, from London to Las Vegas. She introduced such songs as "Some of These Days," "My Yiddishe Mama," "The Last of the Red Hot Mamas," "Blue Skies." The entertainer was married three times, to Louis Tuck (when she was sixteen), to whose surname she added a syllable to get her stage name; pianist Frank Westphal; and Albert Lackerman. She had one son, Bert Tuck. She died of a lung ailment and kidney failure at her apartment in New York, February 9, 1966.

LANA TURNER

Both Lana and her first movie director, Mervyn LeRoy, shatter the myth that the Sweater Girl was discovered at the counter of Schwab's Drug Store on Sunset Boulevard sipping a soda. Julia Jean Mildred Frances Turner, the only child of Virgil and Mildred Turner, was born February 8, 1920, in Wallace, Idaho. Her father died when she was ten. In 1936, her mother took Lana to Hollywood, and worked in a beauty parlor while Lana went to Hollywood High School. The next year, she made her first movie, starting one of Hollywood's more spectacular careers, both offscreen and on. She married bandleader Artie Shaw on her twentieth birthday. Two years later, she married businessman Stephen Crane (divorced 1944), by whom she had a daughter, Cheryl Christine (born July 25, 1943), who stabbed her mother's gangster lover, Johnny Stompanato, in 1958. Other husbands were Bob Topping (1948-1952); actor Lex Barker (1953); merchant Fred May (1960); writer Robert B. Eaton; and most recently nightclub hypnotist Ronald Dante (six months in 1969), all divorced. In the summer of 1970, she made successful summer theater appearances in *Forty Carats*.

HELEN TWELVETREES

Miss Twelvetress added to her shaggy-dog joke by marrying a Hollywood stunt man, later realtor, named Frank J. Woody. Her maiden name was Helen Marie Jurgens, and she was born in Brooklyn, December 25, 1907, daughter of an advertising man for a group of New York newspapers and his wife, Helen Kelly. Upon graduation from Brooklyn Heights Seminary, she studied first at the Art Students League, then at the American Academy of Dramatic Arts for three months, where she met a fellow student, Clark Twelvetrees, whom she married in 1927. The young couple got their first stage experience with the Stuart Walker Players in Cincinnati and Indianapolis. She played opposite film star Charles Ray in a flop play, *Yen*, that closed out of town, and in another play that didn't make Broadway, *Roulette*. But a Fox official saw her and offered her a contract. In 1929, she made her first movie, *The Ghost Talks*, with Charles Eaton and Earle Foxe, and, in 1939, her last, *Unmarried*, with Buck Jones.

As her career progressed, her first husband, whose own career had come to a standstill, tried to commit suicide by jumping out of a window, but his fall was broken by landing on an automobile's canvas top. They divorced in 1931, and she married Mr. Woody, by whom she had a son, Jack Bryan Woody, born October 26, 1932. After her movie days were over, she returned to the stage for seven years. While touring Europe in *The Man Who Came to Dinner*, 1946, she met her third husband, then with the Air Force in Germany, Capt. Conrad Payne. At the time of her death by suicide (sleeping pills), she was living with him at Olmstead Air Force Base, Harrisburg, Pa. She died at a hospital there, February 13, 1958.

LENORE ULRIC

She was born into a German-speaking household in New Ulm, Minn., July 21, 1892, and didn't speak English until she was seven. Her father was Francis Xavier Ulrich (she dropped the "h" from her last name), an Army hospital steward and chemist, and she was one of six children. Leaving St. Anthony's Catholic School in Milwaukee after the third grade, she worked as a cash girl in a department store, while playing walk-ons at night with the local stock company. She then joined stock companies in Chicago and Grand Rapids. As early as 1911, she appeared in movies with the Essanay company, and worked off and on until 1916, when she was billed as "Lenore Ulrich, the magic mistress of a thousand emotions," in such films as *The Better Woman* and *Pallas*. Her lucky association with producer David Belasco began in 1916 when she played an Indian maid in *The Heart of Wetona* (later done by Norma Talmadge in movies), and, until the autumn before Mr. Belasco's death in 1931, she was exclusively managed and directed by him, and her New York appearances were always at the Belasco Theatre in such *femme-fatale* parts as *Tiger Rose*, *The Son-Daughter*, *Kiki* and *Lulu Belle*. After Belasco, her stage career withered away to flop plays and touring companies, except for a Theatre Guild production, *The Fifth Column* in 1940, and as Charmian in *Antony and Cleo-*

patra, 1947. She made her last movie that year, *Northwest Outpost*. She was briefly married to actor Sidney Blackmer. In her last years, she lived alone in a house on Riverside Drive given her by Belasco, but several years before her death, had herself committed to Rockland State Hospital, Orangeburg, N. Y., where she died December 30, 1970.

LUPE VELEZ

Born Guadelupe Velez de Villabos, July 18, 1908, in San Luis de Potosi, Mexico, she was the daugher of Col. M. de Villabos and his wife Josephine, and went to a San Antonio, Texas, convent. At thirteen, she got her start as a dancer in Mexico City, appeared in motion picture prologue shows, and in a musical comedy. Hollywood first saw her in 1926, and Hal Roach began to use her in two-reel comedies. Douglas Fairbanks cast her as the heroine in his *The Gaucho* in 1927. From then until 1943, she appeared regularly in movies, interspersed by some interesting stage appearances. Florenz Ziegfeld cast her as Conchita in his musical *Hot-Cha!*, with Buddy Rogers, at the Majestic in New York in March 1932. Next year, she was Jimmy Durante's co-star in *Strike Me Pink*. She did one London show, a revue, *Transatlantic Rhythm*, with Ruth Etting and Lou Holtz, in 1936. Her last stage appearance was at the Winter Garden in New York in *You Never Know*, with Clifton Webb and Libby Holman, in 1938, and her last movie was *Ladies' Day* in 1943. Famous for her tempestuous romances, she had a long affair with Gary Cooper before she married Johnny Weissmuller in 1933. After their divorce in 1938, she never remarried. She died by sleeping pills in her Beverly Hills home, December 14, 1944.

EVELYN VENABLE

The daughter and granddaughter of teachers, and later in her life a teacher herself, she was born in Cincinnati, October 18, 1913. She went to Walnut Hills High School, where her father, Emerson Venable, a Shakespearean scholar and writer, was head of the English department. At school, she played Juliet and also Rosalind in *As You Like It*, in productions staged by her father. Evelyn won a four-year scholarship to Vassar, but stayed there for only a year, to enter the University of Cincinnati. At nineteen, she joined the touring company of her father's friend, actor Walter Hampden, playing the Dream Child in *Dear Brutus*, the Flower Girl in *Cyrano de Bergerac* and Ophelia in *Hamlet*, which was seen by a talent scout for Paramount Pictures when she was playing the Biltmore The-

atre in Los Angeles. Her movie debut was in *Cradle Song*, with Dorothea Wieck, in 1933, and she stayed on the screen until 1938, when she married cameraman Hal Mohr and became the mother of two daughters. She returned once more, in 1943, as Stuart Erwin's leading lady in *He Hired the Boss*, and then retired for good. After her children had grown, she returned to college, this time at UCLA, and earned her degree. She stayed on there as a faculty member. She and her husband, both vegetarians, live in the Brentwood section of Los Angeles.

HELEN VINSON

The daughter of Edward A. Rulfs, a Texas Oil Co. executive, she was born in Beaumont, September 17, 1907, and went to the University of Texas for two years before going on the stage in Houston in a stock production of *The Charm School*. That same year, 1927, she made her Broadway bow in a play called *Los Angeles*, with Jack LaRue and Alison Skipworth. She continued on Broadway until 1932 and her movie bow in *Jewel Robbery*. Miss Vinson remained in films until 1945. In 1925, she married Harry Neilson Vickerman, a Philadelphia manufacturer, whom she divorced in 1934. Next year, she married British tennis champion Fred Perry. After her divorce from him, she married Donald Hardenbrook, of New York.

NELLA WALKER

She was born in Chicago and went to schools in York, Pa., where she once worked as a salesgirl. After she met and married actor Wilbur Mack, they formed a vaudeville team, touring in *Little Bits of Everyday Life*. Miss Walker made her movie debut in 1929 in *The Vagabond Lover*, and her last recorded movie appearance is in *Sabrina*, 1954.

FREDI WASHINGTON

Born in Savannah, Ga., in 1903, she went to grammar school there, and in Philadelphia, attended St. Elizabeth Convent. Her first job was as a typist at $10 a week. In 1924, she started her theatrical career as a dancer in clubs, and made her Broadway debut as the Negro girl who "passed" in *Black Boy*, Horace Liveright's production of the life of boxer Jack Johnson, with Paul Robeson, 1926. Miss Washington then went to Europe, and joined with Al Moiret in a dance team, Moiret and Fredi, that played clubs in Monte Carlo, Germany, Holland, and Roger Wolfe Kahn's night club in Paris, Le Perroquet. She returned to the U. S. in 1928 to appear in *Hot Choco-lates*. Among her Broadway appearances

have been Hall Johnson's folk drama, *Run, Little Chillun*, in 1933; *Mamba's Daughters*, with Ethel Waters and Jose Ferrer, 1939; a revival of *Lysistrata*, with Etta Moten, Mildred Smith, Rex Ingram, and Sidney Poitier, 1946; and *A Long Way Home*, a Negro version of Gorki's *Lower Depths*, with William Marshall and Ruby Dee, 1948. Miss Washington was one of the founders of the Negro Actors' Guild in 1937, and became its executive secretary. She also served as theatre editor for *The People's Voice*. She married Lawrence Brown, a trombonist with Duke Ellington's orchestra.

LUCILE WATSON

Miss Watson was born in Quebec, May 27, 1879, daughter of Major Thomas Watson, of the Royal Sherwood Foresters, and Leila Morlet, of French descent. She was educated in the Ursuline Convent, and in 1900 entered the American Academy of Dramatic Arts in New York, making her stage debut in New York at the Empire in *The Wisdom of the Wise*, at the age of twenty-three. Among her later famous stage roles were Lady Utterwood in *Heartbreak House*, in 1920; Mrs. Massarene in *Dancing Mothers*; even Mrs. Alving in *Ghosts* (not a "Lucile Waston part"); Mrs. Fanny Townsend in *No More Ladies*; Mrs. Bennet in *Pride and Prejudice*; and perhaps the most famous of all her later roles, Mrs. Fanny Farrelly in Lillian Hellman's *Watch on the Rhine*, 1941, and on the screen in 1943. She made her movie debut as the Comtesse in *What Every Woman Knows* in 1934, and her last film was *My Forbidden Past* in 1951. She was the widow of Louis E. Shipman, playwright, who died in 1933. She lived in one of the smallest of the old New York brownstone residences, at 143 East 63rd Street —just about 12 feet wide. On June 24, 1962, she died at Doctors Hospital.

MARJORIE WEAVER

Daughter of a livery-stable owner, she was born March 2, 1913, in Crossville, Tenn., went to public schools there, and studied at the Universities of Kentucky and Indiana, earning a license to teach French and English. While at the universities, she sang with bands for five dollars a night. She first acted with stock companies, and was a model for the John Robert Powers Agency in New York before she became a "stock girl" at 20th Century-Fox in 1936. Her movie career ended 1943. In October 1937, she eloped from a football game at Goshen, Ind., with Kenneth George Schacht, whom she had known since she was 15. They lived together only sixteen days, and the marrige was annulled in 1941, when he was a Naval lieutenant.

VIRGINIA WEIDLER

The youngest of six children of Alfred and Margaret Weidler, she was born in Eagle Rock, Calif., March 21, 1927. Her mother had been an opera singer under the name of Margaret Theresa Louise, and she tutored her children in languages. At the age of three, Virginia acted in *Moby Dick*, with John Barrymore, but her real acting career began as one of the Wiggs children, in *Mrs. Wiggs of the Cabbage Patch*, 1934. Her last picture was *Best Foot Forward* in 1943. She went East to become a vocalist in night clubs, and appeared in a singing act at Loew's State Theatre in 1943. On Broadway, she played the ingenue in Vina Delmar's *The Rich Full Life*, with Judith Evelyn, 1945. She died, with little public notice, July 1, 1968.

MAE WEST

"The talk of the talkies" (as she called herself in *Go West, Young Man*) was born in Brooklyn, August 17, 1892, the first of the three children to Battlin' Jack West, an Irish prizefighter who later ran a livery stable, and his Bavarian-born, part-Jewish, wife, Matilda Doelger. When she was five, her sister Beverly was born, and a year later her brother John. With encouragement from both parents, she began her career in 1897 with Hal Clarendon's stock company in New York on the road, and for six years played such parts as Little Nell, Lovey Mary in *Mrs. Wiggs of the Cabbage Patch*, and the Angel Child in *Ten Nights in a Barroom*, picking up her formal schooling along the way. Later, she obtained further education privately from the Board of Education's curriculum, enabling her, she said, to write her books and plays. In 1911, she married a jazz singer, Frank Wallace,

teamed with him in a song-and-dance act, but decided marriage wasn't for her. She dissolved the act and left him. (She wouldn't admit this marriage until 1942, when Wallace sued for divorce and $1,000-a-month maintenance allowance.)

Mae made her Broadway debut in 1911, in *A La Broadway*, and until 1926 appeared in revues and vaudeville. Then her mother encouraged her to write her own material, and from then on the Mae West known to the world came into being, with her Broadway plays, *Sex, The Wicked Age, Diamond Lil, The Constant Sinner*—delighting New York and shocking self-appointed censors and the police department. She was arrested in 1926 for writing a "profane" drama (*Sex*), and giving a "suggestive performance." Her eight days in the Welfare Island jail established her as New York's most publicized and popular jailbird. Troubles with the censors never did diminish, and six months after release of her second movie,

MAE WEST

She Done Him Wrong, in 1933, the National Legion of Decency was formed. Thereafter, Mae West had to fudge some of her punches. But her physical qualities as a sexual fantasy were preserved.

HELEN WESTLEY

She was born Henrietta Meserole Manney, or Dutch Huguenot descent, in Brooklyn, March 28, 1875, the younger of two children of a drugstore owner. She aimed to be an actress from the beginning, and prepared herself at the Brooklyn School of Oratory, the Emerson College of Oratory, Boston, and the American Academy of Dramatic Art. At twenty-two, she made her New York debut in *The Captain of the Nonesuch*. The next few years she spent in vaudeville and stock before marrying actor Jack Westley in 1900. The couple separated in 1912, after having a daughter, Ethel. Thereafter, she became a leading spirit in the Bohemian and creative life of Greenwich Village, helping to organize the Washington Square Players in 1915. Three years later, she was one of the founders of the Theatre Guild, acted in at least one Guild play every season thereafter until 1934, and served on its board of directors. She launched her successful movie career in 1934, beginning in *Moulin Rouge*. Her last movie was *My Favorite Spy*, 1942. That year on December 12, she died of coronary thrombosis at her home, Jacques Lane Farm, Franklin Township, N. J.

NYDIA WESTMAN

Born into a theatrical family, daughter of actor-composer Theodor Westman and actress-playwright Lily Wren Westman, in New York, February 19, 1907, she first appeared in her family's act, "Troubles of Joy." Her two sisters and a brother were also members of the act. In 1924, she made her Broadway bow as Mildred in *Pigs*, and her movie debut in 1932 in *Strange Justice*. Thereafter, she alternated between stage and screen. She made her last movie, *The Swinger*, in 1966. Married to Robert Sparks in 1922, and divorced in 1937. She died May 23, 1970, in St. Joseph Hospital, Burbank, Calif., survived by her daughter.

ARLEEN WHELAN

Red-headed Arleen was working as a manicurist at Patrick Regan's establishment on Hollywood Boulevard, when she was seen by H. Bruce Humberstone, director, and recommended to Darryl Zanuck of 20th Century-Fox. Put into training classes, and launched in a failure, *Kidnapped*, 1938, she continued her career off and on until 1957. She was born in Salt Lake City, September 16, 1916, and grew up in Los Angeles (where her father owned a small electrical shop),

and graduated from Manual Arts High School. Arleen appeared on Broadway for a year in a hit comedy, *The Doughgirls*, with Arlene Francis and Doris Nolan in 1942. She also played in the short-lived *Oh, Brother!*, with Hugh Herbert and Catharine Doucet, on Broadway, 1945. She married Hugh Owen, Paramount's Eastern Division manager; actor Alexander D'Arcy; and Dr. Warren O. Cagney, whom she divorced in 1961.

ALICE WHITE

She was born in Paterson, N. J., August 28, 1907, and attended Hollywood High School. She made her debut in 1927 in *Satin Woman*. She returned in the 1940s for *The Night of January 16*, 1941, *Girls' Town*, 1942, and *Flamingo Road*, with Joan Crawford, 1949. She lives in Hollywood. She was once married to writer Sid Bartlett.

ELEANORE WHITNEY

Born in Cleveland, April 21, 1914, she learned how to tap-dance from Bill "Bojangles" Robinson upon his occasional visits to that city. She went on the stage at the age of ten, and later claimed that

she supported her divorced mother and younger sister from that time on. As "the world's fastest tap-dancer" she appeared in vaudeville with singer Rae Samuels, in a special act, and also with Rudy Vallee and Jack Benny, before her screen debut in 1935 (*Millions in the Air*). In 1938, she made her last picture, *Campus Confessions*, and the following year married Frederick Backer, of New York, once assistant U. S. Attorney. In 1946, she turned up on the Broadway stage as Lucille Jourdain in Moliere's *The Would-Be Gentleman*, with Bobby Clark.

DAME MAY WHITTY

The title "Dame" she used with her name from January 1918 was not in recognition of her services to the theater, but for her World War I work. The granddaughter and daughter of newspaper editors (the *Liverpool Post*, the first penny daily in England), she was born June 19, 1865, and made her debut in ballet in the Court Theatre, Liverpool, at the age of sixteen. A year later she began her career in London, and was soon a promising ingenue. For a year she was a member of the Lyceum Theatre Company of Sir Henry Irving and Ellen Terry, and first

Marion Byron, ALICE WHITE, and Sally Eilers

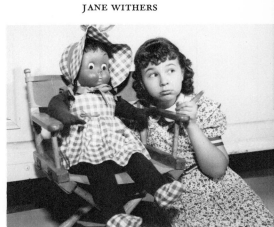

JANE WITHERS

VIRGINIA WEIDLER

came to America with them on tour in 1896. She had married actor Ben Webster, of an old stage family, in 1892, and except for a few years after the birth of their only child, Margaret Webster, later an actress and director, on March 15, 1905, she worked unceasingly on both stage and screen until the year of her death. The role of Mrs. Bramson in Emlyn Williams' *Night Must Fall* was a particularly lucky one for her; she played it in London and New York, from 1935 to 1936, and made her sound debut with it in 1937. In 1940, she played the Nurse to Vivien Leigh's Juliet on Broadway, and in 1945 made her last stage appearance in her daughter's staging of *Therese*, with Eva Le Gallienne. She had made one American film as early as 1915: *Enoch Arden*, with Wallace Reid and Lillian Gish. Her last was *The Return of October*, with Glenn Ford and Terry Moore, released after her death in Hollywood, May 29, 1948.

DOROTHEA WIECK

Although her career flourished in Germany and Austria, she was Swiss-born (in Davos, January 3, 1908), daughter of Hans Wieck, a pianist and painter, and his wife, also a pianist. She spent her childhood in Sweden, and later studied for the stage under Max Reinhardt. In 1932 she married Baron Ernst von der Decken, a year after her triumph in *Maedchen in Uniform*. Her film debut was in 1926. Miss Wieck worked throughout the Nazi regime, and was erroneously reported killed in the air raid on Dresden. She continues to work in German films; one of her latest was *Anastasia*, with Lilli Palmer, in 1965.

DOROTHY WILSON

The stenographer who got a well-publicized movie contract was born in Minneapolis, November 14, 1909, and went to Vocational High School there. She worked there and in Chicago as a typist before going to Hollywood to land a stenographic job at RKO studios at $30 a week. In publicity stories, both producer David Selznick and director Gregory La Cava were individually credited with discovering her. In 1932, after two years in an office, she was given an RKO contract, and worked in movies until 1936. Miss Wilson married Lewis R. Foster, a scenarist, in 1933, and eventually retired to have a baby.

LOIS WILSON

One of the four actress daughters of Andrew Kenly Wilson, she was born June 28, 1896, in Pittsburgh, but raised in Birmingham, Ala., where she prepared for a teacher's career at the Alabama Normal School. She was a teacher for two weeks before getting fired and, going to Chicago, she got a job in the movie industry there, 1916, in director Lois Weber's production of *The Dumb Girl of Portici*, with Anna Pavlova. Miss Wilson appeared steadily in movies for thirty years thereafter, and was joined by two of her sisters, Diana Kane, later wife of director George Fitzmaurice, and Connie Lewis, neither of whom attained her eminence. Her most famous role was that of the heroine, Molly Wingate, in the classic silent Western, *The Covered Wagon*, in 1923. During the 1920s, she spent most of her career at Paramount as the very feminine leading lady to such stars as Wallace Reid, Thomas Meighan, Richard Dix, and Jack Holt. In the late 1930s and during the 1940s she appeared on the stage, notably in John Van Druten's *The Mermaids Singing* in 1946, and at one time had her own TV interview show in New York. She never married. In 1970, Kent State University in Ohio honored her with a "Lois Wilson Day," as part of their silent-screen seminar. Miss Wilson, in turn, donated to the university her collection of film stills, scarpbooks, and clippings collected over a period of fifty years.

MARIE WILSON

Born in Anaheim, Calif., in December 1916, as Katherine Elizabeth Wilson, daughter of Wally Wilson, who died when she was five, she was brought up by her stepfather, Frank White. Wanting to be an actress, but always a flop in school play tryouts, she decided to try to crash the movies as an extra, and went from the extra ranks to a Warner Bros. contract. She was married to director Nick Grinde and actor Alan Nixon, whom she divorced in 1950. She then married TV producer Robert Fallon, with a son, Greg. She died November 23, 1972.

TOBY WING

Her real name is Martha Virginia Wing, and she was born on a farm near Richmond, Va., July 14, 1913, daughter of an Army officer, Major Paul Wing. As a teenager, she lived in Beverly Hills. After her marriage to aviator Dick Merrill in 1937, she retired from the screen. The Merrills live in Miami Beach, where Toby was fifth grade Sunday school teacher at All Souls Episcopal Church, and president of the North Beach Elementary School P.T.A.

JANE WITHERS

She was born in Atlanta, Ga., April 12, 1926, daughter of Walter Withers, an employee of a rubber-manufacturing company, and a stage-struck mother, Lavinia Ruth Elble. Mrs. Withers put her two year-old Jane in Atlanta's Boston Academy to study tap, ballet, and character dancing. Jane landed a regular spot on a radio show, *Aunt Sally's Kiddie Review*, and later the child had her own show, billed as *Dixie's Dainty Dewdrop*, doing imitations of W. C. Fields, Greta Garbo, ZaSu Pitts, and Maurice Chevalier. All this inspired her mother to take Jane to Hollywood in 1932, and her first job there was a $7.50-a-day bit part in *Handle with Care*. After she menaced Shirley Temple in *Bright Eyes*, her salary jumped to $150 a week in 1934. By 1937, she was sixth among the box-office champs, earning $2500 a week. In 1947 (having been out of movies for four years), she married William Moss, Jr., a Texas oil millionaire and part-time film producer. They were divorced in 1953, with three children, Wendy, William and Randy. In 1955, she married Ken Errair, an insurance broker and once member of the singing Four Freshmen, and had two sons, Kenneth and Kendall, before her husband died in a plane crash in 1968. Today, Jane is chiefly known as Josephine, the Lady Plumber, on Comet TV commericals—a run that began in 1963.

CORA WITHERSPOON

She was born in New Orleans, January 5, 1890, educated there and in Paris, and made her Broadway debut at twenty in *The Concert*, the beginning of a long career in New York plays and musicals. She made her movie debut in 1931 and appeared in films for over twenty years. She died of a heart ailment at her home, Las Cruces, New Mex., November 18, 1957.

ANNA MAY WONG

As the movies' longtime bona fide Oriental siren, Anna May Wong saw to it that she retained her image of Oriental sexual mystery and silk sheath-skirt chic, and offscreen always appeared publicly in an Oriental wardrobe. But as an American-born girl, she was as American in her speech, humor, and reactions as any savvy Hollywood actress, and was much enjoyed in the film colony as a witty, delightful woman. She was the daughter of a Los Angeles laundry man and was born January 3, 1907, given a Chinese name that means Frosted Yellow Willow. She received her education at Hollywood High School, and first entered films in 1921 in a small role in Marshall Neilan's *Bits of Life*, with Lon Chaney and Dorothy Mackaill. Next year, she co-starred opposite Kenneth Harlan in what was called a "variation on the Mme. Butterfly theme," *Toll of the Sea*, claimed to be the first Technicolor

ANNA MAY WONG

FAY WRAY and Fredric March

movie ever made. Her first real fame came as the sinuous Mongol slave girl in Douglas Fairbanks' *The Thief of Bagdad* in 1924. Thereafter, she provided atmospheric Oriental menace and/or mystery in a wide variety of silents and talkies, with an occasional offbeat role like Tiger Lily in *Peter Pan*, with Betty Bronson. Miss Wong also made occasional stage appearances, notably in *The Circle of Chalk*, with Laurence Olivier, in London, 1929, and *On the Spot*, a hit, in New York, 1930, as well as in vaudeville. In 1936, she paid her only visit to China. In her last years, she owned the Moongate Apartments in Santa Monica, which she later sold to live in a small house. Her final screen role was a small one in friend Anthony Quinn's film about contemporary Eskimo life, *The Savage Innocents*, 1960. She died in her sleep of a heart attack, at her home in Santa Monica, February 3, 1961.

FAY WRAY

Her birthday has been published as September 10, September 15, and September 25, in the usual manner of film reference books. When asked which one, she said: "Pick September 15." The year was 1907, and the place Alberta, Canada, where her father, Joseph H. Wray, was a rancher. Her family first moved from Canada to California, then to Arizona, and then to Salt Lake City. She went to public schools there, and later Hollywood High School. During a school vacation in 1923, she started to work in movies as an extra, and progressed to leading lady in *Gasoline Love* and in Westerns with such staunch names as Jack Hoxie, Art Acord and Hoot Gibson. Erich von Stroheim chose unknown Fay Wray for the leading role of Mitzi in his *The Wedding March* in 1926. She was nineteen, and he was attracted to her "spirituality and sex appeal." Her long career, becoming a unique one in movie history, was launched. She continued steadily through the 1930s, and into the early 1940s. Later, in the 1950s, she returned for occasional roles. Miss Wray was married to writer John Monk Saunders (*Wings*) in 1927, divorced 1939. He committed suicide in 1940. She married again, in 1942, screenwriter Robert Riskin (*It Happened One Night*), who died in 1955. Miss Wray lives alone in Hollywood.

JANE WYATT

Born into an old socialite family, as the daughter of Christopher Billopp Wyatt and the critic Euphemia Van Rensselaer Wyatt, in Campgaw, N. J., August 12, 1912, she attended Miss Chapin's School and Barnard College in New York. After studying for the stage with Miss Robinson-Duff, she played Freda in *Give Me Yesterday* in her Broadway debut, March 1931, and became a popular young ingenue. In 1934, she made her movie debut in *One More River*, and thereafter alternated stage, screen and television. For nine years, she played Robert Young's wife in the TV series *Father Knows Best*, the greatest success of her career. In 1935, she married Edgar Ward, and is the mother of two sons, Christopher and Michael. Miss Wyatt is a member of the Colonial Dames of America, and lives in Beverly Hills.

339

JANE WYATT

JANE WYMAN

Born Sarah Jane Fulks, in Saint Joseph, Mo., January 4, 1914, she attended Los Angeles High School and the University of Missouri, and worked as a hairdresser, model, blues singer (under the name of Jane Durrell), and in movie chorus lines before getting her first speaking part in *My Man Godfrey* in 1936. She has won three Academy Award nominations for her performances, and an Oscar in 1948 for her deaf-mute heroine in *Johnny Belinda*. In 1937-1938, she was married to dress manufacturer Myron Futterman, then to actor Ronald Reagan between 1940 and 1948, and is the mother of Maureen and Michael Reagan. Her third husband was composer-musician Freddie Karger, whom she married in 1952 and divorced in 1954, remarried quietly in 1961, and divorced in 1965. She was a star on TV in 1955, with *Jane Wyman's Fireside Theatre*, a weekly network show. By 1968, she had made seventy-four movies. She lives alone in an apartment in Century City, Avenue of the Stars, in Beverly Hills.

DIANA WYNYARD

On the stage she could range from Shakespeare to Shaw to Chekhov to Coward, and be in deliberate, exquisite command of any role she acted. A beautiful, brainy woman, she never went in for spectacular, theatrical highjinks. Born Dorothy Isobel Cox in London, January 16, 1906, she went to the Woodford School in Croydon before studying for the stage. In her first engagement, with a touring stock company, she played over twenty parts in her first year, and went on chalking up experience with repertory companies before her official London debut, as Lady Sheridan in *Sorry You've Been Troubled*, at the age of twenty-three. From then on, she was one of the leading players of the London theatre. Her Hollywood career took place between 1932 and 1934. Miss Wynyard married and divorced twice: director Sir Carol Reed (1943-1947) and Dr. Tibor Csato (1951). Working until the end—she was playing Gertrude to Peter O'Toole's Hamlet—she died of a kidney ailment at St. Paul's Hospital, May 13, 1964.

LORETTA YOUNG

A willowy girl with backbone of steel, she was born Gretchen Young in Salt Lake City, January 6, 1912, and was taken to Los Angeles, along with her two older sisters and a younger brother, by their mother, after their father had abandoned them. Mrs. Young opened a boarding house at 9th and Greer Streets, and later, after her divorce in 1920, married a Los Angeles businessman, George Belzer, by whom she had a daughter Georgiana (Mrs. Ricardo Montalban). Whenever they could find jobs, the Young children worked in movies as extras, and in Valentino's *The Shiek* appeared as four Arab waifs. In 1927, she began her real career as a schoolgirl in *Naughty but Nice*, with Colleen Moore, who changed her name to Loretta (without consulting her) because Gretchen sounded "too Dutchy." Twenty-six years later, she had made ninety-one movies, and had won an Oscar for *The Farmer's Daughter* in 1948. Miss Young was one of the first of the big stars to work in television as actress-producer, on *The Loretta Young*

340

LORETTA YOUNG

Show, from 1953 to 1961. A follow-up show, *The New Loretta Young Show*, lasted only one season, and then she retired. In 1930, when eighteen, she eloped with her leading man in *The Second Floor Mystery*, Grant Withers. The marriage lasted less than a year. In 1940, she married advertising man–producer Tom Lewis. She had previously adopted a daughter, Judy Lewis, and by her husband had two sons, Christopher and Peter. They divorced in 1969, after a fifteen-year separation. Miss Young devotes much time now to volunteer work among the underprivileged.

BLANCHE YURKA

She was born June 19, 1887, in Saint Paul, Minn., of Bohemian descent. Her father, Anton Jurka, was a professor of languages. She was educated in New York and began her stage career in 1907. Among her most famous roles were Gertrude to John Barrymore's Hamlet, 1922; Gina in *The Wild Duck*, 1925; Hedda in *Hedda Gabler*, 1929. Miss Yurka made some twenty-one movies between 1940 and 1959. She was once married to actor Ian Keith.

VERA ZORINA

Of Norwegian parents, she was born, as Eva Brigitta Hartwig, in Berlin, January 2, 1917, educated at a private school there, and spent her childhood summers in the coastal town of Kristiansund, Norway, her parents' home town. She studied dancing under Nicholas Legat, and made her debut in Kristiansund as a child of six as a Butterfly in a Flower Ballet. Adopting the stage name of Brigitta, she danced in Erik Charrell's *Lilac Time* in Berlin, 1928, and also in two Max Reinhardt productions, A *Midsummer Night's Dream* and *The Tales of Hoffman*. She first went to England with the Reinhardt *Dream*, and stayed to appear in Rodney Ackland's *Ballerina* in 1933. After changing her name to Vera Zorina, she danced with Col. de Basil's company of the Monte Carlo Ballets Russes in 1934. Her first big part was as the dancer Vera in Rodgers and Hart's *On Your Toes* in London, 1937, and the following year she made her Broadway bow as Angel in *I Married an Angel*. During the 1940s, she made five more movies, re-creating her stage role of Marina in *Louisiana Purchase*, 1941. First married to choreographer George Balanchine (1938-1946), she then became the wife of Goddard Lieberson, president of Columbia Records, and is the mother of two sons.